Social and Political Movements

Social and Political Movements

Readings on Punjab

Edited by

HARISH K. PURI
PARAMJIT S. JUDGE

RAWAT PUBLICATIONS
Jaipur • New Delhi • Bangalore • Guwahati • Kolkata

ISBN 978-81-7033-633-4

Reprinted, 2019

Published by
Prem Rawat for **Rawat Publications**
Satyam Apts., Sector 3, Jawahar Nagar, Jaipur 302 004 (India)
Phone: 0141 265 1748 / 7006 Fax: 0141 265 1748
E-mail: info@rawatbooks.com
Website: www.rawatbooks.com

New Delhi Office
4858/24, Ansari Road, Daryaganj, New Delhi 110 002
Phone: 011-23263290

Also at *Bangalore, Guwahati* and *Kolkata*

Typeset by Rawat Computers, Jaipur
Printed at Nice Printing Press, New Delhi

Contents

Preface

It was in 1995 that we planned to bring together in one volume chapters on the major, social and political movements in Punjab from the time of British annexation of Punjab to the present times.

It has taken us a long time of rescheduling of "deadlines" to collect all the papers from the scholars we approached to write for the volume. An apology is in order to all those who were most supportive in sending their contributions at the earliest. We thank them for bearing with us. Five of the chapters included in the volume are reprints of the published articles. We are grateful to the scholars W.H. McLeod, N.G. Barier and Mohinder Singh for giving us the necessary permission. We are also thankful to Manohar Publishers for permission to reprint the articles by Spencer Lavan, N.G. Barrier and H.K. Puri from three different volumes. The sources are duly acknowledged.

Finally thanks to Rawat Publishers, Jaipur for publication of the volume in record time.

Harish K. Puri
Paramjit S. Judge

Introduction

The study of social and political movements enables us to understand the dynamics of the way a society produces its cultural and political orientations, structures of domination and patterns of resistance. Focus on the notions of 'society' and 'social system' orients us to view the behaviour of actors as indicators of given internal processes of differentiation and integration, suggesting patterns of system-maintenance. A social movement oriented perspective is different. It understands society as "the changing, unstable, loosely coherent product of social relations, cultural innovation and political processes."[1] Alain Touraine, who viewed social movements mainly in terms of cultural struggles, emphasised that such movements do not represent social breakdown or abnormal occurrences. "Instead they make up the fabric of social life by producing and contesting social practices, norms and institutions."[2] Yet these also involve issues of power and hegemony. Political movements, however, are more clearly oriented to stakes relating to power, freedom and legitimacy.

A social or political movement is a collective action by people with a view to change some aspects of their situation. It involves mobilisation and participation of masses and persistence of social action over a period of time. The participants in a movement share common beliefs, interests or ideology. In some cases, the participants may have a homogeneous background in terms of caste, class, language, religion and region. The beginning of a movement is defined by a situation of social or political conflict, reflecting a sort of 'crisis' in the existing socio-political arrangements.

The purpose of a social or political movement may relate to specific issues such as affirmative action for civil rights, formation of a separate state or larger long-term objectives of transformation of existing social and political order including values and attitudes. Creation of a new social and political order as the objective may take the form of 'revolution'. Movements relating to ethnic identity, religious reform and national self-determination may involve levels of mobilisation and solidarities different from those of class-based peasant and workers movements. However, internal contest on the order of priorities in a movement may raise issues of social content of freedom and other political programmes and about the political content of social struggles. Conflicting or polarised perspectives of actors may be prominent in caste, religion and class divided societies such as that of India. Conflicts about the content of desired change and control of the scope of change generally represent conflicts about the state. State, with its ruling ideology and interests, is an inevitable actor in the emergence and the dialectics of a movement. As the activity develops, the purposes may undergo a change and priorities and strategies of action may be contested, often permitting a range of variations, including contrary and conflicting ideas and practices.

In the social science literature social movements are classified into various types. This classification has been made by using certain criteria. For example, in terms of the objectives, social movements may be categorised as reactionary, conservative, revisionary, and revolutionary.[3] Similarly, by examining the social background of the participants, we may classify social movements as dalit, tribal, peasant, working class, etc. Such classifications pose a problem when social movements are examined as a phenomenon of a region. In this regard, the history of the region and its specific and general features acquire greater significance than categorisation. A region presents a case of a more homogeneous unit as compared with the whole which is expected to be complex and heterogeneous. The states as regions may have within them a degree of complexity, but the differences between them make a society, such as that of India—a very complex society. Given the scale of heterogeneity and regional and local variations in levels of development, scholars have noted a significant feature in Indian society: the plausibility of "simultaneity of non-contemporaneous movements". This may not be so in the case of a region. There is no doubt that in the modern era we may be able to visualise movements having an all-India character. However, as Barrington Moore observed, the social and political movements in India have been local in character.[4]

As a corollary to the above, there is a need for the examination of the movements which instead of acquiring an all-India character, remained confined to a region. We can also think of some movements of an all-India magnitude which develop local features. As a result, the region acquires significance for the purpose of comprehending the movements in their generality as well as their specificity.

Why do social movements acquire a regional character? This may be one of the probable queries. It may not be necessary that this definitely happens. In terms of the space, structure and agency, a movement has the probability of becoming local. In this regard, if the complexity of the society results from an aggregation of regional-cultural formations, then the space and agency are expected to be different from one region to another, even though the social structure may be common. For example, caste structure across regions, or market-based inequalities are important dimensions of social structure in India. The regional movements emerge and grow out of the specific conditions of a region. For the understanding of this aspect there is a need to make a distinction between regional movements and national level or country-wide movements.

Regional movements, as stated above, are more or less confined to a definite area and emerge due to the local conditions. Such movements are diverse and have conditions rooted in the local history and culture. In India, instances of such movements are numerous. One may refer to the Telengana movement, the

Moplah rebellion, or the Satnami movement. All these movements had distinct features and were regional in terms of their spatial occurrences. National level or country-wide movements are those which transcend their place of origin and spread to the entire nation. Such movements occur in a wide country such as India when the entire population within the country is integrated through market and communication. The nationalist movement and the Pakistan movement during the last decades of the British rule in India, for example, transcended their places of origin to cover most of the areas. During the post-independence period, the working class movement, the Naxalite movement, the Bhoodan movement and J.P. Narain's anti-Emergency movement were some of the country-wide movements.

In the light of the above one may raise a question whether in the case of a national level movement the dialectics of region and country leads to certain qualitative regional alterations. We cannot ignore the structural plausibility of regional effects on a country-wide movement. At the empirical level, the variations which the regional, cultural and other factors introduced in the all-Indian movements are evident. These can be observed, for example, in the Naxalite movement, working class movements and student movements.

A region is both distinct from as well as integrated with the whole. However, to use a Gramscian expression, the region enjoys a relative autonomy in relation to the country. In India, where socio-cultural diversity is marked by caste, religion and language, the region acquires a significant place in any analysis of a social and political process. Accordingly, social and political movements in Punjab have distinct features and traditions.

It is worthwhile to review some of the dimensions of Punjab. It is important to mention that in this analysis, we may refer only to those factors which are considered relevant to the context.

Punjab occupies a unique position among various states of India for it has undergone a large number of territorial changes. Numerous changes in its territorial boundaries had taken place before the British annexation of Punjab in 1849. The historical memories of expansion and consolidation of the Kingdom of

Lahore under Ranjit Singh, for example, have played a significant role in the shaping of imagination in the contemporary period. After annexation, the British Punjab became a big state embracing the plains between the Jamuna and the Indus rivers but excluded many princely states. In 1947, when India was partitioned, Punjab was divided into two, as its western part was included in Pakistan. After the integration of the princely states, the former states of East Punjab were organised into a separate state, viz., PEPSU (Patiala and East Punjab States Union). In 1956, the PEPSU was merged in Punjab. This was followed by a further intensification of the earlier demand for a Punjabi-speaking state on the pattern of linguistic reorganisation of other states in India. This led to the separation of the Hindi-speaking areas and formation of new state of Punjab in 1966. The boundaries of Punjab have remained unchanged since 1966. However, the struggle for inclusion of certain left-out Punjabi-speaking areas is still going on. All these territorial changes were effected by political decisions and occurrences. These were either consequences of or led to the political movements. The movement for Pakistan and Punjabi Suba movement are two significant movements in this regard.

The changes in the territory of Punjab have also affected the referrent of our study. When we say Punjab, the question automatically emerges: "Which Punjab?" This has also led to the controversies relating to Punjabi identity—the issue that became central to the Sikh discourse in which the conceptual overlapping of language and script led to the appropriation of the former through the latter. The territorial imperative was seriously ruptured by partition in 1947. Further, a considerable number of Punjabis began living outside Punjab after migration from the other part. The construction of identity and then its deconstruction has been a continuous process in the Indian Punjab. Punjab, on the other side of the border, has lost socio-political relevance except for the subjective and historical nostalgia. Since there are religions differentiating between Punjabis of India and of Pakistan, there have been attempts at constructing a community's own culture, history and myths by inventing a past in terms of religious affiliations. The margin of difference became an important aspect of the conscious effort to demarcate the boundary of one community's identity from the others.

Still another consequence of these territorial changes was the uneven character of social formations in the state. What were formerly the princely states experienced different pace of development activities in terms of education, agrarian system, administrative services etc. As an illustration we may refer to the land tenurial system. In the Patiala state *biswedari* system was prevalent whereas in the British Punjab the *ryotwari* and *mahalwari* systems were prevailing. The *biswedari* system was similar to the *zamindari* system of the permanent settlement areas of the country. As a result we find that the agrarian dynamics and subsequent agrarian movements were different in the erstwhile princely states from those of the British administered areas. This fact also explains sub-regional disparities in the region.

Owing to many changes in the physical boundaries of the state, it becomes difficult to understand and examine the dynamics of socio-political movements in the state. One may wonder as to which Punjab is being referred to. A simple solution to the problem is that the movements are viewed as located in the time-space context. In this regard, we can make the following divisions in terms of time and space:

1. *1849-1947:* This phase consists of two areas, viz., the British Punjab and the princely states.
2. *1947-1949:* Punjab is divided into two states, one going to Pakistan. The Indian Punjab, in which we shall remain interested from 1947 onwards, had two geographical units. First, the eastern districts of the British Punjab, and second, the formerly princely states which merged with the Indian Union.
3. *1949-1956:* Punjab consists of two states, viz., (East) Punjab and PEPSU.
4. *1956-1966:* After merger of PEPSU in Punjab, the newly emerged state of Punjab covered a composite territorial area of the former two states.
5. *1966 onwards:* After 1 November, 1966, Punjab refers to the new Punjabi-speaking state which excluded the areas now constituting the state of Haryana and those districts which

were merged with hilly areas to form a new state of Himachal Pradesh. The area which retained the name 'Punjab' was now much smaller.

From 1966 onwards there has been a contest regarding claims to a few areas between Haryana and Punjab; Chandigarh and Fazilka-Abohar being the major areas of contention. This context has been a basis of mobilisation and politicisation. Over a period of time the boundary dispute between Punjab and Haryana as mediated by the Union Government contributed to politics of ethnicity.

The changing character of religious community composition and inter-community dynamics constitute the second significant dimension of Punjab's socio-cultural milieu. To use the recent expression popularised by post-modernist thinking (as a critique of modernisation), there has been a continuous structuration of ethnic communities along religious lines. Demographic composition of these ethnic communities has been influenced by periodic geographic reconstitutions as well as religious conversions and communal displacements. During and after the British rule, religion became central to Punjab's social, economic and political life. As we shall discuss later, the British also classified the people of Punjab as religious communities.

The issues of religious identity and conversion have contributed towards the emergence of various movements. At the time of annexation by the British, Punjab's population was comprised of Muslims, Hindus and Sikhs. The British wrested power from the Sikhs who were numerically the smallest religious community. The British period saw the coming of the Christian missionaries and proselytisation in Punjab. It is argued that conversion to Christianity led to the revitalisation of the three religious communities. In response to conversion, the Sikhs started the Singh Sabha movement. The Ahmediya movement among the Punjabi Muslims and the popularisation of Arya Samaj among the middle-class Hindus could be viewed as partly a response to the conversions to Christianity. The principle of communal electorates introduced from 1909 and the gradual extension of representative assemblies wherein the seats for each community were related to their numbers in the population of the province sponsored emphasis on communal boundaries. The accelerated fear and hatred of the 'other' culminated into the 'ethnic cleansing' in 1947.

The post-independence period saw a new twist to the communal situation. The acceptance of the Muslim League's demand for Pakistan—a separate state for Muslim community—generated an urge for a separate state for the Sikhs. It came to be argued that preservation of a separate Sikh identity in a Hindu majority state required dominant political power for the community in their province. Even though it came to be articulated in terms of a separate Punjabi-speaking (linguistic) state, the exaggerated fears of Punjabi Hindus and the Indian state created conditions of communal apprehensions between the two communities in Punjab.

Could the religious conversion, which was one of the reasons for the development of communalism, effect a change in the social status of the convertees? This question is related with the nature of social structure. The sociologists and social anthropologists regard the Hindu society as characterised by the caste structure. Recent research has shown, however, that caste stratification also exists among the Muslims, Sikhs and Christians.[5] Caste and occupational affiliations cut across religions. Predictably, the low status group in one religion could hardly be high status one in the other. What is significant in the context of lower castes in Punjab is that their conversion was accompanied by a nomenclatural change. For instance, a Hindu Chura came to be known as Balmiki; among the Sikhs he was called a Mazhbi or Rangreta; as a Christian he was called Masih and among the Muslims came to be known as Mussali. Ironically, when the Arya Samaj initiated *Shuddhi* movement, some of the lower castes were reconverted to Hinduism. Most of them were labelled as 'Mahashas'. This did not help them to improve their status. One consequence of the conversion of lower castes was to be gauged, however, in terms of communal tensions in Punjab.

The third issue, perhaps the most complicated one, related to the role of colonial and post-colonial state in the society, culture and economy of Punjab. Punjab was the last state of India to be annexed by the British in 1849. By this time, the British had entrenched their power in the Indian sub-continent. Along with colonial supremacy the British also had a reasonably good idea of Indian material and cultural capital. In certain respects Punjab had the better of the British colonialism.

The British Raj has been responsible for creating institutions and institutional values which remain largely unchanged till today. Similarly, providing administrative identity to the concept of the place of five rivers, agrarian changes, communication networks, and new technology are some of the prominent dimensions which have contributed to the emergence of new Punjabi society. At the same time, the cultural renaissance of Punjab did not occur the way it happened elsewhere in India, particularly in Bengal and Maharashtra. The rejection of Brahmo Samaj in favour of Arya Samaj rang the bell of communalism in which all religious communities got engaged at the turn of the twentieth century. It may be appropriate for our present purpose to know in some detail the role of the colonial rule in Punjab. This aspect of Punjab may, in fact, be analysed in relation to India as a whole. The following aspects demand explication:

1. The British perception of the Indian society had been shaped by the European experience of the evolution of societies. In this regard, the role of Christianity is central. Suppression of heresy and blasphemy, emphasis on correct (official) understanding and observances, institution of inquisition, and witch-hunting are some of the dimensions of the evolution of the West European countries which shaped the European understanding of society. Society, to use Durkheim's expression is "a moral community". It means that society is a collectivity with a degree of homogeneity in a cultural sense. In India, castes and religions became the basis of cultural plurality. In such a context, the notion of a single moral community could be applied to people of one religion leading finally to imagination of a community as a nation. Obviously, for reasons of colonialism, this cognitive perception was found to be useful in transforming agrarian discontent into communal disturbances. The social scene in Punjab did not present a unique

scenario in this respect. Muslims, Hindus and Sikhs were the three major religious communities and the Raj classified the people of Punjab accordingly, but after a considerable pondering over it. Conversely, the people of Punjab had a composite view of their own faiths. It is a well-known fact that in 1881 when the first census enumeration was carried out, a considerable number of Hindus and Sikhs recorded their faith to be the followers of a Muslim Pir's sect known as 'Sakhi Sarvar'.[6] This recording led to reactions among the religious leaders of both Hindus and Sikhs which ensured later a marked shift in the recorded 'belongingness' in the Census of 1891.

We find that the whole process introduced by the British to fit people into different religious compartments contributed to the aggravation in the demarcation of religious boundaries. Its pathological consequences were reflected in the rise of communalism in the third decade of the twentieth century in Punjab. Communal riots, which took place in the aftermath of partition in 1947, bear testimony to this pathology. It may be noted that the titles which the Raj had introduced also carried a nomenclature as per religious boundaries, as for example, Rai Bahadur, Singh Bahadur, and Khan Bahadur. Subsequent to the sponsorship of distinct identities the British also treated them differently. The Sikhs, for example, got preference in army recruitment and land rewards. Further, the Sikh recruits to the army were required to strictly observe religious rituals. After retirement, they continued their routinised life. The entire process furthered the religious revivalism in Punjab.

2. It is in the area of agrarian development that the British played the most significant role. To begin with, the British continued with the already prevalent *mahalwari* and *ryotwari* systems of revenue collection. Secondly, the system of land records was improved without changing the existing system. The British also established the canal colonies in the West Punjab where the land was awarded to the peasants from East Punjab, the soldiers and the loyalists. It was the first set of people who benefited most. At the same time, the increase in revenue raised the level of peasant

indebtedness, the solution to which was found in one of the most discriminatory enactments in 1900 known as the Land Alienation Act. In the light of this Act all the non-agricultural castes became ineligible to buy land. This apparently was done to tackle the problem of indebtedness, but the Act did not prevent the members of the agricultural communities to become moneylenders. The problem of indebtedness was further aggravated by the First World War and later on the economic recession of 1929. It was in this backdrop that the Unionist Party, under the influence of Sir Chhotu Ram, ended this indebtedness. The commercialisation of agriculture and rise in prices of agricultural commodities under colonial political economy led to growth without development. Such a process alienated the peasantry from the British Raj that led to the emergence of agrarian tensions and discontent.

3. The primary feature of the Raj was imperialist exploitation. The creation of the world system, whose centre was London, was unlike the earlier world systems. Most of the earlier world systems were centres of trade, whereas this world system was based on the global exploitation of resources of colonies as well as the distribution of the mass produced goods. In a way, such a process created underdevelopment which was a phenomenon of growth without development. It was in the colonised countries that the simultaneity of non-contemporaneous social formations became the hallmark of their evolutionary process.

Even when the objective of the Raj was to maximise revenue, it required a degree of organisation to do so. As a result, we could witness three areas where the British rule created something new and whose consequences were realised later.

First, a system of communication and transport was created. Within this framework development of roads, rail links and postal services symbolised the beginning of modernisation in the colonial context. It brought people into frequent interaction or, to use Durkheim's expression, 'dynamic density' increased. A dialectical outcome of bringing people together was also the emergence of plausibility structure of people's organisations.

Secondly, the printing technology has had radical

consequences for India. The emergence of vernacular printing created favourable conditions for the spread of ideas among the people at large.

Thirdly, alongside this was the creation of an administrative set-up. For the first time, in the history of Punjab, it became a state with 'administrative boundaries'. In a way, unlike many other states, Punjab as a territorial concept was a colonial construction. Within a few decades the territorial imperative began to work in diverse forms.

As a result of these three developments, we find the emergence of an indigenous middle class. In the beginning, the British brought Bengali Kaisthas and/or *babus* to carry out various jobs as was the case of Assam. We can find their presence, particularly in Lahore, in the form of organisation of the Brahmo Samaj. However, the Brahmo Samaj did not find acceptance among the rapidly increasing Punjabi middle class. It was another sect from outside Punjab which became acceptable. The Arya Samaj, unlike the Brahmo Samaj's emphasis on synthesis between the western and Indian culture, advocated a pride of rootedness in the Vedic Indian culture. It provided not only an anchor to the middle class but also gave impetus to the social, educational and economic development of the Arya Samajis. This kind of thrust is sometimes equated with protestantism. Similarly, the Sikh middle class began to look for its roots in Sikh tradition which found expression in the Singh Sabha. The nationalist movement in Punjab emerged from these two socio-religious movements which within two decades, got routinised and became the basis of Punjab renaissance.

4. One of the notable features of the British rule was the creation of formal basis of legitimacy of the colonial rule. The bringing into existence of judiciary alongwith civil and criminal codes are important events in the history of adjudication in the country. It led to two major consequences in the British India. First, it was able to make a distinction between the legal and the illegal in the light of the laws enacted for the purpose. Secondly, it was able to generate the ideological support to the British rule. *The*

Raj was performing its function in accordance with law. The separation (real or unreal) of powers as portrayed through the western education lent credence to the doings of the rule.

In the context of the political sphere, the British rule provided a degree of liberty to the political activities of the rising middle class while making them aware of the distinction between legal and illegal political activities. We also find certain agitations against certain Acts which the Indian nationalists thought to be anti-people or anti-Indian. A considerable number of nationalists, on the other hand, accepted this legality and thus the framework of their struggle for independence. The coming of Gandhi on the scene is an important event in India. Basing his struggle on the *Satyagraha*—a peaceful way of struggle—he was able to expose the British hegemony with regard to the legal/illegal duality. He was able to demonstrate that even if the colonised remain peaceful and do not violate the law, the colonial state could be suppressive. However, the judiciary and law are the bases of the British rule in India in which the demarcation between the right or wrong way for freedom got overlapped with legal and illegal methods.

5. The birth of independent India was not without pains. Punjab was one of the states to experience the trauma of partition whose memories still act like nightmares for many. In the post-independence Punjab, the demographic composition of communities underwent a change. Now, both Hindus and Sikhs emerged as the major religious communities. The Constitution of independent India provided for equality, liberty and fraternity. In order to help certain sections to come at par with the rest a reservation policy for the scheduled castes was introduced. Punjab had a very large proportion of the scheduled castes.[7] Obviously, the reservation policy was to make an impact in one way or the other.

An important aspect of the state intervention in social relations has been land reform legislations. The Tenancy Act in the PEPSU region had transformed the agrarian relations. However, the ceiling and redistribution of land holdings remained a dream. There is an evidence to suggest that a large number of tenants were dispossessed from land by the landlords under the pretext of self-cultivation.[8] At present, Punjab may be the only state in which the ruling political class has been the most vocal opponent of land reforms.

Punjab drew the attention of scholars when the green revolution became a sustained success. It has been argued that the rural poverty has considerably declined in Punjab.[9] The green revolution has led to two important developments. First, a large-scale migration of casual labour from Bihar and other areas has emerged as a significant feature. In other words, Punjab has emerged as the centre of subsumption of labour in agricultural sector. Second, the farmers' movement has become an important dimension of their economic and political clout in recent years, for continuance and promotion of their class interest. It is argued by some scholars that the terrorist-militant movement was caused by the diverse gains and costs of the green revolution.[10]

6. Before we provide a classification of social and political movements which have occurred in Punjab, it is worthwhile to comment on another important dimension of the Punjabi society. This is related with the Punjabi diaspora. The role of the Punjabi diaspora in fostering the social and political movements has been and continued to be significant. The international migration of the Punjabis dates back to the late nineteenth century. Punjabis did not migrate as indentured labourers in British colonies like the Tamils and the tribals of Chotanagpur area. The Punjabis' migration was voluntary and with a few exceptions involved entrepreneurship, in search of better opportunities.

Owing to various social and experiential factors the Punjabi pioneers were ex-soldiers. It may be argued that at the time of completing his service in the army, a soldier who invariably belonged to the caste and class of peasant proprietors, found himself ill-adjusted in his family in the village. The experience of city life while in service acted like a pull factor, whereas his marginalisation within the village society might have pushed him out of his native place.[11] The ex-soldiers took up menial jobs in port cities, such as Singapore, Hong Kong, Shanghai, etc. On moving into North America at the turn of the century, they found lucrative jobs as farm hands or as labourers working on rail-roads and in lumber mills.

The experience of liberal democracy and the notion of a nation as conceived by these migrants were the reasons for their political mobilisation. What later on became the Ghadar movement was started by the Punjabis in Canada and the USA. They came back in 1914 to organise a large-scale uprisings in Punjab with the help of army. However, their efforts failed and most of them were either imprisoned or hanged.[12] The militant tradition started by the Ghadar movement was kept alive through a series of such movements, viz., Babbar Akali movement Kirti Kisan movement, and Red Communist movement. Later on, the Naxalite movement also made an attempt to use this tradition. The Ghadar martyrs became models for later movements.[13]

Still another wave of Punjabis went to East Africa where they worked as clerks, skilled artisans and entrepreneurs. Mostly, they were employed by the British for rail-road construction where the native Africans lacked the expertise. In the post-independence period, the migration of Punjabis to western countries accelerated to the extent that in some of these countries they emerged as visible minorities. It may be noted that a majority of the Punjabis belonged to the Sikh community. Noticeable numbers among them earned status and wealth as professionals and businessmen. However, most of them experienced certain loneliness and a search for belonging or identity in the midst of material prosperity. Communitarian demands and emotional solidarity tend to become for many the only available measure of worth. Such a stratum of the Sikhs abroad played an important role in the Khalistani militant movement in Punjab. Contribution of money in support of the Khalistan movement was a route for many while some of them actually joined the movement, even through they would rule out the option of settling in their homeland.[14]

In the end, it may be worthwhile to present the plan of this book. There are three parts of the book. Keeping in view the complexity involved in the classification of movements, that, too, which occurred in a region, we have undertaken a simple path to this objective. These parts are chronologically ordered. The rationale may be obvious. Before we come to that it may be appropriate to describe what each part contains. In the first part we have included those movements which originated between 1850 and 1900. The second part covers those movements that emerged during the twentieth century upto 1947. The movements during the post-independent period up to the present have been included in the last part.

The first fifty years of the British rule in Punjab were marked by the slow impact of colonial growth. The process of coping with the problems born of interaction with the Raj was reflected first in the upsurge of revivalism, reform or revitalisation of the believed pre-British values and traditions. The various movements launched during this period had a strong religious content which in one way or the other confronted Christianity and the West. Theoretically, this was a cultural reaction which was channelised through religion in a situation of political and economic subordination.

The beginning of the twentieth century was characterised by a shift away from the exclusive concern with religion towards secular and communitarian political stances. The movements with a pronounced nationalist and anti-British character overlapped, by the third decade, with interreligious and communitarian issues and tensions. The complexity involved in the 1920s could be estimated by the fact that religion, caste and sect seemed to be merging with each other on the fundamental issues of identity and share in political power. Towards the end of 1920s we also find that the princely states came under the influence of the political upsurge in the British Punjab. The partition and independence of India in 1947 became, in a sense, a watershed.

The post-independent period began with hope and expectations alongside apprehensions about the impact of phenomenal new changes. The introduction of universal adult franchise mobilised castes and religious groups along political lines. The emphasis on secularism, planned economic development and nation-building led to new kinds of conflicts and a variety of social and political movements different from those of the British period.

Whereas movements such as the trade union and that of the

farmers in Punjab shared objectives and strategies with similar movements in other parts of India, the movements like that for Punjabi Suba and Khalistan present many peculiar features specific to Punjab.

Each one of the movements enlightens us about the situational issues of perceived threats, the coping strategies, the visions and fantasies, as also the anticipated and unanticipated consequences.

Overall, this collection of studies of social and political movements in one region during the period of a century and a half may help the reader to have a comprehensive understanding of salient trends in articulation of issues, dealing with conflicts and the new shape of challenges and objectives.

Notes

1. Alain Touraine, cited in Jean L. Cohen, "Strategy or Identity: New Theoretical Paradigms and Contemporary Social Movements", *Social Research*, Winter 1985, p. 697.
2. *Ibid.*
3. Wm. Bruce Cameron, *Modern Social Movements: A Sociological Outline*, New York: Random House, 1967.
4. Barrington Moore, Jr., *Social Origins of Dictatorship and Democracy*, Harmondsworth: Penguin, 1966.
5. Imtiaz Ahmad, *Caste and Social Stratification among Muslims*, Delhi: Manohar, 1973. Harjinder Singh (ed.), *Caste among Non-Hindus in India*, New Delhi: National, 1977.
6. Harjot Oberoi, *Construction of Religious Boundaries: Culture, Identity and Diversity in the Sikh Tradition*, Delhi: Oxford University Press, 1994.
7. According to 1991 Census, the scheduled castes constitute 28.31 per cent of the total population of Punjab.
8. S.S. Gill, "Changing Land Relations in Punjab and Implications for Land Reforms", *Economic and Political Weekly*, Vol. XXIV, No. 25 (June 24, 1989).

9. H.S. Shergill and Gurmail Singh, "Poverty in Rural Punjab: Trends over Green Revolution Decades", *Economic and Political Weekly*, Vol. XXX, No. 25 (June 24, 1995).
10. Vandana Shiva, *The Violence of the Green Revolution,* Goa: The Other India Press, 1992.
11. Paramjit S. Judge, *Parvas: Sabhiacharak Sankat* (Punjabi), Jalandhar: NRI Sabha, 2000.
12. Harish K. Puri, *Ghadar Movement: Ideology Organization and Strategy* (2nd edition), Amritsar: Guru Nanak Dev University Press, 1993.
13. Paramjit S. Judge, *Insurrection to Agitation: Naxalite Movement in Punjab,* Bombay: Popular Prakashan, 1992.
14. A.W. Helweg, "The Indian Diaspora" in G. Sheffer (ed.), *Modern Diasporas in International Politics,* London: Croom Helm, 1986.

1

The Kukas: A Millenarian Sect of Punjab

W.H. McLEOD

During the first four decades of the nineteenth century Sikh fortunes prospered. The anarchy which had afflicted Punjab during most of the preceding century had given way to the strong centralised dominion of Maharaja Ranjit Singh. Ruling in the name of the Sikh community and ostensibly as its servant, Ranjit Singh had extended the boundaries of his Punjab kingdom as far as Kashmir, the Khyber Pass and Multan. These conquests were completed by 1824 and for the remaining years of Ranjit Singh's reign Punjab enjoyed an unaccustomed peace. Throughout the turbulent years of the eighteenth century the Sikh community (the Khalsa) had been sustained by the confident assurance that "the Khalsa shall reign" (*raj karega khalsa*). To many it seemed that this prophecy had come true.

Others, however, were troubled. The ascent to military and political power seemed to them to have been accompanied by a corresponding decline from the true glory of the Sikh faith. The Sikh Gurus had insisted on the absolute primacy of devotion to

---

Reprinted from G.A. Wood and P.S.O'Connor (eds.), *W.P. Morrell: A Tribute*, Dunedin: University of Otago Press, 1973.

God. Where now was the fervent, regular remembrance of *nam* (the Divine Name) upon which they had laid such unyielding stress, and where the disciplined purity of life which must inescapably characterise the true believer ? These questions became increasingly acute as the Sikh kingdom slipped into confusion and defeat during the decade following the death of Ranjit Singh in 1839.

One of the troubled was Balak Singh, a resident of Hazro in the north-western corner of Ranjit Singh's domain. Balak Singh had been influenced by another teacher, Jawahar Mal. Like his master, Balak Singh exhorted his followers to return to the simple religious message of the Gurus and in accordance with this message he taught a strict doctrine of salvation through meditation on the *nam*. The sect which was established in this manner has been known by a variety of names. Whereas Balak Singh evidently referred to his followers as Jagiasis[1], their modern descendants prefer the title Namdhari, or "adherents of the Divine Name". Between the earlier and later periods, and particularly during the sect's brief years of prominence, the term most commonly used (at least by outsiders) was Kuka, or 'crier'. The impact of Balak Singh's personality was evidently considerable, for by the time he died in 1862 he had been recognised by his followers as the eleventh Guru.[2] At his death he was succeeded as leader of the sect by Ram Singh, a disciple who had fallen under his spell while serving as a soldier in the army of Ranjit Singh's successors.

Ram Singh transferred the Kuka centre from Hazro to his own village of Bhaini in Ludhiana district and at once the sect began to grow rapidly, both in numbers as well as in prominence. Barely six months after Balak Singh's death the Assistant District Superintendent of Police at Attock drew attention to the sudden change:

> Though the sect seems to have failed in the neighbourhood of Hazru since Balak Singh's death it has thriven in the most remarkable manner in the district adjoining the home of his more energetic successor.[3]

In his comments on this and other police reports T.D. Forsyth, officiating secretary to the Punjab government, mentioned that Ram Singh's activities had first been detected in April 1863.[4] Eight years later Forsyth was to play a leading role in the episode which so abruptly arrested the sect's rapid rise to prominence. In this, the first of his recorded comments, he noted that Ram Singh's numerous converts were "confined chiefly to the lower classes".[5] This vague remark was clarified four years later by Major Perkins, District Superintendent of Police at Ludhiana, who observed in a report on the Kukas that "converts are chiefly made from Juts, Tirkhans, Chumars, and Mazbees" (i.e., Jat agriculturists, carpenters, and outcastes).[6] He added that very few Khatris, Brahmans, or Banyas had been attracted to the sect.[7]

This caste-occupational constituency is of fundamental importance for any understanding of the sudden acceleration in the sect's popularity, and it deserves careful analysis. It was not, however, the aspect which primarily interested the Punjab government. Sedition was the danger which it perceived and which prompted its investigations. In 1863, memories of 1857 were still vivid and any movement which combined rapid growth with a promise of militancy could scarcely escape official attention. This attention it received in abundance. Police officers were instructed to observe members of the sect carefully, informers were employed to report on its activities from within, and narrative accounts of its beliefs and customs were prepared for the guidance of administrators. As early as June 1863, Ram Singh's movements were restricted to Bhaini,[8] a decision which was reversed only when it was realised that this endued him with martyr qualifications and thereby increased his popularity.[9]

Police reports and the narrative accounts based upon them provide much detailed information concerning the sect. The reports are, to some extent, vitiated by the fears and suspicions which prompted them, but the damage is slight and due allowance can be made for it. It is the contemporary analysis which is so commonly awry, not the actual details collected by police officers and their informants in villages with Kuka concentrations. The description of the sect which emerges from their efforts is one which in its essentials is confirmed by later materials produced within the Kuka community,[10] and by recent works dealing with the remnant which survives today.[11]

All agree that the Kuka sect had begun as a religious reform movement within the Sikh community and that in spite of its suspected inclination towards sedition it still preserved this emphasis. Ram Singh, following his master, looked for a return to the pristine purity of the doctrines taught by the Sikh Gurus. In its negative aspect this took the form of a vigorous polemic directed against the corruptions of the contemporary Sikh community. Positively it found expression in a rigorous insistence upon the devotional practice of *nam simran* (meditation on the Divine Name) and upon a strict puritan ethic. Kukas were to rise between 3 and 6 a.m. and having bathed they were to repeat passages from the Sikh scriptures. Virtue and continence were enjoined and to those who abused or struck them they were to respond with meekness.[12] A comprehensive report prepared by the Inspector General of Police at the end of 1867 acknowledges the high ideals of the Kukas. Having sampled the opinions of "the native officers of one of our frontier regiments", he concluded:

> They all seem to have a great respect for the tenets of the sect, and agree that it is an effort to restore the Sikh religion to its original purity, and to do away with the innovations which have crept into it, such as consulting Brahmins as to the proper day for marriages, etc. from what they say, the belief of the sect appears to be a pure disension. They hold that God is one, not made or born, but existing by himself, and they appear to hold in utter reprobation the Hindoo belief of various incarnation of the deity. They inculcate a very strict morality, condemning most strongly lying, theft, and adultery, and appear anxious merely to revive the Sikh religion in its original state of purity and to eradicate the errors which have from time it time, defiled it.[13]

To this extent Ram Singh sought nothing more than a revival of the Gurus' teachings and it is scarcely surprising that at this stage the sample of Sikh opinion taken by the police should have been generally favourable towards the Kukas. Even the vigour with which the Kukas urged the cause of cow protection brought no serious objections until it led to the murder of Muslim butchers in Amritsar and Raikot. Although the Gurus had not attached any evident importance to the issue the ancient tradition died hard and Sikhs who supported it would not thereby mark themselves out as deviants.

It was, of course, inevitable that distinctive beliefs and practices should soon emerge within the sect, but initially even these did not alienate the Kukas from the bulk of the orthodox Sikh community. At first they were regarded as little more than the harmless peculiarities of religious enthusiasts, and protests against them appear to have been largely confined to those members of the Sikh community who were the particular targets of Ram Singh's reforming strictures.[14] The most prominent of these differences was evidently responsible for the appearance of the word 'Kuka'. On important occasions members of the sect would assemble for a ceremony called *Chandi ka Path*, literally "a reading of the epic of Chandi".[15] The ceremony was not, strictly, a reading in the literal sense, although passages from the epic were evidently recited as a part of it. Recitations of this and other passages from the Sikh scriptures were conducted antiphonally around a slow-burning bonfire. Gradually enthusiasm would mount amongst the participants until eventually ecstasy would overtake some of them. In this condition, they would cry out, and from the noun *kuk*, 'a shriek', the sect received its characteristic name.[16] Another distinctive custom was the practice of tying turbans horizontally across the forehead.[17]

None of this bothered the Punjab government unduly, nor did it generate serious concern within the Sikh community until it became evident that the Kuka movement could be an agent of social disturbance as well as religious reform. Even the Kuka disposition to desecrate Hindu temples and Muslim tombs seemed to be no more than the iconoclasm of a few fanatics whose activities were disowned by their leader.[18] What did bother the British from the very beginning of Ram Singh's tenure was the evidence which they soon perceived of territorial organisation. This seemed to add substance to their vague suspicions of sedition, particularly when they began to learn more about the precise identity of Ram Singh's subordinates. In dividing Punjab into Kuka districts Ram Singh was merely following early Sikh precedents, the only significant difference being the title attached to the district leaders. To each district designated in this manner there was appointed a trusted disciple bearing the title of 'subah'. Ram Singh might be innocent of sedition, but could the same be said of his subahs? The police were satisfied that there was sufficient smoke to warrant a strong suspicion of fire. A particular mistrust was attached to Sahib Singh, the heir-apparent of Ram Singh, and to four others "all more or less truculent and ill-disposed to the restraint of constituted authority".[19]

As time passed, however, their fears subsided. By the end of 1868 Kuka influence appeared to be waning,[20] a trend which seemed to be confirmed by the reports received during the following year.[21] A Kuka riot which had occurred in Ferozpore district during that year did nothing to disturb this confidence.[22] Some fresh suspicions were aroused by Kuka enlistments in the army of the Maharaja of Kashmir and by the despatch of an emissary to Nepal, but nothing more than a continuation of regular surveillance seemed to be required.[23]

This crisis began eighteen months later. Although the deeper causes of the outbreak must defy any summary treatment at this stage, at least the immediate issue was plain. This was the Kuka abhorrence of cow killing. In June 1871, a party of Kukas attacked the Amritsar slaughter house and escaped after murdering four of the butchers. A month later the incident was repeated at Raikot, near Ludhiana. One of the culprits apprehended after the second raid turned Queen's Evidence and as a result of his disclosures several arrests were made. All were Kukas and three of them were subahs.[24] At once the tone of the police reports changed. No serious outbreak was yet envisaged, but the growing tendency to treat the Kukas simply as harmless religious fanatics came to an abrupt end.

The climax followed soon after. On 14 January, 1872, a party of Kukas from Bhaini attacked the obscure fort of Malodh in Ludhiana district and then, with augmented numbers, attempted to force their way into the town of Malerkotla.[25] Having failed in their objective, the dispirited party retreated into Patiala territory, where sixty-eight of them surrendered at the village of Rurr.

Meanwhile, L. Cowan, officiating Deputy Commissioner of Ludhiana district, had hastened to Malerkotla, and when the prisoners arrived there, he proceeded to blow forty-nine of them away from guns without trial. This he did in spite of an earlier caution which he had received from T.D. Forsyth, Commissioner of Ambala Division, and a second letter from Forsyth which arrived while the last batch of prisoners was being lashed to the guns. One other prisoner attacked him and was cut down. Two of the total were women, leaving sixteen whom Cowan proposed to execute the following day.

In the letter which arrived during the course of the executions Forsyth had explicitly ordered Cowan to proceed according to legal requirements. Having received Cowan's report, however, he approved the action. He then proceeded to Malerkotla and after a summary trial blew the remaining sixteen prisoners away from guns. Four more prisoners captured during the earlier attack on Malodh were executed the following day.[26]

The result of this episode was a furore. Two separate issues had to be decided and one at least generated a considerable controversy. Cowan had plainly transgressed the bounds of established legal procedure by executing without a trial, and Forsyth had compromised his earlier rectitude by subsequently approving his action. The method of execution was, moreover, irregular and the manner in which Forsyth had tried the second batch of prisoners was not beyond suspicion. Cowan argued vigorously that dangerous situations require impressive remedies, and that because he had been prepared to act with such expedition "a rebellion which might have attained large dimension was nipped in the bud".[27] Forsyth supported this claim,[28] and so too did the Anglo-Indian press, with the notable exception of the *Friend of India*.[29] Many amongst the landed and the titled of Punjab society declared their appreciation of Cowan's action,[30] and even the Lieutenant Governor of Punjab demonstrated an evident willingness to concur.[31] The Government of India did not, however, concur. Cowan was dismissed from the service and Forsyth was transferred to Oudh.[32] This decision was subsequently confirmed by the Secretary of State for India.[33]

The second major question concerned the treatment of Ram Singh and his surviving subahs. In this instance, the primary issue was not one of guilt. It was assumed by the Lieutenant Governor and doubtless by many others that Ram Singh, as leader of the sect, must assuredly have been implicated in the attacks on Malodh and Malerkotla,[34] but it soon became clear that an accusation of complicity would stand little chance in a court of law. The available evidence actually pointed to his innocence. Ram Singh claimed that he had attempted to dissuade his headstrong followers from their rash course, but that they had refused to listen to him. Having failed to convince them of their folly he had immediately visited the Deputy Inspector of Police at Sahnewal and warned him of their intentions.[35]

Forsyth suggested that this action had been no more than "a ruse on his part to try and escape the responsibility of the acts of his followers", that he merely had to wait until they were on their way in order to cover himself without affecting their chances of success.[36] This patently failed to provide evidence upon which a prosecution might proceed. The suggestion was alien to the known character of Ram Singh and had the police officer at Sahnewal acted promptly the entire episode might well have been averted. Ram Singh was probably innocent, and even if guilty of complicity, there could be no chance of establishing the charge. The same result would obviously have followed an attempt to establish his complicity in the earlier murder of the Amritsar and Raikot butchers. The possibility of instituting proceedings against him had been given careful consideration at the time by the Lieutenant Governor, but had been reluctantly rejected.[37]

Against the subahs there appeared to be a strong case, for depositions had been obtained which, if sustained in court, would probably establish their guilt. The situation was reviewed by the Government of India and eventually it was decided not to proceed.[38] The principal objection of the Council was expressed in a note by Sir Richard Temple:

> I am against trial if it can be avoided. I say this with great regret but there is no overlooking the fact that whenever a trial for political crimes takes place there are unhappily found English

> Barristers who not content with justly defending their clients (which is quite right) go beyond all legitimate bounds, and raise a sort of political excitement, very detrimental to the minds of native people.[39]

This decision did not mean that the Government of India was prepared to let Ram Singh and his subahs go free. There was an alternative, one which was speedily adopted in the case of Ram Singh and with greater reluctance in the case of his subahs. The government's principal objective was to deprive the Kuka sect of its leadership "until the movement has lost all vitality and has perished beyond all chance of resuscitation".[40] An alternative method of securing this purpose was provided by the Bengal Regulation III of 1818, a measure which was designed to cover occasional circumstances which

> ... render it necessary to place under personal restraint individuals against whom there may not be sufficient ground to institute any judicial proceeding or when such proceeding may not be adapted to the nature of the case or may for other reasons be unadvisable or improper.[41]

Indefinite detention could thus be imposed on the prisoners without trial. E.C. Bayley, Secretary to the Government of India, offered a justification:

> The opinions expressed above may seem harsh and it may perhaps be deemed a strong measure to use Regulation III of 1818 to the extent contemplated. But it is to be remembered that almost beyond moral doubt all the prisoners have been concerned in crimes which would have subjected them to transportation for life if proved conspiring to wage war against the Queen, seditious preaching and teaching, abetment of murder and of rebellion with murder. These are the offences with one or more of which every one of the prisoners is at least on strong grounds charged. It seems probable now that if it were politic to bring them to trial, proof even for legal conviction (as for example against Burma Singh) could easily be obtained. There seems accordingly no practical injustice inflicting upon them under the Act, for reasons of

> policy, restriction of their liberty which they really deserved by their breaches of the criminal law. It seems only necessary to discriminate between those who as active leaders will be dangerous under any circumstances so long as inflammable marks of ignorance and fanaticism exist in Punjab, and those who are dangerous only in connection with the present movement.[42]

Faced with a choice between the Bengal Regulation III and the freedom, the Viceroy's Council had already invoked the regulation in Ram Singh's case and despatched him to Rangoon.[43] Bayley's argument was accepted in the case of the subahs and in October 1872 the eleven who were regarded as dangers to peace and security were distributed to various British jails, most of them outside peninsular India.[44]

The subsequent history of the Kukas may be narrated very briefly. Religious preaching continued and a few members of the sect endeavoured to sustain a covert agitation against the government. One of them, a subah named Gurcharan Singh, actually reached Samarkand where he established a fitful contact with the Russian governor of Turkestan.[45] The political phase was, however, soon to come to an end. Brief contacts with the restless Maharaja Dalip Singh marked its terminus.[46] Although the Kukas continued to look for the prophesied return of Ram Singh, their activities following the death of Dalip Singh in 1893 occasioned no further concern to the government. During the present century they have been distinguished only by their continuing insistence upon reform of the Sikh religion, and notably by their refusal to permit lavish weddings or dowries. Their horizontal turbans are still to be seen in Punjab and although their numbers are now few the message which issues from Bhaini and Jiwan Nagar remains a vigorous one.[47]

This summary narrative of the rise and decline of the Kuka sect must serve as a basis for our analysis of that rise and decline. The basic facts are clear. A sect which began as a religious reform movement within the Sikh community multiplied rapidly, came into conflict with the British administration in Punjab, and then dwindled into insignificance. The questions which confront us concern the reasons which account for the sudden increase in

Kuka popularity, for the sect's confrontation with the Punjab government, and for the decline which took place thereafter.

Two theories have already been advanced, both of them based upon interpretations which stress the political motivation of the Kukas during the brief period of Ram Singh's leadership. The British administrators who had to deal with the Kuka disturbance quickly produced a theory which, they claimed, was justified by the decline which followed so closely upon the banishment of the Kuka leaders. The events of Malodh and Malerkotla were viewed in the setting of recent military history. Only a quarter of a century had passed since the might of British arms had destroyed Sikh rule in Punjab. Sikh rule meant, above all, the glories of Maharaja Ranjit Singh and it was but natural that the Sikhs should look back to the recent past with an ardent longing. There was, moreover, the conviction amongst the Sikhs that their defeat in the Sikh wars had been the result more of treachery than of British power and the events of 1857 had demonstrated the extent to which that power could be successfully challenged.

And so the Sikhs, or many of them, dreamt of driving the British out of Punjab. Ram Singh provided a focus for this ambition and with the aid of his territorial subahs he set about preparing for the battle. Unfortunately for him, his headstrong subahs moved too soon and provoked a clash which was easily suppressed. The clash proved highly advantageous to the government, for it provided it with sufficient grounds for suppressing the movement before it became a serious problem. Cowan's methods were wholly irregular, but at least they succeeded and the name of the British justice was redeemed by means of disciplinary action. All that was required in order to cripple the movement was to deport its leader. When this was done Kuka numbers and influence declined rapidly. The simple analysis had evidently been correct.[48]

The second theory is a modern nationalist interpretation, and specifically a Punjabi interpretation. During the uprising of 1857-58, the British had received welcome assistance from Sikh troops. This assistance subsequently proved to be an embarrassment to Punjabi participants in the independence struggle and prompted an effort to prove that Punjab had been as loyal to the ideal of freedom as any other part of India. On the one hand it was claimed that the help had been rendered not by the people of Punjab but by the princes; and on the other it was suggested that amongst the people, as opposed to the princes, independence movements were already afoot.

The Kuka episode has, in recent years, been advanced as proof of the second claim. Although indications of this theory appear as far back as 1913 in the propaganda literature of the revolutionary Ghadr Party,[49] the interpretation did not win instant acceptance. Fifty years later, R. C. Majumdar, the historian of the freedom movement, could still dismiss Ram Singh with a brief comment:

> He gave military training to his followers and organised the sect. There is, however, no adequate evidence to support the view that the Kuka movement ever aimed at the subversion of the British rule.[50]

In making this comment, Majumdar had, however, noted a growing tendency to regard various local disturbances as freedom struggles.[51] The tendency eventually emerged in a coherent form when in 1965 two books appeared in support of the freedom struggle thesis. M.M. Ahluwalia's *Kukas* is significantly sub-titled "The Freedom Fighters of the Punjab", and Fauja Singh Bajwa is equally explicit in adding to his *Kuka Movement* the sub-title "An Important Phase in Punjab's Role in India's Struggle for Freedom".[52]

Much of this modern nationalist interpretation is curiously similar to the earlier theory advanced by the British administrators, differing only in points of emphasis. There is, for example, a heavier stress upon the claim that the British owed their earlier victories to treachery within the Sikh ranks, and much attention is understandably devoted to the punitive measures taken by Cowan and Forsyth, and later by the Government of India. The principal difference derives from the attempt made by the two authors to relate the Kuka outbreak to the wider struggle for independence. According to their interpretation it was an early phase of the larger struggle, and because the struggle ultimately succeeded the Kuka sacrifice did not go in vain. Whereas the early British theory had treated the outbreak as an isolated, insignificant, and somewhat sordid failure, the modern interpretation regards it as a heroic setback on the road to ultimate triumph.

The primary purpose of this essay is to suggest a third interpretation, one which shifts the focus of attention away from the political aspects of the Kuka outbreak to the social conditions within which it developed. This is not to deny the existence of political issues, nor their importance. Clearly, the Kuka outbreak must in some measure relate to the annexation of Punjab by the alien British, and it has already been shown that its sudden emergence took the form of political action. There were, however, issues at once more important and more obscure. An examination of these issues raises the possibility that the Kuka movement may be interpreted as a distinctively Indian example of the millenarian pattern. The movement develops within a disturbed social environment; it gathers around the person of a religious leader; it generates a glorious vision of the future; and in pursuit of this objective it moves towards an ill-defined expression of political protest. These features prompt the suggestion that a comparison with characteristic millenarian processes may perhaps lead us to a deeper understanding of the Kuka outbreak.

Protest movements assuming a millenarian form normally pass through four distinct and successive phases of development. The first involves the spread of social discontent within a particular geographical area with the consequent emergence of a substantial group of disoriented and frustrated people. This is followed by the appearance of a holy man, one regarded as inspired and perhaps as divine. The third phase results from a junction of the leader and the group, a connection which produces a fraternity fortified with a social myth adapted to their needs. Finally, the fourth phase issues in "a frantic urge to smite the ungodly", an irresistable impulse to strike out at the person, the group, or the institution identified as the source of falsehood and oppression.[53]

The possibility that this pattern may enlarge our understanding of the Kuka movement arises from an obvious correspondence of three of these phases to the known pattern of

Kuka development. Correspondence at three points suggests the possibility of correspondence at the fourth also. In the case of the Kukas it is the first of the four phases which is obscure, the phase which concerns the origins and motivation of the sect. As we have already seen, the causes of the sect's brief popularity have hitherto been interpreted in political terms as a conscious desire to shake off the British yoke. A comparison with millenarian movements elsewhere implies deeper causes. The political aspects of the sect's activities are not thereby denied, but are instead to be understood as essentially incoherent responses to an underlying social discontent.

The second of the phases outlined above is at once obvious in the case of the Kukas. Ram Singh of Bhaini was the holy man around whom a following rapidly gathered. The fact that Ram Singh evidently disapproved of the violence of his followers does nothing to disturb the pattern. A holy man can serve as a focus for discontent without necessarily sharing the discontent itself or participating in the actions which it provokes.

The third of the four phases is well illustrated by a document which the police acquired in 1863.

The Sakhi of Guru Govind Singh

> I, Guru Govind Singh, will be born in a carpenter's shop, and will be called Ram Singh. My house will be between the Jamna and Sutlej rivers. I will declare my religion. I will defeat the Faringhis and put the crown on my own head, and blow the sankh. The musicians shall praise me in 1921 [1864]. I, the carpenter, will sit on the throne. When I have got one lakh and twenty five thousand Sikhs with me, I will cut off the heads of the Faringhis. I will never be conquered in battle, and will shout 'Akal, Akal'. The Christians will desert their wives and fly from the country when they hear the shout of 1¼ lakhs of Khalsas. A great battle will take place on the banks of the Jamna, and blood will flow like the waters of the Ravi, and no Faringhi be left alive. Insurrections will take place in the country in 1922 [1865]. The Khalsa will reign, and the rajah and ryot will live in peace and comfort, and no one shall molest another.

> Day by day Ram Singh's rule will be enlarged. God has written this. It is no lie, my brethren. In 1922 [1865], the whole country will be ruled by Ram Singh. My followers will worship Wahaguru [God]. God says this will happen.[54]

The parallels with other millenarian movements are self-evident. Guru Gobind Singh (who died in 1708) has declared that he will be reincarnated in the person of Ram Singh the carpenter. To him the righteous of the Khalsa will flock. The enemy is identified (the Faranghi, i.e., the alien, Christian British). The final conflict is imminent, the battle will be bloody, and following its inevitably triumphant conclusion the Khalsa will rule a world transformed, an earthly paradise in which ruler and peasant will dwell together in perfect harmony. All this is expressed in terms derived from the Sikh past and specifically from the period of Gobind Singh—the warrior Guru. It is the Khalsa (the brotherhood founded by Guru Gobind Singh) which will fight the battle. Its forces will number one and a quarter lakhs (1,25,000)—the figure traditionally associated with the triumph of Khalsa arms. The battle will take place on the banks of a river closely connected with the life of Guru Gobind Singh and the war cry to be raised will be one of the Sikh names of God (*Akal*, or "the Eternal One").

Other characteristically millenarian features appear in later police reports. Discontent was directed against the privileged classes and found expression in an attempt to restore traditional values. The targets may have been Brahmans rather than Bishops, and the most compelling of ancient traditions may have been the distinctively Indian reverence for the cow, but the pattern was essentially the same as elsewhere. Religious leaders who were attacked duly retaliated,[55] and so too did the larger landholders when they perceived the social implications of the movement.[56] Amongst the stock criticisms applied to Ram Singh and his followers accusations of sexual immorality figure prominently.[57] Other resemblances are the more striking for being less predictable. The Kuka versions of the *Sau Sakhis* offer a parallel to the Sibylline Books both in their actual usage and in their convenient mutations.[58] A Kuka equivalent of the Heavenly Letter appeared in 1876,[59] and in the claim that Ram Singh was reincarnation of Guru Gobind Singh they produced their own version of the Sleeping Emperor legend.[60] Like many of their European counterparts the Kukas also attached a particular importance to the white colour.

The fourth stage is reached when the impulse to smite the ungodly issues in unplanned conflict and speedy repression. Two varieties of the ungodly served as targets for Kuka anger. The first to be attacked were the Muslim butchers of Amritsar and Raikot, enemies not merely because they were killers of kine (a most abhorrent crime) but also because they were Muslims. Enmity between Sikh and Muslim, greatly strengthened during the eighteenth century, had not been allayed and if a traditional opponent were to be identified the obvious candidate would be a Muslim. This enmity was also in evidence during the later outbreak. Malerkotla was not the most convenient of objectives for a party operating from Bhaini. One reason for selecting it may have been the fact that it was the only Muslim state in Punjab. In this later episode, however, the second enemy was also involved. The new tyrant was the British *mlechchha*, the destroyer of the Khalsa dominion and a more obvious target for the socially discontented during the second half of the nineteenth century.

Three of the four phases can thus be identified in the case of the Kukas. Is it possible similarly to identify the remaining one—the first of the four? What emerges when, following the characteristic millenarian pattern, we look behind the actual incidents for evidence of people disoriented and frustrated ? Is this a description which fits those who participated in the Kuka movement, or are they still to be seen as rebels/nationalists pursuing deliberate and coherent political objectives ?

The answer must be that the Kukas did indeed represent in distinctly millenarian terms the measure of confusion and frustration which one would expect from parallel examples of the same responses. The two decades preceding the sudden surge in Kuka numbers had been for the Sikhs a period of dissolving religious values and slackening communal cohesion. This stood in marked contrast to the preceding century and a half. The eighteenth century had been a stirring period for the Sikh community, as its traditions so vividly demonstrate. This was the century in which persecution and martyrdom had been succeeded first by heroic struggles and ultimately by the triumph of the Khalsa. The triumphs of the eighteenth century were further extended by Maharaja Ranjit Singh, and when he died in 1839 Sikh glory was at its zenith.

This was a powerful myth, one which still retains much of its vitality today. Set against its grandeur, the decades which followed the death of Ranjit Singh, presented a sorry spectacle of failure and decay. Treachery had destroyed the Khalsa army from within. The teachings of the Gurus had been forgotten. Worldliness and immorality consumed the community's leaders. Those who held power and influence had obtained it by unscrupulous means and used it to oppress the less fortunate. Sacred traditions were openly violated. The foreigner who had inflicted the indignity of defeat brought with him not merely his soldiers but also his missionaries. More and more Sikhs were casting aside the visible symbols of their loyalty to the community.

Thus was the myth extended. The brightness of the past was now matched by the darkness of the present. It is scarcely surprising that interpretations of this kind should issue in attempts to arrest the process of dissolution. Balak Singh's Jagiasi movement was one of the earliest of these attempts. For him the earlier glory consisted in the purity of the Gurus' religious teachings, and specifically in the devotional practice of *nam simran*. Ram Singh evidently propounded the same message, but for many of his followers the glories of the past were primarily the military triumphs of the Khalsa. During the eighteenth century the Mughal authority had been extinguished in Punjab and Afghan efforts to invade the land had been resisted. Ranjit Singh had consolidated these successes and then pushed back the boundaries of Punjab in three directions. Even the British, for all their strength, had drawn back from a confrontation. There had been unity and purpose, and for none more than those who were Sikhs. There had also been employment, for Ranjit Singh's army had been a large one.

The two decades following the death of Ranjit Singh were

certainly a period of progressive disillusionment for the Sikhs, and the Kuka attempts to evoke the heroic traditions of Guru Gobind Singh suggest that the development of their sect must be related to this experience of disillusionment. This should not be the end of the analysis, however, for it is possible to proceed further in pursuit of the origins of the distress and disarray. The role of Ranjit Singh's army as an employer of many Jat Sikhs could conceivably imply that the overtly religious aspects of Kuka discontent derived from essentially economic sources. Here too, the example of other millenarian movements may provide a guide. In such instances it is normally economic distress with its attendant social problems which creates the tension leading to distinctively millenarian responses.

At first sight the available evidence is unpromising. The Kuka movement drew practically all of its support from the rural areas of Punjab and if we are to judge from the comments offered by the British administrators of this period these areas were not economically depressed during the years which cover the sect's rapid ascent to its short-lived prominence. The evidence is best presented in the settlement reports produced towards the end of the nineteenth century. These record increases in cultivation and in the irrigation of areas already under cultivation.[61] Population increases are briefly noted, but without evident concern. At this stage it was believed that the agricultural resources of the fertile plains could cope with such increases.[62] The critical test of rural stability was taken to be the degree of willingness with which taxes were paid, and it was recorded, with obvious satisfaction, that revenue collection had generally involved little difficulty during the period preceding the writing of the reports.[63]

It is in just such circumstances that analyses of other millenarian movements can demonstrate their usefulness as guides. A survey of the evidence provided by the settlement reports would suggest that, whatever the reasons for the Kuka outbreak, economic distress was not be numbered amongst them. The parallel pattern which can be observed in other millenarian situations should caution us against accepting this evidence without further analysis. Was rural Punjab really as contented as the British observers believed? There seems to be little doubt that most of the revenue paying landholders must have been in relatively prosperous circumstances, but was this the group which provided the Kukas with the main body of their support? Other millenarian examples direct us to look elsewhere, not to the wealthier grain producing landowners but rather to the humbler orders of the Punjabi society. These are the people who characteristically provide a millenarian movement with its strength. They are also the people who figure prominently in reports concerning the consistency of the Kuka sect.

The dominant caste group within the Sikh community was (and remains) that of the Jats—a rural and agrarian people with strong martial traditions. Some Jats were landlords; others of lesser means cultivated small holdings as tenants. In undivided Punjab, only a minority of the Jats were Sikhs (the remaining being Muslims or Hindus), but within the Sikh community the Jat element has always retained a strong numerical preponderance. These were the people for whom the eighteenth century conditions had proven particularly advantageous and for whom the army of Ranjit Singh had subsequently provided congenial employment. Their poorer members were also the people who offered the strongest body of support to the Kuka movement. Others who joined it were drawn mainly from artisan and other depressed castes which stood in a client relationship to Jat patrons. The line of investigation which must now be pursued concerns these poorer members of the Sikh community. Is there any evidence which might suggest that theirs was a condition of unrest during the period leading up to the emergence of the sect?

A feature commonly associated with millenarian developments is increasing population pressure. This feature was certainly to be found in Punjab of the middle and later nineteenth century. The eighteenth century struggles which opened the way to Khalsa dominance had served, in the usual manner of military disturbances, to impose a check upon population growth. This condition was altered by Ranjit Singh's rise to power. All of his major battles were fought beyond the fertile tract of central Punjab, and after 1824 they ceased altogether apart from some minor skirmishes. Warfare made a brief return during the fifth decade of the nineteenth century, but peace was reimposed in 1849 and was little affected by the events of 1857. By the time Ram Singh emerged as leader of the Kukas Punjab had experienced five decades of relative tranquillity. But for the disturbances which followed Ranjit Singh's death, the total would have been six. Indeed it can be argued that the span was even longer, for the more devastating disturbances of the eighteenth century were over well before the century concluded.

The result was an increase in the population of Punjab. Although no figures exist for the period prior to 1855, it seems safe to assume that the trend which appeared in successive censuses from that year onwards will have been an extension of earlier increases during the preceding half century. Certainly, there is no doubt about the trend during the years immediately preceding the Kuka outbreak. Between 1855 and 1868, the population of Punjab increased by 16.1 percent.[64]

The portion of the province which absorbed the greater measure of this rapid increase was the central tract, the area which already possessed the highest density. Whereas Jalandhar district had a population density of 513 per square mile in 1855, the corresponding figure for the potentially fertile but unirrigated Montgomery district was still only 55.[65] This in itself meant little, for Jalandhar district in 1855 could obviously support a much higher density than areas which lacked either its fertility or its supply of water. A figure in excess of 500 was nevertheless a high one for a rural area to support and its was one which continued to rise in the years following 1855. During the brief period from 1855 to 1868 Jalandhar district had to absorb more than 80 extra persons per square mile. Although the figure for Jalandhar is one of the highest (only Amritsar district with an increase of 96 per square mile is higher), it is clear from a conspectus of the district totals that the major growth was concentrated in the central tract and that the rate of increase dropped away steadily as one moved outwards from it.[66]

These are impressive figures and they can be rendered even more impressive by the observation that during the middle decades of the nineteenth century urban areas absorbed relatively little of any population increase. An overwhelming proportion had to be accommodated within rural society. Against them must be set the statistics for agrarian extension provided by the settlement reports. Although these reduce the force of the demographic argument, they fall far short of destroying it. The situation which thus emerged did not in itself constitute a crisis, but it appears that it did involve a condition of considerable risk. Even the settlement officers perceived this.[67]

In such a situation, a regular succession of adequate harvests was vital. For several years after the British annexation this succession was maintained, but eventually it was broken. Following a favourable year in 1857, the harvests of 1858 were much reduced, and during 1860-61 Punjab experienced a serious famine.[68] This was followed by another period of acute scarcity in 1869-70.[69] In such a situation, those in possession of grain surpluses could secure a handsome profit from the inevitable increase in prices. Others, however, must suffer and for some this was the beginning of the road leading to indebtedness and eventually expropriation.

In such circumstances, the poorer Jats would certainly have experienced distress, and in their case the experience of shared disaster will have been aggravated by two additional features. One was the Jat custom of fragmenting landholdings at death. Large landholders, the heirs of substantial estates from the days of Sikh rule, might survive and flourish. Others must look elsewhere for alternative or supplementary means of support. Such means are usually available and the Jat has been characteristically prompt in utilising them. The second aggravating factor was, however, a temporary blockage of the customary means of supplementary support. During the period of Ranjit Singh and his successors, there was the army—an outlet which was soon to reopen under the British rule. Later, there were the canal colonies, later still the Mercedes trucks and Calcutta taxis, and during recent years there have been opportunities for migration overseas.[70] The period immediately following the British annexation of Punjab in 1849 was, however, a disastrous exception as far as the Jats were concerned. The British had insisted upon disbandment of the large Khalsa army, and although the Indian Army opened its ranks to the Sikhs with surprising speed there was inevitably an interval before this decision could provide a measure of aid sufficient to compensate for the economic problems of the Jat peasants.[71]

Discontent which afflicted the Jat peasants of the central tract would also have affected other rural caste groups of inferior economic status. In addition to the general problem of food shortages anything which affected the Jats could also be expected to affect those who were dependent upon them. If the Jat patrons suffered, the artisan and menial clients must suffer with them. If discontent were to develop within a distinctively Sikh group, the vehicle of that discontent would predictably be a Sikh movement. Its origins might be religious, but the secret of its power to attract evidently lay in economic distress and in the threats to social stability which this involved. The Kuka sect evidently served as a convenient focus for rural unrest. Having won a generous measure of support, the sect was first transformed by its new converts and then shattered by their impulsiveness.

This analysis appears to be the only one which will take account of three fundamental aspects of Kuka history. The first of these is the lowly social and economic constituency of the sect. It was highly significant that Major Perkins should have observed that "converts are chiefly made from Juts, Tirkhans, Chumars and Muzbees".[72] Later police analysis of Kuka membership showed that of these four groups by far the strongest was that of the Jats,[73] and that this element was drawn largely from the ranks of the poorer Jats.[74] These were the people who would suffer extensively from conditions of economic deprivation while yet retaining memories of a more prosperous past.

Secondly, there is the close correlation between periods of food shortage and spurts in Kuka activity. The first serious famine took place in 1860-61, and the sect suddenly surges ahead in 1862-63. In 1868 and 1869, the police report a condition of general tranquillity amongst the Kukas. Another period of scarcity follows during 1869-70 and by the middle of 1871 the outbreaks of violence have begun.

Thirdly, there is the striking increase in the sect's strength which immediately followed the death of Balak Singh. When Balak Singh died in 1862, the focus of the sect's activities automatically moved away from his home in Hazro to Ram

Singh's village of Bhaini. Hazro was a small town situated on the periphery of Punjab in an area which still suffered little from population pressure or social dislocation. Within this area the Sikh population constituted only a fragment of the total population and within the Sikh community itself a majority belonged to mercantile castes.[75] Bhaini, in contrast, lay within the fertile central tract where Sikh traditions were powerful, where most members of the community were Jats, and where crop failure had so recently caused serious problems.[76] A religious leader appears within an area afflicted by famine and immediately attracts a substantial following from the poorer sections of the community. It seems impossible to resist the conclusion that the reason for the sudden growth of the sect must lie in the existing condition of economic distress. And this is precisely what the example of other millenarian movements would lead us to expect.

It thus becomes evident that the Kuka sect is best understood as a distinctively Sikh version of a common millenarian pattern. Social instability had produced discontent, and discontent had found the holy man to whom it could attach its aspirations. Out of this, there emerged the myth which drew together past glories, present frustrations, and future hopes. Battle was joined, not with deliberation but impulsively, and the movement was quickly crushed. The leaders were imprisoned, adherents quickly fell away and although a loyal remnant remained the discontent which had prompted the sect's rapid growth soon found outlets elsewhere. For many the armed forces and the canal colonies provided a sufficient answer. Others found a more convincing purpose in the Gurdwara Reform Movement or in the political channels which fed the Ghadr conspiracy and eventually the Punjab Communist Party. It is, in many ways, a sad story. Like so many other millenarian movements it culminated in tragedy and slipped thereafter into a respectable insignificance. There was, however, more to the later Kuka experience than hopes deceived and fruitless intrigues with a Russian governor. The sect had begun as a religious reform movement and to this exclusive concern it subsequently returned. The contribution of Sikh belief and custom to Punjab society is immense and voices which preach its reform have yet to be wholly ignored.

Notes

1. *Jagiasi*, 'worshipper', from *jagya* or *yagya*, 'sacrifice', 'offering'. In some references the title used is Abhiasi (*abhiasi*, 'student', "one who meditates or devoutly repeats a sacred *mantra*", from *abhias*, 'study, meditation, repetition').
2. According to orthodox Sikh belief the unbroken succession of ten Gurus extending from Nanak (1469-1539) to Gobind Singh (1666-1708) represented the embodiment of a single divine spirit in ten human bodies. Gobind Singh's sons had all predeceased him and according to Sikh tradition he had declared that at his death the spirit which had inhabited the ten bodies would thereafter dwell in the corporate community and in the sacred scripture. The belief which emerged amongst the followers of Balak Singh assumed a resumption of human form by the divine spirit. In Sikh usage the title 'Guru' signifies this divine spirit and within the community it could not be applied to a mere mortal however pious or enlightened he might be.
3. From a report dated 12 June, 1863, included in Memoranda regarding Gooroo Ram Singh, of a new sect of Sikhs, *'Jagiasis'*, compiled by J.W. Younghusband, Officiating Inspector-General of Police, 28 June, 1863, reproduced in Nahar Singh, *Gooroo Ram Singh and the Kuka Sikhs*, New Delhi, 1965, I, 1. Nahar Singh's work is a comprehensive collection of government documents covering the period 1863 to 1881, most of them drawn from the National Archives of India in New Delhi. The other major depository of official documents relating to the Kuka sect (India Office Library, Judicial-Public files and Punjab Government records) largely duplicates the material provided by Nahar Singh. The collection consists of three volumes published by the compiler (vols. I and II, New Delhi, 1965 and 1966; vol. III, Sri Jiwan Nagar, 1967). The collection is cited hereafter as NS.
4. Minute on Younghusband's *Memoranda*. NS, I, 10.
5. *Ibid*.
6. NS, I, 30. The Tarkhan, or carpenter caste, occupies a low ritual and economic status. Chamars are outcaste leather workers (known as Ramdasis when they become Sikhs). Mazhabis are

members of the Chhuhra (sweeper) outcaste group who have become Sikhs. Ram Singh was himself a Tarkhan.

7. *Ibid.*
8. *NS*, I, 11.
9. *NS*, I, 60.
10. Notably Dhian Singh, *Sri Satguru Bilas* (Bhaini Sahib, 1942), Nidhan Singh Alam, *Jug Paltau Satguru* (Delhi, 1947), and Santokh Singh, *Satgur Bilas* (unpub.). For quotations, see Fauja Singh Bajwa, *Kuka Movement*, Delhi, 1965, passim.
11. Fauja Singh Bajwa, *op. cit.*; M. M. Ahluwalia, *Kukas*, Bombay, 1965. Ganda Singh, *Kukian di Vithia*, 2nd ed., Amritsar, 1946; Nahar Singh, *Namdhari Itihas*, Delhi, 1955. Summary accounts of Kuka history and belief are given by Stephen Fuchs, *Rebellious Prophets*, Bombay, 1965, pp. 192-97; and Khushwant Singh, *A History of the Sikhs*, Princeton, 1966, II, 127-35. A brief notice appears in S. Gopal, *British Policy in India 1858-1905*, Cambridge, 1965, pp. 98-101.
12. *NS*, I, 26.
13. *NS*, I, 66.
14. *NS*, I, 56-57.
15. *Chandi di Var*, or 'The Epic of the Goddess Chandi', is a work ascribed to the tenth Guru, Gobind Singh.
16. *NS*, I, 31.
17. Orthodox Sikhs wrap their turbans upwards from each ear to a central point of convergence immediately below the hair line.
18. *NS*, I, 72.
19. *NS*, I, 77.
20. *NS*, I, 98-99, 102.
21. *NS*, I, 111-112, 114.
22. *NS*, I, 105-111.
23. *NS*, I, 115, 119.
24. *NS*, I, 123-127.
25. The number of attackers, originally estimated to have been 500, appears to have been at most 125. *NS*, II, 12.

26. A summary narrative of the episode is given in *NS*, II, 57-72. This narrative, prepared in the Judicial branch, represents a collation of all relevant correspondence received up to 8 April, 1872. For the documents upon which it is based see *NS*, II, 2 ff. One error in the summary narrative is the statement that Forsyth executed the batch of sixteen prisoners by hanging them. It was not until 21 May that the Punjab government realised that Forsyth had followed Cowan's example and had the prisoners blown away from guns. *NS*, III, 75.
27. *NS*, II, 34. Also II, 105, 168-69, 175 ff.
28. *NS*, II, 97. G.R. Elsmie, *Thirty-five Years in the Punjab*, Edinburgh, 1908, pp. 163-64.
29. *NS*, II, 227 ff.
30. *NS*, III, 164 ff.
31. *NS*, II, 125, 151, 194-98.
32. *NS*, III, 18 ff, 29-30, 30-31.
33. *NS*, III, 138.
34. *NS*, II, 14-15.
35. *NS*, II, 4, 134. Sahnewal is six miles from Bhaini.
36. *NS*, II, 50.
37. *NS*, II, 149.
38. *NS*, III, 187-88.
39. *NS*, III, 115.
40. *NS*, III, 107.
41. *NS*, II, 111.
42. *NS*, III, 107.
43. *NS*, II, 204, 226. In 1878 Ram Singh was transferred to Mergui when it was discovered that clandestine communications were being passed between Rangoon and Punjab. NS, III, 368.
44. *NS*, III, 156-68, 187-88.
45. For this episode, see P. C. Roy, 'Gurcharan Singh's Mission in Central Asia', *Indian Historical Records Commission Proceedings*, XXXIV, 2 (December 1958); and 'Sikh Emissary in Russian Turkestan', *Indo-Asian Culture*, 3 (July 1968).
46. Fauja Singh Bajwa, pp. 167-70.

47. The present headquarters of the Namdhari sect are located in the village of Sri Jiwan Nagar, District Hissar, Haryana. The Guru continues to reside at Bhaini.
48. For an example of the British interpretation see David Ross, *The Land of the Five Rivers and Sindh*, London, 1883, pp.225-26. See also *Gazetteer of the Ludhiana District*, 1888-9, Calcutta, pp.67-69.
49. N. Gerald Barrier, *The Sikhs and their Literature*, Delhi, 1970, p.100. For the Ghadr Party see Khushwant Singh, II, pp.181-92.
50. R.C.Majumdar, *History of the Freedom Movement in India*, Calcutta, 1962, I, pp.282-83.
51. *Ibid.*, p. 282.
52. See above n. 11.
53. Norman Cohn, *The Pursuit of the Millennium, Paladin*, rev. ed., London, 1970, p. 60. For a summary of the characteristic pattern of millenarian belief in medieval Europe see *Ibid.*, p. 13. See also his essay 'Medieval Millenarianism' in S. Thrup (ed.), *Millennial Dreams in Action*, The Hague, 1962, pp. 31-43. The literature dealing with millenarian movements in different parts of the world is now immense. One work which deserves particular notice is Peter Worsley, *The Trumpet Shall Sound*, London, 1957.
54. NS, I, 6. This document was supplied by an informer who had been sent to Bhaini by the Cantonment Magistrate of Jalandhar in June 1863. The informer reported having received it from the leading Kuka subah, Sahib Singh. The word *sakhi* means 'testimony'. Guru Gobid Singh, the last of the personal Gurus recognised by orthodox Sikhs, died in 1708. The years 1921 and 1922 are dated according to the Indian Vikrami era. They correspond to A.D. 1864 and 1865.
55. *NS*, I, 56-57.
56. *NS*, II, 224-25, III 164 ff.
57. *NS*, I, 99, 144-45. Cf. Cohn, p.49.
58. Fauja Singh Bajwa, pp. 22-2, 40, 184; Cohn, pp.30-33. An English translation of the version of the *Sau Sakhis* used by the Kukas was made by Sardar Attar Singh of Bhadaur and published under the title *Sakhee Guru Tegh Bahadur and Guru Gobind Singh*, Lahore, 1876, p. v.

59. Fauja Singh Bajwa, pp. 160-61.
60. See above, p. 96.
61. W. G. Purser, *Final Report of the Revised Settlement of the Jalendhar District in the Punjab*, Lahore, 1892, p. 154. T. Gordon Walker, *Final Report on the Revision of Settlement (1878-83) of the Ludhiana District in the Punjab*, Calcutta, 1884, p.183.
62. Purser, p. 1.
63. Walker, p.178.
64. Census of India 1891: The Punjab and its Feudatories, Calcutta, 1892, I, 76. The comparison was possible only in the case of the British territories, the actual figures being 15,161,321 and 17,609,518. It was, however, assumed on the basis of subsequent trends that the population of the princely states must have shown a corresponding increase. *Ibid.*
65. Report on the Census of Punjab taken on the 17th February 1881, Calcutta, 1883, I, 92 (cited hereafter as 1881 census).
66. *Ibid.* It should be noted that these figures relate to the entire area of the district, uncultivated as well as cultivated. In 1881, the figure for Jalandhar district based on the entire area was 597 per square mile. In the same year the figure for the cultivated areas was 762 per cultivated square mile. Purser, p. 2.
67. Purser, pp.2-3.
68. S. S. Thornburn, *The Punjab in Peace and War*, Edinburgh and London, 1904, pp. 232-33; Walker, pp. 123-24.
69. Walker, p.124.
70. Four-fifths of the Indian migrants to the United Kingdom have been Punjabis, a large majority of them Jats.
71. Characteristically several Kukas enlisted in the army of the Maharaja of Kashmir (see above, pp. 89-90). The emoluments were, however, negligible in comparison with those provided by British paymasters.
72. See above, p. 86.
73. A police list of prominent Kukas prepared in 1878 shows the following distribution:

Cultivator	109
Lambardar	18
Carpenter	14
Miscellaneous (occupations shown in each case)	74
None	38
	253

This is an occupational list, not a caste analysis, but it is possible to deduce from it an approximate figure for the Jat constituency of the sect. Almost all the cultivators will have been Jats and likewise the lambardars. Of the various persons grouped above under 'Miscellaneous' at least ten, and perhaps as many as twenty, can be identified as Jats. The category 'None' presumably covers retired persons, and on the basis of the results shown by the other figures may be interpreted as including a majority of Jats. It seems safe to conclude that at least 150 of the Kukas listed by the police must have been Jats. I am indebted to Professors N.G. Barrier and R. Slater of the University of Missouri for the figures given above.

74. The only prominent Jat Kuka of elevated social or economic status appears to have been Mangal Singh, a relative of the Maharaja of Patiala. Mangal Singh subsequently claimed that he had never been a Kuka but that he had become "a believer in Ram Singh" when the Kuka leader cured his ailing son. NS, III, 97. A few other landholders had attached themselves to the movement shortly before the outbreak. NS, I, 143-44. At least some of these recanted as soon as the movement turned to violence and the Government to vigorous suppression, NS, III, 14.

75. Hazro is situated in Attock tahsil which, during the period covered by this essay, was one of the constituents of Rawalpindi district. In 1855, the population density of Rawalpindi District was 114 per square mile, rising to 146 by 1868, and 169 by 1881 (1881 census, I, 92). In 1881 Sikhs accounted for 1.7 percent of the total population of Rawalpindi Division. Of these 68 percent are classified as belonging to relatively wealthy mercantile castes (Khatri, Arora, and Banya). *Ibid.*, p. 139. The population density of the area around Hazro will have been lower than the district average. Cf. the figures for Hazara district, immediately adjacent

to Hazro: 1855 (98 per sq. m.), 1868 (122), 1881 (134). *Ibid.*, p.92. Balak Singh was himself an Arora by caste. *Gazetteer of the Ludhiana District, 1888-9*, p. 68. Ram Singh was a Tarkhan.

76. Bhaini is located in Ludhiana district, a few miles from the boundary of the neighbouring Jalandhar district. For the years 1855, 1868, and 1881 the figures for the population density of Ludhiana district were respectively 383, 429, and 450; and of Jalandhar district respectively 513, 596, and 597. *Ibid.*, p. 92. Sikhs constituted 6.2 percent of the total population of Jalandhar division (the division includes both districts.) Of these Sikhs 72.7 percent belonged to agricultural castes, more than 60 percent of the total being Jats with the remaining 12 percent distributed amongst Sainis, Rajputs, and Kambohs. 14.5 percent belonged to artisan castes, notably Tarkhans (carpenters) and Lohars (blacksmith). 11 percent were outcastes and only 1 percent came from mercantile castes. *Ibid.*, p. 139.

2

The Singh Sabha Movement 1875-1925

N. GERALD BARRIER

Following the annexation of Punjab in 1849, many contemporary observers felt that Sikhism would disappear within a short time and become one of the many sects within Hinduism. The maintenance of outward symbols, the 5 Ks, associated with Guru Gobind Singh and most recently with the Sikh regiments of Ranjit Singh, appeared to be lax. Sikhs and Hindus shared numerous customs and social practices. The traditional Sikh religious leaders, however, showed little interest in articulating a separate and identifiable set of doctrines. While one European scholar declared that "Sikhism is a waning religion, that will soon belong to history", another warned that like a boa constrictor, Hinduism might soon crush and absorb the Sikh faith.[1]

The reversal of this apparent decline marked a decisive turning point in the evolution of Sikhism. By the early 1900s, Sikhs had undergone a dramatic revitalisation in doctrines, institutions, and spirit. Much of this transformation was due to a new and

---

Reprint of "The Singh Sabha and the Evolution of Modern Sikhism 1875-1925", Robert D. Baird (ed.), *Religious Movements in Modern India*, Delhi: Manohar Publishers, 1989 under the new title.

expanding set of organisations loosely referred to as the Singh Sabhas. The accepted view is that the Singh Sabha membership halted the decline of Sikhism, reasserted traditional Sikh values, and put the religion and its followers back on the path that originated with the ten Gurus. Another increasingly persuasive interpretation is that the Singh Sabhas played a more complex role and, instead of asserting a lost orthodoxy, put together elements from diverse and often conflicting traditions so as to enhance the distinct nature of the religion. This resulted in a new and different Sikh identity, complete with ideology and practices commonly associated with Sikhism today.[2]

Understanding the changes among Sikhs in the decades following the formation of the first Singh Sabha in 1875 involves, first of all, the historical context within which the Sikh resurgence occurred. As Punjabi Sikhs attempted to grapple with the challenges accompanying western rule, they did so in light of teachings associated with the Gurus and *Adi Granth* as well as recent religious experience. That in turn led not to the steady spread of agreed upon doctrines and practices but rather to heated in-fighting among Sikhs and appreciable conflict with other Punjabis also experiencing cultural revitalisation, most notably the Arya Samaj. Despite these difficulties, a common set of ideas and institutions began to emerge between 1902 and 1920, which were systematically promulgated by a new central organisation—the Chief Khalsa Diwan. The sudden appearance of the Gurdwara reform campaigns after 1920 brought into prominence a new group of Sikh activists, the Akalis, whose heroic deeds enshrined them as the legitimate leaders of the community. The Akalis and those Sikhs now controlling the shrines and major resources of the community opposed many of the Singh Sabha leaders politically. However, public consciousness that underlay the success of the Akalis and their vision of Sikh religion and history was due in large part to the work of the Singh Sabha movement.

Punjabi Sikhs and the Challenges of Colonial Rule

Sikh traditions and beliefs in nineteenth century Punjab reflected religious changes occurring over four hundred years. The formative phase of Sikhism stretched between the birth of the first Guru - Nanak - in 1469 and the death of the tenth and final Guru - Gobind Singh - in 1708. Guru Nanak emphasised the need for man to meditate on the *Nâm* or name of God, while at the same time combining worship and deep reverence with active participation in daily life, which included raising a family and serving others. His teachings were transmitted and elaborated by nine successors, who invested the Sikhs with a sacred scripture, the *Adi Granth*, complied by Guru Arjan, a tradition of love and sacrifice, and numerous sacred shrines and holy places associated with important events in the evolving tradition. In 1699, Guru Gobind Singh transformed Sikhs into a disciplined body or order called the *Khalsa*, whose members received a new name, Singh, and symbols (the 5 Ks: uncut hair, comb, bangle, sword and breeches). The authority and function of the Guru became vested in the *Khalsa* and the *Adi Granth*.[3]

The subsequent rise of the Sikh *misals* and the control of Punjab by Ranjit Singh (early 1700s-1839) were accompanied by the spread of Sikh political and social dominance in north-western India. Although this turbulent period of change requires more research, the general outline of what was happening to Sikhs and their religion seems clear. First, a loose band of teachers, local saints, and wisemen, often associated with a particular area or shrine, came to be seen as a major source of inspiration and authority among Sikhs. These *bhais, gyanis*, and local dignitaries cooperated with the heads of the families descending from the Gurus, such as the Sodhis and Bedis, to conduct worship, maintain some sense of continuity with the past, and provide spiritual and moral leadership. Although a handful of literary works were produced, most notably the *janamsakhis* or traditional biographies of Gurus, Sikh culture tended to be transmitted orally.[4]

Simultaneous with the spread of the Sikh tradition in the rural areas and particularly among the Jats, the religious doctrines found in the Gurus' teachings were given various interpretations and reflected local custom and social practices. Sikhs could be *sahajdhari*, clean-shaven devotees of Guru Nanak who respected the *Granth* and worshipped regularly in the gurdwaras, or *kesdharis*, those who maintained the symbols associated with Guru

Gobind Singh and had undergone baptism. Worship of local gods and saints was common, and in terms of daily rituals and important events, many Sikhs accepted the role of other Punjabis. Marriage networks and social relations mirrored traditional custom that involved accepted linkages between families and respect for caste. Some attempted, after the late 1700s, to legitimise a particular view of how Sikhs should live by pulling together *rahitnamas* or guides to ritual and practice. This was accompanied by the emergence of sects such as the Nirankaris who opposed caste and tried to define and adopt distinctly Sikh practices. On the whole, however, there was no generally accepted set of traditions, religious beliefs, and social norms among Punjabi Sikhs. Instead, there was a diffuse and often competing group of intertwined traditions perpetuated by local custom and religious teachers.[5]

The transfer of western institutions and ideology after 1849 contributed to the transformation of the world in which Sikhs and other Punjabis lived. The region had always been an invasion zone characterised by a variety of cultures and interactions, with layers of religious belief and an amalgam of lifestyle and values. The British, however, differed from past rulers in that their presence affected major changes in Punjabi society and culture which continue to the present. The most obvious innovations arose from the administrative structures and the political orientation underlying them. Within two decades, the colonial power introduced a new bureaucratic system, complete with western-style executive and judicial branches. These opened up new channels of power and competition, accompanied by emphasis on western education and attainment of skills necessary for new occupations in law, administration, and education. The introduction of municipal and district councils created other arenas of competition, with seats filled initially through patronage and then increasingly by election. The British used these institutions, and less tangible means of influence such as the granting of honors and seating at darbars, to develop support groups that would assist in ruling the province.[6]

After a brief period of disquiet following the end of the two Sikh wars, the Punjab government came to see Sikhs as an important element in their colonial strategy. Sikhs were a mainstay of the army, provided stability in the villages of central Punjab through traditional leaders and social networks, and helped fill the coffers of the revenue department by industrious agricultural activity. Assuming the centrality of religion for the Sikh population, particular care was taken to provide for the adequate administration of shrines, most notably the Golden Temple in Amritsar, and at the same time to control these central Sikh institutions. British officers headed management committees, named key officials, and in general, provided grants and facilities to insure continued Sikh sympathy for the Raj.[7]

The British rule also was accompanied by the rapid spread of Christian missionary activities, thus introducing yet another element in the mosaic of Punjab religious patterns. Prior to the mutiny of 1857, the government openly sympathised with the evangelical programmes of the missionaries. Although the official linkage diminished thereafter, tacit support for the proselytising efforts continued through educational grants and special advantages. Besides posing a threat by aggressively converting Punjabis, the missionaries transplanted more effective methods of communicating their message. The printing press, tract literature, and western world models for organisation and propaganda were new elements that over time were adapted by Punjabis not only to attack the Christians but to assault each other.[8]

One of the most significant consequences of British penetration, however, involved a shift in the way Punjabis viewed their surrounding and traditions. Western social, religious, economic, and political values fostered a new intellectual climate in Punjab. Individuals and sects were challenged to re-evaluate their history, current circumstance, and strategy for survival in terms of foreign categories and agendas. In the area of religion, for example, how missionaries and teachers approached matters such as critical analysis of texts, theological concepts, and the relationship between science and belief, and shaped the debate not only between Punjabis and Christians but within local communities. Also related was the diffusion of a new print culture in the urban areas. The spread of literacy, accompanied by new methods of communication such as journalism, the postal service, and improved systems of transportation, facilitated the rapid transmission of ideas. By 1883, there were over a hundred printing presses in Punjab and over five thousand books and tracts printed annually. Journalism followed suit, with newspapers and journals appearing in several towns.[9] The printed material stimulated and, at the same time, provided new channels for self-examination and debate. Theses intellectual pursuits brought together European rationalism and Indian traditions and mixed western literary styles with local motifs and symbols.[10]

The resulting cultural upheaval in principal Punjab towns, such as Lahore and Amritsar, affected Sikhs from the 1860s onward. Despite their early education in gurdwara schools or through instruction by learned *gyanis* and local teachers, an emerging Sikh intelligentsia began to study western subjects and joined in associations that discussed religious and social issues. In Lahore, for example, Sikhs were members of G.W. Leitner's orientalist Anjuman-i-Punjab, where they became skilled at literary criticism and debate over historical issues. One especially prominent Sikh, Gurmukh Singh, helped foster Sikh concern over Punjabi literature and eventually taught the subject at the Lahore Oriental College.[11] The introduction of Arya Samaj in 1875 seemed to open new vistas for reforming society and modernising Indian religions. A few Sikhs were drawn to the energetic Arya emphasis on personal growth and simplified rituals. For a decade they gave limited support to it before severing bonds in response to its aspersions on the life and teaching of the Gurus.[12]

The atmosphere of questioning theology and current social and religious practices led at least some Sikhs to address the mixture of traditions and sub-traditions prevalent within the community. Differences between the Gurus' teachings and contemporary patterns were obvious, as was the perceived need to revitalise Sikhism before it lost further vitality. Attempts to reform and refine elements of Sikhism already had been made. In the early nineteenth century, for example, the Nirankari sect, descended from the followers of Baba Dyal Singh (1783-1854), opposed the worship of Hindu icons and preached a simple message of devotion and "purified" rituals.[13] Similarly, the Namdhari or Kuka sect, founded by Bhai Balak Singh (1799-1862), was instructed to avoid marriage expenses and dowries, to reject meat, wine, and tobacco, and to lead moral lives. Under Balak Singh's successor, Ram Singh (1816-1884), the Kukas became more militant and openly rejected British authority. Attempting to overturn the custom of worshipping at local shrines and intent on protecting the cow, the Kukas soon ran afoul of the government. After several dramatic encounters, the organisation was dispersed and their leader deported.[14]

The Kuka outbreaks in the late 1860s and the continued missionary success in converting both Sikh students and ruling chiefs set the stage for the creation of a new association in 1873, the Amritsar Singh Sabha. Unintended by its founders, that Sabha and its successors were to inaugurate a new phase in the history of Sikhism that resolved many pressing issues of Sikh identity and conflicting customs.

Evolution of the Singh Sabha Movement

On October 1, 1873, Sikhs from Amritsar and surrounding districts formed the Amritsar Singh Sabha. The mission of the Sabha included propagation of the true Sikh religion, publishing periodicals and encouraging the use of Punjabi, editing and circulating historical and religious books, developing support from well-wishers (particularly the British government), and education.[15] Five years later, a second Singh Sabha was formed in Lahore and by 1900 there were approximately a hundred similar associations in Punjab and neighbouring areas.[16] The spread of the sabhas was uneven, decentralised, and frequently the product of personal interests or ideological disagreement. The Ferozepur Singh Sabha, for example, emphasised scholarly research, female education, and improvement of home life because of the influence of Bhai Takht Singh, a regional leader for almost four decades. To the north in Tarn Taran, Bhai Mohan Singh Vaid's concern with health, the sanctity of shrines, and defense of Sikhism through tract literature set the tone and programme of Tarn Taran group. In Bhasaur, Babu Teja Singh's effort to prune Sikh doctrine and ritual from any suggestion of Hindu influence led to a string of dramatic meetings, resolutions, and social experiments.[17]

Two major constellations existed in the Singh Sabha universe.

The founding Amritsar Sabha was led by a group of traditional leaders that included *gyanis*, *bhais* and aristocrats.[18] These men, such as Thakur Singh Sandhawalia, Khem Singh Bedi and his son, Gurbaksh Singh, and Kanwar Bikram Singh, had suffered some financial loss because of British conquest and felt increasingly under attack from the west and from missionaries. They used an established network of followers and resources to spread western education, love for Punjabi, preservation of historical documents, and generally tried to strengthen Sikhism in response to new cultural challenges.

As "Sanatan Sikhs", however, the Amritsar following recognised the diversity of traditions within the contemporary Sikh community and championed the view that custom provided answers as to who were Sikhs and what they should believe. Anyone accepting the teachings of Guru Nanak, from their viewpoint, was a Sikh, despite any decisions about maintaining the 5Ks, worship of regional saints, or social practice. A major theme in their discourse, for example, was the danger posed to Sikhism by inattention to custom and pollution through indiscriminate marriage alliances. Descendants of the Gurus were held in high repute. At time they were provided with cushions in worship services and treated as though they possessed extraordinary knowledge. Existing divisions among Sikhs were recognised. Udasis, followers of Guru Nanak who often dressed as Hindu mendicants and controlled central Sikh shrines, were to be respected. *Sahajdhari* Sikhs also were seen as being "slow learners" within the Sikh tradition, who someday might undergo formal baptism and with it, the discipline, the *rahit* maintained by the *kesdharis*. Those who accepted the outward symbols and conduct associated with Guru Gobind Singh were applauded, but were not seen as superior to other Sikhs.[19]

Sikhs associated with the Lahore Singh Sabha had a very different perspective on the nature of Sikhism. The members of the Lahore association came from different classes and castes, including aristocrats, lawyers, teachers, publicists, businessmen, and minor officials.[20] They were joined primarily not by economic or occupational interests but rather by a shared experience in anglo-vernacular education and participation in intellectual debate in Lahore, the center of the new school system and an emerging print culture. Aware of western criticism and the vulnerability of a Sikh faith that contained contradictions and few, if any, demarcated boundaries, they sought to present and defend a set of coherent principles and actions that would be adopted by most Sikhs.

Their vision of a rejuvenated Sikh tradition came to be known as "Tat Khalsa", that is, a "true" Sikhism stripped of popular custom and clearly separate from Hinduism. As in the case of the Arya Samaj, which reinterpreted the Vedic period so as to legitimise its programme, the advocates of Tat Khalsa championed a return to a real or imagined golden age of the Gurus in which Sikhs had a clear and definable identity. The Lahore Singh Sabha attacked caste and other social customs that tended to undercut Sikh brotherhood. Similarly, Sikhs were called upon to quit worshipping "living Gurus" such as *pirs*, local saints, and the families connected with the Ten Gurus. A return to original Sikh values meant also a renewal of attention to the *Adi Granth* as the source of theology and authority, the promulgation of rituals devoid of Brahminical and Hindu influence, and a cleansing of sacred space such as gurdwaras and shrines. Portraits or statues of Hindu gods were to be removed from places of worship, as were depictions of the Gurus that suggested Hindu connections. Historical research and discussion of theology were encouraged, but only if they supported the principal tenets of Tat Khalsa Sikhs.[21]

The Lahore and Amritsar Singh Sabhas occasionally attempted conciliation, but because of the divergence of their views and a series of heated confrontations, much of Sikh public life in the last three decades of the century was dominated by internecine squabbles. Sikhs fought in the press, in meetings, and in the courts. An attack might appear in a local paper or tract and then stir controversy and even a civil suit. In 1887, for example, a leading Tat Khalsa publicist, Ditt Singh, lampooned the major Amritsar leaders in a lightly disguised play, *Svapan Natak*. Offensive passages, such as referring to a descendant of Guru Nanak as a pretentious "Guru of Satan", resulted in a slander case that left wounds which festered for years.[22] Any topic or issue could become a battleground. One favourite tactics was to tar opponents with the brush of "sedition" so that official patronage would be withdrawn. The Amritsar Singh Sabha was the target of such a tactic in the 1880s when the efforts of the deposed son of Ranjit Singh, Maharajah Duleep Singh, to return to Punjab created an explosive situation. The location of the first Sikh institute of higher education, Khalsa College, generated similar excitement, as did the proposal in 1897 to light Golden Temple with electrictiy.[23]

The most hotly contested argument within the Singh Sabha movement was whether Sikhs were "Hindu". Sanatanists saw Sikhism as an offshoot of a broadly defined "Hinduism". The Vedas and Hindu epics were judged to be important in understanding man's predicament and relationship with God, although the Gurus' teachings, especially the *Adi Granth*, were to be given more respect. Examples from the *Granth* and accompanying literature were used to "prove" that the Gurus had no intention of separating Sikhs from their Hindu roots or from revered Hindu gods and scriptures. Distinct social and ritual boundaries had not been prescribed by the Gurus but were subsequent additions to the tradition. Therefore, they did not have to be honoured.[24] Arya Samajists supported these views, criticising the assumptions of the Lahore-based group and ridiculing their scholarship. The tract warfare over the issue was heated and prolonged.[25]

"Ham Hindu Nahin" (We are not Hindu) became the battle cry of the Tat Khalsa Sikhs.[26] They published at least a hundred tracts and books on the subject. Quotes from the scriptures and historical analyses were used to combat what was seen as the most dangerous threat to Sikh survival. The Tat Khalsa raised the flag of "Sikhism in Danger" and fought their opponents at every turn.

The divisions among Sikh associations were not limited to ideology. Most of the Sabhas had their own agendas and personal projects and conflicts surfaced frequently regarding where conferences would be held or the degree of respect to be shown to particular individuals. In addition, the race for control of institutions and honour was complicated by the regional orientation of Sikh leaders. Competition between Sikhs from the

Malwa and Majha regions was frequent and bitter.[27]

Despite the time and resources devoted to such controversies, the Singh Sabhas did manage to develop a broad network of new institutions and projects. By 1900, orphanages, a system of Sikh schools, institutions for training preachers and *granthis*, and other self-strengthening efforts garnered broad support from Sikhs in Punjab and especially from migrant communities abroad.[28] In the process, the Tat Khalsa interpretation of Sikh history and religion increasingly came to be viewed as legitimate by both Sikhs and the government. How this was accomplished deserves separate consideration.

Ascendancy of the Tat Khalsa in Sikh Affairs

The Sikhs identifying with the Tat Khalsa tradition defined Sikhism in terms of a theology separate from Hinduism, purified rituals, and distinct norms of behaviour. Social and cultural boundaries had to be demarcated successfully in three separate, but sometimes tangled, spheres. First, the Tat Khalsa message had to reach the Sikh population and be recognised as legitimate. This meant confrontation with Sikh opponents, who had conflicting views and could draw upon time-honoured networks of patronage and support. The Tat Khalsa and Sanatan Sikhs were engaged in a struggle to determine who would control community resources and attain a place of authority. Secondly, the Sikh activists had to defend themselves and their institutions against external attack, particularly that of the Arya Samajists who allied occasionally with sympathetic Sikhs. Finally, the programme centering round the Lahore Singh Sabha had to be accepted and supported by the primary patrons in the Punjab political system, the British rulers. The government was somewhat ambivalent toward encouraging the resurgence of Sikhism, but no matter what its strategy, official perceptions and policies tended to be sympathetic to the maintenance of symbols and separation from Hinduism.[29] The Tat Khalsa had to convert that attitude into active support such as grants and recognition of Sikh claims in legislative and political arenas.

The success of the Lahore group in meeting these challenges

was due in large part to the zeal, sacrifice, and oratorical ability of its leadership. Many exceptional individuals rallied to the Tat Khalsa cause and, in doing so, have been recognised as heroes by their contemporaries and by subsequent historians. Two driving forces in Lahore—Gurmukh Singh and Ditt Singh—became almost legendary for their public service. Writing books and publishing papers, they organised meetings, roamed across Punjab encouraging friends and repelling attacks, and simultaneously laid the groundwork for the creation of new organisations.[30] Singh Sabhas generally had one or more such individuals who provided continuity, money, and spirit. For example, Bhai Takht Singh of Ferozepur who became known as the *Zinda Shahid*, the "living martyr", committed his life to female education. At one point, he left home on a world-wide tour and refused to return until he had collected sufficient funds to maintain his school for girls at Ferozepur. Takht Singh succeeded after six hard and often desperate months of travel.[31] The powerful presence and single-mindedness of Babu Teja Singh Overseer was unmatched. The founder of the Bhasaur Singh Sabha and later the Panch Khalsa Diwan, Teja Singh had the courage and willingness to give and receive abuse, which became part of the folklore of the Singh Sabha Movement.[32] The list could go on to include dozens of talented individuals, who although disagreeing on specific points, were held together by a commitment to a resurrection of Sikhism in the Tat Khalsa image.

Without such devoted Sikhs, the Singh Sabha message would have not taken root. At the same time, however, these individuals also were adroit at controlling the centers of powers and the networks of communication that affected daily Sikh life. Whether aristocrat, businessman, or official, they shared common experiences and acquired new skills vital to their mission. The spread of modern means of communication permitted coordination and continuity over time and space. The postal service, for example, facilitated regular contact. The diaries and correspondence of prominent Tat Khalsa advocates, such as Mohan Singh Vaid, Takht Singh, and Teja Singh Bhasaur, suggest the importance of the mails in planning.[33] The expansion of the railroad meant that leaders could meet personally in private gatherings or public sessions. Such innovations also furnished the backdrop for many of the new experiments and organised publicity efforts of the Tat Khalsa.

The Tat Khalsa created and then dominated the rapidly evolving communication facilities linking Sikhs throughout the world. Secretaries of the Singh Sabhas circulated annual reports and resolutions through the mail and the central body in Lahore helped publish local proceedings. The correspondent system was complemented by the circulation of preaching teams and *jathas*, groups of Sikhs (often with a *granthi* and singers) who travelled widely to encourage baptism, adoption of outward symbols, and an end to *manmat* ("un-Sikh") practices (such as the worship of local saints).[34] The Tat Khalsa missionary efforts followed the railroad lines. As soon as the railway expanded, preachers visited the dispersed Sikhs and tried to influence their actions.[35] Festivals and meetings also became routinised. Sabhas sponsored annual diwans, multi-day occasions that brought together local Sikhs as well as zealots from outside. The larger regional and provincial conferences could attract as many as several thousand Sikhs. Moreover, the regular celebration of the various *gurpurabs* (birth and death anniversaries of the Gurus) and related events in Sikh history were popularised. Such activities provided the chance for discussion, worship, raising funds, and, in general, consolidating the Tat Khalsa position.[36]

Schools, too, were an essential element in the Singh Sabha programme. Not only did Khalsa educational institutions equip Sikhs to compete successfully in the new occupations, but they also served to strengthen Sikh identity. Mixing western subjects with the study of Punjabi and religious traditions, teachers were able to influence generations of upwardly mobile students. Founded in 1894, the Khalsa College at Amritsar became a Tat Khalsa bastion.[37]

Although Sanatanists wrote tracts and published newspapers, both of those important ingredients of modern communication tended to be controlled by Sikhs of the Tat Khalsa persuasion. As in the case of the Christian, Arya Samaj, and Muslim missionary efforts, Sikhs produced an increasing number of small tracts and religious books. Founded in 1894, the Khalsa Tract Society published didactic and polemical pamphlets regularly. Individuals often specialised in that means of disseminating ideas, such as Ditt Singh and Mohan Singh Vaid who wrote over two hundred books and tracts.[38] One variety of tract contained religious scripture and sermons, often with emphasis on an issue such as the non-Hindu nature of Sikhism. Another related set of pamphlets described incidents or told stories that illustrated the victory of Tat Khalsa arguments. A third popular type called for support of associations or a project. Appeals or *benati* were accepted elements in Sikh life and could generate substantial contributions. Finally, the polemic provided entertainment and contributed to literary exchanges that can only be described as tract warfare.[39]

While production of tracts was impressive, the evolving Sikh communication system revolved around an assortment of journals and papers. Many were short-lived, but the newspapers that began to appear with regularity from the 1880s onward reached more and more Sikhs. The *Khalsa Akhbar*, founded in 1883 and surviving until 1904, served as a base for the Tat Khalsa. Many other papers championed specific causes or aimed at particular audiences such as the *Punjabi Bhain* (Ferozepur, on domestic life and female education) and periodicals for one segment of the community—the Ramgarhias.[40]

Approximately fifty Sikh newspapers and journals were published prior to 1900. Most served several related functions. First, the publications circulated news on events and activities of institutions and individuals. In addition, newspapers offered an accepted channel for *benati*, appeal for aid. Increasingly Sikhs were called on to provide money for schools, societies, and special events. The papers also served as scorecards, routinely publishing accounts and lists of donors. Besides providing accountability for funds spent, these reports celebrated public service and good deeds, key fund-raising elements in a society where pride and honour were valued highly. The accounts also kept record of how well particular Tat Khalsa activities were progressing, such as the number of Sikhs who had stopped smoking or quit cutting their hair.[41] Finally, journalism helped mobilise specific groups of the community as a whole on issues and, in general, disseminated a consistent image of past events and current dangers facing Sikhism.

This diverse network for disseminating information and generating support strengthened the Tat Khalsa position among Sikhs. Dozens of meetings and large conferences were held each year and, by 1900, over eighty Singh Sabhas sympathetic to Ditt Singh and his colleagues were active throughout India. Tracts and newspapers applauded victory after victory, ranging from the scattered conversion of Muslim and apostate Sikhs to dramatic incidents such as occurred in Bakapur on June 13-14, 1903. At a large diwan, Tat Khalsa leaders from all over Punjab assembled and gave baptism to 35 Muslims and *sahajdhari* Sikhs. Many of the converts became prominent in Sikh education, religious debate and the gurdwara reform movement.[42] Special committees produced "authentic" versions of historical material, commentaries on the *Granth*, and even went so far as to judge the validity of books and tracts published by others.[43] The mounting pressure for reforms and an end to Hindu practices led to public meetings, petitions for official holidays celebrating the birthdays of Guru Nanak and Guru Gobind Singh, and successful missionary activities in towns and villages. Even foreign collaborators supported the Lahore Singh Sabha's contentions about the uniqueness of Sikh tradition. The most notable example was Max Athur Macauliffe, a former British civil servant, who retired and devoted his life to translating and interpreting early Sikh documents. His multi-volume work, *The Sikh Religion: Its Gurus, Sacred Writing and Authors* (Oxford University Press, 1909) was prepared in close association with Singh Sabha scholars such a Kahan Singh Nabha, and remains one of the most substantial English-language statement of the Tat Khalsa view of their Sikh heritage.[44]

Despite the intensity and volume of such activities, the Lahore Singh Sabha and its affiliates had not managed to supplant the entrenched group of Sanatan Sikhs who controlled shrines and claimed to be the legitimate leaders of the community. The fights were long, bitter, and usually inconclusive. The struggle over location of Khalsa College, for example, was won by the Amritsar Singh Sabha although the better educated Lahore Sikhs came to dominate the faculty and curriculum.[45] Intelligent and articulate defenders of the Sanatan views organised their own newspapers and joined in exchange of tracts. Most notable was Avtar Singh Vahiria, the author of influential guides to Sikh history and practice. He argued in voluminous and well documented books that Sikhism was an outgrowth of Hinduism and should maintain its roots within that religion. The Tat Khalsa innovations were recent additions, he claimed, and artificially separating the two faiths meant confusion in ritual, inappropriate rites, and unnecessary schisms.[46] The vehemence of the attacks on the Lahore leaders accelerated by the late 1890s also suggests their growing power and influence. Battles continued, but in terms of numbers and the ability to control the centre of Sikh news and communication, the Tat Khalsa were beginning to shape the wide range of Singh Sabha activities.

Also accelerating were confrontations with the Arya Samaj. Both the Singh Sabhas and the Arya Samaj launched a campaign of *shuddhi* (purification and conversion ceremonies) after 1890. Aryas openly converted Sikhs and cut their hair in public. The Sikh Shuddhi Sabha in Lahore countered by having Muslim and low-caste Sikhs undergo purification, receive baptism, and then have social relations with Singh Sabha members.[47] The controversy raged, as did the warfare. The titles of typical tracts of the period suggest the tone and content of the works: "a mouth-breaking reply", "the exposure of haughtiness", "a crushing blow", "a real photo of the stupidity of Dayanand", and "as the face, so the slap, or a face-breaking reply",[48] Colloquial Hindi and Punjabi are storehouses of insult and derogatory terms and opponents used them freely to attack sacred scriptures, leaders, and positions. As tensions mounted, the momentum clearly was on the side of the Lahore Sikhs. They managed to sharpen the lines between Sikhs and Hindus and, in doing so, provoked such open attacks on Sikhism that the Arya tracts probably injured the position of their pro-Hindu allies.

The Tat Khalsa success with the government was also mixed, although there too the Lahore Singh Sabha tended to have high visibility and garnered support regularly. The British had reinforced the legitimacy of the *kesdhari* Sikhs through military recruitment policy. Only Sikhs with the 5 Ks could join the army and part of their initiation was baptism and a pledge to maintain "orthodox" practices. Western officers encouraged the celebration of Sikh holidays and, in general, tried to insure the happiness and loyalty of their men.[49] The Punjab government was quite aware of the growing tension among Sikhs and tried whenever possible to steer clear of controversy. However, patronage continued to be given to key institutions such as Khalsa College and schools affiliated with local Singh Sabhas. In a few instances, district officers also sympathised with the Tat Khalsa campaigns to end misuse of gurdwara funds by Udasi managers and to remove offensive symbols and artifacts from the vicinity of shrines.[50] Similarly, the provincial and central governments cooperated in providing limited funds for the publication efforts of Macauliffe and his Sikh friends. Assisting the Singh Sabha in publishing projects was viewed by the British as a necessary corrective to a former act, arranging for Trumpp's translation of the *Adi Granth* in the 1870s. Trumpp had claimed that Sikhs were Hindus and made numerous scurrilous remarks about the Gurus and their teachings. Macauliffe's volumes were seen as restoring the Sikh honour and tradition damaged by the earlier work.[51]

By the end of the nineteenth century, Sikhs stood once again at a critical juncture. Acceptance of the Tat Khalsa message was spreading but as yet had not been institutionalised completely. Sikhs remained disunited. Numerous institutions had been created, but funding and administration often were haphazard and lacked coordination. A surge of energy and resources was evident, but so were persistent patterns of division, competition, and conflict. The Singh Sabhas had raised the cry of "Sikhism in Danger" and highlighted the many problems facing the community, but solutions still had to be worked out. Without unification and focus, as editorials in Sikh newspapers noted: Sikhism still remained vulnerable to both external and internal threats.[52]

The Chief Khalsa Diwan's Contribution to the Sikh Revival, 1903-1919

In November of 1901, a meeting of prominent Sikhs discussed the need for a central body to coordinate and lead the Singh Sabha movement. Many of the earlier generation of leaders had died or passed on their mantles, thus making it easier to bind old wounds and deal with problems plaguing the Sikhs. Officially inaugurated a year later, the Chief Khalsa Diwan (CKD) began with a handful of affiliated Sabhas and by 1919, had over a hundred member institutions. During that period, the organisation was involved in a spectrum of old and new projects and became acknowledged as the major voice for Sikhs.[53]

The CKD had a formal constitution, amended frequently, and a complex set of committees and procedures. Its aims included promoting the welfare of the Khalsa Panth, spreading *gurbani* or the teaching of the Gurus, disseminating information on tradition and current issues, and safeguarding the political rights of Sikhs. Behind the organisation, however, was input from the most active Sabhas, whose leaders, such as Vir Singh, Mohan Singh Vaid, Takht Singh, and Teja Singh Bhasaur, participated actively at one time or another. Sundar Singh Majithia, a Sikh aristocrat long identified with the Lahore Singh Sabha, served as secretary and also helped guide Khalsa College.[54]

The CKD decisions involved both a system of consultation with member associations and a pattern of private decision-making by twenty or so aristocrats and members of western professions. Often questions would be circulated in journals and tracts and then decisions publicised on a specific issue, such as whether it was appropriate to open the *Adi Granth* in public meetings.[55] More controversial decisions tended to be reached in private or sometimes avoided totally if circumstances warranted. The Finance Committee tended to dominate both the public and private proceedings, insisting on full accountability for all CKD operations.

The goals and strategies of the Diwan changed in light of immediate or long-term problems. On the whole, its main function was the coordination of Sikh public activities and the building of a common base on which many, if not all, Sikhs might agree. This was illustrated by an editorial that portrayed Singh Sabhas as stones filled with bits and pieces of material, lacking strength. Only if the elements were fused could Sikhs move forward and be strong like iron. The CKD role was to try and assist cooperation, to pull together and focus efforts.[56]

This task involved insuring the fiscal stability of Sikh enterprises with a growing system of checks and balances. Once accounts and reports were issued regularly, however, the Diwan turned to the more complex task of developing human resources. It elaborated the existing practice of sending out teams and preachers, training personnel in preaching, singing, and publicity. Outreach was also enhanced by more attention to scheduling local and regional meetings, with the result that attendance rose dramatically. Some conferences and diwans had as many as 4,000 to 8,000 Sikhs in attendance.[57]

Concern with panthic resources helped generate new initiatives in studying historical documents and publishing "authentic" material. Committees reviewed books and issued corrections, questioning references to mythology and any link with "non-Sikh" custom. While encouraging debate, the CKD urged that the duty of Sikhs "in days of transition" was the preparation of "standard books and references" based solely on the teachings of the *Guru Granth Sahib*.[58]

Appreciating the importance of influencing communications among Sikhs, the CKD regularised the flow of information by improving links between organisation and publishing more literature. Two newspapers—the *Khalsa Samachar* in Gurmukhi and the *Khalsa Advocate* in English—became its spokesmen and assisted in spreading news and heightening public awareness. The influence of these and related journals was significant. Individuals read material aloud in villages and copies circulated widely among students, the army, and emigrant groups throughout the world. Moreover, the Khalsa Tract Society expanded its operation and soon was joined by several other societies committed to influencing Sikhs in areas such as theology, ritual, and social observance.[59]

The CKD mission of unifying Sikhs and putting self-strengthening projects on a sound footing necessitated creating more institutions. Besides providing aid to old Singh Sabhas and helping form new ones, the Diwan built hospitals and orphanages and launched a drive to expand Sikh educational institutions. Some schools fed into the regular educational system, ending with high school or college degrees. Others such as the *updeshak* (preacher-training) school at Gharjakh and the girl's school at Ferozepur prepared Sikhs for other tasks. The Sikh Educational Conference, first held in 1908, became an annual affair that brought together thousands of Sikhs who discussed educational issues, the spread of Punjabi and related matters. The meetings moved from place to place, thus focusing attention on local activities. The resolutions and speeches usually dealt with history, religion, and current affairs. Besides raising money, the Conference became a symbolic gathering of Sikhs who shared common viewpoints and goals.[60]

The CKD also tried to expand the breadth of the community and at the same time overcome factionalism and conflict. Diwan leaders sponsored the formation of the Khalsa Biradari in 1908, an organisation committed to modifying Sikh attitudes toward untouchability. Low-caste Sikhs such as Mazbhis, Rahtias and Ramdasis had been particular targets for Christian and Arya Samaj conversion attempts. Disturbed by this potential loss in numbers, as well as by the inherent conflict between current social attitudes and the message of equality among all Sikhs, the CKD and the Biradari had some success in improving social conditions and opening gurdwaras to Sikhs who were considered by some to be polluted. A price was paid, however, because this evoked a sharp reaction that included boycotts of CKD activities and public confrontations.[61]

Painfully aware that because of "our self-murdering policy", Sikhs were their own worst enemies (*Khalsa Samachar*, August 16, 1905), the CKD sought to end disputes and resolve internal conflicts. Conciliation teams assisted when groups or associations fought openly. In 1917, for example, even the Educational Conference became an inflammable issue when the site was moved from Montgomery to Lahore.[62] Differences of opinion, rivalries, and affronts to "honour" consumed much of the Diwan's time and energy.

The CKD used its publicity and influence to institutionalise the acceptance of Sikhism as a separate religion with its own rituals, traditions, and sense of identity. Generally pursuing policies that would further demarcate boundaries and remove lingering Hindu influence, the Diwan's efforts helped facilitate the removal of idols from the Golden Temple in 1905 and sparked similar criticism of Hindu accretions in other local shrines. Another CKD victory, the 1909 passage of the Anand Marriage Bill legitimising a distinct Sikh marriage ceremony devoid of Hindu trappings, marked a highpoint in the campaign to spread Sikh holidays, rituals, and daily practices.[63]

Although the Tat Khalsa tradition became increasingly dominant in all Sikh institutions except for the gurdwaras, which generally remained in the hands of Sanatan Sikhs or Udasi managers, the CKD did not consistently argue that the only "true Sikhs" were *kesdhari* or *amritdhari* (baptised) and that others such as *sahajdharis* were in fact Hindu. Given the diversity still existing among Sikhs, the Diwan took the position that those who worshipped in gurdwaras and accepted that Sikhism was a separate religion should be considered part of the larger Sikh community. Fully aware of the persistent minority status of Sikhs (approximately 10.13 percent of Punjab population) and also sensitive to the devotion of many of the *sahajdharis*, the Diwan tried to accommodate and be tolerant of diversity as far as possible. This came out continually in newspaper stories about prominent *sahajdhari* Sikhs, such as Harkishen Lal, as well as in discussions of procedures within the Diwan itself.[64] Although only *kesdhari* Sikhs could serve on CKD committees, special arrangements were made for regular consultation with other groups. Moreover, the Diwan resolved that *sahajdharis* could play a full role in gurdwara affairs and read the *Guru Granth Sahib* in services.[65] To clear up misunderstandings, the official paper of the CKD, the *Khalsa Advocate*, noted that even shorn Sikhs were on the path of religious searching and should be kept within the *panth* and made part of Sikhism (July 15, 1904). The CKD leaders did have a long-term goal of seeing all Sikhs maintain common rituals and symbols, but toleration and openness were necessary. Community interest required such an approach. In the past, *sahajdharis*, such as Sewa Ram Singh and Teja Singh, had eventually been baptised and contributed greatly to Sikhism.[66] Others could do the same in the future.

Accommodation and tolerance did little to reconcile Sikhs who insisted that they were Hindu. Some attacked the CKD in the press or openly sided with Hindus, such as Gurbaksh Singh Bedi, son of Khem Singh Bedi, and the heart of the earlier Amritsar Singh Sabha. Gurbaksh Singh served as the president of the Punjab Hindu Conference in 1910. On the basis of the public record, however, it appears that most Sikhs tentatively approved of the Diwan's posture. A few individuals and organisations did adopt a narrow and increasingly literal interpretation of Sikh tradition. Teja Singh Bhasaur denounced his former colleagues, for example, set up a rival Panch Khalsa Parliament, and tried to rewrite Sikh tradition. Although ostracised and later imprisoned for publishing an edition of the *Adi Granth* with one section, the *ragmala*, excised, Teja Singh persevered in his claim that only *amritdharis* who followed his lead were Sikhs.[67]

For a decade, the CKD consolidated its position and had remarkable success at fostering Sikh identity and strengthening institutions. From approximately 1912 onwards, however, the organisation came under attack from different quarters. The expansion of the elective principle in municipal committees and the Punjab Legislative Council placed fresh emphasis upon numbers and, from the Sikh perspective, underlined their permanent minority status. The Diwan had a policy of working closely with the government because continued British assistance was seen as vital to the future of Sikhism. This seemed to be effective, as for example in 1907 when the British responded positively to the orchestrated Sikh agitation supporting the Anand Marriage Bill. Similarly, the Diwan was able to have more Sikh holidays placed on the official calendar, Punjabi became legitimised in educational and bureaucratic circles, and turbans accepted in the Indian Medical Service and in the London Inns of law.[68] However, growing militancy among Sikh students and British uncertainty about Sikh loyalty created a rift with the colonial power that led to expanded British control over Khalsa College and decisions that limited the influence of Singh Sabha members in Golden Temple management.[69]

The atmosphere of confrontation changed to renewed friendship in 1913 and 1914, when the CKD helped negotiate at least a temporary settlement to the crisis generated by British damage to the Rikabganj Gurdwara in New Delhi. The Singh Sabhas' open denunciation of terrorism and, particularly, the activities of returned Sikhs belonging to the banned Ghadar Party (an US-based revolutionary group) strengthened ties with the British. The First World War also brought Sikhs and the government closer together, at least in the early years. The CKD spearheaded broad-based Sikh support for the war effort and aided in accelerated recruiting for the army.[70]

Although the Diwan continued to be seen by many Sikhs as an authority in political and religious matters, its prominence and close association with the British increased the vulnerability of CKD leaders. The militants who had urged direct action against the government over alleged sacrilege at Rikabganj produced a stream of tracts, against the Diwan's moderate policies and were aided by two newspapers, the *Panth Sewak* and the *Khalsa Akhbar*.[71] By 1917, Sikh concern over recruiting excesses and other wartime injustices led the CKD to launch a publicity counter-attack. More frequently, however, the charge was made that the Diwan had abrogated its responsibilities and engaged in "*unpanthic*" activities.[72]

The keystone of CKD political strategy, influencing British patronage through constitutional agitation and personal contacts, sped up the demise of its central place in Sikh affairs. Open election had not worked for the Sikhs. With only an occasional representative elected to the legislature, frustration over future threats to the Sikh minority became apparent even in *Khalsa Samachar* editorials. The CKD attempted to assert Sikh rights because of their war effort and loyal support for the government, but as a significant transfer of power loomed ahead after the war, the campaign to have one-third seats reserved for Sikhs foundered. The British were being pressured from all directions and could not meet Sikh expectations.[73] The CKD's close association with the administration of Lieutenant Michael O'Dwyer also proved disastrous. His excessive responses to disturbances in the spring of 1919 led to the notorious massacre at Jallianwala Bagh in Amritsar.

The shooting also destroyed much of the CKD's prestige. Still clinging to a policy of toleration and dependence on British support, the Diwan criticised officials but in less than stringent terms and far too late from the perspective of most Pubjabis.[74]

The gurdwara reform agitation grew out of the ashes of Jallianwala Bagh. Distrust of the British was rampant and Sikhs felt the time was right to wrest control of their sacred shrines from the hands of the managers, who generally sided with the government and pro-Hindu interests. Earlier the CKD had attempted to control the gurdwaras through negotiation, legal manoeuvres, and public pressure. Now, losing ground rapidly, its leading members attempted to play a role in a new militant organisation—the Central Sikh League—but there, too, they lost out to more zealous Sikhs bent on confrontation.[75] Since the Diwan opposed the tactic of direct action and possible law-breaking to protect Sikh interest, they came to be seen as hapless and ineffective religious leaders, out of step with contemporary needs of the community. In a short span of time, the organisation that had been at the heart of the Sikh resurgence came to be pictured by its successors—the Akalis—as a threat to Sikhism.[76]

The Gurdwara Campaigns and the Future of Sikhism

The rapid eclipse of the Chief Khalsa Diwan (CKD) and its allies brought to an end four decades of intense soul-searching and intellectual growth. The Tat Khalsa Sikhs had championed Sikhism as a separate religion with distinct rituals and other boundaries. Under the leadership of the Diwan, that view became prevalent among Singh Sabhas and influenced the development of modern Sikh institutions. At the same time, the intellectual excitement and marked degree of literary activity constituted a high point in Sikh cultural history. Because of the zeal of the movement and the evaluation of its communication network, Sikhs became more conscious of both their historical roots and emerging threats. That consciousness has continued until the present, as have the diwans, the conferences, the new festivals and holidays, tracts, and journalistic endeavours that remain important in Sikh public life.

The CKD influenced the direction and tone of much that was written and done. Although firmly committed to the strengthening of a separate Sikh identity, the Diwan supported an open exchange of ideas, a process of accommodation, negotiation and compromise wherever possible, so that differences could be resolved and disunity averted. This accounts for the organisation sometimes avoiding controversial issues and tending to be unspecific and vague when debating doctrines. There were limits to toleration particularly in areas such as editing the scriptures or questioning beliefs about the Gurus that were considered sacrosanct. But, on the whole, the Diwan avoided drawing lines finely or excluding those who wanted to be counted as members of the *panth*. Such an approach meant that many doctrinal issues were not resolved. The Diwan, for example, worked hard to develop a consensus on a set of rituals and practices applicable to Sikhs, but prior to 1920, no definitive *rahitnama* was published. Similarly, the relationship between *kesdhari* and *sahajdhari* remained cloudy, although there was a general sense of each Sikh being able to contribute in his or her own way.

Similarly, in the external political arena, the CKD pursued a strategy combining active defense of Punjabi and other Sikh priorities with an ongoing effort to create linkages and collaboration judged necessary to ensure the Sikh minority's continued access to resources. Sikh identity, from the Diwan's perspective did not mean disrespect for others' views or creating permanent divisions possibly injurious at a future time. When the trust and mutual assistance that had characterised Sikh-British relations broke down quickly in light of the 1919 disturbances and the new reforms, however, the Diwan could not adapt quickly. Some leaders such as Sundar Singh Majithia remained active in Punjab politics and tried to help Sikh interests through alliances with other Punjabis and occasionally, with the British. As an organisation, however, the CKD tended to avoid politics and instead emphasised education and the spiritual dimension of Sikhism.[77]

Acting as a catalyst the Diwan and the Singh Sabhas had helped create the institution, the identity, and the fervour associated with a revived Sikhism. With their task completed, they virtually disappeared from the scene. During the next decades except for interest in the Educational Conference and Sikh schools, the Diwan became inactive in public debate. Without such a forum for focusing debate and exchange of ideas, the intellectual life of Sikhs suffered. There were significant developments in literature, such as the writing of Vir Singh and in scholarship, such as Kahan Singh's monumental *Gurushabad Ratnkar Mahan Kosh* (Encyclopaedia of Sikh Religion, History and Literature, 1930), but, on the whole, the questioning and the stimulation of the Singh Sabha period languished. Only after partition and the creation of new centers of scholarly and religious discourse has there been an attempt to recapture the vitality and literary renaissance associated with the Singh Sabhas.[78]

The Akalis dominated Sikh life during the 1920s, capturing the attention and support of Sikhs everywhere with their heroic deeds and roaring challenges.[79] In a sense, they completed the work of the Singh Sabhas by controlling the centres of Sikh power and orthodoxy, the shrines. The operation of the 1925 Gurdwara Act ensured the ascendancy of the Akali Dal and Shiromani Gurdwara Parbandhak Committee and permanent Tat Khalsa control of Sikh institutions. After the Akalis, there was little doubt as to who were Sikhs, what they wore, and how they worshipped. Without the earlier work of the Singh Sabhas, however, the Akalis' successful confrontation with the British would have been impossible. The spread of Sikh consciousness and the existence of a significant communication network helped the Akalis spread their message quickly and effectively. The Singh Sabha's message of sacrifice and martyrdom paved the way for the Akalis to assume leadership of the community.

Although the Akalis came to be seen as the legitimate leaders of the Sikhs, their attempts to win new political rights met with the same frustration experienced earlier. The world in which they operated placed more emphasis on population percentages and transfer of power to majority groups or broad-based alliances. Driven by Akali zeal and growing fear of Muslim politicians, Sikhs tended to identify more quickly with militant action and intolerance for opponents, especially those within the community who counselled toleration or compromise. Legislative debate and court cases became pivotal events in determining who was a Sikh. Distrusting Hindus and, afraid either of Arya or Muslim dominance, the *kesdharis* insisted that virtually all aspects of community life be led by "orthodox" Sikhs, that is, those who maintained the 5 Ks and ostensibly followed set forms of action.[80] Despite their posturing, however, issues such as authority within the panth and who could legitimately speak for all Sikhs still remained unresolved and, to some extent, have not been settled today. The awkward relationship between custom and a set of accepted practices, *rahit*, continues as a source of contention within the Sikh community in India and abroad.[81]

While the definition of Sikh tradition was worked out in many respects by the Singh Sabhas and finally institutionalised by the Akalis, somewhere in the process, the creative interaction between intellectuals and politicians that characterised the Sikh renaissance became dormant. Sikhism today again stands at a crossroads. Disunity and conflict are evident, as is a renewed sense of challenge and eminent danger. Perhaps a re-evaluation of the recent past and a careful assessment of the successes and failures of the Singh Sabha movement can provide guidance for Sikhs as they struggle with the implications of Sikhism as an evolving world religion.

Notes

1. Views represented in Punjab administration reports, the observations on Sikhs by John Malcolm, Major Leech, Captain Murray, Dalhousie, and especially the assessment of Max Macauliffe, "The Sikh Religion Under Banda and Its Present Condition," *Calcutta Review*, CXLV, 1881, pp. 167-68. Also reflected in Ernest Trumpp's introduction to his translation of the *Adi Granth* (1877).
2. The most recent assessment is Harjot Singh Oberoi, "A World Reconstructed: Religion, Ritual and Community among the Sikhs, 1850-1909" (unpub. diss., Australian National University,

1987). A similar interpretation is summarised in Barrier, *The Sikhs and Their Literature*, New Delhi: Manohar, 1969. [now published: *The Construction of Religious Boundaries: Culture, Identity and Diversity in the Sikh Tradition*, New Delhi: Oxford University Press, 1994].

3. Useful introductions to the period of the Gurus can be found in W. H. McLeod, *Guru Nanak and the Sikh Religion*, London: Oxford University Press, 1968; W. Owen Col, Piara Singh Sambhi, *The Sikhs: Their Religious Beliefs and Practices*, New Delhi: Vikas, 1978.
4. McLeod raises questions and suggests fresh direction for research in *The Evolution of the Sikh Community*, London: Oxford University Press, 1976. A review of traditional leadership is found in Oberoi's "World Reconstructed" and his "Babas and Gyanis: Traditional Intellectuals in Nineteenth Century Punjab," *Studies in History*, II (1980), pp. 32-62. The *rahitnama* literature, guides to correct Sikh practice and ritual, is reviewed in McLeod, "The Problem of the Punjabi Rahit Namas", in S.N. Mukherjee (ed.), *India, History and Thought*, Calcutta: Subarnarekha, 1982, pp. 103-26.
5. Customs are documented in Denzil Ibbetson, Edward MacLagan and H.A. Rose, *A Glossary of the Tribes and Castes of the Punjab and North-West Frontier Province*, Lahore: Superintendent, Government Printing, 1919; articles in *Punjab Notes and Queries*. Evaluated in Oberoi, "World Reconstructed", pp. 49-92.
6. On early British administration and social change, see Ian Kerr, "The Punjab Province and the Lahore District, 1849-72" (unpub. diss., University of Minnesota, 1975); Andrew Major, "Return to Empire: The Sikhs and British in Punjab, 1839-72" (unpub. diss., Australian National University, 1981). Political consequences and strategies are reviewed in Barrier, "Sikh Politics in British Punjab Prior to the Gurdwara Reform Movement", in Joseph O'Connell (ed.), *Recent Studies in Sikh History and Politics*, Toronto: University of Toronto South Asia Monograph, 1988; Barrier, "The Punjab Government and Communal Politics", *Journal of Asian Studies*, 27 (1967-8), pp. 523-39.
7. On administration of the Golden Temple, see Ian Kerr, "British

Relationships with the Golden Temple", *The Indian Economic and Social History Review*, 21(1984), pp. 139-51.

8. The evolution of 19th century tract literature is reviewed in Kenneth Jones and Eric Gustafson (eds.), *Sources on Punjab History*, New Delhi: Manohar, 1975; Barrier, *The Punjab in Nineteenth Century Tracts*, East Lansing: Asian Studies Center, Michigan State University, 1969. On early trends, see Kenneth Jones, *Arya Dharm*. Berkeley: University of California Press, 1975.
9. Press trends and data are found in Barrier and Paul Wallace, *The Punjab Press, 1880-1905*, East Lansing: Asian Studies Center, Michigan State University, 1970; Emmett Davis, *Press and Politics in British Western Punjab, 1836-1947*, New Delhi: Academic, 1983.
10. Theoretical issues and implications of the introduction of a print culture in Punjab is presented in Oberoi, "World Reconstructed". Parallel developments in other regions are discussed in essays, Yogendra Malik (ed.), *South Asian Intellectuals and Social Change*, New Delhi: Heritage, 1972.
11. On the Anjuman, see Jeffrey Perrill, "Anjuman-i-Panjab as a Common Interest Association and Symbol of Social Change in Nineteenth Century Punjab", *Punjab Past and Present*, 16 (1982), pp. 343-70. Gurmukh Singh's background is reviewed in Oberoi, "World Reconstructed", pp. 203-5. Also see Gurmukh Singh's *My Attempted Excommunication from the Sikh Temple and the Khalsa Community at Faridkot in 1897* (privately pub., Lahore, 1898). I am indebted to Harjot Singh Oberoi for a copy of the document.
12. Sikh-Aryan relations are treated in Jones, *Arya Dharm*; Barrier, *Sikhs and Their Literature*.
13. This is discussed fully in John Webster, *The Nirankari Sikhs*, New Delhi: Macmillan India, 1979.
14. On the Namdharis, consult the following: Oberoi, "World Reconstructed", pp. 93-141; W.H. McLeod, "The Kukas, a Millenarian Sect of the Punjab", in G.S.Wood, P.S. O'Connor (eds.), *W.P.Morrell: A Tribute*, Dunedin: University of Otago, 1973, pp. 85-103. Documents in Nahar Singh (ed.) *Gooroo Ram Singh and Kuka Sikhs*, 3 vols. New Delhi: author pub., 1965-71.

15. Background on the Lahore Singh Sabha can be found in the Oberoi dissertation and especially "Bhais"; also details in Harbans Singh, *Heritage of the Sikhs*. Other recent surveys of the Singh Sabha movement include Richard Fox, *Lions of the Punjab*, Berkeley: University of California Press, 1986 and Rajiv A. Kapur, *Sikh Separatism*, London: Allen and Unwin, 1986.
16. The definitive work on the early Singh Sabhas, on which this study relies heavily, is Oberoi, "Reconstruction". The relevant tract and institutional literature, plus interpretation, is reviewed in Barrier, *Sikhs*.
17. The following contain useful biographical information: Attar Singh, *Jinda Shahid Nun Moran Lai Vichar Te Tajviz*, Amritsar: Wazir Hind Press, 1916; Munsha Singh Dukhi, *Jivan Bhai Mohan Singh Vaid*, Amritsar: author, 1939; *Aduti Jivan Britant Panth Rattan Teja Singh Overseer*, Bhasaur: Bhasaur Singh Sabha, n.d.; Harbans Singh, "The Bakapur Diwan and Babu Teja Singh of Bhasaur", *Punjab Past and Present*, 9 (1975), pp. 322-32.
18. Oberoi, "Bhais".
19. This is most clearly enunciated in the following work by Avtar Singh Vahiria: *Sikh Dharm Tat Darshan*, Amritsar: Wazir Hind Press, 1899; *Khalsa Dharm Shastra*, Anandpur: Ram Narain Singh, 1914, and subsequent editions. Sanatan positions on numerous issues discussed in Oberoi, "World Reconstructed".
20. Background on individuals and the general milieu are found in Oberoi, "World Reconstructed", pp. 197-215. Also, summary in Harbans Singh, *Heritage of the Sikhs*, pp. 234-39.
21. *Op. cit.* Also for a discussion of differing views in Oberoi, "A Historiographical and Bibliographical Reconstruction of the Singh Sabha in the Nineteenth Century", *Journal of Sikh Studies*, 10 (1984), pp. 108-30. This comes out most clearly in the tracts of Ditt Singh. Also discussed in Barrier, "Vernacular Publishing and Sikh Public Life in the Punjab, 1880-1910", Kenneth Jones and Barrier (eds.), *Vernacular Publishing in Nineteenth Century India*, New Delhi: Manohar, AIIS, 1988.
22. Amar Singh, *Gyani Ditt Singh*, Amritsar: Kirpal Singh, 1962, pp. 66-68; Oberoi, "World Reconstructed", pp. 287-88. The personalities and conflicts are contained in Bhagat Lakshman

Singh's autobiography, edited by Ganda Singh, *Bhagat Lakshman Singh Autobiography*, Calcutta: Sikh Cultural Centre, 1965.

23. Episodes are detailed in Gurmukh Singh, *My Excommunication*; Ganda Singh, *A History of Khalsa College*, Amritsar: Khalsa College, 1949; Harbans Singh, *Heritage of the Sikhs*.
24. Tracts are cited in foonote 19. Also, see Narian Singh, *Sikh Hindu Hain*, Amritsar: Matbakanuni Press, 1899.
25. Tract warfare is reviewed in several essays in Gustafson and Jones, *Sources*; Barrier, "Vernacular Publishing".
26. Written by Kahan Singh Nabha, first Punjabi edition, 1899. A recent translation with backgournd is Jarnail Singh (ed.), *Sikhs, we ate not Hindu*, Toronto: Sikh Social and Educational Society, 1985. Also, background in W. H. McLeod, *Sikhism*, New York: Barnes and Noble, 1984, pp. 133-36.
27. References to such conflicts are interspersed in the tract and newspaper accounts of the period. An especially important review is in *Khalsa Samachar*, August 19, 1913, pp. 5-6. Also see Chief Khalsa Diwan proceedings, August 19, 1917. Originals of CKD documents are in the Diwan headquarters, Amritsar, but copies are available with the author.
28. For a lengthy analysis of links between Punjab and migrant Sikhs, see Barrier, "Sikh Immigrants and Their Homeland: The Transmission of Information, Resources and Values in the Early Twentieth Century", in Barrier and Verne Dusenbery (eds.), *The Sikh Diaspora*, Ann Arbor: University of Michigan South Asia Series, 1988.
29. British policies are reviewed in Barrier, "Sikh Politics"; Fox, *Lions of the Punjab*; Kapur, *Sikh Separatism*. Also useful is a confidential CID memo. on Sikh politics and British strategy, D. Petrie, "Secret C.I.D. Memorandum on Some Recent Developments in Sikh Politics", *Punjab Past and Present*, 4 (1970), pp. 301-379.
30. References are in footnote 17, and the treatment of publications are in Barrier, "Vernacular Publishing"; "Punjab Politics and the Press, 1880-1910", in Margaret Case and Barrier (eds.), *Aspects of India*, New Delhi: Manohar, AIIS, 1986, pp. 118-33; *Sikhs and Their Literature*.

31. Publications of the Ferozepur Sikh Kanya Mahavidyala, and interviews in December, 1969, with Nahar Singh, M. A., a close associate of Takht Singh and his family.
32. Life and works discussed in Harbans Singh, "Bakapur".
33. Lal Singh, *Kalmi Tasvir*; Dukhi, *Mohan Singh Vaid*.
34. Frequent missionary reports in *Khalsa Akbar*, 1896-1901.
35. For example, missionary activities in Hazara, *Khalsa Samachar*, February 6, 1913, p. 6.
36. The use of such institutions and the spreading network of contacts discussed in Oberoi, " World Reconstructed"; Barrier, "Sikh Immigrants".
37. Ganda Singh, *History of Khalsa College*, Also CID analysis in Petrie's overview.
38. Major tracts catalogued in Barrier, *Sikhs and Their Literature*; Eileen Dimes and Ganesh Saur, *Catalogue of Punjabi Printed Books: Added to the India Office Library 1902-1964*, London: Foreign and Commonwealth Office, 1975. Background in Barrier, "Vernacular Publishing".
39. Based upon extensive study of the major Sikh tracts of the period. The network and particularly its ability to generate funds from abroad is discussed in Barrier, "Vernacular Publishing".
40. Information on Sikh papers is found in Barrier and Paul Wallace, *The Punjab Press, 1880-1905*, East Lansing: Michigan State University South Asia Series, 1970; Barrier, *Sikhs and Their Literature*.
41. Virtually every issue of the *Khalsa Akhbar*, edited by Ditt Singh, had stories on contributions and instances of Tat Khalsa success.
42. Harbans Singh, "Bakapur". Oberoi's various essays and dissertation contain example of similar activities.
43. Dukhi, *Mohan Singh Vaid*, pp. 16-18; Harbans Singh and Jagjit Singh, "Singh Sabha Lahir", in Ganda Singh (ed.), *Punjab 1849-1960*, Ludhiana: Punjabi Sahit Academy, 1962, pp. 127-28, 139. Discussion of the difficulties in preparing the Faridkot commentary and reaching agreement on other matters can be found in Oberoi, "World Reconstructed".
44. Background in Barrier, "Trump and Macauliffe: West Students of

Sikh History and Religion", in Fauja Singh (ed.), *Sikh Historiography*, New Delhi: Oriental, 1978, pp. 155-85.

45. The controversy is discussed in *Bhagat Lakshman Singh Autobiography*, pp. 89-93; Ganda Singh, *History of Khalsa College*. Also, press clippings and manuscripts of Bhagat Lakshman Singh with Dr. Ganda Singh, who has shared his substantial collection and wisdom with me for over two decades.
46. His ideology and writings are discussed in Barrier, "Vernacular Publishing"; Oberoi, "World Reconstructed", pp. 176-84, 278-90.
47. Accounts in *Shuddhi Pattar*, 1986-87.
48. Background is in Barrier, *The Sikhs and Their Literature*; Kenneth Jones, "Ham Hindu Nahin", *Journal of Asian Studies*.
49. See, for example, R. W. Falcon, *Handbook on the Sikhs for the Use of Regimental Officers*, Allahabad: Pioneer Press, 1896; A. H. Bingley, *Sikhs* (British recruiting manual, rep. Patiala, 1970, Department of Languages). Background in monographs by Fox and Kapur.
50. Teja Singh, *The Gurdwara Reform Movement and the Sikh Awakening*, Jalandhar: Desh Sewak Book Agency, 1922, pp. 85-119.
51. Correspondence in Government of India, Home Public Files 192A, August 1902; February 1908, 99-102A; Home-Books, June 1907, 121-2A. Background in Barrier, "Trumpp and Macauliffe".
52. Notes, letters and editorials in *Khalsa Samachar* and *Khalsa Akhbar*, October-December 1901.
53. Background on Chief Khalsa Diwan in Surjit Singh Narang, "Chief Khalsa Diwan" in Paul Wallace (ed.), *Political Dynamics of Punjab*, Amritsar: Guru Nanak Dev University, 1981, pp. 97-108; Surveys in Kapur and Fox volumes. Detailed treatment of CKD and politics is found in Barrier, "Sikh Politics". The primary documents for the period are reports of two newspapers, *Khalsa Samachar* (KS) and *Khalsa Advocate* (KA), along with CKD proceedings.
54. Surjit Singh Narang, op. cit., and a biographical material in Mihar Singh Ravel, *Sir Sundar Singh Majithia*, Amritsar: no pub., 1942.
55. CKD August 5, 1915.

56. KS, March 15, 1905, pp. 5-6.
57. Reports in KS, February-April, July-November, 1906. Background and details are in Barrier, "Sikh Immigrants".
58. KA, February 22, 1905, p. 3.
59. Role of the press is discussed in Barrier, "Punjab Politics" and "Sikh Immigrants". Examples of reports and appeals include material in KS, January 2, 1913 and the special reports and *Masik Pattar* frequently published by the CKD. By 1911, the KTS had issued over 400 tracts numbering at least a million copies. The Sikh Handbill Society issued a flood of small pamphlets, and other agencies, such as Sikh Book Club and the Panch Khalsa Agency, issued dozens of tracts a year. On the general milieu, see Dukhi, *Mohan Singh Vaid.*
60. Education efforts are reviewed in Narotam Singh, "Chief Khalsa Diwan in the Field of Education", *Journal of Sikh Studies*, 8 (1981), pp. 118-129. Also useful is a dissertation by Gurdarshan Singh Dhillon, "Character and Impact of the Singh Sabha Movement on the History of Punjab" (unpub. diss. Punjabi University, 1972).
61. The Khalsa Biradari published annual reports. One interesting note on the outcaste situation is in KS (October 12, 1904, pp.4-5), which stated that if outcastes were given *amrit*, 50,000 new Sikhs would be added. The Sanatan reaction is discussed in the Petrie's CID note, and in the accounts in the KS and KA, 1909-11.
62. Editorials, reports in KS, February-March 1917. Also CKD minutes.
63. Anand marriage agitation and related issues are examined in Oberoi, "World Reconstructed". Also, background material is found in KS. Talwar, "The Anand Marriage Act", *Punjab Past and Present*, 2 (1968), pp. 400-10. Extensive tract literature on the subject is listed in Barrier, *Sikhs and Their Literature.*
64. KS, April 29, 1908, p. 2.
65. CKD minutes, 1902-6. See also CKD October 1, 1916; KA comments, July 15, 1904, p. 3.
66. Background on Teja Singh missionary efforts is in KS, 1908-11. Lala Sewa Ram had been important in the Khalsa Yougmen

Association and took amrit in 1904, KS, March 23, 1904, pp. 2-3. He played a key role in the Rikabganj negotiations and later CKD affairs.

67. Discussed in Harbans Singh, "Bakapur". A typical tract conveying Teja Singh's perspective in *Khalsa Rahit Parkash*, Bhasaur: Panch Khalsa Diwan, 1908. Analysis of ideas in Barrier, "Vernacular Publishing".
68. KS, November 25, 1910, p. 5; KS, September 21, 1904, p. 7; resolutions, CKD, 1904-8. Discussed in Government of India Home Public Proceeding, 1903-5.
69. KA, December 16, 1910, pp. 3-4.
70. On the Rikabganj agitation, Harjot Singh Oberoi, "From Gurdwara Rikabganj to the Viceregal Palace", *Punjab Past and Present*, 14 (1980), pp. 182-98. War effort is reviewed in M. S. Leigh, *The Punjab and the War*, Lahore: Punjab Government, 1922; Barrier, "Ruling India: Coercion and Propaganda in British India During the First World War", in De Witt Ellionwood, (ed.), *India and World War One*, New Delhi: Manohar, 1978, pp. 74-108.
71. Published in Urdu, the Lahore-based *Khalsa Akhbar* emerged as a strong opponent to the CKD during Rikabganj agitation. Edited by Chanda Singh, the *Panth Sewak* launched a series of attacks on moderate Sikhs and was warned repeatedly by the British for allegations and pronationalist activities. Background in annual reports on the Punjab press, CID.
72. Many CKD discussions in 1917-19 focused on these challenges, which included attacks on supports such as Bhai Takht Singh who was charged with mismanaging his girl's school in Ferozepur, CKD, February 11, 1917. Attacks and replies appear frequently in the two major CKD newspapers.
73. CKD, June 3, October 14, 1917. Background on constitutional development in Gurdarshan Singh, "Sikh Politics in Punjab", *Punjab: Past and Present*, 3, (1970), pp. 67-78; Mohinder Singh, *The Akali Movement*, New Delhi: Macmillan India, 1978. Recent analysis in Kapur, *Sikh Separatism*.
74. Discussion in KS, September 16, 1920, p. 3; CKD, August 1, October 31, 1920. Also press commentary in early summer, 1919.

75. The Sikh League and related activities discussed in a series of articles by Sukhmani Bal in the Proceedings of the Punjab History Conference, 1981-83.

76. Kapur, *Sikh Separatism*, pp. 86-100. Akali reaction to the CKD reports on the period, especially V.W. Smith's memo, "The Akali Dal and the Shiromani Gurdwara Parbhandak Committee, 1921-1922", Government of India Home Political File 459/II, 1922.

77. Background on Sikh politics during the 1920s can be found in books by Fox, Kapur, and Mohinder Singh. Two new studies analyse the role of communal politics and the legislative arena; Prem Raman Uprety, *Religion and Politics in Punjab in the 1920s*, New Delhi: Sterling, 1980 and Sarfraz Khawaja, *Sikhs of the Punjab*, Karachi: Modern Book Depot, 1985.

78. Based on a forthcoming study of 20th Century Sikh Literature by N. G. Barrier.

79. Secondary sources include those cited in footnote 77. On the Akali literature and British reactions, Barrier, *Banned*. Columbia, Mo.: University of Missouri Press, 1974, pp. 91, 195-202; "The British and Controversial Publications in Punjab", *Punjab: Past and Present*, 8 (1974), pp. 32-60.

80. Competition in elections and controversies over the definition of "Sikh" in the legislature reflected such an orientation. This is discussed in the studies by Kapur, Khawaja, and Uprety.

81. The "official" *rahitnama* was only published in the late 1940s, and various editions still circulate. The issue of authority and the implications for contemporary Sikh politics assessed in Robin Jeffrey, *What's Happening to India?* New York: Holmes & Meier, 1986.

3

Arya Samaj Movement in Punjab

SATISH K. SHARMA

The uniqueness of Punjab lies in the historical evolution of its social structure and culture amidst an atmosphere of interactions among people of diverse cultures. Unbroken invasions from the North-West have continued till the nineteenth century. Cultural encounters with the Arabs, Turks and the Mughals have significantly altered the social and cultural life of the people of Punjab. The British imperialism and spread of western culture in the second half of the nineteenth century contributed further to the diffusion of cultures. The historical process of cultural evolution has not remained a passive witness to the influences of other cultures. We find that the local forces sometimes resisted as well as accepted, consciously or unconsciously, the other cultures. At times, the local chiefs also militarily fought back the invaders. Despite the resistance, the perpetual interaction with the people of other cultures, imposed either through coercion or the political treaties between the invaders and the local chiefs, left a mark on Punjab in terms of development of new language, culture and values on the one hand and the formation of new set of social relationships, on the other.

Amidst such a changing social, cultural, economic and political scenario, and the emerging contradictions within almost all the spheres of life in Punjab, there has also been a collective concern to resolve oppositions of all kinds at different stages of history through the synthesis of various cultures. It simply meant that good points of each culture could create a better worldview than the existing. Some of the collective endeavours emerged from the religious currents of the period. These were aimed at reforming the human consciousness by providing a reason for doing so from the religious texts. In the nineteenth century, some of the efforts culminated into social and religious reform movements. These were meant either to partially change the existing practices and institutions or to revive the social order which prevailed in the distant past. Such movements derived legitimacy from one or the other scripture. Although these movements were manifestly religious, their latent consequences for the Punjabi society were also political in nature.

Arya Samaj was one such movement in Punjab. It did not only carry on social reform but also generated religious controversies and conflicts. Its founder—Swami Dayanand Saraswati—who originated from Kathiawar in Gujarat, established first formal organisation of Arya Samaj at Bombay in the year 1875. Within just a span of two years, i.e., by 1877, it had captured the imaginations of a section of Punjabis and starting from Lahore it spread to the entire Punjab, including small towns. Its phenomenal rise, if we compare it to other social and religious reform movements, was not a matter of sheer accident. Some historians, with particular reference to Arya Samaj, argue that its development signified 'collective efforts directed essentially at the solution of the common problem of material and psychological adjustment with the Raj[1], the rise of the Hindu consciousness in Punjab,[2] and so on.

It has been argued in this article that Arya Samaj in Punjab was not a movement to provide any solution to the common problem of material and psychological adjustment. It rather entailed deeper meanings the goal of which was to restore the Indian tradition which was perceived as marginalised by other powerful and ruling traditions. One of the motives was assertion of not only the Hindu identity but also to provide it its due place among other religions. Such a need arose at a point of India's history when the existing patterns of relationships began to be perceived in terms of inter-community contradictions. The rise of Hindu consciousness, therefore, cannot be understood only from the ideology of Arya Samaj. It requires analyses of the social structure of Punjab in which the Hindus were placed in relation to other religious communities. The reason being that neither an ideology nor consciousness can be presupposed as actors in the given historical situation. These are rather historically formed on the basis of shared experiences of collectivities. Therefore, the understanding of Hindu consciousness referred to above also requires answers to certain questions such as "consciousness of which class and category of Hindus". Methodologically, the social consciousness of a community heading a particular social movement must be analysed vis-à-vis class and caste background of the rank and file of leadership and the followers.[3]

Arya Samaj, as a social and religious reform movement, arose out of the existing subjective and objective conditions in the nineteenth century. Competing religious communities came into existence owing to various changes brought about by the British rule, one of which was the conversions to Christianity. Religious and social reform among the Hindus could be viewed as a defence against external threats. Ralph Milband has observed that redressing of the distressing conditions are carried out in convergence with the interests of the community.[4] Through such means the dominant section of the community involved in the reforms is not only able to exercise its pervasive powers but also to reassure its predominance. It is in this sense that Arya Samaj in Punjab, besides having a concern for social reforms, was oriented towards meeting the believed threat to Hinduism and thus establishing dominance of the upper sections in relation to others.

In the light of the above assumption, this article attempts at analysing the Arya Samaj movement in Punjab with particular reference to the following dimensions: first, the social structure of Punjab and the rise of Arya Samaj; second, the strategy of reforms vis-à-vis the downtrodden; and third, socio-cultural and political consequences of the movement in Punjab.

Social Structure of Punjab and the Rise of Arya Samaj

To a large extent the rise of a social movement is associated with the social structural conditions prevalent in the society. Described as the subjective and the objective, these conditions are mediated by social consciousness of the masses. Whether this is false or true, the fact remains that the people internalise and legitimise some ideas and ideology. Under certain conditions they would often get completely involved. This is a process which is drawn over a particular historical time and space. Punjab has been a society characterised by religious pluralism since long. As against the popular description of pluralism, which suggests co-existence of different religions in Punjab, it was also marked by a spirit of competition, even conflict. This competition, as pointed out earlier, was partly an outcome of the way the threat of Christianity, perceived to be the religion of the imperial power, was regarded as real.

History was interpreted as a process in which the gradual marginalisation of Hinduism had been occurring since the invasion of Babur. The Islamic leadership and the ruling Mughals were able to assert their influence either through the educational institutions they maintained or the organised and coercive conversions of Hindus to Islam. The historical evidence also indicates voluntary embracing of Islam by the Hindu tribal chiefs and respected men for economic and political gains.[5] As a consequence, the demographic structure was tilted in favour of Muslims in Punjab. Moreover, the lack of political power rendered Rajputs and Brahmins (who, at one point of time, were the dominant segments) insignificant. It is also important to mention here that in the fifteenth century, the process of consolidation of Islam, evoked the Bhakti movement, particularly the Sikh movement. Guru Nanak Dev—the founder of Sikhism—made an attempt to synthesise Islam and Hinduism. The increasing influence of Sikhism also affected those dominant segments of Hindus adversely. The later wars of the Sikhs with Mughals earned the Sikhs honour and respect on the basis of their heroic deeds and by maintaining high moral character. Qazi Noor Mohammed, an accompanist of Ahmed Shah Abdali, described them as the fierce soldiers with highest order of morality.[6] After the foundation of Khalsa empire, gradual emergence of a new consciousness among Sikhs instilled in them a competitive spirit. This new consciousness acquired political and economic overtones in the later years.

The social structure of Punjab presented complexities in the form of segmental divisions, namely, the existence of numerous castes and sub-castes within Hinduism as well as other religions. The divisions were not clearly demarcated as a number of castes could be found simultaneously in other communities also. Each caste was further characterised by heterogeneity in terms of its social status, class position, occupational calling and so on. The caste structure presented combinations of inter-caste and intra-caste hierarchies. The caste Hindus consisted of Khatris, Jats, Brahmans, Rajputs, Mahajans, and so forth. Khatri caste among the Hindus, however, held its domination in education, trade and government services.[7]

On the other hand, there were a large number of other castes called outcastes or untouchables. Among these were Chamars, Mochis, Dumnas and Chuhras, described as leather workers, menials and scavengers respectively. Placed in a socially, economically and politically disadvantageous position in relation to the high castes, these castes had two types of relationship with the caste Hindus. First, they were a part of the Hindu society as they were supposed to serve the Hindus as scavengers, menials and agricultural labourers. Second, they were outside the Hindu society so far as distribution of power was concerned. Exclusiveness of each caste group, whether high or low, was maintained by a set of elaborate caste rules. The gradation of castes into high and low categories depended upon the position of a caste group in the power structure legitimised by the myths of ritual purity and impurity. In the agricultural sector, the Jats occupied high social status owing to the acquisition of landholdings. The untouchables were either engaged in agricultural production as agricultural labourers or as carrying out certain unclean occupations such as scavenging.[8]

In the urban sector, the Hindus were dominant as they were

involved in non-agricultural occupations, such as industry, trade and administration. Being trading castes and also engaged in certain administrative activities, the caste Hindus held an advantageous economic position in the Punjabi society.[9] But, this position could not be sustained after the coming of British imperial power and educated class of Bengali clerks and administrators.[10] The spread of western education, ideas and values not only liberalised the educated sections of Punjabi Hindus but also laid the foundation of their cultural alienation. This gradually added to the threat to their socio-cultural hegemony. The politico-economic conditions of the caste Hindus had already undergone a change. The major threat, however, came from the rising influence of Christianity.

Thus, the Brahmanic hegemony which existed in the traditional society had been questioned by the new religions. In the Brahmanic model of Hindu social system, the untouchables were deprived of various religious and socio-economic rights. This could be one of the reasons for these untouchable castes to get drawn to Islam, Sikhism and Christianity. A great number of the so-called untouchable castes had already started converting to these religions. These conversions were not always voluntary but conditioned by a number of factors including force and allurements. One of the important factors was the difference between the principles of Hinduism and those of Sikhism, Islam and Christianity. The idea of equality of all before God perhaps became the main plank of attack on Hinduism. Hinduism was blamed for the perpetuation of inequality and ill-treatment to the low castes. This attack led to two reactions. Some of the leading persons followed British liberalism, western ideas and education. But, this could not help the caste Hindus to retain their elitist position in the society. The second was to give a jolt to Hinduism so as either to have reforms or create legitimacy for the religion. The latter was perhaps untenable if we examine it from the perspective of positions of strength of other religions.

In the emerging scenario, the caste Hindus needed an alternative ideological framework which could bring about needed reforms. It is in this context that the charismatic personality of Swami Dayanand Saraswati—a wandering seer, who condemned non-Vedic practices—acquires great significance. He condemned Puranas, Smritis, and traditions and all the non-Hindu religions in the society.[11] It is believed that Swami Dayanand—the founder of the Samaj—had emancipated himself from the Brahmanic influence and the authority of Smritis. He called upon all the Hindus to adopt Vedic Hinduism. His slogan was: "Back to Vedas". By this he meant a Hindu society for the Hindus. His belief was that by having such a society, some of the existing problems of ignorance, orthodoxy, darkness and despair affecting the strength of Hinduism could be effectively tackled. He held the authority of Vedas on everything and declared Vedas as the only container of true knowledge.[12]

It is important to mention that Dayanand's model of Hindu society consisted of four classes or *varnas*, namely, Brahmin, Kshatriya, Vaishya and Shudra. Each class had an elaborate list of rights, duties, privileges and prestige based on their relative merits and accomplishments. The Vedic model was based on the *varna* scheme—an open system where mobility was possible for all *varnas*. It was not different from the already existing model. Swami Dayanand emphasised that the division of society into four classes would work in a way that each class has no ill-will against the other.[13] The chances of an individual to move up or down in the social structure depended upon his acquisition of merit and accomplishments. The practice and existence of untouchablity in any form was regarded as non-existent in the Vedic society.[14]

After its establishment at Lahore in 1877, Arya Samaj saw its expansion in other districts of Punjab, including even small towns. In a short span of eighteen months, a large number of branches of Arya Samaj came into existence in Punjab. At the same time, Arya Samaj resorted to mass mobilisation. The target groups, besides the caste Hindus, included the low castes who had converted to Islam, Christianity and even Sikhism. It may be pointed out that the leaders of Arya Samaj belonged, by and large, to the upper castes, such as Khatri, Bania, Arora, Mahajan, Rajput and Brahman as it is evident from census records of Punjab for the period 1881 to 1921. It may be noted that Arya Samaj had a considerable following from among the Sikhs and Muslims. As reported by Kenneth Jones, most of them left Arya Samaj when its founder made critical comments on the Sikh Gurus and Prophet Mohammed.[15] Since Arya Samaj, contrary to Sanatan Dharma, adopted an open door policy, it succeeded in having membership from the low castes, including the untouchables (Census of India, Punjab, 1911). As long as Swami Dayanand lived, the authority remained with him. But, after his death, the leadership of the Samaj was taken over by a section of upper caste Hindus.[16]

Social Reform: Strategies of Arya Samaj

With the given ideology and objectives, Arya Samaj adopted a number of general and specific strategies. The social reform programme of the Samaj included condemnation of idol worship, child marriage, and the practice of *sati*. To improve the condition of widows, it advocated widow remarriage and rehabilitation of the orphans and the destitute. To propagate social integration of the society, it encouraged inter-caste marriages and abolition of untouchability. To instill awakening among the masses, it emphasised removal of illiteracy, dispelling of orthodoxy and superstitions from the society. The practice of untouchability and its related problems, such as large-scale conversion of untouchables to other religions, received special attention of the Samaj. Thus, one of the objectives of Arya Samaj was to ameliorate the social status of untouchables so that their crossing over to other religions could be checked. It may be recalled that conversions to other religions were affecting the strength of Hinduism adversely.

Even before the formation of Arya Samaj, Dayanand had been emphasising the reinstating of Vedas for the formation of a new Hinduism. He also advocated practical action on the part of an individual Hindu for the well-being of himself and his fellow beings. The movement is stated to have called for greater equality and solidarity among all Hindus.[17] One of the planks on which he started fighting the ills of Hindu society was eradication of illiteracy, idolatry, orthodoxy, etc. It was noticed that Dayanand fixed his flag which bore an emblem, '*Pakhand Khandini*', i.e., action for the destruction of sham of rituals and customs of Brahmanical Hinduism. He went to Hardwar on Kumbha festival and spoke on various subjects preaching that Vedas were our scriptures and not eighteen Puranas; idolatry was anti-Vedic; and that bathing in the Ganges did not bear any spiritual or purificatory value.[18] Discourses were held with the orthodox sections of Hindu society. Lajpat Rai—an Arya social reformer—described that the outspoken words and views, noble expositions of the Hindu religion and profound scholarship of the Swami attracted hundreds of Indians to his discourses everywhere. These won him a large number of followers but also invited strong opposition including an attempt on Dayanand's life.[19] His activities have been described as multifarious. It was believed that there had been no field of reform and awakening to which he did not make a contribution.[20]

The religious reform programmes of Arya Samaj included restoration of Vedic religion, protection of cows from slaughter, and anti-Sanatan Dharma propaganda.[21] On the religious front, its campaigns especially against Christianity and Islam, could be observed in terms of organised reconversions of untouchables who had embraced these religions. Such activities brought Arya Samaj into direct confrontation with these religions.[22] Attention was also paid to the eradication of child marriage in Punjab society. In this context, Arya Samaj took legal recourse and met with success. A bill known as Sarda Act, named after Shri Har Bilas Sarda, was passed on 23 September, 1929. Shri Sarda was an Arya Samaj activist who legally fought against the custom and practice of child marriage.[23]

Swami Dayanand also emphasised on the equality between sexes. This to him was the sure way to happiness. In this regard, he quoted Manu's verses which acclaimed:

> When a husband is contented with his wife and the wife with her husband, in that family all prosperity, fortune and happiness perpetually dwell.[24]

The need to uplift the status of women was felt as they were denied high position in the family as well as in the society. Widow remarriage was initiated to rehabilitate the female children who became widows in their childhood. In Punjab alone, as claimed by Radhey Shyam Pareek, 1,099 widow remarriages were conducted.[25] The cause of women became an important aspect of the agenda of various Arya Samaj organisations such as Dayanand Dalitoddhar Mandal whose programme included protection of Hindu girls and widows from goondas and anti social elements.[26] A number of girls were rescued from the clutches of goondas. Rescue homes were also set up for the destitute. Another organisation, known as Bhartiya Hindu Shuddhi Sabha, had reportedly protected 1,451 women and 3,155 orphans from getting into the hands of anti-social elements.[27] A large number of philanthropic activities were also organised in Punjab. These included organisation of orphanages and widow homes. Schools were opened for both boys and girls which imparted vocational training.[28]

Arya Samaj also carried out famine relief works during the later part of the nineteenth and early twentieth century, especially between 1877 and 1910 when about ten famines broke out in India. Distress caused by famines was countered by organising a private movement, known as Hindu Orphan Relief Movement in 1897, which specifically devoted itself to the cause of orphans. In northern India, Arya Samaj is believed to have been a pioneer in organising such social service programmes on a large scale.[29]

In view of the existing illiteracy in the society, another important activity of the Samaj was education for the masses. Arya Samaj explicitly stated that ignorance ought to be dispelled and knowledge be disseminated.[30] The idea of disseminating education was embodied in Dayanand's conception of Hindu society based on Vedic precepts. He found that education in Hindu society had been the monopoly of a few. The western system of education paid no attention to Indian conditions and ideals. He emphasised the desirability of educating not a few individuals but all, including women. For him education consisted of knowledge which meant correct and true idea about things. He was of the firm belief that education by which true nature of things is not revealed and instead a false conception of things is formed only meant ignorance.[31] Educational institutions opened by Arya Samaj were called Dayanand Anglo-Vedic (DAV) institutions. This meant education which included religious, social as well as scientific knowledge. The aim was to build up an individual both morally and spiritually. It was emphasised that without morality and character, education becomes meaningless. This meant a search for democratic, ethical and spiritual values, nationalism, self-reliance, scientific spirit and national integration.[32] According to him, English education imparted by Christian schools infused inferiority complex among the Hindus.[33] By 1962, there came into existence 514 educational institutions run by Arya Samaj throughout India. In Punjab alone, the number of such institutions stood at 240, which included schools and colleges for both boys and girls.[34]

It is significant to know that the maximum number of educated individuals among Hindus in Punjab came from major castes, namely, Arora, Khatri, Brahman, Rajput, Aggarwal and even Ode. The number of educated among the above specified Aryan castes in 1911 stood at 3,613, 5,212, 2,077, 421, 474 and 542 respectively. These castes, otherwise represented a dominant section of the Hindu society in Punjab.[35] But, the education among the Ode caste, which formed an illiterate and untouchable section of the Hindu society, certainly suggests some significant contribution of Arya Samaj. The very objective of DAV institutions was to encourage, improve and enforce the study of Hindu literature, classical Sanskrit and the Vedas, as also the study of English literature and sciences, both theoretical and applied. A study conducted on the role of the educational programmes of the Samaj in Indian education also reveals that in fact little concerted effort was made so far as the education of the untouchables was concerned. It was basically the contribution of the Dayanand Salvation Mission.

Arya Samaj and the Status Upliftment of Untouchables

In pursuance of the objective of equality among all and thereby retaining the untouchables in the Hindu fold, the Arya Samaj leadership organised conferences, lectures and sermons against the practice of untouchability and caste system. This was a historical necessity to make caste Hindus aware of the far-reaching demographic and political implications of the practice of untouchability for Hinduism as a religion. Lajpat Rai, a national leader and staunch Arya Samajist, in one of his speeches, raised the question of lower castes from three angles: one, from the point of view of Hindu community; second, as a question of all-India importance; and third, as an issue of humanitarian bearing.[36] In his opinion, the decline of a nation lay in the oppression of others. In India, too, he expressed the view that the high caste Hindus should open their arms to the persons belonging to the depressed classes. The high castes should build a spirit of human dignity. He was of the firm opinion that no real progress could be made when a large section of a society remained underprivileged. In one of the conferences held at Karachi, Lajpat Rai emphasised the cause of lower sections of the Hindu society:

> No greater harm can be done to a human being than to put him into circumstances which made him believe that he is eternally doomed to life of ignorance, servitude and misery, and in him any sort of ambition for his betterment is a sin.[37]

He further observed:

> No slavery is more harmful than that of mind and no sin is greater than to keep human beings in perpetual bondage. It is bad enough to enslave people, but to create and perpetuate circumstances which prevent them from breaking their chains and becoming free, is infamous... In the insolence of wealth and power, the ancestors of Hindus maltreated people whom God had placed under them to protect and bless.[38]

In his opinion, the fight for the rights of untouchables had been one of the most notable services rendered by Arya Samaj. No other religious sect or organisation ever tried to raise this issue. It launched a strategy called *shuddhi*. It was presumed that untouchability emanated from ritual impurity. Therefore, a ritual for removing impurity could render the untouchables pure castes. By way of this ritual, it was also projected that social status of the lower castes would enhance. Initially *shuddhis* were performed on those untouchables who had embraced Islam and Christianity. When exactly did this strategy come into operation, is not clear. There are some who believe that it was launched after 1888, i.e., five years after Swami Dayanand's death. It was Pandit Ganga Ram, who for the first time solemnised *shuddhi* on 70 Odes—an untouchable caste. In the year 1894, Mahatma Munshi Ram, and his associates Lala Badri Das and Lala Dev Raj purified Rahtiyas, another untouchable caste in districts of Gurdaspur and Jalandhar. In the year 1900, Mahatma Munshi Ram took another 40 Rahtiyas along with him to Lahore and on 3 June assimilated them with Hinduism by way of *shuddhi*. In the subsequent years *shuddhis* were conducted in districts of Ropar and Layallpur.[39]

The Dumnas in district Gurdaspur constituted the maximum number of untouchables. Mahashya Raunak Ram and Mahashya Gokul Ram made considerable efforts for the *shuddhi* of Dumnas. Ch. Ram Bhaj Dutt, who also belonged to the same district, purified Dunmnas and gave them a new identity *Mahashya*. In the subsequent years, he established an organisation, called Mahashya Kaumi Sudhar Sabha, which performed *shuddhi* on an estimated one lakh Dumnas.[40] Another untouchable caste, known as Megh, in district Sialkot constituted one and a quarter lakh of population in 1911. Meghs were considered untouchables. Lala Ganga Ram, a lawyer, purified a large number of Meghs on 28 March, 1903. The Meghs were given the name *Arya* or *Bhagat* after their baptism. A body, known as Megh Uddhar Sabha, was formed in 1912. It later established an exclusive locality for the Meghs in Dina Nagar in district Gurdaspur.[41] According to Radhey Shyam Pareek, during the years 1901-10, about sixty to seventy thousand untouchables underwent *shuddhi*. Some of the major untouchable castes and the number of their persons undergoing *shuddhi* were: Rahtiya (3,000-4,000), Ramdasias (200), Ode (2,000-3,000), Megh (30,000), etc. The places where these ceremonies were organised included: Kangra, Dalhousie, Hoshiarpur and Ambala. In 1923, about 8,000 Chamars were 'purified' at Sialkot through Dayanand Dalitodhar Mandal. Pt. Vishnu Dutt Vakil 'purified' 5,300 Balamikis in 1930 at Lahore. In 1931, another 1,000 Balmikis became *dwija* (twice-born) after their *shuddhi* at Lahore. In 1933, Pt. Vishnu Dutt 'purified' another 1,530 Balmikis. Besides, it is recorded that All India Shuddhi Mahasabha purified 1,83,342 persons within a time span of eight years.[42]

In Lahore, the Arya Samajists concentrated on the ritual

aspects of the sweeper caste and Chamars. After Swami Dayanand's death, Swami Shraddhanand became very active in reforms. A large number of organisations came into existence for carrying out *shuddhis*. One such organisation was Jat Pat Todak Mandal founded by Bhumanand at Lahore in 1922. Similarly, other organisations, such as Megh Uddhar Sabha (Sialkot), Dayanand Dalitodhar Sabha, Achhutodhar Sabha (Amritsar), Arya Dalitodhar Sabha (Dina Nagar), Megh Sabha (Lahore), Asprishaya Nivaran Sangh, All India Mahasha Mahasabha, Achhutodhar Sabha (Meerut), etc. carried on the task of reforms in caste system and eradication of the practice of untouchability. Their main function was to conduct *shuddhis* in different districts in Punjab.[43]

What were the consequences of large-scale "purifications"? Could untouchables acquire equality in social status after they were "raised to the status of *dwijas*?" In other words, what happened to the social status of untouchables in the society after the *shuddhi*? These questions need to be taken up for an examination. For this, the existing conditions of the ex-untouchables are looked into.

The empirical exercise organised to investigate into the consequences with particular reference to the present condition of the purified ex-untouchable castes does not provide a rosy picture. A majority of the individuals contacted still suffered from poverty and the stigma of untouchability. Their educational levels were very low. Occupationally, they were engaged in agricultural labour or were in low-prestige occupations. Their geographical segregation suggested a minimum level of social interaction with the touchable castes. Probably, even after their *shuddhi*, they did not gain anything except for a symbolic right of reading the Vedas and putting on the sacred threat. The ex-untouchables lived in the same social and economic conditions. It is however worth mentioning that there had taken place some amount of social mobility in individual cases. There was a definite departure from traditional caste-based occupations among the 'purified' scheduled castes as well as scheduled castes in general. But, this was limited in extent. Those who had attained high occupational levels, progressed in educational sphere and even acquired political stature in Punjab in post-independence era, attributed this to the constitutional privileges granted by the government and to the efforts of Dr. B. R. Ambedkar. As a result of constitutional safeguards, even the purified ex-untouchables have renamed themselves as scheduled castes—a probable case of de-sanskritisation.[44] On the other hand, the membership of Arya Samaj in two districts, namely, Hoshiarpur and Gurdaspur, did not show any significant number of Balmikis. There were also a few cases where those who became Arya Samajists later became Sikhs.

Concluding Remarks

The examination of the reform activities of Arya Samaj, with particular reference to the status upliftment of the untouchables, reveals a considerable zeal to improve the prevailing conditions. The leadership also did a lot to retain and to reclaim the untouchables into the Hindu fold. This was, as the historical and empirical evidence indicates, due to the conjunction of the social, religious, demographic and the political factors prevalent during this period. The Hindu social system was under attack, at this time, mainly from the Christians. Before this, the Hindus had lost sizable sections of its society to Islam and to Sikhism.

It was fortuitous that the leadership of Arya Samaj and the nationalist movement overlapped in Punjab. The objective interests of both coincided. The Punjabi Hindu elite succeeded, in large measure, to retain the untouchable castes in the Hindu fold thereby increasing their political strength. Some support is lent to the above contention by the evidence available. The Arya Samaj did not continue with programmes to help the scheduled castes. Its last major activity was seen in 1947 when it looked after the refugees belonging to the untouchable castes. Since then, such a policy remained on paper. Furthermore, the investigations into the present conditions of Mahashas and Aryas may indicate that in most of the cases their social, economic, religious and political conditions have remained unaffected. However, as a whole, Arya Samaj made considerable effort to improve the conditions of the depressed castes. It also made significant contribution to the nationalist awakening in Punjab. The educational institutions, which were opened by the movement, have been responsible for an enduring change in the people's awareness leading to economic and political mobility among the people of Punjab.

Notes

1. Indu Banga, "The Arya Ideology and its Socio-political Implications in the Punjab", *Souvenir*, 83rd Indian Science Congress, (January 3-8, 1996), Patiala: Punjabi University, 1996, pp. 141-46.
2. Kenneth W. Jones, *Arya Dharma*, New Delhi: Manohar, 1976.
3. Satish K. Sharma, "Social Structure, Religious Pluralism and Violence" in Gopal Singh (ed.), *Punjab: Past, Present and Future*, New Delhi: Ajanta, 1994.
4. Ralph Miliband, *Marxism and Politics*, Oxford: Oxford University Press, 1977.
5. S.A.A. Rizvi, "Islamic Proselytisation: Seventh to Sixteenth Century" in G.A. Oddie (ed.), *Religion in South Asia*, New Delhi: Manohar, 1977.
6. J.D. Cunningham, *A History of the Sikhs*, New Delhi: S. Chand and Co., 1972.
7. Kenneth W. Jones, *op. cit.*
8. Denzil Ibbetson, *Caste, Races and Tribes of Punjab*, New Delhi: B. R. Publishers, 1974.
9. Kenneth W. Jones, *op. cit.*
10. *Ibid.*
11. *Ibid.*
12. Vaidyanath Shastri, *The Arya Samaj: Its Cult and Creed*, Delhi: Sarvadeshik Arya Pratinidhi Sabha, 1967.
13. Dayanand Saraswati, *Light of Truth*, Delhi: Sarvadeshik Arya Pratinidhi Sabha, 1975.

14. O.P. Tyagi, *Untouchability*, Delhi: Sarvadeshik Arya Pratinidhi Sabha, 1972.
15. Kenneth W. Jones, *op. cit.*
16. Ram Chander Javed, *Punjab Ka Arya Samaj* (Hindi), Jalandhar, 1964.
17. Urusula Sharma, "Status Striving and Striving for Status", *Social Action*, Vol. 3, 1976.
18. Vaidyanath Shastri, *op. cit.*
19. Lajpat Rai, *A History of Arya Samaj*, Delhi: Orient Longman Ltd., 1967.
20. Vaidyanath Shastri, *op. cit.*
21. Radhey Shyam Pareek, *Contribution of Arya Samaj in the Making of Modern India*, New Delhi: Sarvdeshik Arya Pratinidhi Sabha, 1973.
22. J.T.F. Jordens, "Reconversions to Hinduism: The Shudhi of the Arya Samaj" in G.A. Oddie, *op. cit.*
23. Lajpat Rai, *op. cit.*
24. Dayanand Saraswati, *op. cit.*
25. Radhey Shyam Pareek, *op. cit.*
26. *Ibid.*
27. *Ibid.*
28. Lajpat Rai, *op. cit.*
29. *Ibid.*
30. Vaidyanath Shastri, *op. cit.*
31. *Ibid.*
32. Dayanand Saraswati, *op. cit.*
33. Saraswati Pandit, *A Critical Study of Arya Samaj's Contribution to Indian Education*, Delhi: Sarvdeshik Arya Pratinidhi Sabha, 1974.
34. *Ibid.*
35. Census of India, *Punjab Report*, Vol. XIV, Part I Civil and Military Gazette Press, Lahore, 1911.
36. Lajpat Rai, *op. cit.*
37. *Ibid.*, p. 121.
38. *Ibid.*, pp. 122-23.

39. Ram Chander Javed, *op. cit.*
40. *Ibid.*
41. *Ibid.*
42. Radhey Shyam Pareek, *op. cit.*
43. *Ibid.*
44. S. K. Sharma, *Social Movements and Social Change*, New Delhi: B.R. Publishing Corporation, 1985.

4

The Christian Movement in Punjab

JOHN C.B. WEBSTER

Christianity has not been a movement throughout its history in Punjab. Indeed, if one were to look at Christianity in Punjab today, one might wonder whether it had ever been a movement at all. The thesis put forward here is that it was a movement of considerable importance for about sixty years and then, under the impact of events beyond its choosing or control, was transformed simply into a community. This essay describes the process of its development into an important movement and then of its transformation from a movement into a community.[1] The essay is divided into four parts. The first traces the origins of Christianity in Punjab, the second examines the period of its maximum impact on Punjab (ca. 1860-1920), the third describes the transition from movement to community, and the fourth offers some concluding reflections.

I

There is a tradition that one of the disciples of Jesus, the apostle Thomas, came to Punjab. If he did so, he left no known continuing community behind. The same is also true of the priests and missionaries who visited Punjab during Mughal times. Thus, prior to the dawn of the nineteenth century, when Ranjit Singh came to power in Lahore and the British displaced the Marathas in Delhi,

Christian missions to Punjab had been at best sporadic and temporary. The Roman Catholics had established a Prefecture Apostolic in Agra in 1784 but even Delhi, as well as the rest of Punjab, seems to have been neglected. When the first Protestant missionaries arrived in Delhi in 1811, they found only about twenty Roman Catholics there.[2] Thus, the continuing presence of Christianity in Punjab really dates from the nineteenth century.

The Baptists were the first to establish a mission in Delhi. Expanding westward from their base in Bengal, they decided to post a regular missionary—Rev. J.T. Thompson—there only in 1818. The next to establish a mission station was the Presbyterian Church in the United States (American Presbyterian Mission) whose first missionary, Rev. John C. Lowrie, arrived in Ludhiana in 1834. While Lowrie came in response to an invitation from the British Political Agent to establish a school there, he was also convinced both that the Sikhs might be particularly responsive to the Christian message and that Ludhiana would make an excellent centre from which to make preaching tours into Afghanistan, Kashmir and Tibet. The next two missions were created by the two major mission societies of the established Church of England in response to the request of Christian officials on the spot. The Church Missionary Society (CMS) started its Himalaya or Kotgarh Mission in 1840 and by 1852 had established its headquarters in Amritsar. In 1854, the Society for the Propagation of the Gospel (SPG) began its work in Delhi. Sialkot became the initial mission station of two missions in quick succession: the Sialkot Mission of the United Presbyterian Church of North America (United Presbyterian Mission), established by Rev. Andrew Gordon in August 1855, and the Punjab Mission of the Church of Scotland, begun by Rev. and Mrs. Thomas Hunter early in 1857. All of these missions were Protestant. Until the 1880s what few Roman Catholic chaplains were in Punjab confined their activities to the Roman Catholic soldiers and migrants who were serving the British there. As a result, by 1857, what were to become the major mission societies in the region, were already on the scene.

Virtually, all these early Protestant missionaries were Evangelicals, who have been described as

> those who espoused and experienced justification, [i.e., God's grace and forgiveness through the sacrificial death of Jesus Christ] and scriptural authority in an intensified way: personal conversion and rigorous moral life, on the one hand, and concentrated attention on the Bible as a guide to conviction and behaviour on the other, with a special zeal for the dissemination of Christian faith so conceived.[3]

Built into this experientially and Biblically grounded Evangelical faith was not only a strong individualism which emphasised individual moral responsibility, individual conversion, and individual salvation, but also the conviction that religion was the primary variable both in individual and in societal transformation. Bad or false religion resulted in personal immoralities of many kinds as well as in social stagnation or degradation; good or true religion produced good personal and family morality as well as an enlightened and progressive society. This particular Evangelical 'mind-set' shaped not only the missionaries' views of Punjabi religions, people, and society but also the nature of their own work in Punjab.

The primary purpose for which Evangelical missionaries came to Punjab was evangelism, in both senses of that term. On the one hand, they came simply to spread the gospel (literally, 'good news') message to people who had never heard it before that in Jesus the Christ God had acted decisively for the salvation of the world and everyone in it. Thus, one of the major activities of these early missionaries was to go out on tour for months at a time, preaching in towns, villages and even centres of pilgrimage to share this message with anyone who cared to listen. They also distributed large numbers of religious tracts and selected portions of the Bible to those who could read. The aim of this work was to get the message out in an introductory and inviting way to as many people as possible. To this effort there was some response, although it was by no means as great as the missionaries had hoped it would be. Thus, the second aspect of evangelism involved assisting those inquirers, who had become interested in learning more about this message and its implications, to come to the point of belief, commitment, and baptism into the membership of the Christian Church.

The basic Christian message which these Evangelical missionaries preached and taught combined a particular analysis of the human condition or 'predicament' with their own view of 'the way of salvation' God was offering to all of humanity. Their analysis of the human condition, briefly stated, was that all people are not only sinners, deserving punishment from a holy and righteous God, but are also totally incapable of satisfying God's demand for holiness and righteousness by their own efforts. However, despite the serious eternal consequences of the predicament, there was good news. God, out of love for a fallen humanity, had sent his own son, Jesus, to live a sinless human life, to suffer and to die, thus atoning for human sin by taking upon himself the divine punishment which not he, but the rest of humanity, deserved. This atoning act of God in Jesus opened up the way of eternal salvation to all those who sincerely repented of their sinfulness, trusted in God's unmerited grace revealed in Jesus, and united themselves with Jesus Christ in faith, gratitude, and holiness of life as members of his living body—the Church. Both in seeking to convey a vivid sense of how desperate everyone's predicament was, and in pointing out how futile alternative paths to 'true salvation' were, the missionaries considered it necessary to be very critical of the prevailing religious beliefs and practices of the Punjabi people.

The period from the arrival of the first of these missionaries up through 1857 may best be described as one of exploration, preparation, and settling down. These missionaries were not simply visiting Punjab: they considered their work to be both important in its own right and essential foundation laying for its further development by their successors. They therefore travelled throughout the region in order to get to know the terrain, the travel routes, the people, and the best places to establish 'mission stations' where missionaries and their Indian assistants might reside. They also devoted much of their time immediately upon arrival in Punjab to language study. Some of the more gifted among them prepared tracts, translated portions of the Bible, and even wrote grammars and dictionaries to help future missionaries learn the language more quickly and easily. For example, the Rev. John Newton, who arrived in Ludhiana in 1836, produced a fresh Punjabi translation first of the Gospel according to St. John in 1841, and finally of the entire New Testament in 1868. In 1851 he published the first comprehensive Punjabi grammar, and in 1854 a Punjabi vocabulary book as well as the first Punjabi dictionary (the latter with Rev. Levi Janvier).[4] These works, along with the translation of John Bunyan's *Pilgrim's Progress*, marked a significant transition from old to modern Punjabi prose.[5]

By 1857 these missionaries had established mission stations at Ambala, Amritsar, Delhi, Jalandhar, Kangra, Kotgarh, Lahore, Ludhiana, Multan, Peshawar, Rawalpindi, Sabathu and Sialkot. Most of these had a resident missionary, but only a very few had more than two missionary families. The mission in Jalandhar was run by the American Presbyterian Mission's first convert in Punjab—Rev. Goloknath. Most of these mission stations also had a school supervised by a missionary but staffed by Indian teachers, only a very few of whom were Christians. In fact, the mission school offering western education, which included instruction in both the English language and the Christian religion, became throughout most of the nineteenth century, the major sign of the Christian presence in Punjab. The schools were made possible by the resident Europeans who supported them financially, and by Indians of several different religious backgrounds who either taught in them or sent their children to them. They were to become an important means through which Christianity made its social and cultural impact upon Punjab.

Yet, despite this apparent show of strength, the Christian presence in Punjab was extremely small in 1857. Missionaries were very few, no more than fifty in the entire Punjab, and the number of Indian Christians did not exceed a few hundred. Of these, probably, the most prominent were Rev. Goloknath, a Bengali Brahmin, and Professor Yesudas Ramchandra, a noted mathematician of Kayasth background, who taught science at Delhi College. There were at least three reasons why so few people had converted to Christianity during this early period. One was undoubtedly the message itself and the way in which it was presented. Both were strange and had yet to make a meaningful connection with the world in which the vast majority of Punjabis lived. Second, the social sanctions against conversion were extremely severe. Those who did convert were completely cut off from their families and traditional sources of livelihood. Few, except those who already found themselves somewhat marginalised in society, could therefore take the risks or make the sacrifices which conversion entailed. Third, in keeping with their own Evangelical faith, the missionaries put inquirers through a very stringent screening process which included testing not just their understanding of Christianity but also their attitude and lifestyle changes prior to baptism. Since this ordeal could last several years, many initially interested inquirers never made it through.[6] Those who did seem to have come from a variety of backgrounds. For example, of the 46 converts of the American Presbyterian Mission during this period for whom background information is available, 30 percent were Muslim, 13 percent were Brahmins, 25 percent were Sikhs, one was a high caste Hindu, and the remaining 29 percent were Hindus of either low or unspecified caste. They thus represented a fair cross section of the Central Punjab population.[7]

During the 1857 revolt in Punjab this tiny Christian community was generally attacked by the rebels. This was especially true in Delhi where the sepoys who came from Meerut immediately killed as many Christians as they could find. The Church of Scotland missionaries in Sialkot were also killed, whereas the United Presbyterians there managed to escape. The sepoys who mutinied in Jalandhar headed for the mission compound but, after giving the Christians a scare, proceeded on to Ludhiana. There they set fire to all the mission buildings as well as to the homes of three converts. However, both the missionaries and the converts were given shelter and so no lives were lost. In Lahore and Ambala mission work was suspended but no damage was done. Recently, Rajat Kanta Ray has argued, quite convincingly, that 1857 was primarily a religious crusade in defense of *din* and *dharma*, which were perceived as being under serious threat.[8] This would suggest that the Christians were attacked because they were visible symbols of what the rebels believed to be threatening an entire way of life to which they were deeply attached. Whether the Christians either in Punjab or throughout North India actually posed, or were even capable of posing, such a threat at that time is less clear. However, the concern about 'the Christian threat' would continue to be expressed in other forms for another century.

II

The question which Evangelicals put to themselves after the 1857 revolt had been suppressed was, "what was the divine purpose behind this crisis through which we have passed?" The clearest answer, they believed, was that 1857 had been God's chastisement for the government's support of 'heathenism' and reluctance to spread Christianity among the Indian people. This view was especially widespread among officials in Punjab, an unusually high proportion of whom were staunch Evangelicals, e.g., John Lawrence, Robert Montgomery, Donald McLeod, Herbert Edwardes, and Edward Lake, to name only the most prominent among them. As Herbert Edwardes put it in a London speech delivered in 1860:

> In these things we hear the Voice of God. It says: "I gave India to England for the benefit of its 180 million peoples so that you might communicate the light of the Bible and the knowledge of the true God to these my Heathen creatures. You have neglected this charge... and I have chastened you. But I have condoned your offences. I have raised you up, when no other hand could save you. I once more consign this people to your charge... and say take warning from the past." Let us take warning. A Christian policy is the only policy of hope.[9]

This Christian policy, advocated by Evangelical officials, missionaries, and mission societies alike, had two important components. One was to introduce Bible classes into government schools. There was, however, no agreement over whether or not such study of the Bible should be made compulsory. The other was that the government should discontinue giving support to the religious practices and institutions of Hindus, Muslims, and Sikhs (e.g., religious endowments and festivals, caste practices, Hindu and Muslim law). At the same time it should end its discriminatory treatment of converts to Christianity, who had been either denied or removed from government jobs because they were Christians. This opening up of government jobs to Indian Christians was the only aspect of the Christian policy which was implemented.

Beyond that the government would not go. Despite shared views on the Christian task and such good personal relations between Evangelical officials and missionaries in Punjab that one historian has referred to them as "the Evangelical Entente,"[10] the basic purposes of the missions and the government were different. The primary purpose of the missions continued to be evangelism as defined above: that of the government was to rule. Rule meant control and gaining or holding the support of groups within Punjabi society the British considered important but whose religious convictions were at odds with those of the missionaries. Thus, while individual officials could provide personal rather than official support to the Evangelical cause, there was an inherent tension between the missions and the government. For example, there was in the years following 1857 a growing competition between the missions and the Punjab education department for dominance in the field of western education. This was due in part to the fact that key figures in the department were not Evangelicals and in part to different philosophies of education. The missions had government policy, which favoured educating through private rather than government schools, on their side. The department wanted to extend western education among "respectable people who object on religious grounds to send their children to mission schools"[11] and so continued to open new schools, at times in competition with the missions. Government also blocked Christian evangelism if it felt its own interests were threatened. In 1859, some Mazhabi Sikh sepoys in the 24th Punjab Native Infantry became interested in Christianity after acquiring some Christian tracts and books in the sack of Delhi. They approached their officers to learn more. These officers responded to the request and invited a missionary who began an inquirers' class. Some of the sepoys were baptised, but then the Government of India issued an order prohibiting all officers from any involvement with the spread of Christianity among their men. With this indication of government disapproval the conversion movement quickly subsided.[12]

However, as these two illustrations suggest, the Christian movement in Punjab was gaining strength and assertiveness in the years following 1857. The interpretation given to those events by Evangelicals in Punjab, Great Britain, and the United States seems to have fired missionary zeal. On the one hand, converts to Christianity had, with surprisingly few exceptions, proven true to their faith when forced to choose either conversion or death, and many had died as martyrs. On the other hand, the relative quiet in Punjab provided assurance that an open acknowledgement of Christian faith and an assertive Christian movement were not a threat to the empire. The mission societies already present increased their mission personnel and opened 24 new mission stations between 1858 and 1885. New mission societies—the American Methodists, the Roman Catholics, and the Salvation Army—arrived and began evangelistic as well as other work among the Punjabi people. The number of inquirers and converts increased. The 1881 Census of India reported 3,912 Indian Christians in Punjab and its Dependencies. A new era of definitive importance and significant influence for Christianity in Punjab had been ushered in. It made its impact primarily through evangelism, education, and such acts of benevolence as medical and relief work.

Christian evangelism operated at two levels. One was the struggle for people's minds, for the Evangelicals tended to address their message more to the intellect and reason than to the institutions or emotions. Thus, the major emphasis in Christian preaching, teaching or writing was on convincing people that Christianity offered the true way of salvation and that the prevailing religions in Punjab were false in that they offered no genuine solution to the human predicament as Evangelicals had defined it. This particular approach to evangelism inevitably involved not only challenging the religious assumptions an audience brought to an unfamiliar message but also making contrasts between the new faith being presented and those with which Punjabis were already familiar.

Christian evangelists brought their message to the public first through direct preaching in town and city bazars as well as in the villages where they itinerated during the cool season.[13] Preaching was supplemented by the distribution of tracts and selections from the Bible which people could read at their leisure. Published responses to tracts appeared in the vernacular press. However, from the 1870s onwards the opposition became better organised with the rise of the Arya Samaj, the Singh Sabhas, and various Muslim anjumans who trained their own preachers and published their own tracts to set forth their own truth claims as well as counter those of their opponents.[14] In the villages several sects arose which incorporated Christian teaching without converting to Christianity,[15] but the more common response was one of polite indifference.

The other level of Christian evangelism was in the struggle for people's souls, for their ultimate loyalties and allegiances. A highly publicised example of this struggle gives some indication of what could be involved. In August 1866 three boys in the Lahore mission school decided to become Christians and moved into the mission compound. This caused a great uproar in the city. Family members and friends appealed to the boys personally and directly to return to their families. The press supported them and parents withdrew their children from the school in protest, so that attendance dropped from 400 to 100. When that failed, the family of one boy—Dina Nath—requested the court to order that the boy be returned to his family. This also failed because the judge, upon questioning Dina Nath and seeing his determination, felt obliged to allow his baptism to proceed. When a petition to the Lieutenant Governor also failed, Dina Nath and his companions were baptised. In time opposition died down and attendance at the mission school returned to normal.[16] What is unusual about this case was not so much the pressures involved as the outcome. Most often family influence prevailed: inquirers gave up in the face of it and returned home. However, those who returned home after baptism either had to undergo various rites of purification or had to leave. It was not yet possible for caste Hindus, Muslims or Sikhs to convert and remain with their families.

The greatest response to Christian evangelistic work,

however, did not come from the educated urban elites or from their children in the mission schools, but from rural Chuhras primarily in the central Punjab. Chuhras were considered to be at the bottom of the caste hierarchy. Many had previously converted to Islam (Musallis) and Sikhism (Mazhabis) in their search for dignity and respect. Beginning in the mid-1870s a growing number started converting to Christianity, even in the face of quite forceful opposition from the dominant groups within their villages upon whom they were economically dependent. The conversion movement started in several unconnected villages at about the same time. From those individuals who had taken the lead in seeking baptism, it spread through kinship, village and even business connections in the Sialkot, Gujranwala, Gurdaspur, Lahore, Amritsar, and Ferozepur districts. The 1911 census reported 1,63,994 Indian Christians in Punjab, over forty times the 1881 total. A decade later it had almost doubled again (3,15,031). These gains were due almost entirely to Chuhra conversions.

These mass conversions had a great impact upon both Christianity and Punjab in general. The Christian community was changed from a tiny, urban, literate and progressive community into a much larger, but overwhelmingly rural, illiterate, backward and stigmatised community. The movement forced the missions to alter their priorities from the urban elites to the rural menials and it put a permanent Dalit stamp upon the Church. At the same time, conversion made the plight of the Dalits in Punjab, as elsewhere in India, a public issue. Other Punjabis began to realise that if they did not treat their Dalit co-religionists better, they might become Christians. After the British introduced separate electorates for Muslims in 1900, possible conversion became a matter of some political consequence because the number of seats allotted to a community in the legislatures was based in part upon its showing in the decennial census. Hindus in particular feared less that Christians would increase in political influence than that their own community would lose influence in relation to the Muslims and Sikhs. Arya Samaj was the first to see and respond to the impending crisis by initiating what later came to be called "Harijan uplift work" as well as by sponsoring such status-raising events as inter-caste meals and *shuddhi*. The modern Dalit movement in

Punjab, which was picked up later by Mango Ram, the Ad Dharmis, Ambedkarites and others in succeeding decades, had begun.

The Christian missions were pioneers in western education in Punjab. Every town or city which became a mission station had its mission school or schools: in many of them, the mission school was the only recognised school offering a secondary education until the 1880s. Each of the original missions developed a college at the apex of its own network of schools: Forman Christian College in Lahore (American Presbyterian Mission, 1869), St. Stephen's College, Delhi (SPG, 1882), Gordon College in Rawalpindi (United Presbyterian Mission, 1893), Murray College in Sialkot (Church of Scotland, 1889), and Edwardes College in Peshawar (CMS, 1900). Several also collaborated in establishing the Kinnaird College for Women in Lahore (1913).

This growth in the quantity and quality of Christian educational institutions in Punjab occurred in an atmosphere of intense competition because education, to a somewhat lesser degree than evangelism, was also a struggle for the minds and souls of the Punjabi people. Initially, the competition was between the government and mission schools: after 1882 Hunter Commission various Indian religious bodies began to develop their own secondary schools and colleges in order to impart a type of western education which was in keeping with their own religious beliefs and practices. Mission educational institutions had the competitive edge over those of the government in charging lower fees and in their reputation for close contact between Christian staff and students. Government institutions were more stable as they did not wish to offend religious sensibilities either by requiring classes in Christianity or by admitting Dalits into the student body on an equal basis. Hindu, Muslim and Sikh institutions charged even lower fees than did the mission institutions but, being virtually single community colleges, lacked the cosmopolitan student body and atmosphere of the mission and government institutions. Competition between these educational bodies both for students and for influence within education committees led to an expansion of educational opportunities in Punjab, to broader participation in the educational policy-making process, and to greater ideological diversity within the educational system as a whole.

While the Christian missions established asylums in Punjab for orphans, lepers, and the mentally ill, their greatest benevolent work was in providing medical care through dispensaries, clinics, and hospitals, especially for women. By the end of the nineteenth century there were Christian hospitals or clinics in Ambala, Amritsar, Chamba, Delhi, Ferozepore, Gujrat, Gurdaspur, Jalalpur, Jandiala, Jhelum, Kangra, Ludhiana, Sialkot, and at four points along the northwest frontier. Several of these were staffed by women and intended exclusively for women who would not allow a male physician to attend to them. In 1894, Dr. Edith Brown started the North India School of Medicine for Christian Women, which began courses initially for nurses, compounders, midwives, and medical assistants. In 1912, it was upgraded, renamed as Women's Christian Medical College, Ludhiana, and opened to women who were not Christians. Only after independence did it become co-educational.[17] Through these hospitals as well as through the Christian girls schools, Punjabi Christian women came to play a pre-eminent role in both the medical and teaching professions, which was out of all proportion to their percentage of the population and was to continue until after independence.[18]

Christian medical work, while undertaken for evangelistic reasons and producing some positive evangelistic results, did not get caught up, to anywhere near the same degree, in the controversies, competition and conflict which surrounded Christian educational and evangelistic work. In the latter two cases one can discern a pattern of interaction and change running through the end of the nineteenth century. Christian initiatives, undertaken for evangelistic reasons, led to some conversions. These conversions provoked a response from Hindus, Muslims, and Sikhs who believed that their way of life was under serious threat unless properly defended. They therefore entered these fields, often imitating Christian patterns of organisation and Christian methods, to compete for the minds and souls of at least their own people. The result of this competition was that some important socio-cultural and even political changes took place which can only be summarised here.

Christian evangelism, based as it was on individualistic premises, tended to support individualism as a cultural value. Initially Punjabis responded by espousing communitarian values (e.g., one ought to stay with the religion into which one is born), but gradually their tracts also made an appeal to individual reason and conscience, a priority upheld by the courts, as in the Dina Nath case. At the same time, the Christian emphasis upon the decisive importance of religion tended to reinforce the Punjabis' religious identities and communal loyalties at the expense of alternative identities and loyalties. In so doing, it may have made extremist rather than moderate nationalist ideologies more attractive to educated Punjabis. In like manner, Christian initiatives in the field of education and the response which they evoked led to increased availability of western education at lower costs to parents and hence greater opportunity for the social mobility such education opened up. Two groups which particularly benefited from these Christian initiatives were women and Dalits, the condition of both of whom became issues of public concern and whose opportunities for greater dignity and respect were significantly enhanced.

Interaction with other communities also had a significant impact upon the Christian community during this period. The first and most obvious change was numerical growth from several hundred in 1857 to 3,15,031 in 1921. Most of this growth came from rural conversion movements among the Chuhras, but there continued to be a small but steady stream of converts from a variety of other backgrounds as well. The most prominent of the converts in this period was Rajah Harnam Singh, who gave up the throne of Kapurthala to become a Christian, and whose daughter, Rajkumari Amrit Kaur, was Gandhi's secretary and first Health Minister of independent India. These converts brought their own needs and priorities into the church and put their own stamp upon it. In fact, it was both their conversion and then their labour which enabled the Christian community to have the impact it did. A second important internal development was the beginning of a power struggle within the Christian churches in which the best educated clergy started to challenge missionary domination. An open struggle can be traced back to as early as 1862 at the Punjab

Missionary Conference when Rev. Goloknath, in a presentation on "Sympathy and Confidence: How Can Foreign Missionaries Secure, in the Highest Degrees, the Sympathy and Affectionate Confidence of their Native Brethren", called for greater social respect and closer friendship.[19] This developed over time into a national movement within the churches and produced some experiments in power-sharing which by 1919 had not gone very far.

Perhaps, however, the most significant changes within the churches came as responses to the mass conversion of rural Dalits: a change in the social composition of the Christian community, a reordering of priorities in terms of investment of time, energy, people and resources; a gradual withdrawal from the religious controversies which earlier had played so large a role but had proved to be of little value, if not counter-productive; and, perhaps most important of all, a fundamental redefinition of the human predicament in terms of which the basic Christian message had to be reformulated and to which it had now to be addressed. It was Dalit aspirations for basic human dignity as well as for some grounds for hope in this life and in this world which led to a fresh emphasis upon God's unconditional love, embodied in Jesus Christ, for all and especially for those for whom society had the least regard. The themes of God's loving care and mercy, God's law as a new rule of life, as well as God's sovereignty over all forces of evil and adverse circumstances, came to dominate Christian preaching and worship. These were expressed beautifully in a hymn, composed by a Chuhra convert, which reveals a Christian *bhakti* very different in tone from the message of the early missionaries.

> Bring my Jesus to me, O my God!
> To thy door have I come, O my Creator!
> The winner of my heart, Christ the Beloved!
> My Creator, my beloved Lord!
> Let me never forget thee, my Lord, O Christ!
> Twas for me He came into the world;
> My Beloved lost His life for my soul,
> And saved my soul from sin.

I wandered about astray and lost,
But I heard his voice calling me:
Having pity on me, a sinner.
He bore the burden of my sorrows; He injured none.
Yet the cruel ones crucified Him.
O Cruel ones! Why did you commit this dreadful deed?
Did not the fear of God restrain you?
We are all beggars at thy door,
Thou hast fed us all.
In Thy hand is my life,
The shadow of Thy mercy is over me.
O Beloved, show kindness to me,
Who am oppressed by many sorrows.[20]

III

In the years immediately following the close of World War I the Christian movement in Punjab faced a situation dramatically different from the one in which it had grown and thrived. This new era was inaugurated by the Rowlatt Bill, the agitation against it, Jallianwala Bagh, the imposition of martial law, and then the non-cooperation as well as Khilafat movements. Up to this time nationalist agitation in Punjab had been intermittent and there had been no effective Congress organisation in the province. All of that changed as the nationalist movement increased markedly in breadth, depth and intensity between 1919 and 1922. Moreover, the 1919 Constitution, which included communal electorates for both Muslims and Sikhs in Punjab, granted a measure of real power to Punjabi members of the legislature. Both nationalist and communal politics became major pre-occupations of Punjabi public life, whereas the socio-cultural concerns behind the Christian movement no longer captured public attention to the same degree that they had in the past.

Christians in Punjab were not well positioned to deal effectively with these new challenges. While the community had grown dramatically over the past four decades, it still comprised only about one percent of the total population and included a mere 20,000 urban residents scattered throughout the province.

Moreover, Christians had few political resources at their command. Church bodies were still dominated by missionaries and non-British missionaries were required to remain aloof from politics.[21] Their impressive institutional network was of uncertain value in a political struggle. Government reluctance, despite missionary pressure, to recruit Punjabi Christians into the army while conscripting others during the World War had indicated that Christians could expect little help or sympathy from the government. The Indian Christian Association, Punjab, seems to have been the only political organisation they had, but it was small, elitist, and more of a discussion than action group. The Christians' only political asset appears to have been a few very capable individuals.

Things began badly for the Christians, especially in Amritsar where, after the police had fired upon a crowd which had gathered to protest the deportation of Drs. Satyapal and Kitchlew, the atmosphere resembled that of 1857. The religious book depot and church in Hall Bazar were burned, a girl's school and missionary lady were attacked, and Christians feared for their lives. Outside Amritsar, a missionary house in Wazirabad, a church in Gujranwala, and a mission school in Gujarat were also damaged. On the other hand, several Christians were implicated in the rioting and there were reports that Christians were divided in their loyalties. Some Christians believed that the violence was basically anti-Christian in nature while others, including both missionaries and the All-India Conference of Indian Christians, condemned the martial law regime following the Jallianwala Bagh massacre. The non-cooperation movement evoked more sympathy from educated Punjabi Christians but they were too moderate in ideology to accept the recommended methods of non-cooperation. The All-India Conference of Indian Christians, meeting in Lahore in late December 1921 with a majority of Punjabi delegates, adopted a mediating position between the government and the non-cooperators.

A decade later Punjabis in general did not respond to the Civil Disobedience Movement as they had to the non-cooperation and Khilafat movements. Christian participation in it is almost impossible to measure. However, there were clear indications that

Christians were both more sympathetic than a decade earlier and increasingly alienated from a government which either took them for granted or did not take them seriously. Under the 1935 Constitution Christians were granted two seats in the Punjab Legislative Assembly. One of their MLAs, S. P. Singha, came into unusual prominence, was elected Speaker in 1946, and presided over the vote to partition Punjab. His achievement was, however, a personal one, perhaps due in part to the fact that Christians were considered neutral in the raging communal struggle. Certainly, the Christian community was ignored politically by the contending parties and were not even invited to attend the Punjab Minorities Convention in Delhi on May 1, 1947. They could thus only be victims of political decisions in which they had no share. During the partition riots of 1947 some Christians were not only among the victims (at times for giving aid and shelter to Hindu, Muslim or Sikhs neighbours) but also among the most effective public workers because they were trusted for their impartiality.

These political developments had a profound impact upon the Christian movement in Punjab. In effect, they put it on the defensive, forced it to redefine its mission, and turned much of its attention inward. As early as 1919 some far-sighted Christians in Punjab saw that Christianity could not survive there once India became independent unless it got out from under foreign domination and developed its own resources. To others this became increasingly apparent with each passing decade. However, this realisation affected urban and rural churches differently.

The most conspicuous change on the urban scene was the transfer of ecclesiastical power and responsibility from the foreign missions to church bodies in which Indians had the dominant voice. The process and pace of transfer varied from mission to mission but in most cases the basic shift had occurred by 1947. The transfer of administrative responsibility for the many Christian institutions in Punjab to Indians was slower. S. K. Rudra, the friend of Gandhi and mentor of C. F. Andrews, had led the way when he became Principal of St. Stephen's College in 1907; S. K. Datta, a friend of Nehru and Christian representative at the second Round Table Conference, became Principal of Forman Christian College in 1932. With such eminent nationalists as heads of two of the premier institutions in Punjab, a new vision of the Christian mission as service to the nation became more prominent, although it did not replace the old one. Jesus' preaching about the ingdom of God provided a social vision of India permeated by God's holy, righteous, and loving purposes not only in individual lives but also in the political, economic, social and cultural fabric of society. In this vision, the Church and its institutions played the vital role of infusing Christ's vision, spirit, and values into the entire society.[22]

In the rural Punjab the mass conversion movements began to diminish from about the mid-1920s but still continued on through the 1930s. What lay behind this change is not clear; certainly other promising alternatives were being opened to rural Dalits during this period.[23] All rural Christians were put under considerable pressure to declare themselves Hindus, Muslims, or Sikhs when the 1931 census was taken, primarily for political rather than for religious reasons.[24] However, a major emphasis in Christian rural work was developing a viable rural church among an economically impoverished, socially handicapped, and politically powerless people. This involved developing both effective rural church leadership and the rural churches' economic base so that they could support the clergy who served them.[25] However, the Great Depression strained the missions as well as the rural churches' resources to their limits in this endeavour. Each village pastor assumed responsibility for more and more congregations with the result that interaction between rural clergy and laity became increasingly intermittent, perfunctory and superficial. This had serious implications for the quality of religious life.[26] There could be little question of outreach to the unevangelised when those already baptised were not getting adequate attention to keep faith and worship alive. In the reorganised Church councils urban voices and urban concerns tended to dominate, even though the vast majority of Punjabi Christians were rural.

IV

It was the converts who made Christianity a movement in the nineteenth century Punjab. Missionaries preached, taught, healed, organised and even led, but it was converts who, in their quest for the truth of life, decided to break with their past and so shake the foundations of Punjabi society, paving the way for changes which they, by their subsequent labours, helped to promote. It was because their response to the gospel message posed a threat to what Punjabis held sacred that Christians were able to help shape the public reform agenda from about 1860 to 1920. However, the political events following World War I provided a more compelling agenda which displaced it in public life. Some urban Christians were sympathetic to the nationalist agenda, successfully incorporated it into the life of the church, and redefined the church's mission within Punjabi society in the light of it. Neither in the towns and cities nor in the villages did Christians have the resources to compete with it. In fact, as independence approached, it was all they could do to hold on to what they had already attained in the process: the creation of a Christian community.

Notes

1. The author is currently writing a history of Christianity in northwest India during the nineteenth and twentieth centuries. However, it has not progressed to the point where this essay can be based primarily upon fresh research. Instead, it relies mostly upon the research done in writing the following books and articles, listed here according to their date of publication. "Competing Systems of Western Education in the Punjab, 1858-1882", *Indian Church History Review*, I, June 1967, pp.59-63; "Mission Sources of Nineteenth Century Punjab History", in E. Eric Gustafson and Kenneth W. Jones (eds.), *Sources on Punjab History*, Delhi: Manohar Book Service, 1975, pp.171-218; *The Christian Community and Change in Nineteenth Century North India*, New Delhi: Macmillan, 1976; "Christians and Sikhs in the Punjab: The Village Encounter", *Bulletin of the Christian Institute of Sikh Studies*, VI, December 1977, pp.2-27; " 'Arya Evidence': A Study of Christian Influence", *Indian Church History Review*, XII, June 1978, pp.1-19; "Christianity in the Punjab", *Missiology*,

VI, October 1978, pp.467-83; "Punjabi Christians and the Indian Nationalist Movement, 1919-1947", *Indian Church History Review*, XIV, December 1980, pp.66-89 and reprinted in *Indo-British Review*, XV, Special Issue, pp.119-32; "British Missions in India", in Torben Christiansen and William R. Hutchison (eds.), *Missionary Ideologies in the Imperialist Era: 1880-1920*, Arhus: Arso, 1982, pp.38-47; "Presbyterian Missionaries and Gandhian Politics, 1919-1922", *Journal of Presbyterian History*, LXII, Fall, 1984, pp.246-57 and reprinted in *Indian Church History Review*, XIX, June 1985, pp.25-38; "Presbyterian Missionaries and Nationalist Politics in the Punjab, 1919-1935", *Proceedings of the One Hundredth Annual Meeting of the American Historical Association, December 27-30, 1985*, 16 pages; *The Dalit Christians: A History*, Delhi: I. S. P. C. K., 1991 and revised in 1994: "Leadership in the Rural Dalit Conversion Movement", in Joseph T. O'Connel (ed.), *Organizational and Institutional Aspects of Religious Movements*, Shimla: Indian Institute of Advanced Study, forthcoming.

2. *Ye Are My Witnesses 1792-1942: One Hundred and Fiftieth Anniversary of the Baptist Missionary Society in India*, Calcutta, 1942, p.64.
3. Gabriel Fackre, "Evangelical, Evangelicalism", in Alan Richardson and John Bowden (eds.), *The Westminster Dictionary of Christian Theology*, Philadelphia: The Westminster Press, 1983, p.191.
4. James Massey, "Presbyterian Missionaries and the Development of Punjabi Language and Literature, 1834-1984", *Journal of Presbyterian History*, 62, Fall 1984, p.259.
5. Bhupinder Singh Dhillon, *Pilgrim's Progress: The Translation and Punjabi of Padries*, Patiala: Punjabi University, 1969 cited in *ibid.*, p.260.
6. John C. B. Webster, *The Christian Community and Change*, (pp. 53-57) contains a more detailed discussion of this screening process.
7. *Ibid.*, p.49.
8. Rajat Kanta Ray, "Race, Religion and Realm: The Political Theory of 'The Reigning Indian Crusade', 1857", in Mushirul

Hasan and Narayani Gupta (eds.), *India's Colonial Encounter: Essays in Memory of Eric Stokes*, Delhi: Manohar, 1993, pp.133-82.

9. Speech of 1 May 1860 cited in Emma Edwardes (eds.), *Memorials of the Life and Letters of Major General Sir Herbert B. Edwardes*, London, 1886, II: pp.267-68 quoted by Thomas R. Metcalf, *Aftermath of Revolt: India, 1857-1870*, Princeton: Princeton University Press, 1964, p.102.
10. Stanley Elwood Brush, "Protestants in the Punjab: Religion and Social Change in an Indian Province in the Nineteenth Century", Unpublished Ph. D. Dissertation, University of California, Berkeley, 1971, pp.155-179. Some missions worked more closely with the government than did others. The C. M. S., being part of the established Church of England to which most of the officials belonged, was particularly close, whereas the United Presbyterians, with a very strong dissenter tradition, was much more aloof. Moreover, after 1870 the Punjab administration was no longer as Evangelical in sympathy as it had been earlier.
11. D.P.I. *Report-Punjab, 1881-82*, p.57. This competition is discussed at greater length in *The Christian Community and Change*, pp.168-72.
12. *Proceedings of the Church Missionary Society for Africa and the East, Sixty-First Year 1859-1860*, pp.117-18.
13. Christian women also visited *zenanas* to share Christian teaching and simple sociability, but did not seek to break up families by baptising wives apart from their husbands. For a discussion of this see *The Christian Community and Change*, pp.142-45.
14. In 'Arya Evidences', cited above, I analyse some of the tracts of the Arya Samaj, many of which followed a line of reasoning very similar to that of the Christians while at the same time turning the argument very skillfully against the Christians.
15. See *The Christian Community and Change*, pp.122-24.
16. *Ibid.*, pp.135-37 and 170.
17. A popular account of those early years is provided in Charles Reynolds, *Punjab Pioneer*, Bombay: Gospel Literature Service, 1977.
18. The 1911 Punjab Census showed that, while the Christian

community had a slightly lower literacy rate than did the Hindu community (4% vs. 5.5%), there were almost as many Christian as Hindu women who were literate in English (1157 vs. 1296), a reflection of their prominent role in the professions. The number of Muslim (380) and Sikh (127) women literate in English was much lower. These literacy figures are tabulated in *The Christian Community and Change,* p.230.

19. This presentation and the discussion which followed it are found in *Report of the Punjab Missionary Conference held at Lahore in December and January 1862-63,* pp.166-89.

20. John F. W. Youngson, *Forty Years of the Panjab Mission of the Church of Scotland, 1855-1895,* Edinburgh: R& R. Clark, 1896, pp.269-71.

21. In 1917, the British ambassador informed American mission boards that "His Majesty's Government must hold every missionary body responsible for every member of its staff in India, and that should any such member be considered to have acted in a manner hostile to the Government of India as by law established, the Government of India must be considered as justified in ordering the expulsion from India of the entire mission involved", Robert E. Speer to the North India and Punjab Missions, 21 February, 1917. This regulation was not withdrawn after the war but remained in effect until independence. However, it could not apply to British missionaries, some of whom became very critical of government policy and methods. The most notable of these was C. F. Andrews who began his missionary career in India teaching at St. Stephen's College in Delhi.

22. See, e.g., Surendra Kumar Datta, *The Desire of India,* London: Church Missionary Society, 1908. These ideas and those of the Social Gospel became more influential in the 1920s and 1930s.

23. For example, the Punjab census in both 1921 and 1931 showed a considerable increase in the number of Sikh Chuhras and/or Mazhabi Sikhs (57,522 in 1911, 106,709 in 1921 and 169,247 in 1931). In time the Mazhabi figures far surpassed those of the Dalit Christians in the Punjab; the 1981 census recorded 1,221,131 Mazhabis in the Indian Punjab alone.

24. See "Christians and Sikhs in the Punjab" (pp.7-9) for a discussion of this.
25. Many schemes were attempted to achieve each of these aims. One of the most creative and influential was that of the Training School for Village Teachers at Moga which sought to "build the Kingdom of God in our own villages" and so developed a rural educational programme emphasising self-reliance, learning by doing, and a curriculum designed not just for functional literacy but also for improving the conditions of village life. This programme became a model used by the Punjab government and by missions elsewhere in India.
26. In a survey authorized by the Punjab Synod of the United Church of Northern India in 1945 S.N. Talibuddin noted: "The three items of [the rural pastor's] ministry that are affected most by insufficient visitation are, services of worship, preparation of candidates for church membership and church finances." "A Study of Self-Supporting Churches in the Punjab", *The United Church Review*, July 1947, p.326.

5

The Ahmadiyah Movement: An Appraisal

SPENCER LAVAN

Controversial, heretical, polemical, persecuted—all these terms apply to the history of the Ahmadiyah movement in India and Pakistan. The term "effective" applies equally well to the organisational and missionary efforts of the movement. A summary of the history of the Ahmadiyah movement must take into account both the negative and the positive dimensions of Ahmadiyah history.

This study has traced the unusual nature and role of the Ahmadiyah across the spectrum of religious and political events during the period 1876-1936. The advent of Mirza Ghulam Ahmad, with his claims to be the "promised messiah" or *mahdi*, stirred considerable religious controversy throughout Punjab. While Ahmad's message appealed to an increasing segment of Muslims disenchanted with traditional structures incapable of meeting the challenges posed to Islam in the modern world, his claims and teachings about Jesus and *jihad* alienated him and his followers from the mainstream of the Indian Muslim community.

Reprinted from the author's *The Ahmadiyah Movement: A History and Perspective*, New Delhi: Manohar, 1974.

The intense dedication of those who believed in Ahmad and his mission accentuated the sectarian nature of the Ahmadiyah movement. Yet, it is clear that from the earliest times Ahmadis conceived of themselves as preaching and teaching the true Islam. Their widespread missionary outreach, aided by sectarian discipline, justified their assertions. Certainly, during the past century, Sunni Islam on the Indian subcontinent had not been as effective in its preaching efforts.

One essential element growing out of this analysis of the Ahmadiyah movement is that the Ahmadis must be examined on their own terms as much as in the counter-claims of others and in the light of historical events. Mirza Ghulam Ahmad cannot, for example, be judged by the standards which a Christian missionary would employ, thereby to be dismissed as a sincere but deluded claimant of God's revelation. Nor can he be judged, as he has been by so many intelligent Sunni Muslims, as a puppet of the British sent out to divide the Muslims of India. In attempting to evaluate Ghulam Ahmad's motives and drive, it is easy to assert that he had little to lose and much power to gain by deluding people into following him. Such an analysis fails to account, however, for the slow, steady and effective organisation which Ahmad developed at Qadiyan over a period of almost thirty years.

Ghulam Ahmad's firm belief that he was, in fact, receiving God's revelation and that he has God's "truth" to proclaim committed him to a lifetime for preaching that belief, to prophesying on the basis of it, to establishing an organisation of supporters and to making all the claims which he, as promised Messiah, made for himself. Can the non-Ahmadi historian of Ahmadiyah belittle Ahmad for his claims ? Can the historian criticise those mostly middle-class and educated Muslims of Punjab for being inspired by a man who promised to be their messiah or *mahdi*, for promising to restore Islam without bloody warfare against the Hindus or a bloody *jihad* against the foreign rulers of India ?

Ghulam Ahmad spoke to a need prompting responses from men and women. He created a movement significant during his lifetime and which survived a major crisis shortly after his death.

There is little doubt that Ghulam Ahmad could take advantage of opportunities to make a name for himself. The debates against other Muslim *mamlawis*, the virulent Arya Samajist Lekh Ram, and the militant missionaries such as Abdullah Asim and Imad-ud-Din, as well as the opportunities afforded by tract and newspaper publication, provided him with an outlet for his polemics. Those opportunities also helped communication with an expanded audience.

The controversy which Ahmed stirred among the Muslims was in part the result of his teachings and in part due to his very different style of response to the post-1857 Muslim situation. A brief contrast between Ghulam Ahmad and Sayyid Ahmad Khan of Aligarh, illustrates the dynamics underlying such conflict. Sayyid Ahmad developed a "modernist" position on most religious issues while Ghulam Ahmad reinterpreted the *Qur'an* to explain his religious revelations and subsequent claims. Although both supported the British in India, Sayyid Ahmad devoted much of his life to improving the conditions of Muslims generally through the establishment of the college at Aligarh and various Muslim educational organisations. Essentially, Sayyid Ahmad appealed to the Muslims who could respond positively to an educational approach. Ghulam Ahmad, on the other hand, was the son of a middle class Muslim landowner who came from a small village in Punjab. He never associated with academic figures of universities but was educated by tutors during his early years. His approach to communication was not so much through the school although the Ahmadis did found schools even during his lifetime but through public debate and tract. Two types of people, therefore, composed Ghulam Ahmad's audience. One was a literate, though not intellectual, audience which could read his Urdu, Persian and Arabic writings, and after 1898, the various Ahmadi newspapers. While Ahmad addressed audiences in Urdu and occasionally in Punjabi, these constant public appearances and the personal qualities he seems to have communicated brought him to the attention of a non-literate audience in Punjab as well. Through his writings, speeches and personal contacts, Sayyid Ahmad worked to improve the condition of Muslims. He conveyed to the government his firm belief that Muslims were loyal and trustworthy. Mirza Ghulam Ahmad, fearing that the government generally suspected Muslims, devoted much effort to proving his own loyalty to the British. Because he often acted in such a manner, when defending Islam against external threats, Ahmad found himself continuously in an ambiguous position. Condemning the traditional Islamic interpretation of *jihad* while favouring a "verbal" *jihad*, Ahmad's actions in opposing Muhammad Hussain of Batala, the missionary, Abdullah Asim and the Arya Samajist, Lekh Ram nevertheless caused the government to interfere with Ahmadiyah activities.

At a different point in the theological spectrum from Sayyid Ahmad Khan, Mirza Ghulam Ahmad skilfully developed the use of rational argument to press his view of Quranic truth in statements against the *fatwas* of other Muslim *mamlawis* directed against himself. Sayyid Ahmad Khan employed reason to argue a liberal religious interpretation, however, while Ghulam Ahmad's emphasis was essentially conservative. Both men thus applied a similar methodology to buttress a different perspective, both stood for loyalty to the British in India and both agreed that the *khilafat* as represented by the *sultan* of the Ottomans had no religious or political role to play in the lives of Indian Muslims. Ghulam Ahmad advocated these views because he believed that he was the Promised Messiah and *mahdi* of the Muslims. His successors to the leadership of the Ahmadiyah movement took the title *khalifah* for themselves. Sayyid Ahmad Khan rejected the *sultan* as the object of Indian Muslim loyalty because he believed and sought to prove that Indian Muslims were loyal to the British.

Ghulam Ahmad had little in common with the *ulama* who founded De' oband or the Farangi Mahal for they were attempting to re-establish a traditional theological basis for Islam in India through educational institutions, while Ghulam Ahmad was teaching new doctrines about Jesus, *jihad* and the *mahdi* which they vigorously repudiated. Of the movements which specifically identified themselves as "sects" in nineteenth century Islam, Ahmad seems organisationally to have had most in common with the Ahl-i-Hadith, even though the latter strongly opposed him throughout most of his career. The Ahl-i-Hadith were descendants of the *jihadist* movement of Sayyid Ahmad Shahid which the

British had identified with the Wahhabis of Arabia and had taken the name "Wehhabi" during the early part of the century, but their concerns were primarily theological by the 1880s. Muhammad Husain's *Treatise on Jihad* took essentially the same position which Ahmad did and voiced support for the British as long as Muslims were free to practise their religious beliefs. Theologically, the Ahl-i-Hadith had a fundamentalist view of the traditions of Islam. As was the case with the Sunni or Hanafi *ulama* Ghulam Ahmad's theological position became anathema to Muhammad Husayn, spokesman of the Ahl-i-Hadith, once he understood the extent to which Ahmad was deviating from an acceptable Sunni position.

Had Mirza Ghulam Ahmad claimed he was a *sufi* he might have found more acceptance among the *ulama*. He and his followers denied, however, that he was ever connected with *sufis* or *tariqahs*. Although the influence of *sufi* thought and organisational practices is evident in the fact that Ahmad spoke of spiritual stages of *fana* and *baqa* and accepted *bay'ah* from his followers, Ahmad cannot be identified as a *sufi*. What seems most accurate about Ahmad and his followers is that the movement drew inspiration from many sources within the Islamic tradition as its sectarian identity developed.

Beyond the *sufi* influences which affected Ahmad, the approach of the Christian missionaries possibly sifted through the Brahma Samaj missionary work in Punjab—played a role in shaping Ahmad's approach to his own mission. The Ahmadiyah missionary thrust, known as the *tabligh* in the years after Ahmad's death, attests to the utility of a technique not effectively employed by Muslims earlier. The *tabligh* programme did not focus solely on India. Much of its most successful work was carried out in places such as Ceylon, Mauritius, and Hong Kong. Later it spread to England, Africa, Indonesia, and America.

Ghulam Ahmad's missionary zeal, when directed against such a militant Hindu organisation as the Arya Samaj, often was interpreted as fostering communalism. While the Arya Samaj instigated many of the encounters through *shuddhi* (reconversion), cow protection, and pressure for the use of Hindi rather than

Urdu, Ahmad's responses were at least verbally aggressive. Ghulam Ahmad did not address the issues of cow protection, *shuddhi*, and the use of Hindi directly in his fights with the Arya Samaj. Rather Ahmad tended to defend Islam on religious grounds. This he accomplished by his discourses on the *Qur'an* and by challenging Aryas to debates in which they could try to prove the truth of the Vedas. Where Ahmad chose a specific issue for attacking the Aryas, he chose *niyog*. *Niyog*, because of its sexual implications, appealed to the basic emotions of the Muslims and played on their fears and hostility against Hindus. Ahmad never debated cow protection or Hindi-Urdu.

Ghulam Ahmad's reliance on reasoned argument becomes especially evident in his detailed attack on the *Vedas* and Arya Samaj teachings. When he turned his attention to the Sikhs, however, he used different sources to demonstrate that Guru Nanak was a Muslim. Ghulam Ahmad often turned to European writers to buttress his arguments about Guru Nanak or the death of Jesus. Despite the fact that Ahmad knew no European languages, the use of these techniques suggests his familiarity with modern methods of argument prevalent among missionaries and institutionalised by western educational techniques.

The events surrounding Ghulam Ahmad's controversies with Muslim *mawlawis*, Christian missionaries, Arya Samajists and the Sikhs have been a focal point of this study. The political and religious factors underlying opposition to the Ahmadis were enlarged beyond normal proportions by the role of the press. Clearly, it was the traumatic events surrounding the murder of Lekh Ram which led Ahmad and his followers to undertake regular publications. Before 1898 Ahmad published only tracts and books to communicate his position to a broader audience. Communal tension and strife followed the death of Lekh Ram at Lahore in March 1897. Most of the Punjab newspapers commented on Ahmad's prophecy that Lekh Ram would die before 1899, speculating whether he or his followers had any hand in the murder. Since Ahmad had no paper with which to reply, he realised the necessity for the Ahmadiyah community to have a publications network. The creation of *al-Hakam* in 1891, *Review of Religions* in both English and Urdu (1902) and later *Badr*, *Nur* and *al-Fazl* helped close the information gap which Ahmad's *Istifta* first attempted to fill in 1897. While the significance of the Punjab press in affecting public opinion during this period is only now being studied, the contribution which Ahmadi publications made, in spite of limited number of copies per issue, must have been significant in spreading the Ahmadi position to the Urdu reading public.

One final point about Mirza Ghulam Ahmad which his followers employed after his death was Ahmadiyah insistence on loyalty to the British and achievement of goals through peaceful methods. Ahmad's loyalty can be attributed both to his middle-class landowning status and to his realisation, in later years, that without the protection of the government, his movement might have suffered violence at the hands of opponents. The strength of Ahmad's claim that he was propagating the true Islam by peaceful methods became ambiguous at those times when his tactics created tension and conflict with other groups. This tension had its roots in his claims to be the promised messiah or *mahdi* of the Muslims. The ambiguity of Ahmad's role and personality was further complicated by his interpretation of the concept of *mahdi* which explicitly rejected the traditional Sunni conception of a *ghazi* or bloody guide who would direct Muslims to victory against the unbelievers on the final "day of judgement". In contrast to the *mahdi* of the Sudan who led a successful revolt against the British and Egyptians during the 1880s Mirza Ghulam Ahmad was a *mahdi* who came in peace, loyal to the British rulers of India. In doing this, his action was deliberate but also deliberately controversial among Sunni Muslims.

What of the years after Ahmad's death? What was the effect of his personality and ministry on the events that followed? For the first six years, Nur-ud-Din, the first *khalifah*, although a much quieter leader than Ghulam Ahmad, maintained the style of organisation and operation. The public appearance of the movement remained much as it had been under the promised messiah. Internal forces were at work, however, which split the community leading to a more liberal faction emerging in Lahore under Khawajah Kamal-ud-Din and Muhammad Ali. During the 1908-1914 period, the Ahmadiyah community remained aloof, as always from the growing number of politically-oriented organisations active in those years. Where Ahmadiyah later became involved, such as in a Khilafat Conference in 1920 or in the Kashmir Committee in 1931, this activity was directly related to changing Ahmadiyah perception of the world around them.

In those events Bashir-ud-Din Mahmud Ahmad, second *khalifah* and son of Ghulam Ahmad, was more politically and socially astute than his father. His interest in political questions, obvious within five years of his accession to the leadership, is significant. When Mahmud Ahmad became second *khalifah* in 1914, he tended to avoid Ahmadiyah participation in political matters. The "liberal" wing, led by Khawajah Kamal-ud-Din and Muhammad Ali, believed strongly that the movement should turn closer to the mainstream of Islam. Political involvement became an essential element of Lahori party.

While Mahmud Ahmad spoke out on the questions of *swaraaj, ahimsa, khilafat,* and the Simon report, he acted because of his interests as leader of the Ahmadiyah movement. Ahmadiyahs recognised that reforms were needed in India, and that the organisation need not identify with the Muslim League. Mahmud Ahmad's desire to protect a Muslim minority in a Free India spoke just as eloquently for his efforts in protecting an Ahmadi minority within that Muslim minority. Mahmud was an activist, administrator, religious leader and traveller. He was neither an overt agitator nor a communalist as such. He seriously offended many non-Ahmadis by his political and religious stance, even as his father had offended many by the religious claims and support of the British. To a certain extent, Iqbal was correct in his assessment of Ahmadi motives for political involvement, when he suggested that Ahmadis had joined the Kashmir Committee to promote their own organisation.

The two crucial events in Ahmadiyah history after 1930 were the confrontation with Ahrars in the period from 1931 to 1936 (as well as in Pakistan in 1953) and the partition of India itself. In the former case, the Ahrar leaders chose to use the Ahmadiyah as scapegoats to build their own political power in the Islamic community and as a force uniting Muslims in opposition to Hindu rule in Kashmir and to British power throughout India. The continuous five-year struggle with the Ahrar and the persecution suffered by many Ahmadis, the banned publications and government interference with both groups led to solidification of the Ahmadiyah movement never before experienced. Opposition and overt persecution attracted new followers and thereby helped strengthen the movement. This did not mean a great increase in numbers as much as an increase in effectiveness and commitment by those who participated. The most significant outgrowth of this renewal was the creation of the Tarikh-i-Jadid organisation for increased missionary work after 1940.

The partition of 1947, which gave most of Gurdaspur district including Qadiyan to India, set the stage for the decision of the Ahmadiyah community to migrate to Pakistan. There they set up a new community at Rabwah, on the Chenab river near Chiniot. The re-building of the community was a difficult and challenging task. Continued opposition from the Ahrar and later from the Jama'at-i-Islami among others caused setbacks as well as a stimulus to new recruits who admired the courage of the community.

For religious Muslims of middle-class background, Ahmadiyah, whether in the days of the promised messiah, in the 1930s or at present, has offered a sectarian alternative with which one may identify and commit much of his life and resources. Because the community has been comparable to an extended family structure, it offered the religious Muslim adrift in the amorphous and disorganised sea of Indian Islam a home where he would be welcomed, given work to do and a definite programme. For lower class Muslims, the Ahmadiyah offered an opportunity for upward mobility. After the establishment of the community and creation of schools and colleges, anyone who wished to see his son or daughter live a more meaningful life knew that the community provided education that could lead to a career of significance.

Where then do we locate the Ahmadiyah movement? In the 1880's, Ghulam Ahmad began a serious attempt to renew Islam. His dynamic and iconoclastic personality led to controversy almost from the beginning because he referred to himself as *mahdi* of the Muslims. But Ahmad was equally disliked by Hindus both for his claim that the *Qur'an* was superior to the *Vedas* and his later claim that he was an *avatar* or incarnation of Lord Krishna. Similarly, he offended Christian missionaries with his theories about the death of Jesus and the claim that he was the son of Mary. As Ahmad developed the movement, he adapted more and more elements from a variety of sources. Choosing to remain within Islam, however, he and his followers suffered what many who have deviated from acceptable teachings within any faith had to suffer. Baha'i chose to withdraw from Islam and create a universalistic movement of its own. Had Ahmad emerged in Iran or another totally Islamic country, he might well have withdrawn in similar fashion. Because of the large number of religious groups in India and the openness and variety of "Hindu" expressions of religiousness, it was easier for Ahmad, while directing his mission to the Indian community in general, to remain within Islam, which, itself, was in a minority position in India.

In summary, the dynamic of the Ahmadiyah community commenced in the 1880s with the personality and ministry of Mirza Ghulam Ahmad. To many he was an enigma, a threat, a false prophet. To western historical criticism he remains a mystery, full of inconsistencies, and ambiguities. Yet, neither western historical criticism, nor Sunni, nor Christian missionaries can simply dismiss Mirza Ghulam Ahmad. Through an unusual combination of followers, circumstances and organisational talent, he an his successors built a vigorous community whose efforts in spreading Islam to Africa and establishing the first mosques in Europe and America surpassed that of any other Islamic group.

The message and mission of the Ahmadiyah movement often involved polemics and controversy despite its professions to peace and loyalty. Clearly, the involvement of the Ahmadiyah movement represents a difficult and controversial part of that history. The study of history, and particularly the history of religious communities, provides understanding of how and why men believe and act as they do. The history of the Ahmadiyah community demonstrates the complexity of man's religious involvement even within the confines of time and place. The continuing activity of the Ahmadiyah community to the present day testifies to the meaning it has brought to the lives of many.

6

The Ghadar Movement: A New Consciousness

HARISH K. PURI

The Ghadar movement launched among the Punjabi immigrants in North America has been viewed primarily as a dramatic action filled episode in India's struggle for freedom and as a saga of patriotism, bravery and heroic sacrifices. That it was. This may, however, be also viewed as an enterprise in social and political transformation of a politically pre-mobilised traditional community. Those who came under the influence of the weekly paper *Ghadar* were transformed in their social and political orientation. That also made them different from the other members of their community in India and abroad. When they returned to India in 1914-15 to preach and launch an armed rebellion against the British rulers, most of their countrymen thought that the Ghadarites were crazy, 'unfortunate' men, afflicted by some 'pernicious foreign influence'. The British authorities regarded them as "ignorant Sikhs who have been indoctrinated with crude ideas of equality and democracy in America".[1] The Sikh community organisations condemned them

---

Reprinted from Indu Banga (ed.), *Five Punjab Centuries: Polity, Economy, Society and Culture C.1500-1990*, New Delhi: Manohar, 1997.

as apostates and sought to ostracise them from the community.[2] A historian stereotyped their political thinking as 'xenophobic nationalism'.[3] A Ghadar leader looking back expressed satisfaction that everyone who joined the movement became "more secularised and more modernised" than what he was before.[4] It may be appropriate to look into their political culture, structure of social and political beliefs, values and attitudes which the Ghadarites developed and which tended largely to govern their social and political behaviour. This may sensitise us to the dialectics of change in culture and consciousness. Their poems and statements may be taken as a reliable source of what they felt and thought.

I

Emigration of thousands of small peasants from Punjab to Canada, USA and other foreign lands in search of labour opportunities during 1905-1913 carried symptoms of their economic distress at home which had been accentuated by the process of integration of Punjab in the colonial capitalist market economy. Some of the marked features of the economic situation in Punjab were poverty, high rate of land revenue demand, rigid enforcement of revenue collection even during famine years, corrupt and oppressive administration, rising indebtedness of the peasantry which, according to the findings of the Financial Commissioner of Punjab made in 1893, "was already ruined beyond redemption".[5] Their plight was aggravated by the large-scale alienation of lands, recurrent famines, "rigorous operation of the laissez faire policy by the government in times of scarcity", and epidemics (the plague in 1907 alone took a toll of two million lives). It was mainly because "the economic conditions at home were so bad", and the economic 'prospects' advertised by steamship companies and Canadian and American employers were "so good", that these people emigrated to alien lands, staking, in many cases, a major part of their possessions on the venture. It is normal that such a plunge is taken not by the poorest, but by men of that strata which still enjoy a certain capacity for manoeuvre.

There is hardly any evidence, however, that these emigrants

saw at that time any relation of the economic misery and oppression with the British economic interests and governmental policies. Hardly a few had heard of the peasant agitation led by Ajit Singh in 1907. Furthermore, the nationalist political activity was little known to Punjab before the momentous events of 1919-20.

Religious reform movements, like the Arya Samaj among the Hindus and the Singh Sabha among the Sikhs, had been the most powerful influences for the political development in Punjab. Well before the turn of the century, these two movements had begun in the urban areas of the province a process of identity reformation and religious revitalisation, strengthening the existing social divisions and "setting one group against all others". A similar process had started among the Muslims. As observed by the historian, Kenneth W. Jones:

> By the 1890s, Punjab was divided into a series of aggressive organisations, each possessing its own ideology, each containing a unique sense of identity. To protect that identity and its base became the most fundamental drive for educated and marginal Punjabis.[6]

The spirit of community revitalisation and protection of its identity was one of the two important influences which accompanied the relatively privileged among the emigrants to Canada and the USA. Since they were Sikhs predominantly, the early form of community activity and mobilisation in the alien environment centred round the Gurdwaras, and the major social organisation, to begin with, was the Khalsa Diwan Society of Vancouver in British Columbia. Because men of the agricultural classes were not known to be fastidious about observance of external religious norms, prominent among the activities of this organisation were *gurmat prachar*, winning *Sahajdhari* Sikhs and the uninitiated into the fold of *Amritdharis*, and maintaining the purity of Sikh norms in a "corrupting" western milieu. Concerted efforts were made to fight what was described as *mowna lehar*, that is, the marked tendency among the immigrants to get clean-shaven to seek better accommodation in the alien setting.[7]

The Pacific Coast Khalsa Diwan Society included the following in its articles of incorporation in 1912:

(i) To suggest and provide ways and means to assist, help and encourage the spiritual, moral and educational welfare of all Sikhs and other Hindostani workers on the Pacific Coast.

(ii) To initiate and carry out such measures as may ameliorate and improve the moral, social and religious conditions of the labouring classes of all nationalities, but particularly of Sikhs.[8]

An element of exclusivist community identity and its boundary demarcation from other communities was a prominent concern of this Society. The Khalsa Diwan Committee of Stockton in the United States with its gurdwara as the centre of activity was another prominent organisation which followed a similar pattern. The *Aryan* published from Ottawa and the *Sansar* from Victoria tended to advocate similar exclusivist concerns. The Director of Criminal Intelligence recorded in June 1910 that there was a section of Sikhs in British Columbia "whose jealousy and bigotry do much to keep alive the ill-feeling between *mownas* and Sikhs".[9]

The other major influence which these immigrants brought with them related to a notion of the martial traditions of the Sikhs and steadfast loyalty to the British which was considered valuable in facilitating their adjustment and for the protection of their interests in Canada as a part of the British empire. The fact that nearly half of these immigrants had served short terms in the British Indian army also helped, perhaps, to bolster that self-image. The British authorities considered these two influences as complementary. It was believed, as Macauliffe observed, that "the orthodoxy of a Sikh means loyalty to his sovereign".[10]

The markedly different social milieu in North America, however, posed many difficult problems for emigrant Indians. They faced a rather widespread and institutionalised contempt and hostility towards the Asians. Indians were a colonised people and they were regarded as belonging to inferior races. That was also the period when "Social Darwinist thought was prevalent in the western world". In 1907, which was a year of economic depression, there were anti-Asian riots in which the Indians, along with the Japanese and the Chinese, became the victims of mob fury. Riots in lumber camps at Bellingham were more specifically directed against the Indian workers.

In 1908, the Dominion Government of Canada practically banned the further entry of Indians. Whereas thousands of the Chinese and the Japanese continued to pour into that country, it was particularly the 'loyal subjects', including the families of those already settled in Canada, who were denied entry. Cautious moves were also made to persuade a number of these people to move out to the islands like the British Honduras. The question that naturally came to the minds of some of them was: Why the loyal Sikhs were treated so badly in a part of the British empire? Whereas the Chinese and the Japanese were still welcome, why particularly the Indians were denied entry to Canada? The conspicuous contrast of social and economic conditions and political freedom in North America and India, competition with white labourers, and political propaganda by some educated Indians, were gradually creating new stirrings among these people. This was embarrassing for the Khalsa Diwan leadership. For the protection of the Sikh interests, emphasis was laid on the services they had rendered to the empire. In a petition jointly presented in 1911 by the Khalsa Diwan Society and the Hindustan Association for relaxation in the restrictions on the entry of their families, they pleaded:

> Our first claim is that we are British subjects of proven loyalty. More than 90 percent of the Hindustanees in Canada are Sikhs. With the name Sikh is liked-up fidelity and heroic loyalty to the Empire.[11]

The deputation sent to London and India made a similar plea.

II

The new environment and concrete experiences were, however, tending to strain the old clusters of social and psychological commitments. Beliefs and ideas of separate identity of the Sikhs, religious vitality and pride of loyal attachment to the empire, did not appear to provide satisfying answers to the issues that troubled the peace of many. The weekly *Ghadar* published by Lala Har Dayal from San Francisco raised questions and provided explanations which appeared more relevant to the concrete life experiences of these people. The language and idiom of its message, attuned to the cognitive structures of the illiterate labourers and farm workers and often loaded with abuse, eroded many of the old commitments and notions, and made them available for new patterns of political socialisation. Although all the Indian immigrants were not equally influenced, yet thousands of them developed in course of time a distinctly new framework of consciousness.

One element in this framework was a bitter awareness of their own condition and status including a deep sense of humiliation and backwardness and its objective reasons. They were called 'coolies', 'dirty people'. They were bullied, ridiculed and treated like criminals. A regular theme of the lectures, and particularly of their songs, was:

> We are faced with innumerable miseries
> We are called coolies and thieves
> Wherever we go, we are treated like dogs
> Why is no person kind to us?[12]

That was outrageous. But, why did they come to such a pass? A major misfortune was 'betrayal' by the British. The refusal to protect the interests of the people who had been the most loyal and brave in the service of the empire was plain dishonesty. That in the worldview of these people was a serious offence. It was described as *thuggee; badmashi* of the *dhokebaj quam*! Why did they leave their homes? It was because they were poor; because they had little opportunity of earning their livelihood there. They became conscious of the oppression and compulsions back home: that the farmer was burdened with debts and heavy taxes; that little was left to his share at the harvesting of his crops; that the plague and the famine killed crores of people.[13]

Linking of their existing oppression in foreign lands with misery and oppression back home and the backwardness of their country became an important part of the consciousness of immigrants: "Harassed in our land and with no support available abroad, we aliens have no land of our own".

The teachings of the *Ghadar* made them acutely conscious of the contrast between the social and economic conditions in advanced countries and India. The whole world was lit by electric lights. Why did India look so deserted? "The world had manufactured aeroplanes, there was high learning and scientific advancement: the whole world enjoys prosperity and happiness, why is India lying in a stupor".[14] That reality, so conspicuous a fact of their backwardness and poverty, in comparison with what they experienced in USA and Canada, deepened their shame and embarrassment; it became linked up in their minds with their political subjection.

Further questions came to be raised: Why was India so backward? Why were her people famished, sick and ill-clad? The *Ghadar* informed them that it was because their foreign rulers had been draining away the wealth of India to their own country—England. Two regular features of the weekly *Ghadar*, "Angrezi Raj Ka Kacha Chitha" (The British Rule Laid Bare) and "Ankon ki Gawahi" (Evidence of the Statistics), and a series of pamphlets, provided evidence of the British exploitation in India. Its readers now became aware of the excessive expenditure on the armed forces and the wars of expansion, high rates of taxation, decline in indigenous production, frequency of famines and droughts, the staggering toll of lives taken by them, and the practical neglect of education and public health. The agrarian policy of the government was held responsible for the pauperisation of the peasantry. To provide authenticity, most of the statistics and comments were taken from official records or the writings of eminent British and Indian authorities such as William Digby, William Hunter, Alfred Webb, C. J. O'Donnell, C.A. Elliots, Dadabhoy Naoroji and Gopal Krishan Gokhale. The new information shook the immigrants. Deaths from famines during 1891-1900 alone were 19 million and the annual drain of money, according to Digby, was £900 million. Reverend Sunderland was quoted that the reason for famines was not overpopulation; "the real cause was ENORMOUS FOREIGN TRIBUTE".[15] The personal feelings of disgrace harboured by the immigrants got linked up with a whole country's misery.

The readers of the *Ghadar* came to believe that the administration which the British Government conducted in India was plain and simple 'loot', dacoity' and 'thugee'. Their poets sang, for instance:

> In famines our children die of starvation
> And the English live off our income
> We grow wheat to eat, but've to make do with barley
> The revenue collectors do not leave behind a single pie.
>
> ... ...
>
> Cruel English nation is very obnoxious
> They have looted and eaten up Hindustan, Brothers.
>
> ... ...
>
> In India a *kaudi* is not available if you search
> And England has grown enormously wealthy
> The Dogs of the Faringee eat to their fill
> And human beings of India die of starvation.[16]

Incidents of administrative highhandedness, cruelty and oppression by the police, detentions without trial, and third degree methods on undertrials were frequently cited. The British rule was also held responsible for the increasing moral degeneration. Har Dayal said, "we call it British Vampire and not British Empire".[17]

Mark Juergensmeyer hypothesises that, "the hostility towards the prejudice of North Americans was transferred into hostility against the British".[18] Sucheng Chan argues, however, that no 'transference' was necessary because the 'discrimination' suffered by the Sikh immigrants in North America was a validation of "their prior experience of being oppressed back in their homeland by white men as well as Indian elites rather than anything they experienced for the first time".[19] Sucheng's argument is well-grounded, but a different pattern of socialisation was needed to generate that consciousness.

III

The effectiveness of the *Ghadar* lay precisely in its ability to establish such a pattern. Its teachings became meaningful because these appeared to be related to what the people actually experienced. Har Dayal, a well-known radical intellectual, who was invited by leading men among the Indian immigrants, was the editor of the weekly propaganda paper published in Urdu and Punjabi. His craftsmanship as a man of words added to the impact of his message. His biographer, Emily Brown, observed that:

> Har Dayal was able to 'create' the Ghadar movement because he was able to convince the Sikhs that their loyalty to the British ... was misplaced and that it was not the Americans who were making their lives miserable but the British.... If the British treated them like dogs at home, how could they expect to be treated otherwise (*sic*) any place else in the world? Until they were free men, they would be slaves. It was as simple as that.[20]

The situation appeared to confirm the experience of Indian labourers that immigrants of the other countries were protected by their respective diplomatic representatives, and that the Indians were left unprotected because they had no such representative of their own. Their problems sprang from their political subjection.

Sucheng Chan found that some of the Chinese immigrants also saw the connection between their maltreatment in America and the weakness of China.[21] But there was a notable difference. Whereas the Chinese thought of taking their revenge on Americans, when some day their country would be strong, the Ghadarites did not look upon the Americans as their oppressors.

The available evidence suggests that the Ghadarites regarded Americans as their well-wishers. Sohan Singh Bhakna was convinced that Americans wanted Indians to struggle for their independence. One of the couplets in the *Ghadar* poems said that "many Americans suggested to us, through hints, to rise up, but we simpletons did not catch the hint".[22] Har Dayal's writings in the *Ghadar* included many references to the support he was getting from American friends for the national cause. The *Ghadar* cause was often identified with American tradition of democracy and freedom.[23] The Americans had fought a war of independence against the British rule about 140 years earlier. The Ghadarites were preparing for that now. Their suffering and humiliation in America was rationalised: "Americans hate slavery, and we are slaves."

The sense of shame that they were slaves; looted and exploited at home, and ridiculed and hated abroad, with none to sympathise with them or defend them, became deeply embedded in the psyche of these people. "A slave has neither religion, nor dignity", they felt, "it is better to commit suicide than continue to suffer as such."[24] Exploitation and oppression did not in themselves turn the oppressed into rebels; it was the consciousness and shame of subjection which became a force. It is in this sense that 'shame' appeared to Karl Marx as "a revolutionary sentiment". The foremost need was to oust the British from the Indian soil so that the Indians became the masters of their destiny. Then, it was believed, all the miseries would end; then, there would be quick material development and prosperity and spread of education; and then, the Indians would automatically gain respectability in the whole world.[25]

A very significant development in their thinking was a sense of sharing a common fate with the oppressed peoples of other countries. They also felt the need of association with the revolutionary groups of other countries such as the Irish, the Chinese, the Egyptian and the Russian. The revolutionaries of those countries were often referred to as the 'Irish Ghadari', the 'Mexican Ghadari' or the 'Roosi Ghadari'. Inspiration was sought from their activities and it was said, for example, that "even the opium eating Chinese have risen and have launched Ghadar". It was only because the Indians themselves were so fast asleep that no one thought of helping them. Once the Indians took up arms against the British then they would not be alone. There would be many others to help them. That broader orientation of identifying themselves with the oppressed of the other countries developed, in course of time, a sense of solidarity in a common struggle against imperialism.

The only method of struggle, they believed, was of popular

armed rebellion: "See through the pages of the history of the world, you will see that no country ever got freedom without armed struggle".[26] They had before them the examples of the American war of independence, the rise of Japan after her victory over Russia, the persistent struggle of the Sikhs against the Mughals, and of the revolutionary movements in China, Ireland and Russia. Bhagwan Singh, one of the foremost leaders, wrote out a whole treatise on *War and Freedom* which argued in favour of war "as the only alternative".[27] The Ghadarites were, therefore, convinced that the Indian leaders who followed constitutional methods and wanted gradual reforms were no good; the Ghadarites had to follow a different course.

Central to the ideas of the leaders was the 'great' armed rebellion of 1857. The British rulers had contemptuously called it *ghadar*—an Arabic and Persian term for mutiny or betrayal. V.D. Savarkar's *The Indian War of Independence* transformed the event into one of glorious patriotic war. The choice of *Ghadar* as the name of the weekly propaganda paper indicated the preferred image of the movement and the mode of their struggle. "Our name and our work are identical", it was announced. *Ghadar,* the very name of which makes the English shiver, was held up as a glowing example of India's defiance and patriotism. Excerpts from Savarkar's above mentioned history of the rebellion were regularly published and read at meetings. A strong conviction was developed that the British rule would have positively ended, and India would have been free long ago if the Sikh forces had not come out in support of the British.[28] Therefore, now, if the Sikh soldiers also joined in armed rebellion, the end of British rule was believed to be certain. There could be no sitting back until "this base, wretched, evil-doing, vicious government were destroyed", announced the *Ghadar* in its first issue. That became an overriding passion with the Ghadarites.

IV

Another significant dimension of change in their framework of ideas related to attitudes towards matters of religion, religious identity and relation of religion with politics. Most of these people were Sikhs; "the Ghadar movement was practically theirs". Their earlier social maps had been charted largely by their religious traditions and the influence of the Singh Sabha movement. The only important social organisations for them had been the Gurdwaras and their priests. It was natural that even in the process of the immigrants' transformation in coming to terms with new realities, their perception of community heritage would play a prominent role. Karl Marx had also noted, for example, that since consciousness was a 'social product' even when people "seem engaged in revolutionising themselves and things, in creating something that has never yet existed... they anxiously conjure up the spirits of the past to their service...". They used old symbols and attempted fresh interpretations. The significant point, therefore, is to see the nature of the interpretative mediation and of the selection of symbols which they used "in order to present the new scene of world history in the time-honoured disguise and this borrowed language".[29] That selection and mediation may be often consciously organised for that purpose and may, in effect, alter the perception of that legacy, as also the group's self-image.

One element in the new framework consisted of a stress upon some specific cultural and religious symbols of the Sikh community. The headmast of the *Ghadar* regularly carried a popular religious saying of Sant Kabir: *"Je tau prem khelan ka chao, sir dhar tali gali mori aao."* Another popular saying of Kabir which was frequently cited was: "A brave warrior is the one who fights for his faith. He may be cut down to pieces but never leaves the field of battle". Though the original meaning was to exalt the virtues of suffering unflinchingly in the path of devotion to God, a historical consciousness of the battles of the Sikhs against their oppressors had transformed the intent. It now conveyed a combination of martial spirit and sacrifice for a cause held sacred. "For what purpose was the Khalsa created by the Guru? Recollect the words of the Satguru O'Singhs".[30] Inspiration was sought from the Sikh martyrs and warriors such as Banda Bahadur, Dip Singh, Mahtab Singh, Hari Singh and Phula Singh. It was emphasised:

- Adherence to five Ks does not make a Singh.
- One who flees from battle is called a Jackal.

- Singh is the name of lion who fights roaringly.
- When lions are challenged why run away from battle.[31]

Appeals were, therefore, made in the name of the 'panth' to vindicate their heritage and 'the race of heroes' to which the 'Singhs' belonged: "Maintain the honour of the name 'Singh' (Lion) O'Singhs", exhorted the poets.

It has been observed by some scholars that the stress on Sikh symbols by the Ghadarites had the potential for boundary demarcation of this community from others and for the development of the Ghadar movement into a 'militant Sikh movement'. Referring to the *Ghadar* poets, Barrier observes that "the authors frequently did not differentiate clearly between the 'Sikh nation' and the 'Indian nation", nor did they see "the inconsistency of stressing Sikh nationhood at the potential cost of affecting Sikh cooperation with other Indians".[32] It is important to note, however, that the interpretation of Sikh legacy by the Ghadarites was very different from the one upheld by the Singh Sabha movement and the Chief Khalsa Diwan. The Khalsa or panth was to the Ghadarites a force which Guru Gobind Singh created for defence of the great country—Bharat. It was for ending the oppression of the 'Mother Bharat' that the Guru fought fierce battles, it was believed; he sacrificed his sons, and his sons were bricked alive in that cause. The panth and the Khalsa, to them, was a fighting force of the country, as were the Khans and the Rajputs, the Turks and the Marathas.

The panth was to be judged not by what the Sikhs thought or did for themselves but by the objective for which it was created. The worsened condition of the country was attributed to the degeneration of the panth, its great down fall, when the Sikh Sardars turned 'traitors' and betrayed the nation in its war of independence in 1857. That 'dirty' role was regarded as one big 'stigma' on the fair name of the community, a treachery with fellow Indians. The panth was, therefore, reminded of its past and the urgency of washing off that stigma to prove that the Sikhs were the true sons of the motherland:

The people say the Singhs are very bad
Why was the Ghadar of Delhi put off
The country would have, by now, regaled in freedom
Why did these traitors commit such abomination.[33]
The whole world taunts us
Liberate the country soon, O'Singhs
Lest you mistake again as in 'Fifty-Seven'
Fully remember the occasion, O'Singhs
Get up, let's wash the stigma of treachery
If you remember the Guru's words, O'Singhs
Joining with the Mahrattas and the Bengalis
And to the happiness of Hindus and Musalmans, O'Singhs.[34]

True faith, to the Ghadarites, lay not in any of the concerns propagated by the Sikh social organisations of the time, nor in seeing the Sikh community as demarcated separately from other communities, but in its Indian national identity. A regular refrain of their utterances was the destiny of India expressed in 'Bharat Mata', 'Mata', 'Hindostan', 'nation of 30 crores', 'the one Nation of Hindus, Sikhs and Mohammedans' all of whom were 'sons of one mother'. *Bande Mataram* as the major slogan, salutation and war cry, and *Yugantar Ashram* as the name of the movement's headquarters, were also indications of a preference for identification with the then mainstream of militant nationalism which was associated with the Bengal revolutionaries. It reflected an attempt, particularly by the Sikhs, at a new identity formation in a different cultural milieu.

It is interesting to note that whereas in Sikh folklore in Punjab *turk* or *turkara* was a term of opprobrium, the Ghadarites talked of the great Turkish brothers who fought for the national cause:

You are frightened of fighting for the country
And you call yourselves Rajputs and Khans, Brothers
Your brothers are the brave Turks
Musalmans fought for the country, Brothers
Shabash! Shabash! says the whole world to them
Who maintained the dignity of the country, Brothers.[35]

The reference was obviously to the enthusiastic participation of Muslims in the uprising of 1857.

Alongside the heroes from the Sikh community, and the Rajputs, Marathas and Bengalis, references were frequently made to the "sons of the Ghazis", or Muslims. Among the names that were most strongly embedded in the memories of the Ghadarites, because of recurrent references, were those of the martyrs of 1857, the young revolutionaries of Bengal, and the contemporary radical and revolutionary leaders. Among them were the heroes of many different cultural, religious and regional groups. The emphasis was upon their one common passion love for the country and one identity—Indian. Conversely, prominent among those who were particularly marked out for condemnation and ridicule were the chiefs of the Sikh princely states and the leaders of the Chief Khalsa Diwan, or those who looked to British patronage and privileges.[36]

Similarly, among the leaders of the Ghadar movement, all the three major communities were represented, and the membership was inclusive. Conscious attempt was always made to enlist the cooperation of all communities. It is noteworthy that though at least two articles of Har Dayal of the pre-Ghadar phase clearly reflecting a Hindu sectarian orientation, were published by the Ghadar Press, reference to these ideas found no place in the rest of the Ghadar literature, including the writings of Har Dayal himself. It was perhaps a part of their strategy for purposes of ensuring the support of different communities that in their mass meetings Mohammad Barkatullah appeared to address more particularly to the Muslims, Bhagwan Singh to the Sikhs, and Ram Chandra to the Hindus.

A much more striking element related to an unequivocal stress on keeping 'politics in command', and the rejection of pre-occupation with matters of religion. Religious concerns were seen as diversionist and thus positively harmful. A frequently quoted couplet was:

> No Pandits or Mullahs do we need
> No prayers or litanies we need recite
> These will only scuttle our boat
> Draw the sword, it's time to fight.[37]

The exclusivist concerns of social organisations and religious feuds that fouled the social and political life in India came in for a strong condemnation as a 'filthy mentality'. The Ghadarites, it was emphasised, did not think in terms of caste distinctions and did not consider anybody as untouchable or of low caste.[38]

Whereas the British government was blamed by the Ghadarites for contributing to divisiveness among the people, a greater responsibility was placed at the doors of selfish Indians. "Many amongst us are the dogs of the government who abet hostilities amongst us for our destruction". Those who controlled and managed the religious places of the Sikhs were seen as 'commission agents' who exploited their position for material gains.[39]

The Ghadarites viewed themselves as a party of "those who dissolve all caste and religious differences". According to Sohan Singh Bhakna and Harnam Singh 'Tundilat', it was one of the basic rules of the party that no religious issues could be raised at their meetings.[40] Religion was regarded as a purely personal and private matter. For them, the important thing was the understanding of politics: "Why don't we understand the politics of existing arrangements"? Stress was laid on seeing the political implications of the issues of purity, separate identity and Gurdwaras. There is considerable evidence that in their social relations also, the Ghadarities generally discarded considerations of caste and religion. The questions of *kesh* amongst the Sikhs, *jhatka* or *halal*, eating with Muslims or with the low castes, and the observance of any religious norms, now appeared to be irrelevant to them. The Khalsa Diwan Societies in North America and the 'Tat Khalsa' elements, therefore, continued their campaign against the Ghadarites as the 'fallen Sikhs'.[41]

The developing secular orientation was strikingly novel in a period when religious nationalism was the dominant pattern. There was nothing among the Gahdarites of the spiritualism or mystification that was characteristic of the Bengal revolutionaries. There was no invocation of *Kali* or *Durga* as in Bengal or of *Maruti* as in Maharashtra. Although *amre milechhe sab mayer dake* (we have rallied to the call of the Mother) and *jaya kali* or *har har bom*

bom, were familiar battle-cries of those revolutionaries, the Ghadarites adopted no such slogans.

V

As to their conception of struggle, the Ghadarites thought of following the pattern of the 1857 rebellion. But, there was a relatively greater emphasis on a mass uprising. Very frequent references to the heroes of Bengal and Maharashtra, exhortations to the Punjabis to act like them, and stray articles, like Har Dayal's 'Philosophy of the Bomb' suggested a terrorist orientation. However, a more consciously propagated conception was of widespread people's war: "First the Ghadar men must carry open political propaganda throughout the whole country, and then concentrate on collection of arms." No serious thought was, however, given to whether it was to be an organised and properly commanded struggle or a spontaneous one. It may well be 'spontaneous', Har Dayal had thought.[42] The important thing for them was the arousing of revolutionary passion and a readiness to lay down one's life for the cause.

The Ghadarites believed that the real strength of the British government lay in the support and service which Indians rendered to them, particularly the support of Indian soldiers of the British army. There was a certain anticipation of Mahatma Gandhi in their belief that if all the Indians effectively withdrew their support, the British rulers in India would have no legs to stand on. They called upon the Indian people to rise and make a collective onslaught. The Indians were asked not to pay taxes to the oppressor, the foreign rulers. The British "loot you and then beat you" with your resources; "you are the masters of your canals and wells, why should you then pay a tax"? "Stop paying any tax, O' people of villages", and "leave the service" of the government were the common exhortations.[43]

A major focus for that purpose was on the Indian soldiers. The Sikhs constituted a most significant element of the British Indian army and were aware of the great sacrifices they had made in the expansion of the British empire. A very large number of the Ghadarites had earlier served as soldiers. The *Ghadar* teachings now created in them a consciousness of having foolishly contributed to an increase in the power of their enemy. That was a grave mistake and "we suffered because of our own doings":

> We fought against our brothers in Kabul
> We have not forgotten the battle of Chitral
> We conquered China and Africa
> We are doomed because of our own doings.
> Fighting with brothers we created enmity with them
> We have paid for our (wrong) actions.
> Suffering bullets we established the empire
> But we found the cruel rulers to be deceitful.
> ... ...
> We fought many a battle for the Whites
> That has been a grave unwitting mistake, Brothers.
>
> ... ...
>
> You soil your hands with your own blood
> Why don't you understand the wickedness of the foreigner.[44]

They decided not to be fooled any more or sing songs of loyalty.

The Ghadarites had an easier access to men in the Sikh regiments. They knew some of their old colleagues; many had their friends and relatives in those regiments. Fixation with the idea of an armed rebellion on the pattern of 1857 made them attach great importance to the participation of the soldiers in the Ghadar. "Go to India and incite the native troops", was the instruction given to them when they left USA and Canada. Winning over the soldiers was indeed a major part of their strategy. When the Lahore conspiracy case was instituted against them, the first item in the list of the Ghadar operations for which they were charged was "the seduction of Indian soldiers from their allegiance to their King".[45]

One of the factors of which the Ghadarites were very acutely conscious was the damage which the Indian elements, described as 'selfish', 'power-hungry toadies', 'spies' and 'informers of the

British', could do to their cause. They reminded themselves of the treachery of those Sikh Sardars who became instrumental in the British conquest of Punjab in 1849, and the rulers of the Sikh states whose help to the British in 1857 led to the defeat of the rebel forces. "They sold us to the British and themselves became traffickers of the country". Such elements as were associated with the British were held responsible for the degeneration and exploitation of the country. Among them were listed 'Rai Bahadurs' and 'Khan Bahadurs', the 'tailed monkeys', who posed as the saviours of the people but acted as spies and informers. It was generally felt, therefore, that the poor people should join hands to bring about a revolution and not look for support from the *sahukars*.

The Ghadarites were aware that success in their struggle might be very difficult until such traitors were killed. Very often it was said: "We'll deal with the Whites later, let us deal with the traitors first".[46] Such an orientation had a potential for distorting their sense of priorities. That could also become a source of rationalisation of weaknesses in organisation and strategy. Indeed, *mukhbar maar gaya* (spy ruined us) became, for them, the main explanation of the fiasco of their operations in February 1915.

What had seemed as the most important requirement to the Ghadarites was heroism and a readiness to lay down one's life for the cause, *a prem khelan ka chao*. For that, inspiration was sought from the proud heritage of sacrifices: "Only jackals will remain behind; lions will go ahead; either we kill them or get killed but we shall not show our backs like cowards". The accent was on courage. Analysis of the objective social and political situation and considerations of foresight, planning and strategy did not appear to be equally important. They knew very little about the conditions in India and got little support. Most people in Punjab did not understand, much less appreciate, why these people who had left India only a few years earlier to earn money, and had indeed earned well, should suddenly come as a "bolt from the blue", preaching rebellion. "We were under an illusion", as one of the activists said later, that "the whole country felt as we did".[47] It was ironic, indeed, that Punjab which was the main centre of their operations made the maximum contribution towards the defence of the empire they had come to demolish.

The leading sections of their own community vied with one another in tracking down the Ghadarites who were described as 'criminal elements'. The British government of Punjab thankfully acknowledged that the 'great credit' for eliminating the menace of the Ghadarites was due to the members of the Sikh committees.[48] The heavy sacrifices these people made in that venture appear, in retrospect, very tragic, but most of them did not compromise their strong convictions. They in fact became catalysts in eroding and breaking the earlier beliefs and notions of the people in Punjab.

VI

The contribution of the Ghadar movement lay in setting new patterns of political socialisation—a process of learning which marked the beginning of the end of the earlier innocence. The plight of the Indians abroad led, under the powerful influence of the Ghadar movement, to the posing of questions they had rarely raised earlier. In the process they became intensely aware of the linkage between their oppression in foreign lands and the economic and political subjection. Their country's poverty and backwardness was no more a matter of cruel destiny or fate. It appeared to them to be the result of imperialist domination. In their ideas and beliefs there was an unmistakable accent on the understanding of politics and economic relations, and the need for acting politically. It created in them both a convulsive urge to strike at the root cause, and also a confidence in the collective strength and capacity of their people to destroy the old order, and usher in a new era of freedom and prosperity.

"Through a sprinkle on the withered hearts, the *Ghadar* fired a new life into the dead", sang their poets. The Ghadarites did not present any systematic political theory and they were not educated people, but they developed an understanding which altered their perception of things around and their self-image. Many of the traditional concerns appeared trivial and irrelevant. The Ghadar movement created a force for the formation of new identity in place of the separate identity formations being attempted by socio-religious organisations in India in general and among the

Sikhs in particular. A new selection of symbols and mediative interpretation of their heritage weakened the dissonance between cultural identities and political identity. Religious concerns now appeared as obscurantist designs of the vested interests. This contributed substantially towards the secularisation of consciousness and politics. Revivalism could never appeal to them and there was hardly any Ghadarite who could be persuaded into 'communal' politics in later life. They identified themselves not only with the oppressed of the country as a whole, but also felt that they had a common cause with the oppressed of other countries. Though they failed in armed action, the awakening that their teachings and actions gradually brought to Punjab countryside shook the British off their balance. The British could no longer rely upon the former loyalty of the Punjabis, particularly the peasant in uniform.

VII

The above study of an episodic movement sensitises us to the dynamics of change in culture and consciousness. It is axiomatic that culture is not an 'objective' or 'given' package, nor is identity-formation an unmediated outcome of primordial ties.

The forms of identity, values and political orientations developed among the Ghadarites were strikingly different from those of large sections of the Sikh community in India who came under the influence of the Singh Sabha movement and the Chief Khalsa Diwan. This underlines the point that culture and consciousness do not evolve independently of the life lived by the people and the socio-historical context. "There are no traditions", as Richard Fox observes, "except those that enter into consciousness in the present".[49]

Ideological mobilisation by the leadership of a social or political movement can be a potent force in the transformation of perceptions, values and attitudes. The rhetoric and ideas propagated by leaders of the Ghadar movement played, as we have seen, a crucial role in altering the structure of consciousness of the Punjabi Sikh immigrants on the Pacific Coast of North America. However, the effectiveness of such a mobilisation and the nature of the evolving structure of consciousness is determined by a complex dialectic of its relationship with objective conditions of existence and subjective orientations.

Most of these pioneer immigrants were sojourners. They went there to earn and return home, not to settle there permanently. Pull of the home was an ever present aspect of their lives. The daily experience of discrimination and shame could not persuade them to fight against the structures of domination in USA and Canada. Given the expectations of support from the British government in the light of the believed loyalty and extraordinary services rendered by their community in the service of the empire, the incidence of discrimination against them in Canada appeared to be a breach of faith. The frequent use of words like *thuggee*, deceitfulness, trickery, false appearance, guile, hypocrisy in the Ghadarite protest spoke of a hapless simple peasant's deep personal feeling of insult and anger against the ungratefulness of a believed patron. Such a wrench within would affect sojourners more deeply than those determined to settle in foreign lands. Not all of them were, however, affected in the same manner. The freedom for radical political propaganda enjoyed by Indians in USA before the American entry in the World War also appeared to have been crucial. Such a freedom was not available in Canada. The Punjabi immigrants in British Columbia were radicalized more by the events relating to the treatment of the *Kamagata Maru* passengers than by the Ghadar network of ideas.

VIII

After the end of the war when the Ghadar Party was revived in 1919, the life situation of the Punjabi immigrants was very different. Most of the Punjabis were not sojourners any more. Their primary concerns related to settling there and making good. Even though the more attractive economic opportunities of farming the leased or owned lands were being restricted, the threat of deportation loomed large and public antipathy against them was mounting, yet there were few who thought of returning home. That made a major difference. Increasing British repression in India disturbed the peace of many; the mass political upsurge for

India's freedom stirred them, and the brave deeds and sacrifices of the Ghadar heroes were a source of some vicarious dignity, but only a few were inclined to follow the party leaders beyond the contribution of funds. Though the party continued to function up to 1947, its impact remained marginal. The weakness of available leadership was as much a consequence of the changed objective conditions as of the powerful reasons for a nominal political activity.[50]

More significant for our purpose here is the manner in which people came to understand and absorb new ideas and beliefs. The process was neither simple nor smooth. It was mediated through cultural symbolism of the people in the process of transforming themselves. Paul Brass, in his studies of the formation of ethnic identities, has brought to focus the catalytic role of political leaders in the selections they make from the storehouse of symbols and their skilfull manipulation for political change.[51] The importance of the leaders' role was evident both in the Ghadar movement and the Singh Sabha movement in the development of diverse patterns of consciousness. Beyond that, however, as we have seen in the above study, is the nature of change which the activists introduce by translating the ideas propagated by the leaders into the 'mother-tongue', so to say, of the rank and file. This may be a more significant part of the process when the gap between the cultural equipment of the leaders and followers is wide or when the tension between the held values and images and those desired to be absorbed creates problems for the activists.

From the mid-1920s, when the Ghadarites turned to adopt the Communist ideology under the direction of the Communist International, such a tension remained a part of the mental equipment of most of the leaders. This kept the Ghadar-based Communists of Punjab ideologically and organisationally apart from the Communist Party of India for a long time.[52] Sohan Singh Josh discusses in his autobiography his prolonged struggle to overcome his fascination for individual heroism and sacrifice and the tension between the deeply entrenched religio-cultural impulses and conscious anti-religious secular ideological preferences.[53] Such a serious tension at the level of one's cultural equipment and consciousness may not be a normal feature of the life of a majority of activists. Further, a certain lack of a fit between political consciousness and social consciousness is not unusual in the political movements. As evident from our study of the Ghadar movement, the tenacity of traditional structures of thought and behaviour make the transformation of consciousness a very complex dialectical process.

Notes

1. 'Punjab Government's letter', cited in Sedition Committee Report, 1918 New Age Publishers, Calcutta, 1973, p. 155.
2. NAI, *Home/Political Proceedings,* B, April 1915, Nos.416-19.
3. Khushwant Singh, *A History of the Sikhs,* Vol. II, OUP, Delhi, 1973, p. 191.
4. Gobind Bihari Lal's Address at the University of California, Berkeley, 9 May 1973. *Ghadar Party Collection.* Center for South and Southeast Asia Studies Library (CSSEASL), Berkely.
5. Cited in C.J.O'Donnell, *The Causes of Present Discontent in India,* London, 1908, p. 94.
6. Kenneth Jones, *Arya Dharam: Hindu Consciousness in the 19th Century Punjab*, New Delhi: Mahohar Publishers, 1976, p.315.
7. Ganda Singh (ed.), *Amreeka Vich Hindustanee* (in Punjabi), Vancouver, 1976, pp. 48-61, 66-69.
8. Pacific Coast Khalsa Diwan Society, "Articles of Incorporation (1912)". *Ghadar Party Collection* CSSEASL, Berkeley.
9. NAI. *Home/Political Proceedings,* B, August 1910, Nos.10-17.
10. Cited in Baldev Rai Nayar, *Minority Politics in the Punjab*, Princeton N J: Princeton University Press, 1966, p. 65.
11. S.A. Wiaz, *Indians Abroad*, The Imperial Indian Citizenship Association, Bombay, 1927, pp. 654-56.
12. *Ghadar di Goonj*, No.21, p.1,2,7.
13. *Ibid.* Poem 1, p.1.
14. *Ibid.* Poems 1,2,10, p.1,2,7.

15. William Digby, *Few Facts about British Rule in India*, San Francisco: Hindustan Ghadar Press, 1915, pp. 3-5.
16. *Ghadar di Goonj*, No.1, pp.5-17; No.2, p.8.
17. Har Dayal's speech at Astoria. *The Astorian*, 5 June, 1913. Also NAI, *Home/Political Proceedings*, B, November 1913, Nos. 62-66.
18. Mark Juergensmeyer, "The Ghadar Syndrome: Nationalism in an Immigrant Community", *Punjab Journal of Politics*, Vol. 1, No. 1, 1977, p. 2.
19. Sucheng Chan, "Overseas Sikhs", in Mark Juergensmeyer and N.G. Barrier (eds.), *Sikh Studies: Comparative Perspectives on a Changing Tradition*, Berkeley, 1979, p. 203.
20. Emily Brown, 'Ghadar Leadership: Elitism and Mass Participation'. Paper presented at a symposium on the 'Public Policy Process and the Development of Ethnic Identity: The East Indian Experience', University of California, Berkeley, 23 June, 1979.
21. Chan, *op. cit.*, pp. 203-4.
22. *Ghadar di Goonj*, No.2, p.11.
23. Mark Naidis, "The Propaganda of the Ghadar Party", *The Pacific Historical Review*, Vol. XX, No. 3, 1951, pp.304-5.
24. *Ghadar di Goonj*, No.1.
25. *Ghadar di Goonj*, No.2, pp. 15, 29,31.
26. *Ibid.*, No.1, Poem 20, p.19. Also Bhagwan Singh, *Azadi Aur Jang*, Ghadar Press, 1915, pp. 5-7.
27. *Ibid.*, p. 47.
28. *Ghadar*, 1 November, 1913. Also *Ghadar di Goonj*, No.1, pp.6,19.
29. Karl Marx, *The Eighteenth Brumaire of Louis Bonaparte*, in Karl Marx and Frederick Engels, *Selected Works*, Moscow: Progress Publishers, 1973, I, p. 398.
30. N.G. Barrier, *The Sikhs and Their Literature*, New Delhi: Manohar Book Service, 1970, p. 106; *Ghadar di Goonj*, No.2, p.19.
31. *Ghadar di Goonj*, No.1, p.26.
32. Barrier, *op. cit.*, pp. 102, 110.
33. *Ghadar di Goonj*, No.1, pp.6, 11.

34. *Ibid.*, No.2, p.19.
35. *Ibid.*, No.1, p.17.
36. *Ibid.*, No.1, pp.9, 17.
37. *Ibid*, No.1, p.17.
38. *Ibid*, No.1, p.19.
39. *Ibid.*, No.2, pp.11, 23.
40. Sohan Singh Bhakna, *Jeevan Sangram*, Yuvak Kendar Prakashan, Jalandhar, 1967, p.41. Also Harnam Singh Tundilat. Unpublished manuscripts, Desh Bhagat Yadgar Library, Jalandhar.
41. NAI. *Home/Political Proceedings*, B, May 1916, Nos. 577-80; January 1917, Nos. 270-72; February 1917, Nos. 552-55.
42. Cited in Emily Brown, *Har Dayal: Hindu Revolutionary and Rationalist*, Tucson: University of Arizona Press, 1975, p. 159.
43. *Ghadar di Goonj*, No.2, p. 8, 18, 23.
44. *Ibid.*, No.2, p.14, 15.
45. NAI, *Home/Political Proceedings*, A. October 1915, No.91.
46. *Ghadar di Goonj*, No.2, p.16.
47. Gurmukh Singh Lalton in his interview with the author, Jalandhar, 5 November, 1967.
48. Michael O' Dwyer, *India As I Knew It 1885-1925*, London: Constable & Co., 1925, pp. 183 and 198.
49. Richard G. Fox, *Lions of the Punjab: Culture in the Making*, Berkeley: University of California Press, 1985, p. 198.
50. Harish K. Puri, *Ghadar Movement: Ideology, Organisation and Strategy*, Amritsar: GND University, 1993, pp. 223-76.
51. Paul R. Brass, *Ethnicity and Nationalism*, Delhi: Sage Publications, 1991, p. 100.
52. Puri, *op. cit.*, pp. 246, 248-50.
53. Sohan Singh Josh, *My Tryst With Secularism: An Autobiography*, New Delhi: Patriot Publishers, 1991, pp. 110-12, 133-34.

7

The Gurdwara Reform Movement

MOHINDER SINGH

The Gurdwara Reform Movement (1920-25) began with the attempts of Sikh reformers to liberate their religious places from the hereditary control of the Mahants[1]. It came to be popularly known as the Akali movement because of the large-scale participation of *Akali Jathas*[2] in the struggle for reform. What began as a purely religious movement turned out to be a major force for India's liberation at the provincial level, for the British administration in Punjab lent its support to the Mahants and the Congress and other nationalist forces came out in open support of the Akali reformers. As a result of the alliance with the nationalist forces, the Akali leadership was able to broaden the scope of the movement and launch two-pronged struggle, directed against the corrupt Mahants on the one hand and the British administration in the province on the other. During their five years' peaceful struggle in Punjab, the Akali reformers succeeded not only in wresting control of their historic shrines but also in strengthening nationalist forces in the country through their passive sufferings. Mahatma Gandhi was so impressed by the Akali reformers' strict adherence to their vow of non-violence that he often quoted their

---

Reprinted from Ravi Dayal (ed.), *We Fought Together for Freedom: Chapters from the Indian National Movement*, Delhi: Oxford University Press, 1998.

example to other satyagrahis, such as those of Munshi Peta and Malegaon, who failed to keep their vow.

A careful study of the movement shows how past Akali leaders rose above narrow communal interests and channelled a popular religious upsurge into a powerful instrument for India's struggle for freedom. As will be seen from the discussion in the following pages, three distinct features of the past Akali movement made it more effective than later Akali movements in independent India. First and foremost, the Akali leadership eschewed violence from the very beginning and quickly disowned the violent activities of splinter groups of the Babbar Akalis. Secondly, they appreciated the value of the press and public opinion. And thirdly, the movement was never allowed to take a communal colour. Before discussing the nationalist implications of the Akali struggle for Gurdwara reform, it is relevant to briefly discuss the circumstances leading to the origin and development of the movement and the peaceful manner in which its leadership launched and directed the long-drawn struggle.

Origin of the Gurdwara Reform Movement

Though corruption in the Sikh shrines existed much before the launching of the Akali struggle in the 1920s, no organised effort for their purification could be initiated earlier for lack of the necessary awareness among the masses. The cumulative effect of the internal forces of purification among the Sikhs, such as the Nirankari, Namdhari and the Singh Sabha movements, as also external influences such as the rise of nationalism in the country, the propaganda of the native press, the impact of the Ghadarite activities and above all the tragedy of Jallianwala Bagh, set the stage for the Akali struggle for reform. Reform was initially initiated by the local Akali Jathas in their respective areas, but soon two representative bodies of the Sikhs—the Shiromani Gurdwara Prabandhak Committee (SGPC) and the Shiromani Akali Dal—came into existence. From 1920 to 1925 these two bodies were not only able to obtain control over all the important Sikh shrines through peaceful agitations, but also strengthened the forces of nationalism in the province by ejecting the Mahants, priests, government-appointed managers and other pro-British interests, and by providing a new, nationalist leadership to the Sikh community.

The Golden Temple and the Akal Takht, Amritsar

After successfully gaining control over the Gurdwara Babe-di-Ber in Sialkot through peaceful methods, the Akali Jathas next paid attention to the premier Sikh shrines at Amritsar. Corrupt and non-Sikh practices in the precincts of the Golden Temple and the Akal Takht[3] and official control over its management had been sources of great discontentment among the Sikhs much before the beginning of the Gurdwara Reform Movement. While the reformers were anxious to free these premier shrines from evil influences and indirect official control as early as possible, British officials in the province carefully tried to forestall any effort at reform or change in the existing system of management. The loyalty and support of government-appointed priests and other vested interests was treated by the British government as symbolising the 'proverbial loyalty' of the Sikh community as a whole. These priests of the Akal Takht were made to issue *hukamnamas* against Ghadarite heroes that described them as thugs and which called upon the Sikh masses not to give them any shelter. After the massacre of Jallianwala Bagh, Arur Singh, the government-appointed manager of the Golden Temple, invited General Dyer to the temple and after honouring him with a *saropa* (robe of honour) declared him a 'Sikh'. The dialogue, which took place between Arur Singh and other priests on the one hand and General Dyer on the other, is worth quoting here:

> "Sahib", they said, "You must become a Sikh even as Nikalseyan Sahib (Nicholson) became a Sikh".
>
> The General thanked them for the honour, but he objected that he could not, as a British officer, let his hair grow long.
>
> Arur Singh laughed, "We will let you off the long hair", he said.

General Dyer offered another objection, "But I cannot give up smoking".

The priest conceded, "We let you give it up gradually".

"That I promise you", said the General, "At the rate of one cigarette a year".[4]

According to General Dyer's biographer, "the priests chuckling proceeded with the initiation. General Dyer and Captain Briggs were invested with the five *kakas*, the sacred emblems of that war-like brotherhood and so became Sikhs".[5]

On the basis of this honour at the hands of the priests of the Golden Temple, General Dyer later boasted that his action at Jallianwala Bagh had been 'approved' by the Sikhs. In fact, Arur Singh's action greatly scandalised the Sikh community and brought home to the advocates of Gurdwara reform the necessity of putting a stop to the prevailing system of Gurdwara management and with it the greed, licentiousness and misdeeds of the hereditary custodians of the Sikh shrines.

While the reformers were agitating for the termination of official control over the Golden Temple and the authorities were trying to soft-pedal the issue by deferring the question till the implementation of the reforms scheme in the council, the walk out of the priest of the Akal Takht in protest against the entry to newly baptised low-caste members of Khalsa Biradari into the premises of the Golden Temple virtually brought these important shrines under the control of the reformers, who appointed a representative committee for their management.

The Nankana Tragedy and Its Impact

Thus far the Akalis had gained control over important Sikh shrines through peaceful means and without shedding much blood. But, the tragedy of Nankana,[6] in which over 130 peaceful Akali reformers were done to death by Mahant Narain Das and the mercenaries hired by him, proved a turning point both in the annals of the Akali struggle for Gurdwara reform as also in the official policy towards the movement. The involvement of British officials in the Nankana tragedy, particularly that of C. M. King, Commissioner of Lahore Division, and the support extended to Mahant Narain Das by officials convinced the Akali leadership that the bureaucracy was supporting the influence of the vested interests in the Sikh shrines.

The Government of India's criticism of the Punjab government's failure to deal with the Akali movement "firmly and consistently from the beginning" and of the local officials for not having taken the necessary precautions to avert the tragedy, provided British officials in the province with the excuse to come out in open support of the Mahants. In consultation with the Viceroy and other members of his Council, the Punjab government now inaugurated a 'strong policy' towards the movement with the two-fold objectives of (i) suppressing the reformers by force, and (ii) weakening the growing Akali agitation with promises of 'suitable legislation'. The implementation of this new policy resulted in the subsequent agitation over the keys' affair and later opened new fronts, first at Guru-ka-Bagh and then at Jaito in the erstwhile state of Nabha.

Akali Agitation over the Keys' Affair

After taking over the management of the Golden Temple and the Akal Takht at Amritsar, the Akali reformers formed a provisional committee for their management. Sardar Sunder Singh Ramgarhia, who held the dual office of secretary of the newly established committee of management under the SGPC and also the government-nominated *sarbrah* (custodian), still controlled the keys of the Toshakhana. To ensure its complete control over the shrines, the SGPC asked Sardar Sunder Singh Ramgarhia to hand over the keys of the Toshakhana to its president. But before the *sarbrah* could do so, the Deputy Commissioner of Amritsar forestalled the Akali move by immediately sending Lala Amar Nath, an Extra-Assistant Commissioner, who took away the keys from Sardar Sunder Singh Ramgarhia.

This action created a stir within the Sikh community, which was already agitated over the tragedy of Nankana and official involvement in the affair. A period of intense protest through the press and on the platform followed the official taking over of the keys and the Punjab press, particularly the pro-Akali papers, expressed its opinions very strongly.[7]

Noticing the flood of protest and indignation in the central districts of Punjab and the increasing sympathy of various sections of the Sikh population with the Akali movement, the Government of India advised the Punjab authorities that the only way of severely rebuffing the increasing non-cooperation of the Sikhs was to successfully prosecute five or six leading men, especially Dan Singh and Jaswant Singh.[8] Accordingly, the Deputy Commissioner of Amritsar arrested these leaders when they were addressing a Sikh *diwan* (congregation) at Ajnala, near Amritsar, on 26 November, 1921.

The Akali reaction to the arrests of these leaders was immediate. As soon as the news reached Amritsar, the SGPC, reached Ajnala and continued the proceeding of the *diwan*. The authorities declared the assembly illegal and arrested all its members. However, instead of checking the advance of the movement, the arrests gave a fillip to the Akali agitaion. The SGPC, by a resolution, called upon the Sikhs "to hold religious *diwans* everywhere to explain the facts about the keys' affair".[9]

When the government realised that instead of weakening the movement, its 'strong' policy had made the movement increasingly popular and that the Akalis had joined the Congress programme of non-cooperation at the provincial level, it thought of solving the Akali problem by appointing a committee of a few moderate Sikhs to get the keys back from the government. But, in the face of determined opposition form the Sikh masses, moderate leaders also refused to accept the official offer. The SGPC passed a resolution on 6 December, 1921 saying "no Sikh should agree to any arrangement about the restoration of the keys unless and until all the Sikhs arrested in connection with the keys' affair are released unconditionally".[10] According to Mahatma Gandhi, the Punjab government was in a real dilemma: "If it releases the Sikhs arrested it would be ridiculed and the strength of the Sikhs will increases ten-fold. It must, therefore, decide whether it should be wiser for it to allow the Sikhs' strength to increase ten times or to release the Sikh prisoners and be laughed at, taking consolation in the fact that the strength of Sikhs will then only be doubled".[11]

To get out of the dilemma and to check the increasing movement of non-cooperation among the Sikhs, the government thought of negotiating with their leaders. Suddenly and dramatically, all those arrested in connection with the keys' affair were released unconditionally on 17 January, 1922.

Even after securing the unconditional release of all the prisoners, including Pandit Dina Nath, President of the Ajnala District Congress Committee and other Congress workers, the Akalis were not prepared to go to the Deputy Commissioner to collect the keys. A gazetted officer was thus sent by the Deputy Commissioner to hand them over to Baba Kharak Singh, President of the SGPC, at a specially arranged *diwan* at the Akal Takht. The unconditional release of prisoners and the return of the keys to the Akali leadership was described by a contemporary European writer in the following words: "Never was there a more shameful defeat. One thinks irresistibly of the capture of Calais by an English king, when the leading citizens had to bring the keys to him clothed only in their shirts and with ropes round their necks. The Punjab government had the Prabandhak Committee...".[12]

The nationalist leaders in the country, who had been backing the Akalis in their struggle against the bureaucracy, saw the defeat of the government as a decisive victory for Indian nationalism. Mahatma Gandhi sent the following telegram to Baba Kharak Singh, President of the SGPC: "First Battle for India's Freedom Won. Congratulations".[13]

In its anxiety not to alienate the Sikhs further or to allow their movement to gain momentum, the government virtually surrendered to the Akalis. In its effort to win back the Sikhs, the government changed its earlier stand. The actions of the leaders of the Akali movement, whom the judicial machinery had sentenced to rigorous imprisonment for 'political activities' and 'treason against the King-Emperor', were now explained away as "excitement based on the action taken by the government in respect of the Durbar Sahib rather than due to a desire to join in any campaign of disobedience to the law".[14] In the light of the statements given by Akali leaders earlier at the time of their prosecution, the changed official version appears incongruous. These leaders had more than once proclaimed that "they were non-cooperators and were not prepared to offer any defence as they had no regard for a foreign government, its courts and the law".[15] Baba Kharak Singh's statement in the court made this stand crystal clear: "As the government is a party to this prosecution and the judge is one of its servants, I, therefore, do not wish to make any statement".[16]

That the whole Sikh community was giving expression to its feeling of resentment against foreign rule through the struggle for reform in the Sikh shrines is borne out from statements of other Akali leaders too. Thus, Sardar Dan Singh proclaimed: "I have no regard for the present government nor do I consider these courts as places of justice as they belong to a government which is made under the intoxication of power...".[17] Sardar Dan Singh also had the courage to tell the judicial machinery that the justice administered in the courts was arbitrary: "Announce to us the sentence which you have already decided in the club a day earlier".[18]

It seems that in administering justice the judiciary was doing nothing more than implementing preconceived decisions of the executive, which were based less on the merits of the case and more on political expediency. Other leaders equally defied the law: "I do not consider this court as a place of justice nor do I expect any justice from the British government. Making a statement is useless", said Sardar Bhag Singh Vakil.[19] And Master Sunder Singh bluntly announced: "There is no government, no justice and hence no statement".[20]

This was the spirit of non-cooperation which the Gurdwara Reform Movement created among the Sikh community. The statements of the Akali leaders show how the awe for authority, officials, judges and the police had disappeared from the minds of the people in Punjab. The attempt of the government to win back the Sikhs failed. The hope expressed in the communique that "the cordial relations which have hitherto been maintained between the government and the Sikhs may continue uninterrupted for the perpetual benefit of the government and the community" proved a cry in the wilderness. Professions of "goodwill and friendliness" could no longer deceive the Akali leadership, which, during this early phase of the struggle for reform, had travelled far from "unfailing loyalty and staunch support" to "open defiance of authority". The community had now awakened from its slumber and its religious places could no longer be misused either for the pleasures of the Mahants or to strengthen a foreign government. No *saropas* could now be offered to the Prince of Wales and no prayers held for his well-being. Even his scheduled visit to Amritsar had to be cancelled and receptions arranged in his honour at Lahore and elsewhere were boycotted.[21]

The official stand on the keys' issue and unconditional release of the Akalis and other prisoners arrested in this connection made the government feel that, in its efforts to suppress the Akalis and thus set an example to the forces of nationalism in the country, it had suffered a political defeat and humiliation. In a circular to Deputy Commissioners, the Chief Secretary to the Punjab government wrote that "the release of the Akali prisoners had been misunderstood", and desired them "to bring the Akalis to their senses by strictly enforcing the law and order".[22] With a view to achieving this objective a vigorous campaign of repression against the Akali reformers was launched in various districts.

Guru-ka-Bagh Morcha

Finding the Akalis isolated as a result of the suspension of non-cooperation movement and the arrest of Mahatma Gandhi and other nationalist leaders who supported the Akali cause, the government thought of launching a vigorous attack on the reformers. To implement this scheme it ordered the arrest of some Akali reformers for cutting wood from the dry *kikkar* trees attached to Gurdwara Guru-ka-Bagh,[23] on the pretext that they had committed a 'theft' of private property. This action of district officials, done in anticipation of the Mahant of the Gurdwara lodging a formal complaint with the local police, points to a preplanned policy of the government. In the implementation of this, Sunder Das, the Mahant of Gurdwara Guru-ka-Bagh, became a mere tool in the hands of the local British officials.

The unprovoked action of the district officials was seen as a fresh challenge by the Akali leadership. In protest against official high-handedness and to assert their right to cut wood from the land attached to the Gurdwara for use in the free kitchen, jathas of five Akalis each started marching daily towards Guru-ka-Bagh. A new wave of enthusiasm prevailed among the reformers and soon Akali Jathas from surrounding areas reached Guru-ka-Bagh and began helping in the cutting and storing of wood for the community kitchen.

To check the continued influx of Akali Jathas and their supporters and sympathisers, police pickets were placed on all the roads leading to Guru-ka-Bagh. Arrangements were also made to stop jathas travelling to Amritsar by rail or road. By an order of J.M. Dunnett, the District Magistrate of Amritsar, assemblies of Akali volunteers gathered at Guru-ka-Bagh in Ajnala tehsil, were declared illegal and consigners and carriers taking supplies to them were warned that "they were engaged in the commission of a cognizable offence under Section 143/109 of the Indian Penal Code" and prevented from doing so. The District Magistrate also directed the police officers in charge of pickets at the Ranewala and Chinnawala bridges on the Lahore branch of the Upper Bari Doab "to prevent the transmission of such supplies to the illegal assemblies at Guru-ka-Bagh".[24]

Despite these preventive measures, the Akalis continued pouring in at Guru-ka-Bagh. Jathas of fifty, sixty, one hundred and sometimes even two hundred Akali volunteers started marching to Guru-ka-Bagh daily after taking a vow of non-violence at the Akal Takht in Amritsar. On the way, these jathas were stopped by a group of police officials and beaten till they became unconscious or otherwise unable to stand on their legs and proceed further towards Guru-ka-Bagh.

Criticism of the oppressive measures by the Indian and the foreign press, secret reports about the adverse effects of these beatings on Sikh soldiers in the Indian army, and the fear of alienating moderate Sikhs, unnerved the authorities in Punjab and the higher bureaucracy in Delhi and London. They wanted an immediate escape, without further loss of prestige. A wayout was soon found when Rai Bahadur Sir Ganga Ram, a retired government engineer, offered his cooperation. He arranged for the disputed land to be leased out by the Mahant and for the Akalis to cut wood[25] for use in the community kitchen. On Sir Ganga Ram informing the Deputy Commissioner that the police was no longer required, the government withdrew its contingents from Guru-ka-Bagh. The barbed wire around its enclosures was immediately removed and the Akali reformers took possession of the land attached to Guru-ka-Bagh. Thus ended the long-drawn struggle between the Akalis and the government in which over 1,500 reformers were injured and over 5,000 imprisoned.[26]

Struggle in the Sikh States

The Akali struggle in the Sikh States—an outcome of Maharaja Ripudaman Singh of Nabha's anxiety to win over the radical section of the Sikh community and the response of the Shiromani Akali Dal and the SGPC to take up the question of his restoration—is an important phase in the Akali struggle against British imperialism. Apart from the fact that the rulers of two important Sikh states (Bhupinder Singh of Patiala and Ripudaman Singh of Nabha) were closely involved one way or another with the Akali movement right from its inception till the finale, it was in the Sikh states that the Akali leadership, after its initial successes in the keys' affair and at Guru-ka-Bagh, offered a fresh challenge to the authorities on an issue of doubtful relevance. During their agitation in the Sikh states, the Akalis met the strongest opposition from British officials, who decided to put an effective stop to their activities by declaring the SGPC, the Shiromani Akali Dal and the various jathas affiliated to them as 'unlawful associations' and by arresting the top leadership on charges of 'treason against the King-Emperor'.[27] It was in the Sikh States, again, that the Akalis, who had humbled the powerful bureaucracy in Punjab during earlier phases of their struggle, were put to the severest test by the official policy of suppressing their Movement through Sikh groups and institutions—the Sikh princes, particularly Maharaja Bhupinder Singh of Patiala, Sikh troops, the Sikh Sudhar and Zila

Committees consisting of loyalists and other vested interests in the Sikh community—who rallied round the British in weakening a popular people's movement.

The Akali struggle in the Sikh states started with the Akali leadership taking up the issue of the restoration of Maharaja Ripudaman Singh of Nabha to his throne.[28] It took a serious turn when Nabha officials disrupted the *Akhand Path* at Gurdwara Gangsar, Jaito, while forcibly removing the priest reading the Holy Book.[29] This action caused a stir among the Sikhs who were already sore over the forced abdication of the Maharaja and arrest of the organisers of the Akali *Diwan* at Jaito.

The Jaito Morcha

The action of the Nabha officials resulted in the launching of a bigger *morcha* at Jaito, a village in Nabha state, when jathas of twenty-five Akalis each started marching there in protest against the official action in disrupting the *Akhand Path* and for the restoration of the Maharaja. The Jaito agitation took a serious turn when, on 21 February, 1924, a *Shahidi* Jatha of 500 was fired at by the Nabha police, killing in the process about forty Akalis and wounding over a hundred.

While official action at Jaito was still being criticised by the nationalist press and the Akali leadership, and the demand for an independent inquiry was being repeated, the SGPC continued sending jathas to Jaito, even though Mahatma Gandhi and other national leaders advised them not to do so.[30] In these circumstances, the second Shahidi Jatha left for Jaito on 28 February, 1924, and over 40,000 people gathered to give them a send off. More Shahidi Jathas, including the Military Pensioners' Jatha and the Canadian Sikhs' Jatha, continued marching to Jaito. While these activities were going on and outwardly the morale of both sides seemed to be high, Akali and official sources reveal that there were in fact signs of weariness in both the camps. At this juncture, the Akali leadership was facing several difficulties. The SGPC's decision to defend the Akali leaders' case; their opening of another front at Bhai Pheru in Lahore district while the Jaito *morcha* was still on; Malcolm Hailey's new policy[31] of creating divisions among the ranks of the Akali leadership and organising powerful opposition to their movement in the name of the loyalist Sikh Sudhar Committees, all these combined with other factors, created serious difficulties for the Akali leadership. On the other hand, the government was also getting tired of the increasing number of Akali prisoners resulting from the continuance of the *morcha* at Jaito.

The Gurdwara Bill and the Finale

In these circumstances, the Akali leadership, the administrator of Nabha and the Punjab government were anxious to find a solution to the Akali problem. While the government was prepared to negotiate with the Akali leadership through Pandit Madan Mohan Malaviya and Bhai Jodh Singh, the main difficulty was the Akali stand regarding the Maharaja of Nabha. Though the government was prepared to permit the completion of the interrupted *Akhand Path* on certain conditions, it insisted that the Akalis drop the question of the restoration of the Maharaja of Nabha for all time to come. While negotiation between the administrator of Nabha and the Akalis were still going on, the Punjab government introduced the Sikh Gurdwara and Shrines Bill in the Punjab Legislative Council. It was unanimously passed on 7 July, 1925, and accepted by the Akali leadership.[32] On successful passage of the bill, Sir Malcolm Hailey, the Governor of Punjab, made an important declaration and permitted bands of Akalis to proceed to Gurdwara Gangsar in Jaito to complete the interrupted *Akhand Path* on certain conditions.[33] This announcement was followed by the release of most of the Akali prisoners arrested in connection with the Jaito *morcha.* On 21 July, 1925, two jathas of Akalis from Amritsar and Delhi arrived at Jaito and on the 27th more jathas reached after their release from various jails. The deadlock finally ended with the Akalis completing 101 *Akhand Paths* on 6 August, 1925 in place of the one that had been interrupted by Nabha officials. Thus ended the struggle between the government and the Akalis, in which over 30,000 men and women went behind bars, 2,000 were wounded and over 400 died in various peaceful agitations. A large number of sympathisers of the movement had faced dismissal from service, the withdrawal of *jagirs* and pensions, the imposition of fines to the tune of Rs. 15 lakhs and forfeiture of properties.[34]

Impact of the Gurdwara Reform Movement

The Gurdwara Reform Movement, though itself a product of the general awakening and growing political consciousness in the country, greatly strengthened the nationalist forces by rejecting the Mahants, the landed aristocracy and other pro-British and vested interests in the Sikh community who had been declared the 'natural leaders' of the Sikhs by the British. The movement provided the Sikh community with a new type of middle-class nationalist leadership, consisting of barristers, *vakils*, school and college teachers and retired military officers. This new leadership, instead of playing into the hands of the British officials as the previous leadership of the Chief Khalsa Diwan had done, preferred to join the mainstream of nationalism in the country. It was not surprising, therefore, to find a majority of the Akali leaders turning from the original Akali programme of Gurdwara reform and linking it with the non-cooperation movement launched by Mahatma Gandhi and the larger programme of the country's struggle for freedom. It was mainly due to the emergence of this new type of leadership that the Akalis could secure the active sympathy and support of the Indian National Congress and other nationalist forces in the country in their own struggle against imperialism.

The new leadership also saw the need for the press and public opinion to further the cause of Gurdwara reform. Besides enlisting the support and sympathy of some important nationalist papers like the *Tribune, Independent, Swarajya, Kesari, Milap* and *Bande Matram,* they also started two vernacular dailies of their own, *Akali* and *Akali te Pardesi*. Later, an English daily, *Hindustan Times*, was also started by the Akali leaders from Delhi to carry their message to their countrymen outside Punjab. Well-known Akali radicals like Mangal Singh, Master Sunder Singh Lyallpuri, Sardul Singh Caveeshar and Master Tara Singh managed these papers in one capacity or the other.[35] The SGPC also acquired shares in *The Nation,* the daily then published from Lahore. Similarly, the Akali leadership appreciated the value of carrying with them the non-Sikh population and its leaders. Apart from important national leaders like Mahatma Gandhi, Jawaharlal Nehru, the Ali brothers, Swami Shraddhanand, Hakim Ajmal Khan, Pandit Madan Mohan Malaviya and C.F. Andrews, the Akali leaders also enjoyed the sympathy and support of non-Sikh leaders in the province. Lala Lajpat Rai and Pandit Dina Nath strongly supported the Akalis, and Professor Ruchi Ram Sahni looked after the publicity programme of the Gurdwara Reform Movement. An Akali Sahayak Bureau was also set up with the help of the Congress; it was looked after by A.T. Gidwani, K.M. Panikkar and other Congress leaders. Perhaps, the wisdom of the collective leadership prevented violence from creeping into the Akali struggle. When splinter groups like the Babbar Akalis resorted to violent means, the Akali leadership quickly disowned acts of terrorism perpetuated by these and reiterated its declared faith in non-violent agitation.

It was mainly due to the Akali-Congress association during the initial phase of the Akali struggle that the leaders of the two major Sikh groups came closer to each other and the Sikhs became inextricably involved in Congress activities. Actually, the two groups—the Akali advocates of purely religious reform, and others who looked upon Gurdwara reform only as a part of the larger programme of the country's freedom—remained united till 1939, initially under the leadership of Baba Kharak Singh and, later, that of Master Tara Singh.

In the Gurdwara Reform Movement, the Congress found an opportunity to further its own programme of non-cooperation launched by Mahatma Gandhi and to strengthen its position in Punjab. By winning over the Akali leadership the Congress was able to influence a large section of the Sikh masses who had till then remained aloof from the Congress programme. As Maulana Mohamed Ali remarked in the course of his presidential address at the Kakinada session of the Indian National Congress on 31 December, 1923: "A better opportunity for civil disobedience at least on a provincial scale never presented itself since the arrest of the Mahatma".[36]

To give moral support to the Akalis in their non-violent struggle against the government, the Congress leadership passed formal resolutions supporting them in whatever they did. An attack on the SGPC and the Shiromani Akali Dal was described by the Congress as a direct challenge to the right of free association of all Indians and a blow aimed at all movements for freedom. Dr. Kitchlew, the convener of Satyagraha Committee, emphasised that "the Akali struggle was now a national struggle and defeat of the Akalis for want of help from the Congress would affect the national assembly". The Akalis were also eulogised as "the only living wing of the national movement" and "the strongest community in India because of the triumph of *satyagraha*, of which they had given full proof".[37]

Apart from passing formal resolutions lending them moral support, the Congress leadership also rendered the Akalis solid practical help by sending Congress volunteers to assist in publicity work. The Akali-Sahayak Bureau was set up at Amritsar to coordinate Akali-Congress activities and to help the Akalis organise their propaganda machinery. Almost all the important national leaders, including Mahatma Gandhi, Pandit Madan Mohan Malviya, Jawaharlal Nehru, Maulana Mohamed Ali and Hakim Ajmal Khan visited Nankana, Amritsar, Guru-ka-Bagh and other places of Akali activity to obtain first-hand information about events and to help the Akalis with advice and moral support. In the special session of the Congress held at Delhi in September 1923, a resolution was passed supporting the Akali agitation in the State of Nabha and it was also decided to send Congress observers to get first-hand information about developments there. Jawaharlal Nehru, A.T. Gidwani and K. Santhanam, who were sent there for the purpose, were arrested as soon as they entered the state's territory and put behind bars for having entered it without the prior permission of the British administrator of Nabha. During their stay in Nabha jail and their subsequent trials, the Congress observers not only gained first-hand knowledge about the Akali cause and the genuineness of their suffering but also got a chance to observe the high-handedness of bureaucracy and the arbitrary nature of justice in Nabha, then under the control of a British administrator. In an emotional hand-written statement, in which he was highly appreciative of the Akalis, Nehru attacked the British administration of Nabha and the judicial machinery in the state for their "unscrupulous and crooked ways". Having gained first-hand impressions about the Akalis, Nehru became their great admirer and wished to prove "worthy of their high tradition and fine courage". The last paragraph of his original statement drafted in Nabha jail on November 1923, reads:

> I was in jail when the Guru-ka-Bagh struggle was gallantly fought and won by the Sikhs. I marvelled at the courage and sacrifice of the Akalis and wished that I could be given an opportunity of showing my deep admiration of them by some form of service. That opportunity has now been given to me and I earnestly hope that I shall prove worthy of their high tradition and fine courage. *Sat Sri Akal.*[38]

In return for the help extended to the Akali movement, the Congress leadership was able to establish an influence with the Akali leaders and, through them, the Congress programme was carried to the Sikh masses. It was mainly due to nationalist influence upon the Akali leadership that the SGPC was able to adopt non-violent non-cooperation as a weapon with which to fight the powerful bureaucracy in Punjab and to broaden the scope of its earlier programme of Gurdwara reform. A formal resolution in favour of non-cooperation and passive resistance was passed by the SGPC on 11 May, 1921. Resolutions were also passed at this meeting to boycott liquor and foreign goods and to substitute panchayats for courts of law.

With the election of Sardar Kharak Singh, a professed non-cooperator and a die-hard nationalist, as president of the newly elected SGPC in July 1921, and the formation of a new executive committee consisting of nationalist and non-cooperators, the non-cooperation movement in Punjab was further strengthened. This new element in the Akali leadership, to whom the cause of religious reform differed little from extreme nationalism, was able to introduce national politics into the movement for Gurdwara reform and thereby broaden the scope of the Akali movement.

Perusal of the court proceedings against some prominent Akali leaders shows that the ideology of non-cooperation had taken deep root. Most of them did not defend themselves in the courts. During interrogation they neither admitted nor denied the official charges. Whatever they said in court was not by way of defence but to tell the official machinery that, as non-cooperators, they had no regard for the British judicial system which they, considered arbitrary and biased. The following extract from Baba Kharak Singh's speech in court serves as an example: "As the government is a party to this prosecution and the judge is one of its servants, I, therefore, do not wish to make any statement. My position as President of the Sikh Panth is like that of the President of the United States, France and Germany".[39]

A strong link and reciprocal relationship had thus been established between the two movements. The Akali movement became a part of the national movement—in effect a manifestation of the Congress programme of non-cooperation at the provincial level—and in return received active sympathy and support from the Congress leadership in its struggle against the government. Growing Akali-Congress cooperation is evident from the fact that, while in 1919 there was not a single Sikh on the AICC, in 1920 there were two and in 1922 nine Sikhs on it.

The Akali movement also clearly demonstrated the efficacy of the doctrine of non-violent non-cooperation when the Akalis in Punjab were able by peaceful means to dislodge the Mahants from their hereditary positions in the Sikh shrines, and the government from its unreasonable stand. A contemporary paper thus summarised the contribution of the Akali reformers to the struggle for freedom: "The Akalis have shown to the Indians how a most arrogant, oppressive, cunning and deceitful bureaucracy can be brought to its knees by means of non-violent *satyagraha*. By sacrifices at Guru-ka-Bagh, they have destroyed the prestige of the bureaucracy and raised the dignity of India".[40]

Notes

1. According to Mahankosh (*Encyclopaedia of Sikhism*, p.700), Mahants were those heads of Deras, Akharas or Gurdwaras, who controlled these institutions and admitted followers.
2. *Akali Jathas literally* means "bands of deathless warriors". This term was used for those Sikh reformers who were prepared to sacrifice everything, including their lives, for the liberation of Sikh shrines from the control of Mahants.
3. For a detailed account, see Mohinder Singh, *The Akali Movement*, New Delhi, 1978, pp.20-23.
4. Colvin, *Life of General Dyer*, p. 201. Confirmed by *The Tribune* (article on 'Gurdwara Reform', 9 May 1925), and the *Akali*, 17 December, 1921.
5. *Ibid.*
6. For a detailed account, see pp. 27-36 of *The Akali Movement*.
7. For details see Punjab Press Abstracts ending 30 November, 1921, NAI.
8. Note 26 November, 1921 by H.D. Craik, File I-17/1921, Home-Pol., NAI.
9. Quoted in the *Akali,* 30 November, 1921.
10. Quoted in the *Collected Works of Mahatma Gandhi*, Vol. XXII, p.170.
11. *Ibid.*, pp.208-9.
12. Komma, 'The Sikh Situation in the Punjab', *Fortnightly Review,* September 1923.
13. Ganda Singh (ed.), *Confidential Papers of the Akali Movement*, p.11.
14. Punjab Government Communique, 12 January, 1922, file-459/II/1922, Home-Pol., NAI.
15. Partap Singh, *Gurdwara Sudhar: Arthat Akali Lehar*, p.142.
16. *The Civil and Military Gazette* (4 December, 1921) gives the following account: "Sardar Kharak Singh asked whether the case against him was by the government, and being told that it was, he said that as the government was the prosecutor and the court its

servant, he did not want to make any statement to the court, because a party could not arrogate to itself the functions of the judge. The accused's position as President of the Panth (the Sikh Nation) was similar to that of the United States of America, France and Germany". This is confirmed by most contemporary accounts, such as the *Gurdwara Reform Movement, the Gurdwara Sudhar, Akali Morchian da Itihas* and *Baba Kharak Singh Abhinandan Granth.*

17. Court Proceedings in Crown v. Kharak Singh and others, *The Civil and Military Gazette*, 4 December, 1922.
18. *Ibid.*
19. *Ibid.*
20. *Ibid.*
21. According to *The Civil and Military Gazette* of 15 February, 1922, Master Tara Singh and other extremists in the Akali leadership threatened to persuade the students of Khalsa College, Amritsar to go on strike in case the Managing Committee of the college invited the Prince. The college authorities had to give up the plan of welcoming the Prince to the college.
22. File No.459-II/1922, Home-Pol., NAI.
23. For a detailed account of the Guru-ka-Bagh *morcha*, see Mohinder Singh, *The Akali Struggle,* New Delhi, 1988, pp. 52-65. Also see G.A. Sundram, *Guru-ka-Bagh Satyagraha,* Madras, 1923.
24. For full text of the order, see *The Akali Struggle,* p. 220.
25. Shiv Narain Mishra's booklet, *Akali Darshan* (in Hindi), Kanpur, 1923, gives an interesting inside story of a secret understanding between the Deputy Commissioner of Amritsar and Sir Ganga Ram.
26. Proceedings, Punjab Legislative Council, 1922, Vol. IV, pp. 468-69.
27. See for details, order no.23772 dated 12 October, 1923 in file no. 23 of Nabha State Records and quoted in *The Akali Movement*, p. 198.
28. For detailed account about the circumstances leading to the Maharaja's abdication, see the author's paper, 'The Nature of the Abdication of the Maharaja of Nabha', *Proceedings of the Punjab*

History Conference, Patiala, November 1973.

29. There are divergent views about the disruption of the *Akhand Path* at Jaito. The SGPC alleged that "armed soldiers in uniform literally dragged the man reading the Granth" (*Tribune*, 18 September, 1923). The official version contradicts the Akali charge. According to the statement of Gurdial Singh, Assistant Administrator of Nabha, published in the *Pioneer*, 6 October, 1923: "The *Path* was not interrupted even for a second. The Akali who was reciting at the time was asked to leave his place when our man had taken his seat by the side of the Akali and had begun the recital..." Nazim of Phool and evidence of Mir Muhammad Ali, in *Crown* v. *Mehtab Singh and others*, mention the name of Bhai Atma Singh, who took over the *Path* from Inder Singh, *The Civil and Military Gazette*, 16 January 1924. The evidence of the Superintendent of Police, Nabha, in the court of Lala Amar Nath, Sessions Judge, Nabha also confirms the above view, *The Civil and Military Gazette*, 16 May, 1924.

    From a perusal of the initial official reports about the incident it appears that the *Path* was disturbed when the state soldiers tried to remove the Akalis from the place where the *Path* was going on. See the letter of Wilson-Johnston, the administrator of Nabha, to the Viceroy about the incident: "The place where they were holding the Diwan is now turned into a camping ground for our soldiers. Sri Guru Granth Sahib was removed and taken to the Dharmsala with all honours by five Sikh soldiers who were ready for the purpose beforehand...". The fact that the Granth Sahib was removed establishes that the reading of the *Akhand Path* had come to a stop for some time. It appears that at a later stage, when the officials realised the serious consequences resulting from their action, they issued a statement in the press that "the *Path* was not interrupted even for a second". Gurdial Singh's statement in the *Pioneer* is dated 6 October while Wilson-Johnston's letter was written on 1 October, 1923 (D.O.II.C.D.L., 1 October, 1923), File No. 623-P-3, Foreign-Pol., NAI.

30. Mahatma Gandhi's letter dated 4 March, 1924 to the Secretary of the SGPC, quoted in Ganda Singh (ed.), *Confidential Papers of the Akali Movement*, pp. 45-46.

31. Malcolm Hailey, who replaced Edward Maclogan as Governor of Punjab, believed that the Akalis had a typical mentality. They described every concession as a defeat of the government. He followed a double-edged policy of creating divisions in the Akali leadership and suppressing the movement with an iron hand. See Hailey Papers in IOL, London (MSS Eur E. 220/5-D, 6-A, B, C, 7-A and B, 8-A and B and 35-7, 41-5). For detailed discussion of the subject, see the author's paper, 'British Policy towards the Akali Movement', *Journal of Sikh Studies,* Vol. IV, No. 1, February, 1977.
32. For a detailed study of the circumstances leading to the passage of the bill, see pp. 133-44 in *The Akali Struggle.*
33. *Ibid.*
34. On the basis of a statement by Tara Singh, Member in the Punjab Legislative Council, 7 May, 1925. *P.L.C. Proceedings*, May 1925, p. 1,105. While the *Collected Works of Mahatma Gandhi* confirm the above figures on the basis of a news item in *Young India*, 26 February, 1925, Vol. XXVI, p. 197, Giani Nahar Singh, a near contemporary, puts the figures as 40,000 arrested and 500 dead; see Ganda Singh (ed.), *Punjab*, Vol. II, p. 234.
35. For details, see *The Akali Movement,* pp. 91-92.
36. Report on the Coconada Session of the Indian National Congress, quoted in *Tribune*, 1 January, 1924.
37. *Ibid.*
38. For full text see S. Gopal (ed.), *Selected Works of Jawaharlal Nehru,* Vol. I, pp. 369-74.
39. *The Civil and Military Gazette*, 4 December, 1921.
40. *Akali te Pardesi*, 25 December, 1923.

8

The Congress in Punjab

K.L. TUTEJA

The Indian National Congress was the main political organisation that spearheaded the struggle against the British rule and thereby made an important contribution to the achievement of India's independence in 1947. Established in 1885, it successfully mobilised Indian people from particularly all sections of society irrespective of caste, class, creed or regional affiliations. The birth of the Congress was the product of the nationalist consciousness that initially grew in the presidency towns in the second half of the nineteenth century.[1] It is important to note that nationalism in India as in most countries of the West is intimately related to the emergence of a broad collectivity formed through enlargement of market beyond local limits, establishment of capitalist relations of production and the enunciation of the enlightenment ideals and values of modernity such as rationality, freedom, equality and progress.[2] But, along with this, the primary factor behind the emergence of the idea of nation and the ideology of nationalism in India was resistance to and struggle against the colonial rule in the country. The beginning of nationalist consciousness signified a loose sense of collectivity based on shared experience of subjugation and a desire to resist oppression and exploitation by the colonial rule underlying an inclination to overlook or ignore their internal divisions at the social level. Therefore, it has been rightly observed that nationalism in India was the product of the contradiction between colonialism and the interests of the Indian people.[3] This character of Indian nationalism was best reflected in the ideology and the activities of the Congress during the course of the freedom struggle. The social base of the Congress slowly expanded beyond presidency towns, particularly under the leadership of Mahatma Gandhi. This change transformed its character from an elite to a mass organisation of the Indians. Although the Congress operated as a strong, unified and well organised body at the all-India level, its activities and programme differed at the provincial and local levels. As a matter of fact, the Congress movement in local areas was largely influenced by the specific conditions that prevailed at a particular place and time and also by the kind of leaders who held the strings of the movement in their hand. Apart from this, the strategies and the attitudes of the colonial state had a strong bearing on the struggle. Keeping these complexities in mind, the present paper attempts to examine the nature and growth of the Congress movement in Punjab.

I

Punjab was taken over by the British government in 1849. It was gradually "converted into an agrarian appendix of the British metropolis".[4] Large amount of capital was invested by the government in building canal irrigation system in the northwest Punjab that brought new areas under cultivation and greatly increased agricultural production. Agriculture in this region was transformed into a capitalist venture where production was geared to the market.[5] Major part of agricultural produce was transported through the newly established railway system from Punjab to port cities for export to the overseas market. This included export of grains and raw cotton to England in large quantities which made the province important for the metropolis.[6] Punjab also became crucial for the imperial system of control because the British army made its home in this province after 1880. A large number of persons belonging to the peasantry began to join military service, and soon their number swelled.[7] In order to ensure regular supply of manpower for recruitment, the government considered it essential to maintain its hegemonic hold over the rural society. Any attempt to challenge the colonial authority in the countryside was perceived by the British officials as a 'seditious' activity that needed to be ruthlessly suppressed.[8]

Under the conditions, the main object of the colonial state was to tighten its grip over the rural society in Punjab. For this purpose, it chose to make an informal alliance with the rich landed classes, which held dominant influence over the local societies through social and economic ties. The landlords responded favourably, and often acted as intermediaries between the state and the rural masses.[9] The government also patronised them in different forms. But a significant step by which government intended to win larger section of the rural people was the Land Alienation Act (1900).[10] The new legislation disallowed permanent alienation of land owned by the agriculturist castes to the non-agriculturist moneylenders particularly belonging to Khatri, Arora and Bania castes. Later Michael O'Dwyer, the Lt. Governor of Punjab, who harboured strong prejudice against the urban middle classes, granted to the agriculturists a preferential right of recruitment in the government service.[11] This attitude of favouring agriculturists became further evident when the Montagu-Chelmsford Report recommended larger representation for the rural population in the Punjab Legislative Council.[12] It is in pursuance of this policy that the British government, as we shall see below, chose to maintain cordial relations with the Unionist Party which claimed to represent the interests of the peasantry in Punjab.

It is important to mention that the logic behind the pro-agriculturist policy followed by the British in Punjab underwent a change at the later stages of its rule. In the earlier phase, as stated above, the government endeavoured to maintain its hold over the rural society in order to ensure regular export of agricultural products needed for the metropolis, and also to ensure a regular supply of manpower for the army. But, when the anti-imperialist forces started gaining strength after the turn of the century, the government realised that an ideology which favoured the agriculturists against the non-agriculturists could also serve as an effective device to frustrate the nationalists' attempt to bring unity among the Indian people.[13]

The urban society in Punjab also underwent major transformation following the establishment of colonial rule. The economic and social changes, which took place during this period, threw up new social classes with their distinctive interests. First of all, a large trading class, which included big traders, moneylenders and petty shopkeepers, sprang up as a powerful section of society. The urban Hindus belonging to the intermediate castes such as Khatri, Arora and Aggarwal formed a major component of this class. Some Khatri and Arora Sikhs, and Khoja and Piracha Muslims also constituted a small section of the emergent trading community. On the whole, Punjab witnessed a significant expansion of the trading class as a result of the sharp increase in the import and export trade under the colonial rule.[14] But, similar phenomenal growth did not take place in the case of industry. Its pace of development remained rather slow in Punjab.[15] In view of this, the industrial bourgeoisie could not take shape as a distinct formation and play a leading role in giving a direction to social and cultural life of the urban society. In fact, the entrepreneurial class in this province in the beginning of the twentieth century, does not in any case qualify to be described as industrial bourgeoisie with its own distinctive character. It can at best be classified as a segment of the newly assertive middle classes.[16] One of the most significant changes in Punjab, however, came as a result of the growth of education in the late nineteenth century. A number of schools and colleges were established in different parts of the province. Lahore, the capital of Punjab, became a leading centre of education attracting students from all parts of north India.[17] The number of literates significantly increased in the urban society of Punjab. The establishment of British colonial regime created opportunities for the newly educated sections in the form of government jobs and in other liberal professions. The urban Hindus who formed the largest number of the literate in Punjab acquired a predominant position in jobs and professions in comparison to the Muslims and the Sikhs.[18]

II

The new western educated elite and other sections of petit bourgeoisie took keen interest in the emergence of the nationalist movement in Punjab during the closing decades of the nineteenth century. The first nationalist organisation known as India Association was established in Lahore on the advice of Surendra Nath Banerjee who visited this province in 1877.[19] It was, however, after the founding of the Indian National Congress in Bombay in 1885 and the subsequent setting up of its provincial and district branches that the social base of the nationalist movement was considerably widened in Punjab. The provincial and local leadership in the early phase was selected by the criteria of education and social status.[20] The growing popularity of the Congress in Punjab came to notice when for the first time the session of the Congress was held in Lahore in 1893. The pavilion of the Congress having the capacity of 4,000 persons remained filled with visitors on all the days of the session. Almost similar enthusiasm was witnessed when the Congress assembled here again for the sixteenth session in 1900.[21] However, the pace of politicisation in Punjab was quite slow in comparison to that of the presidency towns. After the turn of the century, however, one noticed a decline in the popularity of the Congress.[22] A section of the Hindu elite got disenchanted with the Congress when the latter did not take a clear position on the Land Alienation Act which, as stated above, favoured the agriculturist castes against the non-agriculturists.

In 1907, a powerful agrarian movement was launched in Punjab in which a large number of peasants from the canal colonies and a section of urban middle class actively participated. However, barring Lala Lajpat Rai and a few others, the participation of the provincial Congress as an organisation in this movement was marginal. When the government resorted to the extraordinary measure to deport Lajpat Rai without any trial, members of the Congress were badly demoralised. They even temporarily withdrew from the nationalist movement. Moreover, a section of Hindu middle class was seriously perturbed over the assurance of separate communal representation to Muslims under the Morley-Minto reform scheme of 1909. A prominent Hindu leader, Lal Chand, who was also associated with the Congress, even suggested the substitution of Hindu Sabhas for Congress committees in Punjab.[23] For the next few years the popularity of the Congress was at a low ebb in this region, and the activities of the provincial Congress were not "more than annual gatherings in which few interested people participated".[24] However, the Congress slowly expanded its social base particularly in the urban areas. The number of its branches increased particularly after the first constitution of the Congress (1908) was implemented to strengthen its organisational structure.[25] The growing number of the nationalist newspapers and periodicals also helped the Congress to mobilise masses in its favour.[26]

The Congress-led national movement was weak in Punjab during this phase because its provincial leadership became more interested in sectarian issues than the issue of larger national concern.[27] This observation is based on the assumption that communitarian consciousness is incompatible with nationalist perspective. It was noticed that apart from the nascent growth of nationalism, there was an attempt among different segments of the middle classes belonging to the Hindus, Muslims and Sikhs to define their respective sectarian identities on the basis of religion. In fact, however, the communitarian consciousness that emerged in Punjab had a real potential for the evolution of a nationalist perspective[28] The relationship between communitarian assertion during the colonial period and the nationalist struggle was actually defined by the specific historical context. It is indeed true that Mahatma Gandhi was the first national leader who consciously attempted to achieve an effective linkage between communitarian loyalties in the political field with commitment to the larger collective interests of the nation.[29] In Punjab, such a transformation had already started taking place in the pre-Gandhian phase.

The main thrust of the Congress at the time was to build an anti-imperialist consciousness as a long-term objective. But, along with this, the Congress took up issues like the larger representation of Indians in the local and provincial bodies, and greater employment opportunities for them in government jobs.

In other words, the immediate goal of the Congress was to secure some concessions for the Indians in the existing political and administrative structure. Thus, the Congress provided space to all those who, without giving up the anti-imperialist framework pursued a politics of securing concessions as a short-term objective. That is why, from its very inception, the Congress maintained a broad character and carried within its fold such active members and leaders who also had pronounced communitarian leanings. The Congress, however, always took care to project itself as a secular organisation, and the Muslims in particular, were assured that by joining it their interests would always be protected.[30] The majority of its members in Punjab came from Hindu urban middle classes particularly those belonging to Arya Samaj. However, its overall perspective allowed space for the unity of Hindus, Muslims and Sikhs in the nationalist movement without giving up the pursuit of sectional interests at the local and provincial levels.[31]

The dominant form of political consciousness in Punjab at this juncture was both nationalist and communitarian at the same time. It was on account of this reason that some Congress members could easily remain associated with the Muslim League or the Hindu Mahasabha in the early decades of the twentieth century. For instance, Dr. Saif-ud-Din Kitchlew was office-bearer of both local Congress committee and district branch of the Muslim League in Amritsar in 1919.[32] Similarly, Dr. Satyapal had close association with the local Hindu Sabha and the district Congress committee at the same time.[33]

The nature and strategies of the colonial state had also some bearing on the movement of the Congress in Punjab. Since Punjab was highly important for the British rule, the British took maximum care to check the growth of political consciousness in this province.[34] Therefore, unlike other major provinces, the system of legislative councils based on the Indian Councils Act of 1861 was introduced in Punjab only in 1897.[35] As a matter of fact, from the very beginning, a distinct colonial ideology was developed in Punjab which "emphasised firm paternal rule by an elite of self-confident administrators who conceived their duty as that of bringing order and prosperity to a contented peasant society".[36] Apart from paternalism, it also embodied the necessity of taking firm actions against the people if they ever tried to pose a challenge to the authority of British rule. It was in pursuance of this policy that Michael O' Dwyer imposed severe restrictions on the nationalist activities particularly during the First World War.[37] Indeed, all this weakened the Congress as an organisation in this province. But, the embargo enforced by O' Dwyer was lifted at the instance of Montagu, the Secretary of State during his visit to India in 1917. As a result, participation of people in the nationalist programme of the Congress again became possible. The growing anti-imperialist consciousness in both its secular and religious-communitarian variants was evident form the fact that the Punjab Provincial Congress Committee extended an invitation to the Congress in 1918 to hold its next session in Amritsar. This resurgence of nationalist activities was noted with great satisfaction by the nationalist press.[38] There was a groundswell of nationalist sentiments in Punjab and this led to a large scale participation of urban people in Rowlatt Satyagraha in 1919.

III

The emergence of Mahatma Gandhi as the leader of the national movement in 1919 deeply influenced the nature and activities of the Congress in Punjab. It is well known that his decision to launch a *satyagraha* against the draconian Rowlatt legislation received popular support in Punjab, particularly in urban areas like Amritsar. The provincial Congress as a body was not actively involved in the movement, but a large number of local Congress leaders and other members took a leading part in it. The movement appeared to have successfully converged the elite and popular anti-colonial consciousness. What actually proved decisive in the movement was the popular perception of Gandhi's charisma and strength.[39] The masses openly defied the colonial authority and took some initiatives which were not strictly in accordance with the programme given by Gandhi.[40] The increasing erosion of the ideological hegemony of the colonial state was perceived by the British officials as a dangerous phenomenon which needed to be ruthlessly crushed.[41] This explains the massacre of a large number of innocent people at Jallianwala Bagh by General Dyer. During the movement, deep communal harmony was witnessed between the Hindus and Muslims in Punjab.[42] This social phenomenon was an inevitable consequence of the communitarian nationalist perspective, which had gained ascendancy at this point of time.

After a year, Mahatma Gandhi launched another agitation called the non-cooperation movement, which received favourable response from people in Punjab, particularly in the cities of central and the eastern parts of the province. One of the important reasons for this successful mobilisation was the changes which took place in the organisational structure of the Congress following the amendments made in its constitution in late 1920. Under the new amendments, four *anna* membership was introduced and Congress branches were set up in small towns and villages to bring masses into its fold.[43] In Punjab, Gandhi's call to boycott the government educational institutions was quite successful as large number of students in cities like Lahore and Amritsar left such colleges and schools.[44] But, the Congress programme of boycotting the elections of the council received popular support mainly in the cities of central Punjab. For instance, merely 8 percent voting took place in Lahore.[45] On the whole, barring a small section of upper classes, the urban people belonging to middle and lower classes took active part in the movement. The response of urban Muslims was no less significant in view of their emotional involvement on the issue of the khilafat which Gandhi took up for launching the non-cooperation movement against the colonial rule.[46] However, the rural Muslims in the western part of Punjab did not take much interest in the movement. They were more under the influence of the local sufi saints and the universal Islamic identity represented by the Khalifa did not carry much importance.[47] Part of the reason was that the provincial Congress had neither cared to establish its branches in deep areas of the northwest Punjab nor made serious efforts to mobilise the Muslim masses. The Sikhs participated in a large number in the non-cooperation movement. Many of them were closely associated with the Congress and some even held high offices in its organisational structure. Besides, at this stage the Sikhs were also engaged in the Akali movement which aimed at reforming the Gurdwaras. Since this movement was largely anti-colonial in character, the Congress gave all kinds of support to the Sikhs. In other words, the Akali movement in Punjab became an auxiliary to the non-cooperation movement of the Congress.[48] An important aspect of this movement was the massive participation of the Sikh peasantry in this anti-imperialist struggle.[49] Yet, the Congress in Punjab failed to bring large sections of the peasantry in its fold. As stated above, its social base lay mainly in the urban areas. Its middle class leadership therefore neither took interest in the social and economic problems of the agriculturists nor made genuine attempts to mobilise them. Nevertheless, the non-cooperation movement was quite effective in Punjab if it is compared with the subsequent Gandhian movements.

However, the forces of nationalism represented by the Congress came under great strain on account of the growing communal division in the province during the 1920s. The communal tension between the Hindus and Muslims resulted into the outbreak of communal violence at many places in Punjab—an aspect that has not been adequately explored so far. Different reasons are given for this growth of communalism in the province. The government blamed the press (particularly, the vernacular papers) for fomenting hatred between the communities. Some contemporaries, however, believed that the movements like *Shuddhi* and *Sangthan* among the Hindus, and *Tabligh* and *Tanzim* among the Muslims proved instrumental in accentuating Hindu-Muslim tension at the social and political levels.[50]

David Page argues in a recent study that it was primarily the working of dyarchy, particularly in the Muslim majority provinces, namely, Punjab and Bengal, which proved crucial in the rise of Hindu-Muslim tension. Under this scheme of dyarchy, introduced under the Montagu-Chelmsford reforms, some departments such as local government, agriculture, education, etc., were transferred to the control of ministers responsible to the legislature. This intensified competition for power between different sections of the elite and the council chamber became a battle ground "between those who had access to transferred subjects and those who did not".[51] It is also significant to note that the Muslims (particularly, the rural Muslims) had larger share of seats in the legislature, but the government retained balance of power in its own hands through the nominated members who constituted 30 percent of the total strength. Under the circumstances, the success of a minister depended both on the goodwill of the rural Muslim members and the government. Fazl-i-Husain, who was appointed minister of education and self-government, enjoyed the goodwill both of the Muslim members and the British government nominees in the legislature. With such support in the legislature, it became quite easy for Fazl-i-Husain to introduce various measures favouring Muslims in the province. This policy was strongly resented by some urban Hindus and Sikhs who saw in it an attempt to establish 'domination of Muslims' in Punjab.[52] They organised a number of meetings to protest against the partisan pro-Muslim decisions. Their strong feeling at this stage was that the system of separate communal representation needed to be replaced by joint electorate since this alone would work as a check on persons like Fazl-i-Husain.[53] The Muslim leadership, however, was not prepared to yield to this kind of pressure. The Muslim League, at its session in 1924, reiterated its original position demanding that the separate communal electorates be retained in the Muslim majority provinces, that is, Punjab and Bengal.

Under these conditions, some Hindu members of the Congress in Punjab, including Lajpat Rai, were convinced that it was essential to protest against the policies of the education minister and to raise strong voice against the statutory majority being enjoyed by the Muslims in the Punjab Legislative Council. They had strong apprehension that the Congress leadership at the national level including Mahatma Gandhi might reach an agreement with the Muslim League ignoring the interest of minorities in Punjab. They were also highly sceptical about the outcome of the unity conference being organised by the Congress to diffuse the increasing communal tension. Lajpat Rai even went to the extent of alleging that Gandhi did not properly take up the cause of Hindu victims of the riot which took place at Kohat in 1924.[54] Some Hindus Congress members of Punjab developed a strong belief that the Congress as an organisation was unable to protect the Hindus against the growing power of the Muslims in the society and politics of the province. Moreover, the working of the Punjab Legislative Council also convinced them that the Swarajists' programme of obstructing its proceedings was rather harming the interests of the Hindus.[55] Therefore, persons like Lajpat Rai decided to quit the Swaraj Party and joined Madan Mohan Malaviya's Independent Congress Party which claimed to work both for the "interest of Hindus" and the nationalist movement.

The decline of the Swaraj Party became quite evident from the fact that it could secure only two seats in the elections of the Punjab Legislative Council held in 1926. On the other hand, its opponent, Independent Congress Party won nine seats.[56] It is important to note that there was not much difference between the two parties as both intended to capitalise on the fear of 'Muslim dominance' in Punjab politics. Both the parties projected themselves as defenders of 'Hindu interests' with a view to winning over the goodwill of Hindu urban middle class voters.[57] The Swarajists did not make much efforts to strengthen the position of the party among the Muslims and for all practical purposes it was largely a body of Hindu middle classes and a small number of Sikhs in Punjab. On the other hand, the Independent Congress Party included both Hindu communitarian nationalists as well as Hindu comunalists.[58] It is significant, however, that the communitarian nationalists never gave up their ideological commitment to the national movement and preferred to remain within the Congress, as and when the contingency arose. For instance, when the appointment of Simon Commission was announced, Hindu communitarian nationlists like Lajpat Rai took active part in the agitation against it and strongly criticised all those who were favourably inclined towards the Commission.[59] In other words, the communtarian nationalists had no hesitation in going along with the secular nationalists. This explains their effective intervention in the recommendation of the Nehru Committee appointed by the all parties conference in 1928. It was under the pressure of such communitarian nationalists (who were also working within the Congress) that the Nehru Report refused to agree to the Muslim League's demand of statutory majority for the Muslims in the Punjab legislature.[60] In other words, the

Congress in Punjab carried both the secular nationalists as well as communitarian nationalists within its fold and both sections, despite their differences over the issue of Muslims, were always ready to join hands against the colonial rule.

IV

The Congress in Punjab faced strong opposition from the Unionist Party which was formed in 1923 as the main political organisation to represent the interests of the agriculturists in the province. The leaders of the Unionist Party—Fazl-i-Husain and Chhotu Ram—always asserted that all agriculturists irrespective of socio-economic differentiation within them formed a distinct social group having identical interests. The origins, ideological programme and the political activities of the Unionist party have been much explored by now. This party believed in collaboration with the Raj and its primary objective was to safeguard mainly the interests of rich and middle peasantry of the province.[61] Its constant effort was to project the non-agriculturists, that is, moneylenders and urban middle classes as the main enemy of peasantry in Punjab. It is through this ideological campaign based on rural-urban divide (which was also the central point in the strategy of the colonial state in Punjab), that the Unionist Party tried to maintain its hegemonic dominance over the rural society.[62] It painted the Congress as a champion of the interests of the moneylenders and other urban middle classes. The Unionists also resorted to the use of caste and community in their campaign against the Congress. In south-east Punjab, Chhotu Ram used the ideology of Jat caste to retain hold over the large section of peasantry and to prevent them form coming under the influence of the Congress. On the other hand, the Muslim leadership of the Unionist Party maintained their strong sway in the countryside by invoking the idiom of tribal fraternity and by aligning themselves with the local *Pirs* who had immense religious authority over their Muslim rural society. Besides, the Muslim leadership of the Unionist Party often indulged in propaganda saying that the Congress was above all a Hindu organisation which was primarily interested in the welfare of Hindu moneylending class and propertied sections of the urban society. The Unionists' ignored the primary contradiction between British imperialism and the Indian people, by highlighting antagonism between agriculturists and non-agriculturists.[63] Since this ideological programme of the Unionist Party converged with the colonial interest, the British government gave it all support to weaken the nationalist forces spearheaded by the Congress in the province.[64] In such circumstances, the Congress in Punjab could not effectively expand its social base in the rural society and Gandhi's constructive programme such as khadi did not evoke much response in Punjab's villages.

The Civil Disobedience Movement was started by Mahatma Gandhi in 1930. The Congress' efforts at that time to expand its social base by enrolling new members failed to produce favourable results.[65] It carried the mass struggle as decided by the AICC, after constituting a War Council, which included representatives from different sections of society. Factional disputes within the Congress were temporarily pushed into the background. The movement was strong in Lahore, Amritsar and some other towns of central Punjab, but it was weak in Multan and Rawalpindi of the north-west region.[66] In rural areas, the Gandhian movement was successful in those parts of central and eastern Punjab where the Congress had established its organisational structure effectively. The Unionist Party opposed the Congress by using all tactics against the movement. In the south-east Punjab, for instance, Chhotu Ram carried anti-Congress propaganda in the countryside warning that non-payment of land revenue would provide opportunity to the government to confiscate their lands.[67] The Unionist landlords kept tight control over the Muslim peasants by a campaign against the Congress. On the whole, the majority of people who took part in this movement were Hindus and Sikhs living in the cities, and the participation of the Muslims remained negligible.

The politics of the Congress in Punjab underwent a major transformation following the announcement of the Communal Award in August 1932. The Award retained the system of separate communal electorates on the ground that it was needed to protect the interest of the minorities. It also provided statutory majority to the Muslims in legislative councils of Punjab and Bengal. It seems that the British government prepared this scheme partly to counter the Civil Disobedience Movement which Gandhi had resumed in early 1932.[68] Indeed the Award was welcomed by large sections of Muslims, but the Hindus, particularly of Punjab and Bengal, were unhappy with it as it reduced them to permanent minority in the legislatures. The Congress was opposed to the Award since the whole scheme was contrary to the national interests. Its working committee, however, resolved that the Congress would neither accept nor reject the Award as there was strong division among the communities on this issue. The provincial Congress had no alternative but to accept the decision of the AICC on the Award. The stand taken by the AICC was however resented by some of the local Congress members belonging to the Hindu and Sikh minorities in Punjab. They even participated in the conferences and meetings organised in the province to denounce the Award. Outside Punjab, Madan Mohan Malaviya was strongly opposed to the position taken by the Congress. He criticised the AICC when the latter directed the Congressmen not to vote against the Award in the legislatures and abstain from making representations against it to the British government. In Punjab, Gopi Chand Bhargava and his associates who had earlier developed Hindu communitarian-nationalist perspective joined Congress Nationalist Party formed by Madan Mohan Malaviya to oppose the Congress in the forthcoming elections to the Central Legislative Assembly in 1934. The Congress Nationalist Party won three out of four seats in Punjab, which clearly established that the stand taken by the Congress was not acceptable to the upper and middle class Hindus in this province.[69]

The Congress tried its best to revive its position in Punjab when the elections of the provincial legislature were held under the Government of India Act of 1935. Of course, the Congress at the all-India level rejected the Act in its entirety, but it also took the decision to contest the elections in the provinces "in order to combat the government from inside and outside the legislature and render it inoperative". The Congress Party's manifesto, which was prepared by Jawaharlal Nehru underlined its commitment to the goal of achieving complete independence and promised radical economic measures including land reforms for peasants and tenants.[70] Actually, the elections provided a solid opportunity to the nationalist leadership through their rallies, pamphlets, etc., to erode the colonial hegemony and to counter the politics of collaboration being followed by the upper classes particularly the Unionists for safeguarding their vested interests. The Congress socialists strongly favoured an alliance with all those parties, which were anti-imperialist in nature.

The Congress in Punjab continued to suffer from local problems and internal rivalries. As mentioned above, there was bitter resentment among the urban Hindus on the issue of Communal Award and the position taken by the Congress camp in Punjab. When the Congress President, Jawaharlal Nehru conveyed to the provincial Congress in Bengal, the party's latest decision concerning the rejection of the Award,[71] it pacified the Hindu communitarian natinalists headed by Gopi Chand Bhargava. Similarly, the Sikhs too felt satisfied with the amended stand of the Congress. In such conditions, the provincial Congress found itself in a better position to contest the forthcoming elections. Some of the Muslim associates of the Congress expressed their unhappiness on its changed position in the case of the Award. They alleged that the Congress succumbed to the pressure of the Hindu communal elements. However, the Congress succeeded in forming a broad alliance with all those who were anti-imperialist in nature. In particular, it contested election in collaboration with the Shrimoni Akali Dal and the socialists. As expected, the Congress was successful largely in urban areas and it over all secured 19 out of 175 seats of the Punjab Legislative Assembly. However the Congress and its allies formed a group of 40 members and worked as an effective opposition in the house.[72] They took up all those issues, which strengthened the cause of the nationalist movement in Punjab. It supported the premier's decision to convene the unity conference, but strongly condemned the pact of Sikander Hayat Khan with Jinnah (1937).[73]

The provincial Congress found itself in a very delicate situation when the Unionist ministry introduced certain agrarian bills particularly favouring the rich section of the peasantry. Some of these measures were indeed detrimental to the interest of the money lending classes. There was strong criticism of these bills both within the legislature and outside. A section of the press particularly representing the Hindu viewpoint took a communal position saying that these bills were meant to favour the Muslim peasantry against the Hindu moneylending classes. The Congress leadership in the province could not reject these bills out-rightly since the party at the national level was committed to work for improving the conditions of the peasantry in the country. This, however, did not prevent some local Congress members to express their resentment over these measures of the Punjab government. For instance, Satyapal criticised the bills on the ground that these would not give sufficient relief to the poor peasants and tenants as the Unionist government was more interested in the welfare of upper sections of the peasantry. However, he did not support those Hindus and Sikhs who described the bills as 'pro-Muslim'. Gopi Chand Bhargava, on the other hand, took the position in favour of the Hindu urban traders and moneylenders. He suggested the members of the provincial Congress to join in their individual capacity the Non Agriculturist Association which was formed by Gokul Chand Narang as a representative of the Hindu traders and moneylenders to oppose the bills. This kind of position taken by a section of the Congress leadership indeed alienated some of the Muslim members within the Punjab Congress. For instance, Mohammad Alam, the deputy leader in the Assembly decided to resign saying that the Congress in the province was no better than the Hindu Mahasabha.[74]

At the national level, the Congress was desperately trying to establish its credibility as a secular organisation. Jawaharlal Nehru disapproved the formation of the government in UP in collaboration with the Muslim League in 1937 on the ground that the latter represented communal and vested interested in the country. At the same time, the Congress commenced a mass contact programme to mobilise the Muslim masses in its favour. This programme failed in its objective as large number of Muslims in UP and Punjab did not enthusiastically respond to the Congress.[75] In 1938, the Congress, in order to underline its secular character decided to put a ban on the members of both Muslim

League and Hindu Mahasabha to join or remain associated with it. These two bodies were now clearly viewed as communal organisations.[76] On the other hand, since the recent activities and programme of the Congress posed a serious threat to these communal organisations, both adopted highly aggressive attitude towards it. The Hindu Mahasabha, which recently changed its creed and became an ardent champion of 'Hindu nation', decried secularism of the Congress on the ground that it was merely a strategy to appease the Muslims at the cost of the majority community. Simultaneously, the Muslim League also carried a virulent campaign against the Congress alleging that the latter was above all a 'Hindu organisation'.[77] Though the Congress claimed to be committed to secularism, yet a section of its members were associated with the Hindu communal elements in the Muslim majority provinces, both Bengal and Punjab.[78] When the Muslim League came out with the demand of separate state of Pakistan and it started gripping the imagination of the Muslim masses, many of these Hinduised Congress members in Punjab began to feel that the idea of a unified nation was more a myth than a reality.

V

The Congress was again engaged in a confrontation with the British government following the outbreak of the Second World War in 1939. The Viceroy, Lord Linlithgow had unilaterally announced that India being a part of the British empire was also associated in the war against Germany. The Congress would not agree to support the British in the war if India was not granted independence. The offer made by Linlithgow in this regard did not satisfy the Congress leadership. As a result, the Congress ministries resigned in the provinces to protest against the decision taken by the Viceroy. After a lot of hesitation, the Congress under the leadership of Gandhi decided to launch individual Civil Disobedience Movement against the colonial state with a "limited and deliberately ineffective programme".[79] A number of important persons were selected to court arrest by making speeches against the war. In Punjab, the Congress leader, Iftakhar-ud-Din, initiated the individual *satyagraha* by offering himself for arrest. The total number of Congress men arrested in this movement from Punjab was more than 2000.[80] But, the movement was not well organised because of internal rivalries and factionalism within the Congress. Akalis' participation in the movement was more symbolic than real. In fact, they openly supported recruitment of the Sikhs in the army since this was seen as an important avenue for employment. Besides, the Akalis expected this pro-recruitment stance would keep the Sikh community relevant for the empire.[81] Even then, a number of Sikhs participated in this movement. On the whole, the movement was strong only in the cities of eastern and central Punjab. By the middle of 1941, however, this movement was almost over in Punjab as in other parts of the country.

Mahatma Gandhi launched a more powerful struggle in the form of Quit India Movement in August 1942. The situation of the war underwent a major change when the Japanese joined it against the allied powers. Japan sent its forces towards South-East Asia and also posed a danger for the British empire in India. The Churchill government in England under the American pressure sent Cripps Mission to India to recommend some constitutional changes with the object of softening the opposition to the war efforts by the Congress and some other elements in the country. But, the Cripps proposals failed to satisfy the Congress demands and the latter resolved to start a mass struggle under the leadership of Mahatma Gandhi. The government from the very beginning adopted suppressive policy. The Congress leaders including Gandhi were immediately arrested. In Punjab too, the leading Congress members were put behind the bars and the Congress was declared an illegal organisation. In such circumstances, the movement went underground and the enraged mobs sometime resorted to actions, which did not fit into the Gandhian programme of non-violence.[82] There were incidents of attack on railways and other government property which represented symbols of British authority. The people in urban areas appeared more enthusiastic in their participation. On the other hand, the rural population remained comparatively quiet in Punjab. The Unionist government which was supporting the British war effort took extra care to maintain peace and ruthlessly suppressed anti-British activities in the countryside. The communists' opposition of this Gandhian movement also prevented peasants in the central Punjab from participating in it. On the other hand, the Akalis' attitude towards the Congress was vacillating and they took little interest in the Quit India Movement. In fact, they were practically a part of the Unionist government as Baldev Singh had joined the ministry after an agreement with Sikander Hyat Khan. As a result, the participation of the Sikh peasantry in the movement was checked to some extent.[83] The involvement of the Punjabi Muslims in the movement was almost negligible since the activities of the Congress did not interest them. Yet it would be wrong to conclude that the whole of peasantry in Punjab remained away from the movement. In fact, some lower sections of the peasantry were active in central and eastern parts of Punjab. However, the Quit India Movement in Punjab almost petered out by the middle of 1943.

The more serious issue for the provincial Congress at this stage was the demand of Pakistan raised by the Muslim League. Since early 1942, Jinnah's endeavour had been to strengthen the position of the Muslim League in the Muslim majority provinces of Punjab and Bengal. In fact, by this time the Muslim League had gained considerable weight in Indian politics and this encouraged Jinnah to directly intervene in these provinces. In Punjab, he activated the Muslim League immediately after the death of Sikander Hayat Khan in December 1942. The new premier, Khizar Hayat Khan, found it extremely difficult to resist the expansionists pressures of the League and his position became quite vulnerable. Actually the Muslim League's idea of a unified Islamic community aspiring to be an independent separate 'nation' slowly gripped the imagination of the Muslims particularly in the western parts of Punjab where as stated earlier the Congress had failed to extend its influence. This of course led to the weakening and eventual disintegration of the Unionist Party in the closing years before the partition. Indeed, under the circumstances, the Muslim League in Punjab emerged as the main representative body of the Muslims. A large section of the Muslims were gradually carried by the propaganda that the Congress was a Hindu organisation in the province.[84] What is important here is that the provincial Congress leadership could not do much to remove this impression. In other words, the Congress' commitment to secularism appeared doubtful in Punjab.

The spectre of Pakistan was haunting large number of Hindus and Sikhs in the province. Within the Sikhs, the Akalis also came out with proposals such as Azad Punjab state and separate Sikh state primarily to counter and weaken the demand of Pakistan.[85] As stated above, their relations with the Congress were not cordial in Punjab at this stage. But they were committed to the cause of Indian nationalism and were not willing to dissociate with the Congress at the national level.[86] They felt seriously perturbed over the role of the Congress when Rajagopalachari came with his formula to resolve the issue of separate state for the Muslims. The Congress in Punjab had significant following in the Sikh community and would not like to give up their cause. In fact, the provincial Congress leadership was convinced that the scheme of Pakistan posed a serious threat to the very existence of the Sikh and Hindu minorities and therefore needed to be opposed at all levels. In such conditions, some Hindu and Sikh Congress members in the province with strong communitarian consciousness tended to move towards a sectarian view of the Muslim community as their 'enemy'. Under the conditions, the Congress in Punjab appeared as the leading 'non-Muslim' organization which alone could provide security to the minorities against the growing forces of Muslim communalism. In particular, a large number of Hindu peasants in the south-east Punjab moved towards the Congress after the death of Chhotu Ram in 1945.[87] The Congress was no more seen by them as an organisation of urban moneylenders alone. The Unionist ideology based on urban-rural divide appeared irrelevant to the Hindu peasants under the changed conditions. Moreover, some Hindu conservatives shifted their allegiance to the Congress for another reason. The radical content in the movement led by the Congress at the national level had considerably declined by this time. Under the changed conditions, the negotiations with the British rulers for the transfer of power became the main issue on its agenda. Within the party, there was a growing influence of the right wing and some Congress leaders under the fear of popular upsurge in the post-World War II period became committed to the path of negotiations and compromise. In Punjab, the conservatives felt more secure since Jawaharlal Nehru's socialist programme for which he vigorously campaigned a decade ago was not at present on the primary agenda of the Congress. As a result, the conservative Hindus did not find any inconvenience in moving towards the Congress when polarisation on communal lines was on the rise.

Therefore, the social base of the Congress had considerably expanded in the post-war phase. This phenomenon is evident from the fact that in this province the Congress won 51 seats in the assembly elections held in 1946. It was certainly a remarkable success in comparison with 1937 elections when the Congress had secured only 19 seats.[88] This success is explained in terms of the nationalist wave that was fast blowing in central and south-east Punjab after the return of large number of INA soldiers to their villages. As stated above, the end of the British rule appeared certain to large sections of people and they looked towards the Congress with lots of hope and aspirations. However, the Congress at this stage was practically an organisation of the Hindus and Sikhs in this province. Its following among the Muslims in this area was almost negligible. In 1946 elections, the Congress President, Maulana Daud Ghazanivi was the only Muslim who secured the east Punjab labour seat. But he too left the Congress soon on communal grounds and joined the Muslim League.[89] A large number of Muslims in Punjab were convinced by this time that the Congress only represented the interests of non-Muslims and was the main hurdle in the achievement of Pakistan.

Indeed, the Congress in Punjab was facing serious challenge from the Muslim League, which had considerably strengthened itself by extending its social base among the Muslim peasantry in particular. The League won 73 of the total 84 Muslim seats in 1946 elections of the Punjab Legislative Assembly whereas in 1937 it had just secured two seats. But, despite such a massive success, Muslim League was not able to form the government as it did not have sufficient number in the legislature. As a result, a coalition government comprising of the Congress, the Akalis and the Unionists was formed under the leadership of Khizar Hayat Khan.

But, due to the deteriorating communal situation in the province, the new government could not survive for long. Khizar decided to quit the office on 3 March, 1947. Punjab now came under the direct control of the Governor but the communal violence escalated following the announcement of Lord Mountbatten regarding partition of the country. Undoubtedly, the provincial Congress was opposed to the partition. But, the basic position of the local Congress leadership was that if the demand of Pakistan was accepted its endeavour would be to ensure the division of the province with a view to safeguarding the interests of the Hindu and Sikh minorities. Here, it is important to mention that unlike Gandhi who had personally gone to Noakhali risking his life to restore communal harmony, the Congress leadership in Punjab did not do much to check the escalation of violence. On the contrary, there is sufficient evidence to show that some Hindu Congress members secretly or otherwise joined hands with the workers of Hindu Mahasabha and the RSS workers against the Muslims in the communal riots. Actually they became communal to such a degree that the difference between them and the RSS workers was blurred and practically obliterated in 1947 Punjab.[90] Yet, at the national level, the Congress under the leadership of Mahatma Gandhi and Jawaharlal Nehru was committed to follow the principle of secularism in independent India.

Notes

1. See Anil Seal, *The Emergence of Indian Nationalism: Competition and Collaboration in the Later Nineteenth Century*, Cambridge, 1968.
2. For a recent debate on the emergence of nationalism, see E.J. Hobsbawm, *Nations and Nationalism Since 1870*, Cambridge, 1990.
3. Bipan Chandra, "The Long-Term Dynamics of Indian Nationalist Movement", *Proceedings of the Indian History Congress*, Amritsar Session, 1985, p. 5.

4. Bhagwan Josh, *Communist Movement in Punjab,* Delhi: Anupama, 1978, p. 2. Also see Gaukovasky, Yu. V., *The Peoples of Pakistan: An Ethnic History,* Moscow, 1971; Mustapha Kamal Pasha, *Colonial Political Economy,* Karachi, 1998.
5. See Imran Ali, *The Punjab Under Imperialism,* New Delhi: Oxford University Press, 1989.
6. For instance, at the turn of the twentieth century, an average 840 thousand tons of wheat and wheat flour was exported to England. *Punjab Census Report*, 1921, part 1, p. 20.
7. Ian Talbot, *Punjab and The Raj,* New Delhi: Manohar Publications, 1988, pp. 41-46.
8. For the repressive policy followed by the colonial state in Punjab particularly during the First World War, see Michael O' Dweyer, *India As I Knew It,* London, 1925.
9. Ian Talbot (1988), pp. 48-64.
10. See N.G. Barrier, *The Punjab Land Alienation of Land Bill of 1900* (Duke University, n.d.).
11. Ian Talbot, *op. cit.*, p. 57.
12. Virinder Singh, *Dyarchy in Punjab,* New Delhi, 1991, Chapter II.
13. See Prem Choudhry, *Punjab Politics: The Role of Sir Chhotu Ram,* Delhi, 1984.
14. H. Calvert, *The Wealth and Welfare of the Punjab*, Lahore, 1936, pp. 102-48; J.S. Grewal, "Business Communities in Punjab", Dwijendra Tripathi (ed.), *Business Communities in India,* New Delhi, 1984, pp. 209-23.
15. Amiya K. Bagchi, *Private Investment in India,* London, 1976, p.436. For industrial growth in Punjab, see H. Calvert, *op. cit.*; A.C. Badnech *Punjab Industries,* Lahore, 1917.
16. Richard Fox, "Urban Class and Communal Consciousness in Colonial Punjab: The Genesis of India's Intermediate Regime", *Modern Asian Studies*, 18, 3, 1984, pp. 459-89.
17. See H.R. Mehta, *A History of the Growth and Development of Western Education in the Punjab,* 1846-1884, Lahore, 1929.
18. Among the urban Hindus, the increase in literacy was at a high rate. For instance, in 1891 they accounted for 89 percent of the total literates in Punjab. N.G. Barrier, *Punjab Politics and the*

Disturbances of 1907, Ph.D. Thesis, Duke University, 1966, pp. 16-17; Kenneth W. Jones, *Arya Dharm: Hindu Consciousness in the Nineteenth Century Punjab,* New Delhi, 1975, pp. 59-60.

19. Azim Husain, *Fazl-i-Husain: A Political Biography*, Bombay, 1946, p. 71.
20. Gopal Krishna, "The Development of Indian National Congress as a Mass Organisation, 1918-1923", *Journal of Asian Studies,* XXV, 3, May 1966, pp. 413-30.
21. A.M. Zaidi and S.G. Zaidi (eds.), *The Encyclopaedia of the Indian National Congress,* Vol. 2, 1891-1895, New Delhi, 1977, pp. 245-46. See also *Idem,* Vol. 3, 1896-1900, New Delhi, 1977, pp. 499-502.
22. For instance, when the Congress session took place in Lahore in 1909, the number of delegates from Punjab was merely 76 where as in 1893 their strength was 421. Annie Besant, *How India Wrought for Freedom,* Adyar, 1915, p. 162, 311 and 491.
23. See Lal Chand, *Self Abnegation in Politics,* Lahore, 1939.
24. Duni Chand, *The Ulster of India,* Lahore, 1936.
25. Gopal Krishna, *op. cit.*
26. N.G. Barrier and Paul Wallace, *The Punjab Press, 1880-1905* (Monograph), Michigan State University, 1970.
27. Kenneth W. Jones, *op. cit.*, pp.280-30; N.G. Barrier, "The Arya Samaj and Congress Politics in Punjab 1894-1908", *Journal of Asian Studies*, 1, 26 (1966-67), pp.365-77.
28. For details, see K.L. Tuteja, "Hindu Consciousness, Communalism and the Congress in Pre-Partition Punjab", *Proceedings of the Indian History Congress* (Bangalore session, 1997), pp.425-73.
29. Ravinder Kumar, *Essays in the Social History of Modern Indian,* New Delhi, 1983, pp. 47-48.
30. For instance, at its session of 1900 held at Lahore, the Congress decided not to take up the issue of Land Alienation Bill because it feared that such a step would alienate a section of Muslims in Punjab.
31. K.L. Tuteja, *op. cit.*
32. Toufique Kitchlew, *Saif-ud-Din Kitchlew,* New Delhi, 1987; p.11; K.L. Tuteja, *op. cit.*

33. This aspect was quite evident in the peasant struggle that took place in Punjab in 1907. See Shyamala Bhatia, *Social Change and Politics in Punjab, 1898-1910,* New Delhi, 1987.
34. Harish K. Puri, *Ghadar Movement: Ideology, Organisation and Strategy,* Amritsar: Guru Nanak Dev University Press, 1993.
35. Satya M. Rai, *Legislative Politics and the Freedom Struggle in Punjab,* Delhi, 1984.
36. Thomas Metcalf, *The New Cambridge History of India: Ideologies of the Raj,* New Delhi, 1995, p.288.
37. Michael O'Dwyer, *op. cit.*
38. *The Tribune,* 9 January, 1919.
39. K.L. Tuteja, "Jallianwala Bagh: A Critical Juncture in the Indian National Movement", *Social Scientist,* Vol.25, Nos.1-2, January-February1997.
40. *Ibid*; Home Political File, Deposit, October 1919, No.28 , National Archives of India.
41. *Home Political B,* January, 1920, No.513 (NAI).
42. K.L. Tuteja, 1997; M.K. Gandhi, *An Autobiography Or My Experiments with Truth,* Ahmadabad, 1927, p.349.
43. Gopal Krishna, *op. cit.*
44. Sumit Sarkar, *Modern India* (1885-1947), New Delhi, 1983, p.210; See also, S.L. Malhotra, *Gandhi and the Punjab,* Chandigarh, 1970.
45. Sumit Sarkar, *op. cit.*, p.206.
46. See Mushirul Hasan, *Nationalism and Communal Politics in India 1885-1930,* New Delhi, 1994; G. Minault, *The Khilafat Movement: Religious Symbolism and Political Mobilization in India,* Columbia University Press, 1982.
47. See David Gilmartin, *Empire and Islam: Punjab and the Making of Pakistan,* London, 1988.
48. See K.L. Tuteja, *Sikh Politics,* 1920-40, Kurukshetra, 1984; Mohinder Singh, *Akali Movement,* New Delhi, 1978.
49. Sohan Singh Josh, *Akali Morchon ka Itihas,* in Hindi, Delhi, 1975.
50. G.R. Thursby, *Hindu-Muslim Relations in British India,* London, 1975, pp. 72-177.

51. David Page, *Prelude to Partition,* Delhi, 1982, pp.30-72.
52. *The Tribune*, 8 March, 1923.
53. K.L. Tuteja (1997).
54. V.C. Joshi (ed.), *Lala Lajpat Rai, Writings and Speeches*, Vol. II, Delhi, 1966, pp. 170-220.
55. *Ibid.*
56. K.C. Yadav, *Elections in Punjab,* Delhi, 1987, pp.52-66.
57. See Dunichand (1936).
58. Statement of Raja Narendra Nath in *Hailey Papers* (India Office Library, London) No.MSS/EVR/E/220/9A.
59. V.C. Joshi, 1966, pp.299-322.
60. Mushir-ul-Hasan, 1994, pp.279-81. See also Uma Kaura, *Muslims and Indian Nationalism,* Delhi, 1977.
61. See Prem Choudhary, 1984.
62. *Ibid.*
63. *Ibid.*
64. See Ian Talbot, 1988.
65. Judith M. Brown, *Gandhi and Civil Disobedience,* Cambridge, 1977, p.52.
66. S.L. Malhotra, *From Civil Disobedience to Quit India,* Chandigarh, 1979.
67. See Prem Choudhry, 1984.
68. *File no. 174/32-R&KW, Reform Office* (NAI); Viceroy to Secretary of State 21 March, 1932, *Templewood Papers* (Nehru Memorial Museum Library, New Delhi).
69. K.L. Tutuja, 1997.
70. S. Gopal, *Jawaharlal Nehru: A Biography,* Delhi, 1993, pp.108-15.
71. Letter of Jawaharlal Nehru to Bengal Provincial Congress Committee, cited in Satya M. Rai (1984) p.218.
72. See K.L. Tuteja (1984); Harmohinder Singh, "The Congress in Punjab Politics and Elections of 1937" in *Proceedings of the Punjab History Congress,* Patiala, 1979, pp.271-76.
73. K.L. Tuteja (1984); Satya M. Rai (1984) pp.215-77.
74. G.A. Heeger, "The Growth of the Congress Movement in Punjab", *Journal of Asian Studies*, XXXII, I (1972).

75. Mushirul Hasan, "The Muslim Mass Contact Campaign: Analysis of a Strategy of Political Mobilization" in Mushirul Hasan (ed.), *India's Partition: Process, Strategy and Mobilization,* Delhi, 1984, pp.133-59.
76. See Ashok Mehta and Achyut Patwardhan, *The Communal Triangle in India.*
77. See Anita Inder Singh, *The Origins of the Partition of India, 1936-47*, Delhi, 1987.
78. K.L. Tuteja, 1997; Zoya Chatterjee, *Bengal Divided: Hindu Communalism and Partition, 1932-47,* Cambridge, 1995.
79. Sumit Sarkar, 1983, p.381.
80. S.L. Malhotra, 1979, pp.102-39.
81. For details on the issue of recruitment policy of the Akalis, see K.L. Tuteja, 1984.
82. *Home Political File: Fortnightly Reports,* Oct.1942, NAI; Sumit Sarkar (1983), pp.388-408.
83. S.L. Malhotra, 1979, pp.141-61.
84. See Ayesha Jalal, *The Sole Spokesman: Jinnah, the Muslim League and the Demand of Pakistan,* Cambridge, 1985: Ian Talbot, *Khizr Tiwana: The Unionist Party and the Partition of India*, Richmond, 1996; see also, D. Gilmartin, *op. cit.*
85. J.S. Grewal, *The New Cambridge History of India: The Sikhs of the Punjab,* Cambridge: Cambridge University Press, 1990, pp.157-80.
86. For this view, see Sukhmani Bal, *Sikh Politics, 1937-47,* unpublished Ph.D. thesis, Jawaharlal Nehru University, 1996.
87. Prem Choudhry, *op. cit.*
88. *The Tribune*, February 24, 1946.
89. *Home Political File: Fortnightly Reports*, July 1946.
90. *AICC File No. CL-9, 1946-47* (Nehru Memorial Museum and Library).

9

Ad Dharm Movement

MARK JUERGENSMEYER

It is a rare moment in history when marginal groups perceive that they have the opportunity to advance their role within society—or even to reconceive it altogether. The 1920s provided such an occasion for Punjab's Scheduled Castes. An ambitious circle of activists within this community reached out and utilised a resource for mobilisation that is often available for the poor and the socially marginal in the absence of more tangible means for achieving change: religion. This is the story of the 'original religion' they created—Ad Dharm.[1]

The early twentieth century was a time of change throughout India as the colonial government, defensive in the face of rising anti-British sentiment, was open to new alliances from below. At the same time the emerging Indian National Congress desperately needed lower caste support. Both groups vied with each other to provide incentives for the untouchables, and new Scheduled Caste movements emerged throughout India in response.

Punjab presented a particularly volatile form of social politics due to a roughly equal distribution of upper caste Sikhs, Hindus, and Muslims. Each group comprised a fourth of the population, with untouchables of whatever religious identification providing the crucial remaining quarter. The innovation of provincial elections in 1920 exacerbated this competition and spawned new political parties: the Unionist—spokesman of Muslim landed interests, and the Sikhs' Akali Dal. Foreign missionaries spreading Christianity were entering the last phase of their mass expansions, and the urban Hindu reform movement, the Arya Samaj, turned its attention increasingly to the problems of numbers, the census, and elections for legislative councils.

Politics were in the air. Cadres of the revolutionary movement, the Ghadar Party, formed by expatriate Indians in California who returned to Punjab, and violent anti-British Sikh activists, the Babbar Akalis, roamed through the villages. The Congress non-cooperation movement had begun, and Gandhi's tour of Punjab in 1921 received enthusiastic crowds. The nationalist newspapers, the *Punjabee* and the *Tribune*, nurtured a growing nationalist elite. It was a time for political opportunity and change, one especially ripe for ambitious members of Punjab's Scheduled Castes.

Mangoo Ram and the Founding Circle

In the early 1920s a handful of educated young untouchable activists began meeting together in Jalandhar to discuss the possibilities of political organisation. At the heart of the group were Vasant Rai, Thakar Chand, and a Swami Shudrananad (also known as Vasant Singh, Thakar Das, and Shiv Charan).[2] These three came from central Punjab's new affluent leather-working caste, the Chamars, whose tanning and boot-making businesses had boomed with government army contracts. With their relative wealth came new educational opportunities—thanks in part to schooling provided by the Arya Samaj.

The Arya Samaj had provided young untouchables with ideas of social equality not only by allowing them to attend its schools but also by creating service organisations such as the Dayanand Dalit Udhar at Hoshiarpur and the Achhut Udhar at Lahore. These movements for the uplift of untouchables spawned even more radical movements, in part because of a growing disillusionment with the paternalistic attitudes of the groups' upper caste benefactors. The Jat Pat Torak Mandal (Society for the Abolition of Caste), for example, was organised within the Arya

Samaj in 1922 by Sant Ram, but split from it in 1924. Punjab's new Muslim movement—the Ahmadiya sect—is also said to have encouraged untouchables to leave the Arya Samaj.[3]

Swami Shudranand, influenced both by radical Arya Samajis and Ahmadiyas, gave a firebrand speech in a Chamar neighbourhood of Jalandhar city in 1925, calling for mobilisation and action. Following the speech, the first group of activists came together to begin discussing what might be done.[4] Other meetings followed—one lasted for four days and ended only when upper caste men in the area attacked the participants for utilising the village pond.

The most significant new member to be recruited into these conversations was a young Chamar who had recently returned from travels abroad and had become something of a folk hero—Mangoo Ram. On returning he had created a small school near his home in village Mugowal in Hoshiarpur district, and it was there that the Ad Dharm movement had its first official meeting on June 11 and 12, 1926. Mangoo Ram was elected president of the organisation, a title he never relinquished throughout the movement's history, and to a large extent the Ad Dharm movement reflected his values and aspirations.

Mangoo Ram was in some ways characteristic of his generation of activist Chamars: bright, young, educated, and financially independent. His father had developed a flourishing trade in raw hides for the leather market. Despite these assets, however, Mangoo Ram was still regarded by upper caste society as an untouchable. When he attended elementary school he was not allowed inside the building. He had to squat in the doorway to listen to the teacher's lessons. Even so, he graduated with the second highest marks.[5] He decided to look elsewhere for opportunities, and did what few of his caste fellows were able to do at that time—journey abroad.

When Mangoo Ram was 23 years old his father arranged through a labour contractor to have him work in America and send money home. Part of the money for the passage was paid up front, the rest to be reimbursed to the labor contractor when Mangoo Ram began working. In 1909, he arrived in California and was sent to the fruit orchards of Fresno and other parts of the state's central valley. It was in California that Mangoo Ram became associated with a newly created movement for India's independence—the Ghadar Party. He accompanied a boatload of weapons sent by the party from San Diego to India, where it was to be used in what was hoped to be a revolutionary uprising. The rebellion was foiled, however, by British agents, and Mangoo Ram's boat was captured in the Philippines. He escaped, and by 1925 he had managed to work his way back to India where he received Arya Samaj support to open a school for Scheduled Caste children in his home village. It was this school, and Mangoo Ram's revolutionary leadership, that would be the base for the radical new political religion of untouchables—Ad Dharm.

The Ideology of a Political Religion

In their initial meetings, Mangoo Ram and his colleagues surveyed their potential bases of influence and concluded that they had only three resources: *qaumiat* (communal pride), *mazhab* (religion), and *majlis* (organisation).[6] These were embryonic sources of power, however: the organisation had to be created, the communal pride had to be brought to consciousness, and the religious ideas had to be articulated in such a way to reveal their social strength.

The group laboured over creating an ideological theme on which they could build a political organisation. The social politics of Punjab suggested that the untouchables should think of themselves as a community—*a qaum*—similar to Muslims, Sikhs, and Hindus. The rise of *adi* (original) movements around India at the time suggested a historical feature of this community: that it was a modern manifestation of the original people of India. This idea, which would later be treated at length by Dr. B. R. Ambedkar, was particularly appealing to the Punjabi activists after news of archeological discoveries at Harappa in western Punjab in 1921 and the historical speculation regarding the role of Punjab as the portal for ancient Aryan conquests over the original people of the region. The wording on a poster announcing one of the first meetings of Ad Dharm summarises their ideological position:

> We are the original people of this country, and our religion is Ad Dharm. The Hindu *qaum* came from outside and enslaved us. ... Brothers, the time has come: wake up, the government is listening to our cries.[7]

Their myth of origin postulated that the birthplace of ancient civilisation was India—once a utopian land where all inhabitants dwelt in amicable equality. The story went on to say that one branch, however, split off and migrated to the region we know as Europe. From there, as Aryans, they returned to India to conquer the true inheritors of the original civilisation "with so much cruelty and injustice" that these *adi* people—now treated as untouchables—"forgot their own identity".[8] From there this mythic account of history paused only briefly to denounce Manu, the legendary codifier of Hindu law, before advancing to the present period where it showed how the Aryans—upper caste Hindus in general and members of the Arya Samaj in particular—continued to subjugate those *adi* people who had descended from the original inhabitants of India. The Arya's efforts to reconvert untouchables to Hinduism and provide social service organisations for them were singled out as examples of ways that the Aryans were continuing to try to "seduce" the untouchables and set traps to snare them "like falling into the clutches of elephants' teeth".[9]

Mangoo Ram made clear, however, that Ad Dharm as a religion was not exclusive to untouchables. It was a religious community similar to Hindus. It was not the expression of a particular caste but the manifestation of what it regarded as the original egalitarian society of India. For that reason the movement's first report proudly listed twenty Brahmins and two Jains among its membership.[10]

The theology of Ad Dharm was straightforward. There was a creator god, *Adi Purkh* (Original Being), whose wisdom was communicated through the great saints of medieval India, including Kabir, member of the weaver caste, and Ravi Das, a Chamar, who became the patron saint of Ad Dharm. Since Ravi Das had already been highly revered within Scheduled Caste communities this amounted to an appropriation of traditional lower caste religiosity. Nonetheless, the Ad Dharm leaders urged their followers to practice their reverence for Ravi Das in as disciplined and faithful manner as Hindus worshipped their gods and Sikhs revered gurus: they were to meditate regularly, pay obeisance to the guru, and keep a chaste and disciplined life.

Other aspects of religious identity were invented as well. The Ad Dharmis' salutation to one another was *Jai Guru Dev* (victory to the divine guru), to which the appropriate response was *Dhan Guru Dev* (blessed be the divine guru). The followers were to adopt the Upanishadic phrase *soham* (I am that) as a *mantra*, presumably because it implied the basic unity and equality of the world. They were also urged to wear the colour red, either as turbans or as arm bands, in part because upper caste Rajputs in the area near Rajasthan refused to allow lower caste members to wear such a regal colour. With this portfolio of distinctive theological ideas and an array of external symbols of religious identity, therefore, Ad Dharm was ready to present itself as a movement representing a great and significant *qaum*.

Schisms, Census, and an Epic Fast

Three events marked stages in the early history of the movement. The first was a series of internal schisms and leadership disputes, followed by the grand mobilisation to have Ad Dharm registered in large numbers for the government's census of 1931, and finally a counterfast in opposition to Gandhi. Although vastly different, each of these demonstrated how Ad Dharm was trying to carve out a distinctive niche within Punjab society.

The early leadership squabbles were basically over strategy—whether to compromise with the Arya Samaj and other moderate elements of the wider society, or to take a harder, more separatist line. Mangoo Ram, the old Ghadar revolutionary, maintained a strident stance. Others were not so sure. With the rise of nationalism throughout India, the Ad Dharmis' refusal to support the moderate service organisations set up by the Congress movement appeared to some as collusion with the colonial government. The Arya Samaj had been making new overtures to Ad Dharm leaders, offering them an expanded role in the movement if they would return, and in 1929 several were lured back. The exodus included the Ad Dharm founders, namely, Thakar Chand, Vasant Rai, and Swami Shudranand. In 1930, another group left the Ad Dharm to establish a rival All-India Ad Dharm Mandal, with headquarters in Lyallpur, in western Punjab. The Lyallpur group survived for only three years, disbanding in 1933 to merge with Dr. Ambedkar's national movement. Though buffeted, the Jalandhar office of Ad Dharm under Mangoo Ram's leadership survived, resisting the temptation to compromise with the wider society's politics and to accept even implicitly their prevailing social assumptions about caste and the stigma of untouchability.

Taking the hard line turned out to be an important stand in the second critical event in the movement's early years: the census of 1931. The census was important not only as a demonstration of the movement's strength and legitimacy but also as a basis for mobilisation. In central Punjab, where the Ad Dharm was based, the numbers of Muslims, Hindus and Sikhs were almost equal, and untouchables were relatively evenly distributed among the three communities. But untouchables were marginal to the religious life of upper castes, and if they could be persuaded that their true religious identity was something else—Ad Dharm, for example—this new religion would hold considerable electoral power. Before 1931, census takers had been instructed to use the category "Hindu" for any untouchable respondents who were uncertain how to answer the question about religious affiliation. In 1909, when Census Commissioner Edward Gait issued a circular suggesting that the "depressed classes" ought to be listed separately from Hindus, the response from the upper caste bordered on panic. The circular was rescinded, but in 1930 when the government's census commissioner accepted Ad Dharm's petition to have its name listed as an option on the list of religions, the upper caste fears were revived.

Sikhs took the census threat from Ad Dharm more seriously than Hindus. "The Hindus treated the Sikhs badly, by taking some of their people into Hindu census rolls, so the Sikhs took it out on us," one old Ad Dharmi recalled.[11] Several angry Sikhs interrupted an Ad Dharm rally at Nankana Sahib, destroyed the kitchen where meals were being prepared, threw hot rice at the participants, and beat up several Ad Dharm followers.[12] Other Ad Dharmis were also attacked—some say several were killed—but the effort to have untouchables record their religion as "Ad Dharm" persisted. A song was composed for the occasion:

Leave the bickering behind,
And tie your turban red;
We do not have to record
Any *qaum* other than our own,
So, Ad Dharmi, be strong.[13]

The final tally of Ad Dharmis reported in the 1931 Punjab census was 4,18,789. In certain areas of Punjab Mangoo Ram and his colleagues had reason to feel victorious: over eighty percent of lower castes in Jalandhar district declared themselves members of Ad Dharm, as did about a tenth of the number of lower caste people eleswhere throughout the state. There were two epicenters of Ad Dharm support: the *doab* area, including Jalandhar and Hoshiarpur districts and the state of Kapurthala, and the area in western Punjab around Lyallpur, including districts Sheikhapura, Multan and Montgomery—many of these canal colonies to which lower caste people from the *doab* area had migrated. In these districts Chamars were the largest group among the Scheduled Castes. In Amritsar and Lahore districts, the largest Scheduled Caste group were Chuhras (sweepers), who apparently saw the Ad Dharm as a largely Chamar affair. Non-Chamar lower castes in the mountain areas of Kangra and the north-western areas of Shahpur and Gujarat, however, offered the Ad Dharm a modicum of support (18 percent in the case of Kangra).

Throughout Punjab the number of people returning their religion as Ad Dharm was roughly equal to the number of Christians, also largely from Scheduled Castes. Mangoo Ram pointed out that Christianity had been trying to convert untouchables in Punjab for over fifty years, and the Ad Dharm had succeeded as well in only five.[14] Moreover, he said, the census had proved that untouchable castes were capable of mobilizing for their own benefits, and of organising in ways that permitted them to compete in the wider socio-political arena.

These efforts to create an independent political base for untouchables were threatened, however, by other political forces in Punjab that saw the participation of untouchables as numerically and ideologically vital to their existence. The Arya Samaj was one such force, as we have seen; the Independence Movement was another.

Since Congress was dominated by upper caste Hindus, leaders of the Ad Dharm thought that an independent India controlled by them would not be a significant improvement over British rule. In some cases, this indifference to the independence movement bordered on hostility. According to one Scheduled Caste Congress supporter, a group of Ad Dharmis attacked a salt satyagrahi in Jalandhar in 1930: they vandalised the heavy salt kilns, beat up several of the Congress men, and stole several pots and kettles.[15] Earlier, in 1928, Ad Dharm leaders had rejected Motilal Nehru's call for the abolition of separate electorates. When the issue was raised again at the Round Table Conference in London, Mangoo Ram sent telegrams to the government pledging the Ad Dharm's support for Dr. Bhim Rao Ambedkar, the untouchables' representative at the conference.[16]

At the Round Table Conference, Gandhi had adopted a position opposite to that of the untouchables. In Gandhi's view, independent India should become a land of caste equality that would incorporate all communities within it without discrimination—but he radically differed with untouchable leaders over how this utopia would be achieved. Gandhi advocated a united front of all castes as the way to bring about this transformation; but Ambedkar and Mangoo Ram thought that untouchables first had to establish a separate political base from which they could demand respect.

Nothing illustrated these differences of strategies more than the response to the British suggestion of communal representation as the way to provide untouchables with a voice in India's legislative assemblies. The untouchable leaders embraced the idea. Gandhi rejected it, claiming it was an effort to legitimise the institution of untouchability. He vowed to go on an "epic fast" in opposition. On September 20, 1932, the fast began, accompanied by a great deal of publicity. Mangoo Ram went on a counterfast of his own. He also went to Simla to raise his demands directly to the British government's summer headquarters; he wrote a letter to king George opposing Gandhi; and he threatened massive disturbances throughout Punjab.[17]

On September 26, 1932, the Poona Pact provided a compromise that both Ambedkar and Gandhi could accept. The untouchables would forfeit their claim to separate electorates provided they were given reserved seats in open electorates. The pact did not guarantee how many seats would be allotted in Punjab, however, so Mangoo Ram continued his fast and threats of disturbances until he felt an appropriate figure was reached. The rift between the liberal Gandhians and radical untouchables was not healed however, since each continued to perceive the other as an obstacle to achieving inter-caste harmony. Gandhi thought the untouchables' militant separatism was reinforcing the concept of caste, and the untouchables thought Gandhi was trying to whitewash existing differences and to deny untouchables their legitimate base of power. Both the perceptions were to some extent correct.

Politics and the Decline of Ad Dharm

Eventually, the radical untouchable position was eroded not by the moral persuasion of Gandhian liberals but by the exigencies of politics. By the mid-1930s there had been a political shift away from the direct interaction of communal organisations to the creation of political parties and the competition of electoral politics. The extreme separatist position persisted, but was increasingly identified with the creation of new communal states along the lines of the Muslim proposal, which came to be known as "Pakistan". Discussions were held in the Sikh Akali Dal about demanding a separate Sikh state as well—which some called "Sikhistan" or "Jatistan", a state for Jat Sikhs—and some untouchable activists talked about also proposing "Achhutistan".[18]

The more immediate political task, however, was to secure adequate representation in the new legislative councils. This meant forming—or allying with—political parties. The first election following the Government of India Act of 1935 occurred the following year, and Ad Dharmis entered into an alliance with the (Muslim) Unionist Party to secure support for their candidates, who ran as independents in the eight constituencies reserved for Scheduled Castes. The Ad Dharmis mounted a campaign reminiscent of the 1931 census drive, and swept all but one of the seats. In the urban Jalandhar constituency, they defeated their Congress rival by a resounding 1,400 votes. The victorious candidate was Seth Kishan Das, a wealthy leather merchant in the Chamar neighbourhood of Boota Mandi, who had supplied the building for the Ad Dharm headquarters and served as Mangoo Ram's press agent during his counterfast against Gandhi.

The lustre of the victory was tarnished somewhat by the alliance with the Muslims' Unionist Party, which had so consistently controlled Punjab politics since the late 1920s that it took on the aura of the political establishment. The alliance between the Unionists—led by Muslim landlords—and the untouchables was a marriage of convenience: both opposed upper caste Hindus, Sikhs, and the Indian National Congress. Mangoo Ram had received support from the Unionist leader, Sikandar Hyat khan, for his counterfast against Gandhi in 1932, and he felt obliged to support Sikandar as chairman of the legislative council in 1934.[19] In 1936, when the Unionist Party came into power in the Punjab Legislature and Sikandar Hyat Khan became Chief Minister, the Ad Dharmi alliance appeared to have paid off.

But it was a short lived success. Within a few brief years, the political climate again changed as independence loomed near and no resolution to the Muslim-Congress dispute was apparent. The Muslim League—more aggressively separatist than the Unionist Party—gained power and propelled the surge towards the creation of Pakistan. In the Punjab Legislative Assembly elections of 1945-46, on the eve of independence, the Muslim League triumphed with 79 seats. Congress followed with 51, the Sikhs' Panthic League with 22, trailed by the Unionists and independents with 10 each. Mangoo Ram was one of the Unionists' ten. Thus, the Ad Dharm faced independent India with scarcely a voice. It was burdened by alliances with fading political powers—the colonial government and Muslim landlords—and as a regional entity in an increasingly national arena, it had become obsolete.

In June, 1946, Mangoo Ram closed the Jalandhar office of the Ad Dharm. The Ad Dharm leaders told Dr. Ambedkar that the Ad Dharm Mandal had decided to change its name to the Ravi Das Mandal and to leave the politics to Dr. Ambedkar and his All-India Scheduled Caste Federation. Ambedkar's organisation thanked Mangoo Ram for his decision to "confine the activities of the Ad Dharm Mandal to social and religious matters" and to "entrust" the Ambedkar organisation with "the political work".[20] Eventually, the building became a high school for Scheduled Caste children named in honour of Sant Ravi Das, the patron saint of Ad Dharm. The name "Ad Dharm" continued to live on as the caste name adopted by Chamars in many parts of Jalandhar and Hoshiarpur districts.

The Ad Dharm movement had been a composite of two kinds of activity—religious and political. Both of those activities continued. When the movement disbanded in 1946, the efforts to mobilise Punjab untouchables around Ravi Das and other symbols of cultural unity continued. A thriving Ravi Das Ashram near Jalandhar expanded, Punjabi activists were instrumental in locating the birthplace of Ravi Das near Banares and building a temple on the spot, and a new generation of leaders were involved in linking the devotion of Ravi Das to the social identity of Chamars and other Scheduled Castes.

The political momentum that Ad Dharm initiated also continued. Old Ad Dharmis became active in other organisations. Seth Kishan Das helped to found the Punjab branch of Dr. Ambedkar's Republican Party. Sadhu Ram became involved in the Scheduled Caste Federation, and then joined the Congress Party. Master Gurbanta Singh also became a leader in the Congress Party, serving in the cabinet of Chief Minister Pratap Singh Kairon. Eventually, even Mangoo Ram turned towards the Congress party, accepting, as he put it, that "without Congress we could no longer do anything".[21] He served in the Punjab Legislative Assembly until 1952, where he attempted to secure legislation providing for land redistribution, increased government jobs for the lower castes, and the establishment of public holidays on the birth dates of lower caste gurus.[22]

Although the Ad Dharm organisation ceased to exist, Mangoo Ram felt that it played an important role in the development of Scheduled Caste identity and political power in Punjab. He summed up its contributions to the Scheduled Caste community this way: "We gave them a better life and made them into a *qaum*. We gave them gurus to believe in and something to hope for".[23]

Ad Dharm Anew

In 1970, the Ad Dharm movement was revived. On December 13, a rally at the Ravi Das Ashram in village Ballan near Jalandhar proclaimed the renewal of the Ad Dharm organisation. Mangoo Ram was brought out of retirement for the occasion, and a series of conferences called for a renewal of efforts aimed at creating cultural identity and supporting social activism on behalf of the Scheduled Castes. A new magazine, *Ravidas Patrika* was launched.

Like the leadership of the original Ad Dharm, the organisers of the revived movement were educated, financially secure activists who felt that their community deserved better social recognition and political clout than it had heretofore received. In addition to the financial successes of the community's traditional occupation, the leather trade, the new money came form two sources: a new middle class and expatriate communities. A suburban Scheduled Caste community had begun to flourish in larger Punjab cities, comprised of administrators, businessmen, teachers and others who had become successful in the middle class occupations increasingly available to members of lower castes, thanks in part to government reservations in schools and jobs. The new *Ravidas Patrika*, for example, was housed in the comfortable suburban home of its editor, Mangu Ram Jaspal, in Jalandhar's Model Town.

But Jaspal had not achieved his financial success in Jalandhar: he earned it in Wolverhampton, England. There he was part of the other source of support for the new Ad Dharm: a thriving Punjabi Scheduled Caste community that had established its own Ravi Das temples, often in abandoned Anglican churches. The pride that the community felt in developing the symbols of their culture in

England became linked with a pride in the history of Scheduled Caste social activism in Punjab. Mangoo Ram was invited to tour Wolverhampton and was feted as an early pioneer for their cause. It was fitting, therefore, that expatriate Punjabi Chamars would want to return to Punjab to revive the movement that they regarded as instrumental in their community's social development.

Yet, the revived movement did not develop in quite the same way as had the old Ad Dharm, though it did do much to provide financial support for emerging Ravi Das temples in Banaras and Punjab. The social politics of Punjab in the early 1970s was not like it was in the 1920s, where political power was based in modern organisations that were grounded in religious communities, like the Hindus' Arya Samaj. By the end of the 1970s, however, a new religious politics had begun to emerge in Punjab—the Khalistan movement—and a decade later movement for Hindu nationalism arose throughout India. These were not, however, opportunities for untouchables in the same way that the religious politics of the 1920s had been.

For one thing, the new religious politics was more violent. The extremism of the Khalistani movement in the 1980s sobered most lower caste activists. Urban members of the Chamar caste tried to avoid siding with either the rebels—largely young rural Jats—or with the police, many of whom were recruited from Scheduled Castes. Members of Chuhra caste in Sikh-dominated rural areas of Amritsar and Gurdaspur districts would sometimes side with rebels—especially if they were pressured into doing so. Known as *mazhabi* (faithful) Sikhs, they at times felt called upon to prove their loyalty to the Sikh tradition. Such appeals were said to have been made to Beant Singh, the bodyguard for Indira Gandhi, who came from a *mazhabi* family in Gurdaspur and was persuaded to participate in her assassination. A *mazhabi* Sikh military unit was among those that rebelled following Operation Bluestar in 1984.

In the 1990s, social politics changed again as the Khalistan movement was under siege and Hindu nationalism was on the rise elsewhere in India. Though this movement also had a violent side—sometimes aimed at keeping the Scheduled Castes in line—some activists saw the time as again ripe for asserting the social and political independence of Scheduled Caste communities. A Punjabi Chamar, Kanshi Ram, founded the Bahujan Samaj Party, based in part on his attempt to organise middle class administrative workers and government employees from Scheduled Caste background in Delhi-based Backward and Minority Communities Employees Federation (BAMCEF). The Bahujan Samaj Party enjoyed considerable electoral success in Delhi, Uttar Pardesh and Punjab, in part through strategic alliances with other parties.

The form of social and political activism generated by the Ad Dharm movement continued into the twenty first century, albeit through other names and sometimes other means. The movement was remembered as having helped to raise the consciousness of lower caste people throughout Punjab and instil an awareness of the possibilities of social change. It also demonstrated the efficacy of religion as an instrument in social transformation. It helped the members of Scheduled Castes to come to terms with the cultural, as well as economic and political aspects of their oppression, and to assert the distinctiveness of their community and tradition. It also helped them reconceive the social whole and to think optimistically about their role within society—a more sophisticated ideological position than the grievance politics of most forms of self-interested protest. In this way the religious imagination of Ad Dharm allowed its Punjabi adherents to assert not only what they disdained but also to articulate a vision of what they and all of society should become.

Notes

1. My information on the Ad Dharm movement comes from government records, newspaper reports, original documents, and interviews conducted in Punjab in 1970-97. See my *Religion as Social Vision: the Movement Against Untouchability in 20th Century Punjab*. Berkeley: University of California Press, 1982,

revised edition published in India as *Religious Rebels in the Punjab: The Social Vision of Untouchables*, New Delhi: Ajanta Publications, 1988. This article is a revised and condensed version of information first presented in this book.

2. According to my interviews with Principal Ram Das, Hoshiarpur, April 18, 1971 and Sant Ram, MLA, Jalandhar, June 12, 1971.
3. Interview with Sant Ram, B.A., Sadhu Ashram, Hoshiarpur, April 18, 1971. See also his autobiography, *Mere Jivan Anubahav* (My Life Experiences), Varanasi: Om Parkash Beri, Hindi Pracharik Prakashan, n.d.
4. Interview with Swami Shudranand, Jalandhar, May 15, 1971.
5. Interview with Mangoo Ram, Garhshankar, April 17, 1971. See also "Appendix A: The Early Life of Mangoo Ram" in my *Religion as Social Vision*.
6. Interview with Mangoo Ram, Garshankar, April 17, 1971.
7. *Mugowal Zila Hoshiarpur de Ad Dharm Skool: Wadda Bhaari Diwan* (Mugowal, Hoshiarpur district, in the Ad Dharm School: Huge Public Meeting) a poster announcing an Ad Dharm meeting in 1927 in the collection of Mangoo Ram, Garshankar.
8. *Report of the Ad Dharm Mandal, 1926-1931* (in Urdu, translated by Mark Juergensmeyer and Surjit Singh Goraya), Jalandhar, 1932, 7. An excerpt of the report is reprinted as an appendix to my *Religion as Social Vision*. I am grateful to L. R. Balley, Ambedkar Mission Society, Jalandhar, for access to the copy of the Report he has in his possession.
9. *Ad Dharm Report*, 10.
10. *Ad Dharm Report*, 70.
11. Chanan Lal Manik, "Adi Dharm Bare" ("About Ad Dharm"), *Ravidas Patrika* 1:46, December 29, 1970.
12. Manik, "Adi Dharm Bare".
13. Manik, "Adi Dharm Bare".
14. Interview with Mangoo Ram, Garhshankar, April 17, 1971.
15. Interview with Prithvi Singh Azad, who claimed to have witnessed this event, April 13, 1971.

16. Lahore *Tribune*, 51: 240, October 11, 1931. I have seen a copy of one of Mangoo Ram's telegrams in support of Dr. Ambedkar, which Mangoo Ram had in his possession.
17. Interviews with Mangoo Ram, Garhshankar, January 29, 1971; and Gurbanta Singh, Jalandhar, May 8, 1971. See also Manik, "Adi Dharm Bare".
18. Interview with Mangoo Ram, Garshankar, January 29, 1971; Sant Ram, MLA, June 12, 1971; and L. R. Balley, Jalandhar, April 3, 1971.
19. A letter of appreciation from Sir Sikandar Hyat Khan, dated March, 1934, was among the memorabilia of Mangoo Ram at his home in Garhshankar.
20. Letter form D. B. N. Shivaraj, President, All India Scheduled Caste Federation, New Delhi, to Mangoo Ram, June 24, 1946; in Mangoo Ram's personal collection.
21. Interview with Mangoo Ram, Garshankar, April 17, 1971.
22. *Ibid.*
23. *Ibid.*

10

Communist Movement in Punjab, 1926-47

BHAGWAN JOSH

The 'left' in Punjab before the Meerut conspiracy case (1929-32) was constituted by individuals drawn from Muhajirs, nationalist youth, Akali militants and members or sympathisers of the Ghadar Party. What brought them together was their desire to organise the oppressed sections of the society in an uncompromising struggle against imperialism and communalism. They conceived of complete independence as the establishment of workers' and peasants' government in India. Of these four currents, individuals from the latter two were not only the larger in numbers but also played a significant role in the organisation of Punjab Kisan Committee (PKC).

To evaluate the ideas of these individuals, especially those grouped round the *Kirti* magazine,[1] we must understand, firstly, that the lives of these revolutionary nationalists had been shaped by the popular principles of Sikhism; and secondly, that these practical men evolved their ideas more under the influence of the achievements of the Russian revolution than under the influence of Marxist theory. There is a huge gap between the recognition of the general principles of scientific socialism and the practical achievements of a revolution in a particular country at a specific historical conjuncture, even though staged under the guidance of the same general principles. This distinction between the two modes of influence is not a formal one, but, as we shall see, it will help us to understand various aspects of the contradictory elements fused in their consciousness.

Ideas can travel across the oceans but not the conditions of which they are the product. When a set of ideas which are the product of certain historical process at a particular place they not only influence the already existing ideas with which they come into contact but also themselves in turn get influenced and consequently modified. These modified ideas in order to first exist as a tendency among limited political circles in the form of political consciousness and then ultimately to become a motive force to change the society must dig below themselves their labyrinth roots to the inner most psychological springs of the masses. That is to say, instead of existing as abstract theoretical formulas to be remembered or parroted at different occasions they must exist in a psycho-theoretical form. In retrospect we can say that Marxism failed to dig its roots deep into Punjabi society and remained a superficial discourse of abstract theoretical formulas among a small but very vocal section of the Punjabi intelligentsia.

Members and sympathisers of the Ghadar Party in America were mostly Sikhs having a theological cast of mind. The founder of the *Kirti* magazine, Santokh Singh, read Marx's *Capital* and recited *Gurbani* simultaneously. The mind of the wooden plough and the primitive myth was physically severed and thrown into a world of science and industry. But, the idea of the limited nature of their sojourn in America kept feeding their natural nostalgia keeping alive the desire to go back to their natural surroundings in their respective villages. In spite of this, their political mentality was affected by the new environment though because of the nature of their work in America and the relatively short period of their stay there, elements of their subjective world could not be properly sucked in, digested and thus dissolved by the centres of industrial civilisation.

The return of the emigrants provided the human channels through which the ideas of the outside world were injected into the life of certain limited strata of rural Punjab. The emigrants were mostly Jat Sikhs and no wonder the left movement remained limited only to the Sikh peasantry. But, the effect of the infusion of the new ideas proved to be very weak on the small landholder with his conservative self-sufficiency and indifference to the greater issues of the age. This was the social base on which the Kirtis operated and as we shall see the ideology of this base ultimately manifested itself in their programme and organisation. This was also the fertile ground of the Akali movement. No wonder, at the very beginning, the militant "Akali" and "Kirti" were embodied within the same person.[2] Thus, a section of the Punjabi communists have always looked up to *Gurbani* and Sikh traditions in order to nurture their convictions. But they have always avoided the fundamental questions: In what way Marxism as a vision and worldview is related to their Sikh beliefs and Sikh identity? Coming to terms with their own identity at a deeper level could have compelled them to come to terms with the actually existing historical consciousness created and lived within the framework of Sikh praxis and ideology of "Jatism". Consciously or unconsciously, many of them lived a two-fold tension in their daily lives: between *Gurbani* and Marxism and between Jatism and Marxism. Historically speaking, Punjab had been a region where many sects with different lifestyles have thrived on the margins without having any significant impact on the wider society. Gorakh Panth was one such sect which was a small but certainly a very vocal sect. Punjabi communists reproduced themselves in that marginal tradition. This Marx Panth sect did not challenge at the level of ideas and psychological moorings the actually existing Punjabi social consciousness but those working towards creating a wider impact on Punjabi society would be forced to enter into a dialogue with them. In cultural terms Marx Panth was a continuity of Gorakh Panth in modern times and provided a suitable channel for those who were deeply dissatisfied with contemporary life styles and oppression. Thus, they continued to play the role of a catalytic agent as well as of a steam value for social grievances and thus forcing others to come to terms with the aspirations of the poor and marginal people in Punjabi society.

The *Kirti* was not only a propaganda journal but a mobiliser and organiser also. It tended to organise the youth, workers and peasants around the journal. The *Kirti* management had decided to build an organisation of the youth and had brought out a poster signed by Bhag Singh Canadian and Sohan Singh Josh for that purpose in March 1928 and they were making preparations to hold a youth conference in the Jallianwala Bagh from 11 to 13 April, 1928.

The Naujawan Bharat Sabha (NBS), Lahore, founded by Bhagat Singh, was mainly confined to the students in the Lahore colleges and was active only for a short period from March 1926 to April 1927. The programme of the NBS comprised of debates on moral, literary and social subjects, the popularisation of *swadeshi* goods and inculcation of a sense of brotherhood and the stimulation of interest in Indian languages and civilisation. Towards the end of this first phase, Ram Chandra acted as President, Bhagat Singh as Secretary, Bhagwati Charan Vohra as Cashier and M.A. Majid and Kidar Nath Sehgal were among the members. S.A. Dange and Philip Spratt spoke at some of the meetings organised by the NBS on the meaning of Indian independence. Recapitulating the short history of the NBS in 1929, the provincial CID noted: "Beyond holding a few public meetings at which intemperate speeches were made, the Sabha during this period accomplished nothing".

By the efforts of the Lahore communists and *Kirti* group, the NBS was revived in April 1928. The declared aims and objects of the newly constituted NBS were:

1. to establish a completely independent republic of the labourers and the peasants of the whole of India;
2. to fuse the spirit of patriotism into the hearts of the youths of the country in order to establish a united Indian nation;
3. to express sympathy with and to assist the economic, industrial and social movements which while being free from communal sentiments are intended to take us near to our ideal, namely, the establishment of a complete independent republic of labourers and peasants; and
4. to organise labourers and peasants.

Prominent leaders of the NBS such as Abdul Majid, Sohan Singh Josh and Kidar Nath Sehgal visited places, held meetings and helped interested persons to organise local *sabhas*.

The notion of martyrdom occupies a supreme position in the system of Sikh philosophy, as elaborated by the various Gurus. The self-sacrifice of the determined individuals or "heroes" to uphold the cause of the oppressed is considered to be necessary in order to arouse the slumbering people. The first article contributed to *Kirti* (December 1926) by S.S. Josh, one of the future leaders of the Communist Party of Punjab, was concerned with the meaning of "martyr". The article provided an insight into the psychological situation and isolation in which the politically most advanced youths of this part of the country were placed. The article also indicated the psychologically nurturing influence of Sikh conceptions for those who had superficially accepted the goals of economic equality annunciated by Marxism. The article runs as follows:

> The martyr is far higher than his time, and his views are far loftier than those of other people. The people who are tightly bound with the chains of conservative views cannot understand his lofty flights and independent views. They, therefore, rain condemnation on him and boycott him.
>
> The martyr sees a hidden and obscure truth, and he wishes to make the world look more charming than before by propagating the truth... . People laugh and jeer at him. And then they call him mad and misguided.... They consider the system in vogue stable and well founded, whether it may be religious, social or political. They have special love for the old system... . It is not known why people are the worshippers of the absurd policy of following customs of their forefathers into the 20th century.... To support these customs is to become a reactionary.
>
> The martyr breaks as under the stout chains of blind obedience to the customs of forefathers making them produce a sound. He does not care for public approbation and public criticism. He revolts against all this. He is the lover of truth, progress and freedom... . After consideration, he comes to the conclusion that

> sacrifice is required to rouse people from sound sleep. For this reason he sacrifices himself. People get a severe shaking through this sacrifice and they begin to think. As they think, their faith in blind obedience to the customs of their forefathers becomes somewhat slack and their eyes open gradually and they come to realize that the martyr was not "misguided" but "well guided", was not mad but a national asset and an inestimable diamond.[3]

Thus, the alienated youth of rural society only dimly aware of the complexity of urban life, first and foremost thinks of his own martyrdom as a way out of the trap of small peasant household miseries.

After the NBS had functioned a few months, two main trends emerged in it. Bhagat Singh and his comrades were so dismayed with the slow moving nationalist parties that they were impatient to do something spectacular. The teachings of the Russian anarchists, Kropotkin and Bakunin gripped their impressionable minds. The patent argument of all terrorists, i.e., "the action will rouse the masses and strengthen the movement", became a pivot of their world view. Implicit in this argument was a conception of politics in which the state apparatus was seen as a purely external organ of coercion having no roots in the social organisation itself. This was how the Russian autocracy had appeared to the revolutionary terrorists in Russia. Because of the foreign nature of the state in India, the strength of this conception was redoubled and it seemed even more convincing. Once the state was conceived of as a mechanism operated from outside, the focus became concentrated on mechanical means, i.e., dynamite, to explode this strait-jacket. To perform this task heroically, Bhagat Singh and his comrades derived inspiration from the courage, self-sacrifice and dedication of the Ghadar heroes. In an article "History of Anarchism", Bhagat Singh repeated and defended the arguments of Bakunin and Kropotkin. In the same article he promised to write about communists but the promise was not fulfilled because of fateful events. His main line of argument that "a single deed makes more propaganda in a few days than a thousand pamphlets" and how series of such actions ultimately lead to breaking out of the revolution remained unchallenged. The reason why no one could counter Bhagat Singh's views is given by Sohan Singh Josh, the then working editor of *Kirti* magazine as follows:

> I too was raw and immature. I did not know so much of Marxism then as to differentiate between terrorism and Marxism. The Ghadar Party ideology of armed struggle and Ghadar heroes' unprecedented sacrifices had a hold on my thinking.

The foregoing account may leave an impression of Bhagat Singh being a terrorist and remaining one till the end. However, after his imprisonment, Bhagat Singh underwent a radical metamorphosis in his political views and conceptions as a result of an intensive study of Marxist works which initiated a process of deep introspection. Consequently, by the time that he was hanged, he could be considered a creative Marxist thinker and ideologue. Bhagat Singh remains a permanent source of inspiration for all those who preach the idea of violent revolution, despite his condemnation of violence for advancing a political cause. Can Bhagat Singh's life and activities teach any lesson to the youth of Punjab? Today, I am asking this question with all the awareness that when I was young I did not learn any positive lesson form his life except using it as source of inspiration for violent activities. Yes, it can teach us the following two important lessons:

- Those who go through the "method of terrorism" do at the end become aware of its shortcomings as a political method and finally, its utter futility. But they are all destroyed by the state before they are able to correct their mistakes and invent new methods of mass struggle. The advantage of other political methods are that they give political workers enough time to correct their mistakes and thus evolve more effective methods of struggle for advancing their goals. Bhagat Singh did not have the time to implement his own new thinking and thus testing its validity.
- It is not enough to sacrifice one's life; one must do so at an appropriate moment of time. "Dying is not enough, one must die in time". (Sartre) *Manas janam durlabh hai* (human life is very precious).

Kirti Kisan Party

In September 1927, the *Kirti* informed its readers that a conference would be held in Hoshiarpur on the 6th and 7th of October, 1927 under the presidentship of Sohan Singh Josh in which the problems of Kirtis would be discussed. It was also announced that similar conference would be held in Lyallpur in the last days of September 1927. The League Against Imperialism sent hearty greetings to the Hoshiarpur Kirti conference.[4] The conference coincided with the Sikh League Conference and was attended in large numbers. President S.S. Josh talked at length about the squalid living conditions of the Punjab peasantry, corroborating his points with statistics from M.L. Darling. Akali leaders such as Darshan Singh Pheruman, Jathedar Udham Singh Nagoke, and Gurmukh Singh Musaffir offered themselves for work in the cause of the Kirtis and the Kirti group leaders hoped to raise a Kirti organisation under their leadership.[5] The new organisation was to establish close links with the national Congress and thus become a part of the anti-imperialist movement. It was resolved at the conference that after creating their permanent organisation with a political programme they would help the national Congress in every way. They would accept whatever the Congress might say, and would always support the left-wing of the Congress.[6]

Some held the opinion that the biggest task before them was the organisation of the workers. Among the "workers" in Punjab 90 percent were peasants. In other words, workers organisation in Punjab primarily meant the organisation of the Sikh peasants. In due course, large number of Kirti Kisan Conferences were held in various districts of Punjab and they succeeded in establishing a foothold in some of the villages of Punjab. But despite their best efforts, large number of villages remained untouched by "Kirti ideas".

Programme of the Kirtis

The Kirtis did not put forward a systematic and coherent programme to be followed. It is scattered in various issues of *Kirti* (monthly) and can be summed up in the following items:

1. All means of production should be nationalised.
2. Land should be taken away from the landlords without compensation and it should be divided among the cultivators.
3. The revenue should be reduced. It should be imposed on production and not on land. On small holdings there should be no revenue at all.
4. The wages of the industrial workers should be increased. Working time should not be more than eight hours.
5. Government should give loans to the cultivators. It should also open departments which should provide the peasants with machines, seeds and scientific assistance.
6. Village Panchayats should be reorganised and they should include the elected representatives of cultivators and other rural workers. They should be entrusted with authority to impose revenue on the peasants.
7. Establishment of a "Kirti" or "Bolshevik type" state.

In the course of three years (1933-35) eight Moscow trained members of the Ghadar Party were intercepted and interrogated by the Punjab police. They were brutally tortured to extort information about the network of Ghadar Party, training in Moscow and instructions which they had brought for their Indian compatriots. Till 1935, the police authorities were able to establish the identity of some 15 to 20 of the 40 trained communists who had returned to India and were working at different places. These returned communists included some of the more active members of the Ghadar Party such as Teja Singh Swatantar, Gurmukh Singh, Prithivi Singh, Iqbal Singh Hundal, Harbans Singh Basi, Chanan Singh and Bhagat Singh Bilga. According to Williamson, the number of Ghadar Party students in Moscow in 1935 was 60. This did not include those who had already finished their courses and left USSR. The Kirti Kisan Party's offices were raided on 22 June, 1932 and amongst other literature, the police seized copies of a cyclostyled Urdu pamphlet entitled, "The Programme of the Indian Communist Party".

Members of the Kirti Kisan Party who were outside jails continued to pursue their activities. A Kirti Kisan Conference was held at Nankana Sahib on 12 and 13 November, 1932. It was attended by 2,000 people. Speakers criticised the Congress and said that the Congress movement was designed to substitute a "white" bureaucracy by a "brown" one. Processions and meetings to protest against the judgement in the Meerut conspiracy case were organised by the NBS in Lahore and Amritsar. According to the police sources, the audience did not exceed 900 persons on either occasion. On 10 February, 1933, a body known as the *Rajsi Qaidi Chhurao Committee* (Committee for the Release of Political Prisoners) was organised with the object of securing the release of the prisoners' of 1914-15 (first Lahore conspiracy case) and to assist all political prisoners. Delegates were sent to organise meetings in connection with "May Day" celebrations in Amritsar and Lahore. In the latter half of the year 1933, a few conferences were held in Amritsar and Hoshiarpur districts. Police orders restricted the leading participants to their respective villages under the Punjab Criminal Law (Amendment) Act.

After the ban, individuals sought to regroup themselves under the banner of Punjab Kisan Qarza Committee, the first meeting of which was held at Amritsar on 3 March, 1935. A general committee of 52 members was elected. The proposal was to organise small committees in rural areas to assist the peasants to obtain as much benefit as possible from the relief provided by the Indebtedness Act. A number of conferences and meetings were held, and the Jalandhar District Qarza Committee established 60 branches at various places in the district. It held small village meetings at which speakers "combined agrarian agitation with communist propaganda".

The Doaba rural uplift conference was organised by the communists at Patara (Jalandhar district) during the month of October 1935. It was attended by more than 4,000 people. The conference demanded cancellation of debts and assessment of land revenue on the basis of income tax. It denounced the oppressive methods of the government, criticised the Congress for being the party of the capitalists and urged the villagers to establish Qarza Committees.

Before the emergence of the Punjab Congress Socialist Party the various socialist groups in the province were rent by personal feuds and were full of mutual distrust. Their activities were confined mainly to carrying on propaganda work. So far as organisation was concerned, little headway was made. Many issues of the monthly *Kirti* (Punjabi and Urdu) were proscribed and securities were demanded from the Kirti press. The control of funds coming from the Ghadar Party was in the hands of a group of Ghadarite communists known as Kirtis. It was this group which constituted the Managing Board of the *Kirti* magazine. This group strove to maintain its relatively autonomous position in the matter of using these funds. The Communist Party, which was a very small group of roughly five to ten members, wanted the larger group of the Kirtis to dissolve its separate identity and made efforts to bring this group and its funds under its own control. As far as ideological differences were concerned, there were none because, both the groups claimed that they were following the line laid down by the Third International, one through the CPI, the other through the Berlin centre of the Ghadar Party. However, from 1936 onwards, the activities of both these communist groups merged into the general stream of Congress activities in the countryside. Consequently, it is extremely difficult to distinguish between strictly "communist activity" and "nationalist activity".

Alongwith Akalis and the Congressmen, the Punjab communists organised number of *morchas*. Following are some of the peasant agitations by them:

Peasant Agitations

The year 1938 was the year of active agrarian agitations. Like the peasant organisations in many other provinces, the Punjab Kisan Committee took an active part in organising, and, to a large extent, providing leadership to all the peasant agitations throughout the state.

Multan, Montgomery and Nilibar

In some of the areas of the districts of Multan and Montgomery, the government used to invite tenders in order to allot definite acres of land to the highest bidders. These tender holders further divided these lands among the rent paying cultivators. After the depression, tenders of government land by leases had so risen through competition that lessees, in order to make a profit, had been adding to the standard rents various other exactions. About 25,000 tenants of Nilibar went on strike and refused to pick cotton or sow wheat.[7] Similarly, the tenants of 20 or more villages in Talamba thana (district Multan) struck work in September 1938 and the strike lasted for about a month.[8] Jalawant Singh, Kartar Singh, Harbans Singh and Amir Huq were some of the Kisan Committee workers who carried on propaganda in these areas.[9] In both cases government and tender holders were compelled to negotiate and concede many of the immediate demands.[10] The more important demands were: (1) *Begar* of all kinds be stopped at once. (2) No tender holder shall have the right to exact illegal taxes from his tenants. (3) No tender holder shall eject any tenant for his participation in the strike. The tenants shall pay the price of green fodder at rupees three per unit instead of rupees six. (4) Cotton and other crops shall be divided half and half in the field itself. (5) Water for drinking purposes would be provided to the tenants by the tender holders.[11]

In the month of March 1938, tenants of the various *chaks* in the Montegomery district sent applications to the Commissioner threatening "kisan satyagraha" if their rents were not reduced.[12] A member of the PKC advised the peasants to get organised and form local committees.[13] Two months later, they ceased to work as a protest against the exaction of the temporary lessees of the government land and demanded that the same concessions may be granted to them as the government recently accorded to the tenants in the Nilibar.[14] Tenants of fifteen *chaks* in the Khanewal tehsil went on strike under the leadership of District Kisan Committees of Multan and Montegomery. They refused to pick cotton and sow the wheat crop.[15] Tenants struck work for about 20 days when ultimately a settlement was reached. According to the police, the agrarian unrest in this tehsil was "instigated by local Congress Committee".[16] The British Cotton Growers' Association was willing to discuss matters with the tenants and to meet their demands as far as possible but it refused to allow the Congress or any other outside body to act as an intermediary.[17]

In order to pacify the movement, the government started

arresting the workers of the PKC on the ground that "they had no interest in colony affairs beyond that of creating a revolutionary mentality".[18] On the other hand, it decided to split up some of the colony lands to be auctioned for temporary cultivation into small plots to suit lessees of slender means. The Kisan Committee could see through the government plan of diverting the attention of the tenants and tried to dissuade the small tenants from submitting tenders.[19] This gave rise to fresh problems. A great difficulty arose where tenant lessees succeeded in getting land which at that time was being cultivated by other tenants who had to be ejected because they wanted to cultivate the land themselves.[20]

The process of finding a foothold among the tenants of a few villages of Montegomery and Multan began in January 1938 and by the beginning of next year, the PKC was able to create some pockets of influence.[21] Tenants under the leadership of PKC put up resistance when a number of times armed attempts were made to eject them. According to a police report, on several occasions armed police had to be despatched from the district headquarters to various places to "prevent breach of peace".[22] Agrarian agitation in Multan district came to a head on 12 April, 1939 when the colonisation officer sought the help of the police in ejecting the old tenants from certain plots. Sixteen tenants were arrested for obstruction. Next day about 100 tenants entered the fields and began to plough them. They were dispersed with the help of the police and 18 of the more active tenants were arrested. It is interesting to note that the Congress leaders of some standing including a few members of the Legislative Assembly avoided any association with this "ill-advised agitation".[23]

Lyallpur

The spasmodic agitations of the peasants of the Lyallpur district which aroused the demands for reduction of land revenue and water rates gained considerable momentum in July 1938, when the irrigation department remoulded the canal outlets. Six *jathas* varying in strength from 60 to 550, aggregating in all to over 15,000, marched from various points in the district to headquarters, where a procession was taken out on 10 June, 1938.

Some papers claimed that the processionists numbered about 40,000 and that 90 percent of them were Sikhs.[24] The agitation became more vigorous in the next month and numerous meetings were held in the villages.[25]

In the beginning of July 1938, it was decided by 164 villages of Rajbaha area to begin a boycott of canal waters in order to compel the government to increase the water supply.[26] Because of the dire necessity of water in the summer for human beings and livestock, the boycott had to be ended on July 29, 1938. Socialists in the Amritsar Bandobast Committee toured the villages and advocated agitation over the remodelling of canals outlets on the lines of the Lyallpur agitation.[27]

Amritsar

In July 1938, kisan demonstrations at Amritsar had overshadowed all other forms of agrarian agitations. Leaders of Bandobast and Kisan Committees brought out a poster stating that the government planned an addition of four lakhs rupees per annum to the land revenue of the district, that the canal outlets of a number of villages in the Rayya area had been reduced and that the peasants were groaning under the burden of *malba, chowkidara, chahi* and local taxes.[28] Members of the Bandobast Committee and allied bodies decided to stage a big demonstration on these issues on 20 July, 1938, in the civil lines outside the canal and settlement offices. An order under section 144 was imposed on 19 July, prohibiting any procession in the areas around these offices.[29] On 20 July, after a big peasant gathering in the Jallianwala Bagh, 500 peasant volunteers under the leadership of Udham Singh marched through the city to express their grievances before the broader public and to make them known to the government.[30] When volunteers defied section 144, police lathi charged to disperse them. About 300 peasants received injuries and 145 prominent workers were arrested.[31] A war council consisting of two members each of the District Bandobast Committee (Akalis) and the Kisan Committee (Socialist), and one member of the Congress was formed to intensify the struggle. It was decided to send out *jathas* of twenty-five men everyday to defy the order under 144 CrPC.[32]

A mammoth meeting of the Amritsar citizens declared support to the kisan cause and condemned the repressive policy of the Sikandar Hayat government.[33] On 21 July grain and cloth markets of Amritsar observed *hartal* in sympathy with the victims of police lathi-charge. Saifuddin Kitchlew assured the Kisan Committee of Congress support.[34] Here again, the government made use of the dual tactic of force and clemency. It released 70 persons but arrested important socialist leaders. Kartar Singh Gill, the secretary of the PKC was interned in his village for an indefinite period. Prominent leaders of the PKC were arrested.[35] The All-India Kisan Sabha condemned the Unionist government for adopting the repressive policy of interning, externing and imprisoning workers of the PKC.[36] On 9 August, the agitation came to an end with assurances from the authorities.[37]

Reviewing the role of socialists in these agitations, a state police report submitted to the Central Government concluded:

> There has been intense rural activity on Communist lines in the Central Punjab districts and a series of small meetings have been held by the district Kisan Committee in the Lyallpur district with a view to stirring up disaffection among the peasants against the system of land revenue and other cognate forms of taxation. In the Sikh villages affected by recent agitation and by the propaganda, land revenue has not been collected with the usual promptitude. In the Montegomery district also the Kisan Committee has been trying to exploit differences between the lessees and the tenants. In all forms of rural agitation, the chief agitators have been communist Sikhs, many of them members of the Ghadar Party trained in Communist schools in Moscow.[38]

Lahore

The Lahore agitation was a result of increase in the revenue. A general impression of the poor economic condition of the large sections of the peasantry can be gathered from the simple fact that during 1938-39 scores of *lambardars* (headmen) and hundreds of peasants of Lahore district were arrested because of their inability to pay revenue in time[39] In the second half of March 1939, Lahore

District Kisan Committee declared in advance to mobilise 50,000 tenants to stage a protest demonstration; but according to the police only 300 persons turned up.[40] According to another source, the number of demonstrators was 8,000.[41] A contemporary government report stated that the Premier offered to receive a deputation of the peasants but refused to allow certain "professional agitators" who themselves were not peasants, and were not residents of Lahore district, to act as spokesmen of the deputation.[42] When demonstrators defied section 144 CrPC, 103 of them were arrested on the spot. The demonstration was staged on 23 March and till the end of the month 374 persons had been arrested.[43] Small batches of peasant volunteers gathered daily to defy section 144 and demonstrated before the legislative Assembly. Congress members of the Assembly and city "riff-raffs" openly supported the demonstrations.[44] The kisans were determined to continue their civil disobedience until their demands were met. They demanded that action on the new settlement should be postponed for three years. The Akalis actively participated in this agitation and till the end of April, 100 persons were arrested, including 24 Akalis.[45] Kisan Committees in the Kasur sub-division of Lahore and Dipalpur teshil of Montegomery refused to use canal water as a protest against the enhancement of revenue under the new settlement in Lahore.[46]

In the first half of May 1939, control of the agitation was taken over by the PKC in order to give a state-wide dimension to the agitation.[47] A charter of demands which listed, apart from general demands, the specific demands of peasants of various areas was presented to the government.[48] District level committees were directed to send volunteer *jathas* to court arrest at Lahore. Volunteer *jathas* from various districts such as Ferozepur, Ambala, Jalandhar, Amritsar, Gurdaspur and Lyallpur proceeded towards Lahore and on their way passed through villages denouncing the high-handedness of the "landlord ministry" in Punjab.[49] Almost all the *jathas* were intercepted by the police and later on arrests of prominent agitators started in the villages. War was approaching and the government decided to take firm action against the volunteers in order to stop further misleading.[50] All India Kisan Sabha (AIKS) decided to observe June 4 as the "All-India Punjab

Kisan Day" in order to express their solidarity with the Punjab peasants.[51] On June 17, The government issued a warning that firm action including the use of ordinary criminal law and Criminal Law Amendment Act would be used against the organisers of "kisan satyagraha" in Lahore.[52] Though the agitation continued for three months and about 4,000 persons were thrown behind bars,[53] and internal dissensions weakened the movement, it was mainly the iron heel of imperialist repression that crushed the agitators.

The Second Provincial Kisan Conference met at Sargodha from 5 to 7 September, 1939 under the presidentship of Baba Rur Singh, MLA.[54] The conference expressed its determination to carry forward the struggle by further mobilisation and organisation of the peasantry under the banner of the PKC. But, the big war had already started and this completely altered the whole situation.

Anti-Recruitment and Anti-War Agitation

During the later 1930s, the struggle against British imperialism in Punjab took the form of an agitation against the Unionist government which suppressed nationalist activity with a heavy hand and stood for all out support to the British rulers in the event of war. Everywhere in the province leaders of the Congress Socialist Party and other leftists asked the people not to enlist in the army. The Unionist ministers toured various districts to encourage their supporters in resisting and countering Congress propaganda. Keeping in view the anti-war agitation, the tours were designed to mobilise people belonging to the rural areas to rally behind the "peasant government". A police report on the anti-war agitation, submitted to the Central Government in November 1937, records:

> Speakers at meetings have shown an increasing tendency to declaim against enlistment in the Army. Leaders from outside the province were the first to speak on this subject but it has now been taken up by local Congress speakers of all ranks. The rumours of war serve to spurt on socialist and communist agitators in their denunciations of imperialism and in their

appeals to make the empire's difficulty, India's opportunity.[55]

Yusuf Meharally set the tone at Amritsar on 3 September, when he declared that "in the event of war, neither a single man nor a single pie would be provided to the British government by Indians". At about the same time, Professor N.G. Ranga addressed a series of socialist meetings in the Jalandhar district and advised the people not to render any help to British imperialism in any future war. Towards the end of September 1937, in the Mazoor Kisan Conference at Barapind, Swami Sehjanand presided and repeated the same injunction. At the Kisan Conference at Nowshera Pannuwan on 29 September, Jaya Prakash Narayan advised the audience not only to refuse to help the British Government in the event of war, but also to take advantage of the pre-occupation of the British in the next war to make a bid for liberty.

Thanks to the efforts of extra-provincial socialist leaders, anti-war propaganda was well under way in Punjab by the beginning of October 1937, when Pandit Jawaharlal Nehru made another of his meteoric appearances in the province and gave fresh impetus to the agitation. Speaking at the Garhdiwala Conference to an audience of 50,000 on 11 October, he said that clouds of war were hovering over the world and India should avail itself of the troubled times to set its house in order. A provincial police officer reported:

> The significance of this visit is obvious even though its immediate effect was negligible. A friend of mine told me that he had heard Dr. M. Ashraf (who accompanied Nehru on his tour) at a social function at Lahore saying that the Congress intended to concentrate on the Army recruiting areas in the West Punjab in order to cut the supply of manpower at its source. Dr. Ashraf himself advised the students at Amritsar on the 19th of October to exert their influence in the villages and educate the masses against the recruitment in the Army.[56]

In November 1937, the League Against Fascism was formed at Lahore.[57] The League gave a call to observe an "Anti-War Day" on Armistice Day. Only eight districts responded with meetings, at which 24 speakers made anti-war speeches. Afzal Haq, one of the leaders of Ahrar Party, talked of triple boycott which included the boycott of the army. Between April and December, 115 persons had made anti-war speeches at 71 meetings in various parts of the province.[58] At the end of December 1937, the Rawalpindi division unit of the Congress Socialist Party deputed a group of its members to tour the districts of Gujarat, Jhelum and Rawalpindi to conduct anti-war propaganda.[59]

The provincial police authorities observed: "The infection is spreading and it looks as if 'not a single man, nor a single pie' is going to be the principal Congress slogan in Punjab in the days to come".[60]

Throughout the year 1938 anti-recruitment propaganda formed an integral part of the Congress and Socialist activities. According to a police report 310 meetings had been held in Punjab for that purpose.[61] The speech delivered at a meeting organised by the Amritsar Kisan Committee at Chheharta Sahib by Giani Sajjan Singh can be taken as typical of all the left popular speeches delivered. It ran as following:

> People will prolong their subjugation by helping the government in the next war. Peasants and workers of the world have decided to refuse to participate in any war in which these governments are involved. They (workers and peasants) expect employees in utility services to go on strike simultaneously and to utilise the opportunity to subvert their governments and to establish popular rule. Indians should like-wise render no assistance to the British in the next war but should keep in readiness to launch their struggle for independence.[62]

In the middle of 1938, military observers were worried about the adverse effect of the propaganda.[63] The police department, however, held a different opinion. In a note prepared in July 1938, it observed:

> Sporadic propaganda of this type is not having any real effect on Punjab. Public opinion in the province attaches far too much importance to military service as an economic asset and to be

induced to give up such a valuable tradition and the attempts to dissuade Punjabis from enlistment are regarded purely as a Hindu move to weaken Mohammedan contribution to army.[64]

In an atmosphere of communal tension, this was the government's most powerful weapon to fight the anti-recruitment propaganda.[65] However, the potential of the kisan movement in drawing into its orbit the military bases of the British empire was an alarming development for the authorities, both of the British government in India and the Unionist Party government in Punjab. So, the Unionist Party moved in a big way to claim for herself the position of the only real champion of the interests of the peasantry and to give a deadly blow to the Congress Party and its anti-recruitment campaign. It is in that context that the agrarian legislation carried on by this party in 1938 along with severe political attacks on the Congress must be understood.[66]

Agrarian Legislation and the Punjab Congress

The Unionist Party and the Punjab Provincial Congress (excluding its small left wing) constituted two polarities, the former defending the interests of the rural landlords, and the latter defending the interests of the urban commercial and money lending classes. The new agrarian legislation was designed to wean away the peasantry from the newly established influence of the Congress and the PKC. The Punjab Legislative Assembly's summer session which concluded on 23 July, 1938, passed various bills such as the Restitution of Mortgaged Lands Bill, the Registration of Moneylenders Bill, the Agricultural Produce Markets Bill and the Alienation of Land (further Amendment) Bill.

The agrarian problem in Punjab was not less acute than in the other provinces of British India. However, during the election campaigns in Punjab, the leaders of Congress never specifically mentioned anything about the agrarian question, the predominant problem of the province. This was logical as the top leadership of the provincial Congress was greatly under the pressure of the urban moneylending and trading sections. The Unionist Party, as against it, claimed to "follow a consistent and vigorous policy for ameliorating the condition of the masses, particularly their backward sections", and a policy of relieving the agricultural and labouring classes of their burdens of debt.[67]

The introduction of various agrarian bills placed the Punjab Congress in a paradoxical situation. If it did not support the bills actively and criticised them as being inadequate, it ran the risk of giving the impression that the Congress was opposed to the measures which helped the agriculturist. On the other hand, consistent stand along the lines of the Congress programme regarding amelioration of the conditions of the agriculturists would have certainly incurred the wrath of the moneylending, commercial and professional sections of the urban population. The big landlords of Punjab were intensely pro-imperialist. The problems before the imperialists was how to safeguard the interest of the landlords and at the same time pacify the peasants so that Punjab might be preserved as the recruiting ground for the imperialist army. The bills referred to above, provided no relief to the small-holding peasantry against the agriculturist moneylenders. They were designed to check the exploitation of only one section (though by far the biggest section) of moneylenders. Nor was anything done about the two major and long standing demands of the peasantry, that of reducing land revenue and water rates. The demands of the tenants-at-will who cultivated more than 50 percent of the arable land were totally neglected.

The non-agricultural moneylending and commercial sections called meetings and *hartals* throughout Punjab to express their opposition to these bills. An All-India Non-Agriculturists Association, with Mahasha Krishan of the *Partap*, as President, was organised at Lahore to agitate against the bills. But, the bills were welcomed by all sections of the agriculturists and they came in thousands to listen to the speeches of Chhotu Ram during his tour to the districts in the south-west and central Punjab. All Muslim papers, strongly supported the bills and condemned the anti-bill agitations. The papers controlled by the Sikh leadership also refused to take any part in the agitation. The socialist members of the Legislative Assembly, under instructions from the CSP, gave their qualified support to the Bills. The Congress Socialist Party and the Punjab Kisan Committee supported four agrarian bills passed by the Punjab Legislative Assembly to the extent that they benefited the tillers of the soil. The Punjab Kisan Committee, however, warned the peasantry that unless and untill the Land Alienation Act was revised to benefit all the genuine kisans (who had not been covered by the definition of statutory agriculturist); protection against the kisan moneylenders was afforded to the poor kisans; a moratorium was declared on all agrarian indebtedness of the small holders; and finally, all settlements were stopped and land revenue was replaced by income tax on agricultural incomes, they would have to continue to struggle against the Unionist ministry. The committee also at the same time denounced the agitation organised by the non-agriculturists against the bills. It called upon all its branches to conduct an intensive campaign simultaneously against the non-agriculturists and their anti-kisan propaganda; as also against the anti-kisan economic and political policies of the Punjab government.

The provincial Congress was ridden by factional wrangles between the groups led by Dr. Gopichand and Dr. Satyapal. The Satyapal group had the support of the CSP including the Kirti group of the CPI and the Radical League and a CPI section led by Sohan Singh Josh was inclined towards Dr. Gopi Chand.[68] The party elections in 1938 had brought their differences in the open. This naturally divided the leftists also. Ajoy Ghosh and Yusuf Meharally who had come to attend the fourth session of the All-India Congress Socialist Party at Lahore on April 12-13, 1938, attempted in vain, to mediate between the dissidents and the provincial CSP leadership. The Kirti group accused Sohan Singh Josh of being closer to the right wing in the Congress and also of hobnobbing with Master Tara Singh when the latter invited Maharaja of Patiala to a tea party.[69] So, when the issues came to a head in the fight against the Unionist government's zamindara ideology and agitation against the agrarian bills, the Congress found itself unable to act boldly.

The Unionist Party organised conferences in various districts to convince the peasants that the Unionist ministry was a "zamindara government" working for their welfare and best interests. The conference at Lyallpur was attended by about 50,000 people. The Unionist leaders characterised the arguments of the

Non-Agriculturist Association as the "arguments of the disappointed capitalists" and pointed out that the legislations had been designed to bring practical benefits to small holders.[70] Referring to the Congress stand on the agrarian legislation, Chhotu Ram said: "The so-called Congressmen in this province are a gang of traders and capitalists, who are working not for the liberation of the country, but to grind their own axes... *It is the Unionist Party which has been following (implementing) the Congress programme in this Province*".[71]

Every conference was concluded with a warning that any attempt to undermine the "supremacy" of Punjab in the army would be firmly resisted.[72] Thus, under the cover of ameliorative measures, through deliberate and calculated efforts, agriculturist sections of the province were once again tied to the war-chariot of British imperialism. The provincial Congress was pushed into giving up the most significant plank of its anti-British struggle, i.e., the anti-recruitment campaign.[73] The onus of exposing the landlord Unionist ministry which was acting as an ally of imperialism, was also on them. They attempted to launch peasant agitation on the general demands of the peasantry like the reduction of land revenue and water rates. However, the CSP (consisting of left Congressmen and communists) leading the PKC were entrapped in a situation where the projected image of the Congress acted as a deterrent to their attracting all those sections of the peasantry who were in the grip of moneylenders and were more attracted to the Unionist government. The whole peasant movement suffered a severe set back.

At the end of August 1939 Sikander Hayat declared that he guaranteed that the manpower and resources of Punjab would be unhesitatingly placed at the disposal of Great Britain.[74] He was joined in his expression of loyalty by Sardar Ujjal Singh, a prominent Sikh leader. The repressive machinery of the state was brought into full-swing against the opponents of war. The press was terrorised and stringent measures were taken to prevent political demonstration. In spite of this suppression, however, on 20 December, 1939, about 20,000 peasants of Jalandhar district staged a demonstration in the city under the leadership of Hari Singh Saundh in order to express their grievances. The inconstancy of the water level and failure of the rains had spelt utter ruin of crops in the doaba region, but the taxes continued to press down heavily. Peasants poured into the city from the villages shouting slogans: "supply us water", "we are bending under the weight of taxes" etc.[75] But, in effect, the peasant movement and the anti-recruitment campaign which had brought the peasantry into the larger stream of anti-imperialist struggle became weak.

People's War Period

On June 22, 1941, Germany attacked Russia and for CPI, this transformed the character of the imperialist war into People's War.[76] The new party line was derived from two important documents which the Communist Party of Great Britain (CPGB) published in the first month after Hitler's attack on the Soviet Union. These documents were circulated by the Central Committee of the CPI in a party letter of December 1, 1941. "These documents make us realise as in a flash that in formulating our policy, we have allowed ourselves to be misled by our own 'theories' and 'speculations' which were the product of our bourgeois nationalism, rather than by the Proletarian Internationalism of Marx and Lenin".[77] In a self-condemning tone, it stated as follows:

> We went wrong because our blind bourgeois nationalist hatred of British imperialist government prevented us from grasping the simple fact that the government was now in the same progressive camp with the Soviet Union and ranged against Hitler-Racism. It dimmed our Marxism-Leninism for a time and we were unable to see that this fact had to be recognised and made use of for the very purpose of liberation of our people from the national enemy.[78]

The CPI leadership was well aware of the fact that their arguments to justify this new line would not convince the people.[79] The Punjab government decided to release eight of the leading communists of the province on 1 May, 1942 because of a visible increase in the volume of pro-war propaganda.[80] The communist appeals for cooperation in the war-efforts, however, were making little headway. Poorly attended meetings were held to celebrate 'May Day' and 'Anti-Japanese Day'.[81] The new trend in communist policy had aroused bitter opposition from the Congress and CSP.[82] A meeting of the Punjab Kisan Committee was held at Lahore on 20 and 21 May. It was attended by 450 members. Instructions were issued to all kisan workers in the province to support the war effort, demand the formation of a National Government and the release of all security prisoners.[83] In the first half of June, an All India Detainees Release Conference was held in Rawalpindi at which B.P.L. Bedi, S.S. Josh and others urged resistance to the axis powers. The conference was interrupted by the Congress socialists.[84] Keeping in view the hostility of the Congress workers, later on communist leaders devoted the larger portion of their speeches to criticism of the British government.[85]

In the second half of July 1942, communists were very active in conducting propaganda and organised as many as seven rural meetings. Their argument was that it was imperative to resist Japanese aggression. They stated that support for the British rulers was a matter of expediency. It was said that joining the army in huge numbers would transform it into a national army paving the way for the seizure of power at the end of the war.[86] It was at this conjuncture that the communists belonging to the CPI and Kirti group joined hands for the first time with "mutual trust" and "full faith"[87]

Although the communists continued to hold conferences throughout the month of July, it was becoming increasingly difficult for them to conduct effective pro-war propaganda in the face of the reports assiduously spread by the Congress and by the Akalis that they (communists) had purchased their release from jail on the understanding that they would back the war-effort of the government.[88] The ban on the CPI was removed on 23 July, 1942. With the removal of the ban the systematic organisation of the Communist Party started in Punjab.

Meanwhile, the AICC session passed the famous 'Quit India' resolution at Bombay on 8 August, 1942. The resolution challenged the government to act immediately. Within hours after the AICC meeting had concluded, Gandhi and all the members of the Congress Working Committee were arrested. Public reaction was immediate and spontaneous. There were demonstrations and processions everywhere. At Amritsar, Congress workers made speeches asking the people and the police to stage a revolt. There were *hartals* in many towns of Punjab and telephone lines were cut at many places. There were clashes between the people and the police and lathis were used freely to disperse the crowds.[89] In spite of all the stringent measures the government could not completely suppress the Civil Disobedience Movement. The PCSP leader, Puran Chand Azad, after talks with Yusuf Meharally, Secretary AICSP, declared the intention of his party to follow whole-heartedly the Congress move. Many of its members had already gone underground.

Following the lead given by P.C. Joshi, communists in Punjab issued a press statement in which they accused the Congress of following a path of national suicide but blamed the government for precipitating the crisis. They declared that they would force the government to release the Congress leaders and open negotiation for the establishment of a National Government.[90]

To spread nationalist and anti-British views in the armed forces had always been one of the essential elements of the Kirtis' programme in Punjab. The anti-recruitment and anti-war agitation was steered precisely towards the achievement of the purpose. But their shift to the new line of People's War created a paradoxical situation. The fact was that soldiers on leave from the Far East campaigns were spreading anti-British 'loose-talk' in the villages. The desertions from the army were presenting a problem of increasing gravity. The monthly total of provincial combatant deserters had risen steadily from 1,600 in January to 4,000 in June 1942. The deserters of all kinds at large in the province, on 30 June numbered no less than 15,442. Ironically the Kirtis had waited for this golden opportunity for fourteen years, but when it appeared on the historical juncture, they were asking the people to join the army in record breaking numbers.[91]

There was a major shift in the nature of communist political work within a few months. By October 1942, communists in Punjab had almost abandoned the conduct of anti-facist propaganda and were concentrating on strengthening and enlarging the party organisation.[92] In their open meetings the main emphasis was on demands for the release of Congress leaders and the establishment of a National Government. Surveying the political situation in the province, a political report observed: "Communist influence was undoubtedly helpful in exercising a moderate effect on the Congress campaign during the critical phases; it now remains to be seen whether or not communists have outlived their usefulness".[93] The communist organ *Jang-e-Azadi* continued to conduct propaganda in favour of national unity, to criticise the government, to demand the release of Congress leaders and to issue appeals to resist Japanese aggression.[94]

The mobilisation of limited sections of the peasantry in the agitations discussed in this paper points to the mass base of the PKC (headed mainly by the Kirti group and the Punjab branch of the CPI). Like the mass base of the Akalis and the Congress Party, the limited mass base of the communists in the countryside was also among the Jat agriculturists mainly of the central Punjab districts. As to the social bases of the leadership, the impression one gathers from the reminiscences or memoirs written later tends to point out that local leadership was mostly provided by well-to-do-peasants who in a number of cases had acquired a certain level of formal education and were now engaged in agriculture. It was thus able mainly to agitate on those issues which were central to the concerns of the relatively well-to-do peasants. It could not successfully mobilise them for the demands of the tenants against the big landlords. Whereas the united front with the Congress brought the socialists of the Congress, and the communists together in the peasant movements, the factionalism of the Congress and connections of its leadership with the moneylending and trading interests tended to dilute the character of the agitations. On the other hand, the Unionist Party found it easy to sell the 'zamindara' ideology, confuse the issues dear to the left, and isolate and suppress the communists. The People's War thesis further eroded the identity of the communists. Though mobilisation of the peasantry and their agitation for their specific demands continued on a low key, the thrust of the movement was blunted by the successful campaigns for recruitment to the army.

Notes

1. The first issue of *Kirti* was published in February, 1926. For details see Bhagwan Josh, *Communist Movement in Punjab 1926-47*, Delhi: Anupama Publications, 1979.
2. At the initial stages important Akali leaders such as Jathedar Udham Singh Nagoke, Darshan Singh Pheruman and Gurmukh Singh Musafir had close links with Kirti management. Master Tara Singh, the future leader of the Sikhs, wrote some articles in *Kirti* during this period. See his article 'Bolshevik Propaganda in India', *Kirti*, February 1929.
3. Meerut conspiracy case (1929-33) (English translations of Gurmukhi exhibits). It were these lofty intentions which inspired the militancy of Punjabi youth in the first quarter of the twentieth century and led some of them to embrace the terrorist method of political struggle.
4. *Kirti*, October 1927.
5. *Ibid.*
6. *Ibid.*
7. *Kirti Lehar*, December 11, 1938.
8. *National Front*, December 4, 1938.
9. *Kirti Lehar*, August 7 and September 8, 1938.
10. *National Front*, November 27, 1938.
11. *Ibid.* Also see *Kirti Lehar*, July 10, 1938.
12. Home (Political), File No.18/3/1938.
13. *Ibid.*
14. Home (Political), File No.18/6/1938.
15. Home (Political), File No.18/10/1938.
16. Home (Political), File No.18/11/1938.
17. *Ibid.*
18. Home (Political), File No.18/2/1939.
19. *Ibid.*
20. *Ibid.*
21. A police report, commenting on the activities of PKC workers, records: "The danger of intemperate and inciting agitation by

workers of the Kisan Committee is well illustrated by an incident which occurred in the Montgomery district on the 15th February 1939. Kisan agitation has given rise to the idea that tenants who remain in a particular plot of land for over six years become entitled to proprietary rights. To safeguard their own interests, a few land owners of village Suchan arranged for some of their tenants to exchange plots of land. This action by the landlords led the tenants to believe that the agitators were correct and so they refused to change. The relations between the parties became strained and the landlords eventually attacked their tenants. The few policemen who were present, were unable to prevent the clash. Ten workers who are to be blamed for the whole incident, are now exploiting the unfortunate incident in order to create further unrest". Home (Political), File No.18/3/39.

22. Home (Political), File No.18/3/1939.
23. Home (Political), File No.18/4/1939.
24. Home (Political), File No.18/6/1939.
25. Home (Political), File No.18/7/1938. See also *Kirti Lehar* July 3, 1938 and July 10, 1938.
26. *Kirti Lehar*, July 10, 1938.
27. Home (Political), File No.18/6/1938.
28. Home (Political), File No.18/7/1938.
29. *Ibid.*
30. According to *Kirti Lehar*, July 31, 1938, about 20,000 peasants participated in the Jallianwala Bagh gathering.
31. *Ibid.*
32. *National Front*, July 31, 1938. The members of the war-council were Sohan Singh Josh, Sohan Singh Bhakna, Hakim Sikandar Khizer, Darshan Singh Peruman and Partap Singh Kairon.
33. *National Front*, August 7, 1938.
34. *Ibid.*
35. *Kirti Lehar*, July 31, 1938.
36. *National Front*, October, 1938.
37. The premier addressed crowded meetings of the zamindars at three places in the district on 9 and 10 August, 1938 and attacked

the leaders of the agitation. He emphasised that the anti-government demonstration at the present moment amounted to an expression of disapproval of zamindars and of the policy of the present government which had recently carried through agrarian legislation in the interests of the agriculturists. Home (Political), File No. 18/8/38.

38. Home (Political), File No. 18/8/1939.
39. *Kirti Lehar*, June 4, 1939.
40. Home (Political), File No. 18/3/1939.
41. *Kirti Lehar*, April 2, 1939.
42. Home (Political), File No. 18/3/1939.
43. *Ibid.*
44. *Ibid.*
45. Home (Political), File No. 18/4/1939.
46. *Ibid.*
47. *National Front*, May 28, 1939.
48. *Ibid.*
49. Kirti Lehar, July 31, 1939; also see *National Front,* August 27, 1939.
50. Home (Political), File No. 18/6/1939. On June 16, 1939, Subhash Chandra Bose sent a long message to PKC in which he expressed the fullest support for the Lahore *morcha*. He stated: 'Due to the over-bearing, unsympathetic and oppressive conduct of the Unionist Government, the District Kisan Committee of Lahore has felt compelled to launch the civil disobedience movement against the enhancement of land revenue. I am told that upto date 1,700 persons have been arrested and sentenced to various terms of imprisonment. They include 200 kisan ladies also, out of whom 75 ladies are still in jail. During these three months of struggle four persons have died in Jail including a seven months old child of Comrade Yog Raj. The sacrifices are sterling and heroic and the determined manner in which struggle is being carried on gives credit to the organisers of the movement.

    "The so-called Kisan government of the Punjab stands exposed and unmasked as the instrument of oppression in the hands of foreign imperialism. As such the kisans are fighting the battle of all progressive forces of the province and deserve fullest support and sympathy of the Public". *National Front*, July 9, 1939.

51. *National Front*, July 11, 1939.
52. *National Front*, June 25, 1939.
53. *Kirti Lehar*, July 9, 1939.
54. *National Front*, September 10, 1939.
55. Home (Political), File No. 18/11/1937. Outside leaders who first specifically spoke on this issue were Jawaharlal Nehru, Dr. M. Ashraf, Jai Prakash Narayan, J.D. Bukhari, Yusuf Meharally, Swami Sahjanand and Prof. N.G. Ranga.
56. *Ibid.*
57. *Ibid.* Following were the members of the League: B.P.L. Bedi, Hiteshi Chander, Kishen Chander, Jai Gopal, Inder Dutt, Narender Nath Pleader, Mian Iftkhar-ud-Din, Dev Raj Sethi, Abdullah Safdar, Raj Bans Krishen, Ram Lal, Mulk Raj Anand, Master Raja Ram, Sardul Singh Pleader, and Karam Singh.
58. *Ibid.* Punjab Congressites who spoke twice or more than twice on the subject were Mian Iftikhar-ud-Din, Chaudhri Afzal Haq, Sohan Singh Josh, Sultan Ahmed, Asghar, Gian Sagar, Inder Dutt, Mange Ram Vats, Master Raja Ram, Dr. Sant Ram Sethi and Dr. Saif-ud-Din Kichlew.
59. *Ibid.* Members of the group were: Abdul Kasuri, Ahmed Din Qassab, Abdul Aziz, Mohan Lal, Sheikh Mohammed Hayat and Master Raja Ram.
60. *Ibid.*
61. *Ibid.*
62. *Ibid.*
63. *Ibid.*
64. *Ibid.*
65. *Ibid.* On May 6, 1938, Ram Manohar Lohia issued the following press statement: "The Governor of Punjab in course of a speech to the Lahore Old Soldiers' Association, expressed his distress at the attempts to discourage enlistment to the Indian Army. He referred in particular to the motives of the non-martials who were trying to disaffect and mislead the races of Punjab. I belong to what the British government pleased to call the non-martial

races and it was less than a month ago that I spoke in Lahore on the necessity of refusal of military service. Many others like me, who concern themselves with the freedom and peace of the world and their own country have to speak in Punjab on the subject of the Indian Army. Our motives are now suspect to the Punjab Governor. Is the Punjab Governor suggesting that we non-Punjabis are desirous of replacing the Punjabis in the military services of the country? I look upon the Indian Army as one of the greatest instruments of reaction that the world has ever known. In the event of a future world war, the Indian Army will be used to keep India in bondage and to help to win the war for the British empire. Therefore, we don't want our countrymen to enlist in the Indian Army. Inevitably, we address our appeal to the Punjabis, for the British government has degraded the Punjab into a recruiting ground of its military forces". Home (Political) File No. 58/1938.

66. Appealing to the peasantry to enlist in the army and defending the bills at Sonepat before a gathering of 30,000 peasants, Sikander Hayat declared: "I am a soldier and I am always prepared to serve you. There are people who tell us that it is against the interest of the country to enlist in the Army. I ask these people if it is proper to demilitarise the people of Punjab who are the sword men of India and will defend India against foreign invasion". *National Front*, July 3, 1938.
67. Sir Sikander Hayat's speech quoted in *The Tribune*, January 17, 1937.
68. Home (Political), File No. 18/1/1939.
69. *Kirti Lehar*, July 9, 1939.
70. Home (Political), File No. 18/9/1938.
71. Madan Gopal, *Sir Chhotu Ram: A Political Biography*, New Delhi: Sterling, 1977, p. 116.
72. Home (Political), File No. 18/8/1938. Bhai Parmanand, MLA, in an open letter published in the *Hindu* of September 9, 1938, stigmatised the agrarian legislation of the Unionist Party as communal oppression and Bolshevism. Similarly, Akali Party's attack on the Unionist Ministry from the rightist standpoint, pushed the illiterate Muslim peasant masses towards the Unionists.

73. Home (Political), File No. 18/8/39.
74. *National Front*, August 27, 1939.
75. *Kirti Lehar*, January 1, 1939.
76. Joshi, P.C., *CPI: Its Policy and Work in the War of Liberation*, September 1942.
77. Home (Political), File No. 44/32/1942.
78. *Ibid.*
79. *Ibid.* Jail document was written by some of the CPI members in Jail to convince the outside party members of the correctness of the new line.

    In jail document it was categorically asserted: "Should the Indian proletariat refuse to join this battle, because it is not yet nationally 'free', because even the most elementary rights are denied to it? The Indian proletariat should not allow itself to be deluded by such false nationalist considerations. As a party of the International, it looks upon the USSR as the only fatherland. Its defence is the most sacred, the most vital task. It fights for national freedom to secure international freedom for its entire class. Its international freedom hinges on the safety of USSR. National struggle is only a part of the international struggle and not vice-versa".
80. Home (Political), File No. 18/5/1942.
81. *Ibid.*
82. *Ibid.*
83. The only exception was Dr. Satyapal, member of Provincial Assembly, former President of PPCC who in a letter offered his services to the government to tend the wounded in the overseas theatres of war. He wrote: "I have no faith in the satyagraha movement which has produced practically no effect on Indians or on the government; in the Punjab the movement has miserably failed and humiliated the Congress in the eyes of the government and the public". Home (Political), File No. 4/8/41.
84. Home (Political), File No. 18/6/1942.
85. *Ibid.*
86. Home (Political), File No. 18/7/42.

87. *Ibid.*
88. A secret note dated 19th June, 1942 by DIG of Police, CID Punjab informed the Central Government that he had a long talk with Teja Singh Swatantar, Achhar Singh Chhina and Sohan Singh Josh. He wrote: "Their main object in seeing me was, of course, to demand the release of more members of their party. They are being hounded by the Congress, CSP and Akalis and feel that they are too few to be able to put across their propaganda. The fact that only eight members of the party have been released in the Punjab has made them suspect and they are being accused of being government agents".

    Home (Political), File No. 7/2/42 (Pol.1) and K.W.

    They told the DIG that if they supported the British whole-heartedly, they would be as impotent a political force as Roy's Radical Democratic Party. But they promised to damp-down their anti-British speeches at public meetings.
89. Home (Political), File No. 18/8/42.
90. *Ibid.* The statement was signed by Sohan Singh Josh, Teja Singh Swatantar, Karam Singh Mann, Bhagat Singh Bilga, Achhar Singh Chhina, Ferozdin Mansur, Iqbal Singh and Fazal Illahi Qurban.
91. *Ibid.*
92. Home (Political), File No. 18/10/42.
93. *Ibid.*
94. *Ibid.*

11

Praja Mandal Movement in East Punjab States: Notes on the Elite Political Culture

M.S. DHAMI

The Praja Mandal Movement in the east Punjab states which formally took birth in 1928 was a reaction against "double oppression" resulting from colonial rule and autocratic regimes in the princely states. Geographically, the main locus of the movement was the Punjabi-speaking areas of the Patiala state, the largest of all these states. Soon the movement spilled over to the other contiguous states of Nabha, Jind and Malerkotla.[1] In the later period the movement spread to the princely states of Faridkot and Kapurthala as well.[2]

In the first decade of its emergence (1928-38), the movement was primarily led by the rural based Akali leaders who earlier participated in the Gurdwara Reform Movement of 1921-24. In 1938, an important section of the peasant leadership in the movement, linked to the communist-led Punjab Kisan Committee, Amritsar, led a militant *muzara* (tenant) movement against *biswedars* (landlords) of the Patiala state. Around this period (1938-39) the social base of the movement was broadened by the inclusion of pro-Congress, mainly Hindu, professionals and businessmen.[3] For a while the movement looked like a broad democratic front of 'militant' Akalis, pro-Congress Praja Mandalists, and communists. This front also presented a possibility of the emergence of a secular political culture during the heyday of the movement. This possibility could not materialize subsequently but it did leave behind a trail of this broad-based front alongwith traces of secular political culture.[4]

In the early 1940s, certain exogenous factors (including the circumstances associated with the transfer of power) and the internal dynamics of the movement released certain forces which led to the disintegration of this broad front. By 1945, the three constituents of the movement separated into three independent political groups: Akali Dal, Praja Mandal and the communists. Commenting upon this development Romesh Walia writes that Praja Mandal in 1945 had now become a Hindu urbanite movement whereas in the initial stages it was a Sikh peasant movement.[5]

The major concern of this brief paper is to explore the elite political culture, that is, the political orientations, values and ideology of the leading actors in this movement. For this we will have recourse to the statements of the prominent leaders and the overall programme and strategies of the Punjab Riasti Praja Mandal. As the Praja Mandal during its heyday was a federal body encompassing three important constituents, we shall naturally look into the changing programmes and policies of these constituents from 1928 to 1945.

The other objective of this study is to explore why this movement, which had the potentialities of developing into a broad democratic front, failed to do so. And, why this movement—which went some way in the direction of the development of secular political culture—ultimately failed in building such political culture. For the purpose of this study, we define secular political culture of a movement as a certain degree of uniformity in terms of goals, aims and ideology which makes possible mutual collaboration amongst leaders despite their social diversity in terms of community, caste and other primordial loyalties.

Lastly, we make some tentative observations regarding the

factors that go into the making of elite political culture. Firstly, we argue that the elite political culture or their ideology is seldom independent of the social structure and its modern institutional appendages, especially the educational institutions and the mass media. Secondly, the situational factors, including the nature of political institutions, obviously play an important role. Finally, the political elites or party ideologies who lay down the ideology and programme of political groups do represent, to a considerable extent, the interests of the social formations they come from.[6]

With this brief overview of the Praja Mandal Movement in the east Punjab states, and the objectives of this study, we first draw a brief sketch of the socio-economic structure of Patiala state. This is followed by the study of elite political culture in the three phases[7] of the movement. Finally, we sum up our findings about the elite political culture of this movement, and the contribution of the movement to the post-independence political development.

Socio-Economic Structure of the Patiala State

Patiala being the largest of the east Punjab states, its socio-economic structure may be taken as more or less representative of the other contiguous princely states. According to the 1931 census, the total population of the state was 1,625,520 having a total area of 5,992 sq. miles.[8] Religion-wise, Sikhs were around 39 percent, Hindus little over 38 percent and Muslims 22.3 percent. The next decennial census recorded the Sikh population as 46 percent of the total while Hindu population went down to 31 percent. Muslim population kept around the previous figure.[9]

One of the peculiar features of the east Punjab states was that out of the three major religious communities, only the Sikhs came under the influence of a powerful Gurdwara Reform Movement led by Akalis in 1921-25. The Sikh population of the states was greatly stirred and politicised by Akali *morcha* at Jaito in Nabha state during 1923-25.[10] The Arya Samaj movement made comparatively lesser impact on the Hindus of the princely states—Sanatan Dharam being the predominant persuasion amongst the Hindus as compared with those of the British Punjab. Muslims, the least numerous of the three communities, were also the most backward educationally and socially. Majority of the Muslims were artisans or tenants growing vegetables in and around towns.[11] In view of the overall backwardness of the Muslim community, and the politico-religious origin of the Praja Mandal Movement, Muslims took little notice of it.

As compared with the adjoining British territories, the land revenue demands of the state were very high. At times revenue authorities had to use police force in order to realise land revenue.[12] The state administration took little interest in providing roads, hospitals, educational institutions and other welfare facilities, to its subjects. The literacy level of the people was very low—only 4.9 percent of the state subjects were literate in 1931.[13]

The agrarian set up was most oppressive. The Patiala (and other states) had two main forms of land tenures. In one type of villages, the land was cultivated by peasant proprietors. This type was designated as *bhaichara* tenure and also covered *pattidari* tenure. In the second type, the *biswedari*, biswedar (or the landlord) was the proprietor. The second system worked under two types of tenancies. In some villages the cultivators had hereditary cultivating rights but no proprietary rights. They paid fixed rent as *malikana* to the owner, and were designated as occupancy tenants. In the second type, villages belonged to the biswedars and the land was cultivated by tenants-at-will who had no hereditary cultivating rights, and their tenure was at the will of the owner.[14] The *biswedari* system had its origin in the conferring of *jagirs* (of villages) on high state officials and close relations or kins of the state ruler.[15] As to the extent of biswedari land tenure, there are different estimates. The *Census Report of Patiala State, 1931* claims the prevalence of this system in 746 villages, which comes to around 21 percent of the total villages in the state. In addition, the rulers had huge area under their personal management. As early as 1909, the Settlement Commissioner affirms that the "relations between the landlords and tenants in the Patiala State were strained and bitter long before this settlement commenced".[16] The position of the tenant was further aggravated by "a strong offensive and defensive alliance between the *ahlkar* (official) and *biswedar* (landlord) classes".[17]

The other most oppressed group was that of landless Harijans who would often be compelled to do *begar* (forced labour) by police and other state officials. Thus, tenant cultivators, poor peasants and the landless Harijans comprised the most oppressed and exploited classes which subsequently gave birth to a militant peasant struggle in the states.[18] We now present the three phases of the Praja Mandal Movement in the east Punjab states.

First Phase: Akali-based Praja Mandal, 1928-38

The people in the east Punjab states, particularly in the Patiala state, not only suffered economic and social hardship but they were also denied the most elementary civil rights. After the end of Akali movement in 1925, the Punjab government released most of the Akali leaders, and in 1926, Sewa Singh Thikriwala, an extremist Akali Sikh leader of the Patiala State was also released from the Lahore jail without any condition. But, immediately after his release, he was arrested by Patiala police and detained in Patiala jail.[19] Maharaja Bhupindra Singh in 1928 also signified his refusal to release Sewa Singh Thikriwala. This unleashed a movement for the release of Thikriwala throughout the Phulkian states. This movement got full support from the Master Tara Singh-Kharak Singh faction of the Akalis in Punjab. The moderate faction of S.B. Mehtab Singh and Giani Sher Singh collaborated with the Maharaja.

It was under these circumstances that a big public rally was held at Mansa and Punjab Riasti Mandal came into being on 17 July, 1928. Sewa Singh Thikriwala was elected its President and Bhagwan Singh Longowalia—who too was product of the Akali movement—was designated as its General Secretary. The speeches at the first meeting of the conference fully testify the secular credentials of its programmes and policies. The new movement aimed at ending autocratic rule in the states, defending democratic rights and liberties of the common people and ameliorating their economic conditions.[20] Jaswant Singh Danewalia, the acting President said: "Let us agitate against exploitation of the states' people and establish Panchayati Raj".[21] The Riasti Praja Mandal was linked to the All-India States' People's Conference (AISPC), and its membership was open to any state subject irrespective of one's religion, caste or community.

The protracted agitation by the people of the states, especially the Sikh peasantry, led to the release of Sewa Singh Thikriwala in August 1929. After his release, Sewa Singh Thikriwala conveyed the message of the Praja Mandal through Akali *dewans* (religious congregations), and he maintained his links with the national leadership through AISPC. Sewa Singh Thikriwala and other leaders of the Riasti Praja Mandal were also instrumental in the setting up of enquiry committee by AISPC to look into the misdeeds of the Maharaja of Patiala, and maladministration in the state.

As early as 1929, a Muzara Committee was set up at a secret meeting at village Sekha in 1929. In 1931, in an Akali Praja Mandal Dewan held at Dhuri leaders like Wazir Singh Daftriwala and Harnam Singh Dharamgarh made inflammatory speeches attacking the *biswedars* (landlords).[22]

The Independence Day in 1930 was also celebrated earlier at many places by Akali Jathas and national flag hoisted at various places. It seems that the "anti-imperialistic and anti-feudal character" of the Akali movement of 1920s was maintained by the Panjab Riasti Praja Mandal. The overall ethos of the movement was secular, although its social base as yet was limited to the Sikh peasantry, and it conveyed its message through *dharmic dewans* (congregations in the presence of holy *Guru Granth Sahib*).

In order to keep its repressive hold on the movement the Maharaja issued *Hidayat* 88 in 1932. According to this decree no society, organisation or association could be formed without formal recognition from the government. In view of the mounting campaign against the Maharaja, the Patiala government, on 9 August, 1933, arrested Sewa Singh Thikriwala and Bhagwan Singh Longowalia, the two top leaders of the movement. In view of his maltreatment in the jail, Thikriwala resorted to hunger strike which led to his death on 20 January, 1935. The Maharaja in order to meet the difficult situation entered into a secret agreement with the Punjab Akali leader, Master Tara Singh. As a result of this agreement (also called 'pact'), the government released most of the

Praja Mandal workers (including Bhagwan Singh Longowalia). The important leaders of Praja Mandal, such as Bhagwan Singh Longowalia, Jagir Singh Joga, Harchand Singh Jeji denounced the Tara Singh-Bhupindra compromise, characterised it as a shameful betrayal on the part of the Akali leader.[23] It appears that the Amritsar-based Akali leaders, who were not actively involved in the movement, resorted to the politics of bargaining and manipulation. And, moreover, leaders like Master Tara Singh were more concerned with religious issues and *panthic* (community) interests.

After the passing away of Sewa Singh Thikriwala, the Praja Mandal movement got divided into two groups: one led by Harchand Singh Jeji, a landlord persecuted by Maharaja Bhupindra Singh, and the other led by Bhagwan Singh Longowalia who was now linked to the leftist Punjab Kisan Committee. This division became evident at the Shahidi Conference held at Anandpur Sahib on 25-26 March, 1937.[24]

Longowalia group was more representative of the Praja Mandal Movement. It had in its fold leftist peasant leaders like Jagir Singh Joga, Giani Sardara Singh Uthap, and also 'militant' Akalis, such as, Jagir Singh Phaguwalia, Bhagat Singh Dhatogal. The leftist and pro-peasant orientation of this group is evident from Jagir Singh Joga's speech in which he said:

> Aristocratic government of 14th century should be ended and a government by elected members from labour classes (sic) should be established which should concentrate on their betterment.

After dilating on the various socio-economic demands of the states' people, he demanded that the "land be distributed to the tenants". He further stated that his party (group) is "the sympathiser of the poor and that of Harchand Singh Jeji's is the friend of capitalists".[25]

The other group of Praja Mandal led by Harchand Singh Jeji included leaders like Rulia Singh Bargar (Faridkot), Ujagar Singh Bhaura (Patiala state) and Pt. Bijla Singh (Malerkotla). On the second day of the Shahidi Conference at Anandpur, they held their meetings separately. The speakers of this group "concentrated merely on personal issues and sidetracked the basic economic and political questions".[26] Interestingly, the Jeji group's meeting was presided over by an unknown figure, Baba Lal Singh who was characterised as "millionaire" and "moneylender" by the other group.

The second half of 1930s saw the stepping up of muzara (tenant) agitation under the influence of the communist-led kisan movement. After the death of Maharaja Bhupindra Singh, his son Yadvendra Singh succeeded to the Patiala *gaddi* (throne). The young Maharaja wedded the daughter of Harchand Singh Jeji, the old Praja Mandalist. This also led to the withdrawal of Jeji and his group from the Praja Mandal leaving the field clear for the communists to capture the organisation. The militant Akalis led by veteran leaders, Pritam Singh Gojran and Jagir Singh Phaguwalia kept their links with the Praja Mandal Movement till the early 1940s.

At the end of the first phase in 1938, young urban professionals and businessmen (mostly Hindus) joined the movement, and for a while it created hope for the emergence of a broad democratic front accompanied by an overall ethos of secular political culture.

Second Phase: Radicalisation of the Movement, 1938-41

With the loosening of the repressive regime in Patiala after the death of Bhupindra Singh, and the general awakening in the country as a result of the Freedom Movement, the Praja Mandal Movement, for the first time, made its dent in the urban areas of the east Punjab states. Most of these urban Hindu leaders were inspired by the ideology of the Congress in general and Jawaharlal Nehru in particular. The important urban leaders included Seth Ram Nath (Jaito) who was interested in Harijan uplift programme of Mahatma Gandhi, Sunder Lal (Bassi), Brish Bhan, (Sunam) Harbans Lal (Bhatinda), Des Raj (Mansa), Tirath Singh (Dhuri)—all the last five being practising lawyers.[27]

After mid-1930s, Praja Mandal leaders like Bhagwan Singh Longowalia and Jagir Singh Joga laid emphasis on the organisation of Kisan Sabhas in order to take up the cause of tenants. At the end of 1937, a violent clash took place between the police and tenants in village Qila Hakima over the payment of *batai* (landlords share of the produce) which led to two deaths and injuries to nine persons. In this struggle, the tenants were led by Praja Mandal leaders having communist orientations. In December 1938, the Muzara Committee was formed which took upon itself the task of coordinating, guiding, and doing propaganda on behalf of the muzara movement.[28]

In 1939, the muzara body advised tenants not to pay *batai* to their landlords. This brought leaders with radical views into the forefront—Harnam Singh Dharamgarh, Dharam Singh Fakkar, Jagir Singh Phaguwalia, Wazir Singh Daftriwala, Pritam Singh Gojran.[29] The last three belonged to the Akali Dal but they were not affiliated to the Shiromani Akali Dal, Amritsar (then under the control of Master Tara Singh). These more radical Akalis or 'militant Akalis' formed a separate Malwa Riasti Akali Dal which at that time, did not toe the collaborationist policy of the Akali Dal, Amritsar. These kisan leaders were given moral, material and legal help by urban leaders like Brish Bhan, Des Raj and Harbans Lal. Writing about this the Inspector General Police (IGP) reported to the Patiala government: "A gradual fusion of the ... Parja Mandal, Congress and kisan workers appears to be in the course of making. Although retaining separate outward identities".[30]

In February 1939, AISPC was held at Ludhiana and the Punjab Riasti Praja Mandal acted as host to it. At this moment, the communists were the dominant force in the Riasti Praja Mandal. Baba Karam Singh Dhut (radical kisan leader) was the chairman of the reception committee. Urban leaders like Brish Bhan, Sunder Lal, Tirath Singh were attending the session for the first time.[31]

As to the composition of the Praja Mandal leadership on the eve of the Second World War, it included Congress Praja Mandalists, Akali Praja Mandalists (affiliated to the Malwa Riasti Praja Mandal) and the communists. The meeting of the Patiala state branch of the Praja Mandal showed that out of ten members who attended the meeting three were Congressite, two Akalis, three communists, and two without any definite affiliation.[32]

After the beginning of the Second World War, most of Praja Mandal leaders (including the 'militant' Akalis) were arrested, and the movement, as a result, suffered a setback. In late 1939, Shiromani Akali Dal adopted a policy of cooperation towards the British government and organised the Sikh Defence League, and on the whole followed a policy of cooperation towards the Maharaja of Patiala. In early 1940s Master Tara Singh, for the first time after 1935, renewed his activities in the east Punjab states in order to wean away the states' Akali leaders from the Praja Mandal. This new stand of Master Tara Singh, according to Walia, was in sharp contrast to his earlier posture, when he "championed the cause of the states' people ... and supported their demand for responsible government, his emphasis now was on Sikh rights and the independent entity of the panth".[33]

Third Phase: Fragmentation of a Broad-based Movement

In the changed situation, the community-based issues and demands acquired greater salience, and the vocal and dominant middle class leadership of every community was trying to get the better of the other communities. In this atmosphere, Master Tara Singh and other Akali leaders followed a policy of cooperation with the Maharaja of Patiala, and extended tactical support to the British government's war efforts. Master Tara Singh and his group of Akalis held series of religio-political conferences at different places in early 1940s, and succeeded in weaning away 'militant' Akalis from the Praja Mandal. In October 1940, Master Tara Singh presided over a big religious conference at Bhawanigarh (Patiala). These were followed by a series of other conferences at Mansa, Talwandi Sabo, Sirhind etc., where "Akali leaders eulogised the Sikander-Baldev Singh pact and acclaimed it as a great victory of the panth".[34] They also demanded, and later agitated for more jobs for the Sikhs in the states which appealed to the newly emerging educated Sikh middle class.

The most important watershed in this development was the holding of the fourth All-India Akali Conference at Bhawanigarh on 14-15 March 1943. By the time this conference was held, Master

Tara Singh succeeded in bringing to the fold of Shiromani Akali Dal, Amritsar almost all the Praja Mandal Akalis. The emergence of an altogether new political orientation amongst the old Praja Mandalist Akalis and the newly mobilised Sikh middle classes—with their emphasis on Sikh rights and Sikh interests—is evident from the deliberations of this important conference.[35] The purpose of the Bhawanigarh conference, as stated in a poster, was to think for the interest of the small Sikh community at this time of intense struggle between communities so that Sikhs and the Sikh nation is able to maintain its dignity and self-respect in the future set up.[36]

The proceedings of the Akali conference at Bhawanigarh shows the salience of religion-oriented demands. Immediately after the flag hoisting ceremony, Giani Sher Singh in his speech said:

> Dear Brethern, you know that the sign of nations that are alive is their flag.... This flag symbolises freedom, panthic glory and spirit of courage. It flew in the four corners of the world... from Punjab upto Kabul, from the Jumma upto Jamraoa (sic) .... Those who are opposed to the Azad Punjab are following their selfish motives.[37]

The achievements of the Akali Dal cited in a poem, recited at the conference, included, removal of a Muslim Prime Minister in Patiala, fulfilment of the Sikh demands by Sir Sikander Hyat Khan, the Premier of Punjab, inclusion of a Sikh member in the Viceroy's Executive, the abolition of the Nazool land laws in the Patiala state, etc.

One speaker from Punjab eulogised the present Maharaja of Patiala and his ancestors. "The ancestors of Shri Hazoor Maharaja of Patiala were *Jathedars* and your ancestors were sepoys under their *Jathedarship.* You should feel proud of this land". The gallant resistance of the Akalis from early 1920s to mid-1930s against the princely oppression was in sharp contrast to the loyalty demonstrated in some of these speeches. The Maharajas of the Sikh states were strongly taken to task for not observing *rehats* (religious practices) and symbols. A resolution was moved to the effect that Sikhs be given majority share in the State cabinets, and greater share for Sikhs in services—not less than 60 percent in the Patiala state.

Some Akali leaders, with Praja Mandal background in the states, such as Wazir Singh Daftriwala and Pritam Singh Gojran put forth some economic demands for the reduction of irrigation rates, relief from indebtedness and raised the issue of muzara problem. Another saving grace of the conference was a resolution in favour of the demand for complete independence for the country.

The success of this Akali conference proved to be a turning point in the history of the Praja Mandal Movement in the states. The Akalis took away with them a big chunk of the rural peasant base of this movement. The peasant base of the Praja Mandal was further depleted with the exit of the communists from the Praja Mandal in 1945. Its social base got limited to urban areas though its leaders still maintained their old links with communist leaders—some of them even maintaining close links with the erstwhile Akali Praja Mandalists. In view of the militant muzara movement[38] which continued till the early 1950s, the urban leaders, like Brish Bhan, Des Raj and Harbans Lal, who were sympathetic to this movement, kept their links with the kisan leaders for quite sometime.

Conclusion

The leaders who took part in the first phase of the Praja Mandal Movement (1928-38) belonged to the rural peasant stock and most of them were politicised by the Akali movement of 1921-25. But, in view of the objective conditions of double oppression of the colonial rule and princely order, the movement took a more radical turn. And, the general political orientation or political culture of the leaders was secular, anti-princely and nationalist. At the end of the thirties, a section of peasant leaders like Bhagwan Singh Longowalia, Jagir Singh Joga, Harnam Singh Dharamgarh developed a radical political orientation. The other section of leaders with religious orientations, Pritam Singh Gojran and Jagir Singh Phaguwalia, too worked with this radical wing. And for a time this leadership pulled on well with newly mobilised urban leaders like Brish Bhan, Des Raj, Harbans Lal and Seth Ram Nath. Around 1939 a broad-based front of 'militant' Akalis, communists and Congressite urban Praja Mandalists took shape and presented the possibility of the development of secular political culture. But in early 1940s, under the influence of Punjab-based Akali leadership and the circumstances associated with the future transfer of power to Indians, Akali constituent left the Praja Mandal; and thus the hope for the development of a broad-based secular political front could not get materialised. In mid-1940s the Praja Mandal was further weakened by exit of the communists. Now the question may be posed, why this happened. One general explanation is that religious cleavages were in-built in the Punjabi society ever since the end of the nineteenth century. In this connection Jones writes:

> By the end of century, competition between religious movements had become an institutionalised part of Punjabi life. Each religious community possessed one or more aggressive movement. The commitment to these movements rested on educated Punjabis and their sense of alienation from traditional society.[39]

It seems these religious movements exercised far-reaching influence on the subsequent developments on the mainstream politics in Punjab. In the colonial period, the community-based interests, reflecting religious cleavages, may get moderated during periods of freedom struggle or during the heyday of radical mass movements but these interests were reactivated at critical junctures, especially at times of political reforms under the aegis of colonial rule. The modern institutional appendages of the social structure such as denominational educational institutions, mass media, especially the vernacular press, also exacerbated the cleavages and acted as a damper on the development of a secular political culture. This, however, in no way forecloses the possibility of a composite secular political culture in the given situation provided the major political forces adopt a more pragmatic approach.[40]

In the context of this general explanation we briefly study the role of the three main constituents–the Akali Dal, the Congress Party and the communist groups–of the erstwhile Praja Mandal Movement in understanding political developments in the east Punjab states from the early 1940s to the formative years of the post-independence period.

In the years preceding the transfer of power, Master Tara Singh was able to win back a big chunk of Akali leaders of the east Punjab states who earlier cooperated with the Praja Mandal Movement. The reason for the development was the changed political scenario on the eve of the transfer of power. Master Tara Singh was able to play on the fears of the Akali rank and file that the Sikhs would not get justice through the Praja Mandal that was now being increasingly identified with the Hindu urban elements. He was able to appeal to the Sikh pride by emphasising Sikh tradition and Sikh history. It is also likely that in the prevailing ambience of community-based interests amongst the significant sections of the Hindu and Sikh middle classes, coupled with the unfavourable social situation of the Akali ideologues,[41] Punjab Akali leaders in the changed circumstances emphasised Sikh interests and Sikh *(panthic)* solidarity with greater force. To a certain extent protection of minority rights and its cultural heritage may be innocuous but it carries the danger of losing sight of common secular interests in the domain of governance.

In the post-independence period Akali leadership was more preoccupied with protest movements for protecting Sikh interests; it rarely addressed itself seriously to the issue of governance in the common parliamentary domain.[42]

Secondly, in view of Master Tara Singh's concern for *panthic* unity he wanted to take all sections of the Sikh community including the Sikh Maharaja(s) and the Sikh landed and business notables with him. This prevented the Akali Dal from taking up the cause of the Sikh tenants of the east Punjab states unambiguously. This also gave a rightist stance to Akali Dal's policies in the socio-economic domain which persists to the present.

The post-1945 Praja Mandal and its incarnation into the Congress in 1948 lost its composite secular character to a considerable extent. It is true that the party was led by liberal and left-oriented leaders like Brish Bhan and Des Raj and a Gandhian freedom fighter Seth Ram Nath. The explanation for this transformation can be traced to the social and political milieu under which these leaders had to work. The compulsion of excercising control over the party machine through loyal persons in key positions converted the District Congress Committee in Sangrur, the home district of Brish Bhan, virtually into a Hindu body. Brish Bhan did maintain cordial relations with leftist kisan leaders, and he also enjoyed personal electoral support from a section of the peasantry for some time but the peasant support to the Congress as a party remained insignificant. The Congress government at the centre and the party high command tried to shore up the party's fortunes for a time by coopting Sikh influentials and administrators of the erstwhile princely states into the Congress party but this failed to achieve any lasting success.[43]

The communists maintained some pockets of support amongst peasants but a large majority of the peasants supported the Akali Dal.

Mirdula Mukherjee, in her study of the peasant movement in the east Punjab states[44], depicts the Congress party and the Akali Dal in black and white. She squarely blames the communist leaders for their failure to continue alliance with the leftist Praja Mandalists such as Brish Bhan, Des Raj and others; they instead hobnobbed with the rightist Akalis in the post-independence period thus encouraging the rise of rightist and communal forces. This explanation of communal politics in terms of ideological and 'nationalistic' perspective is too facile and unrealistic. It seems to ignore the political and social realities which condition and limit the role of the parties and their leaders. It may be reiterated that ideology cannot work in a social vacuum; it has to take into account the ground realities.

In evaluating the role of the Praja Mandal leaders one cannot help mentioning the role of Seth Ram Nath, a Gandhian who perhaps was more aware of the ground realities of the east Punjab states politics and therefore adopted a more discriminating attitude towards the Akalis' demands. He probably was the first important

Congress leader who supported the demand of the Punjabi *suba* in early 1950s. The dismissive attitude of a prominent section of the mainstream publicists and leaders towards regional aspirations and the local cultures of the people under the garb of nationalism is a real hindrance in the way of building an ethos of composite secular political culture.

Notes

1. Except Malerkotla State, all the other states had Sikh rulers.
2. For this paper I have consulted only selected files (relating to the Patiala State) at Punjab State Archives, Patiala. I also had the benefit of a few personal interviews. But for detailed information regarding this movement I relied on two studies: Ramesh Walia, *Praja Mandal Movement in East Punjab States,* Patiala: Punjabi University, 1972; Mridula Mukherjee, "Peasant Movement in Patiala State, 1937-48", *Studies in History*, Vol.1, No. 2, July-December 1979, pp. 215-83.
3. The movement made little impact on Muslims and Harijans in view of their poverty, general backwardness and low politicisation.
4. The Congress in the post-1947 period tried to build a composite secular coalition in this region and the Punjab state but it could not strike deep roots.
5. Ramesh Walia, *op. cit.,* p.205. This characterisation of later day Praja Mandal as a 'Hindu urbanite movement' is criticised by Praja Mandal leaders like Brish Bhan and others. It is true that Praja Mandal of post-war years continued to enjoy some peasant support, and also the overwhelming support of the Harijan masses.
6. Karl Mannheim, *Ideology and Utopia: An Introduction to the Sociology of Knowledge*, London: Routledge & Kegan Paul, 1960, p. 45.

7. The three phases are adapted from the Ramesh Walia's study cited above.
8. *Census Report of Patiala State*, by Sirdar Arjan Singh Shah, Lahore, n.d.
9. *Census Report 1941*, Patiala State, by Lt. Col. Sukhdev Singh, Patiala, 1944. It seems that the increase in the Sikh population may be mainly, due to the continuation of a trend in favour of Sikhs ever since 1901, and secondly, it might be at the cost of scheduled caste population whose religious affiliations are ambiguous. Hindu population of the state was concentrated in the Hindi-speaking areas.
10. For the detail of this *morcha* see, Ruchi Sahni, *Struggle for Reform in Sikh Shrines,* Amritsar, nd.
11. Ramesh Walia, *op. cit.*, p. 34.
12. *Ibid.*, p. 36.
13. *Census Report of the Patiala State, 1931*, op. cit., p.152.
14. *Punjab States Gazetteers, Vol.17-A, Phulkian, States: Patiala, Jind and Nabha 1904*. Lahore, 1909, pp. 314-15.
15. Chhaju Mal Vaid, "PEPSU Che Muzaraian da Ghol te Communist Party" in *Fifty Years of Struggle,* Publication of Communist Party of India, 1976.
16. *Final Report of the Settlement of the Patiala State (1900-1908)* by F. Popham Young, Ajmer, 1909.
17. *Ibid.*, p. 27.
18. See also Walia, *op. cit.*, p. 97.
19. Fauja Singh, *Eminent Freedom Fighters of Punjab,* Patiala: Punjabi University, 1972.
20. Walia, *op. cit.*, p. 56.
21. *Ibid.*, p. 57.
22. *Ibid.*, p. 95.
23. *Ibid.*, p. 115; p. 126. (The government even exercised control over the correspondence of the leaders through post offices).
24. Patiala State Records, *Prime Minister's Office*, File No.744.
25. *Ibid.*
26. Walia, *op. cit.,* p. 136.

27. *Ibid.*, p. 140.
28. Mridula Mukherjee, "*Peasant Movement in Patiala State, 1937-48*, p. 228; p. 230.
29. *Ibid.*, p. 237, Ghhaju Mal Vaid, *op. cit.*
30. Patiala State Records, *Prime Minister's Office*, 1939, Folio No. 1553.
31. Walia, *op. cit.*, p.150.
32. One of the two was Pt. Narain Datt, advocate (Sunam) who earlier organised Hindu Mahasabha unit in the state, and the second was Mansha Ram, an old Praja Mandalist, Patiala State Records, *Prime Minister's Office*, File No.1553.
33. Walia, *op. cit.*, pp. 155-56.
34. *Ibid.*, p. 157.
35. Patiala State Records, Report of the IGP Patiala State, File No.772.
36. *Ibid.* For the organisation of the conference: it was earlier proposed to include *Lambardars*, *Safedposhs* and *Zaildars*. Later, however, this proposal was dropped. It showed a new policy of cooperation towards the Patiala ruler on the part of the Akalis.
37. Azad Punjab plan of the Akalis envisaged a fresh demarcation of the pre-independence Punjab so as to ensure that no one community (out of the three) has majority in the population of the proposed province.
38. For an exhaustive account of the peasant movement in the Patiala State, see, Mridula Mukherjee, *op. cit.*
39. Kenneth W. Jones, "Social Changes and Religious Movements in Nineteenth Century Punjab", in M.S.A. Rao (ed.), *Social Movements in India*, Vol.2, New Delhi: Manohar, 1979, pp. 11-12.
40. In a society like that of the Punjab where we discern the coexistence of political subcultures, I consider it more appropriate to use the term composite political culture. Terms such as secular political culture, secularism vs. communalism signify absolutist connotation.
41. M.S. Dhami, "Political Parties and State Autonomy: A Case Study of Akali Dal", in K.R. Bombwall (ed.), *National Power and*

State Autonomy", Meerut: Meenakshi Parkashan, 1978.

42. Some present-day Akali ideologues might argue that unless the issue of national question of Sikhs / Punjabis in the Indian federal set up is suitably thrashed out it is pointless to discuss the issue of governance. This is merely confusing the two issues. Issue of governance just cannot be wished away.
43. For the role of the Congress High Command on the political development in the east Punjab states (and later PEPSU) I was helped by my interviews with Om Parkash Garg, Patiala, 3 January, 1982; and Dara Singh, Advocate, Chandigarh, 4 February, 1982.
44. Mridula Mukherjee, "Communists and Peasants in Punjab: A Focus on the Muzara Movement in Patiala, 1947-53", *Studies in History*, Vol.3, Nos.1 & 2, January-December, 1981, pp. 401-46, *passim*; also M. Mukherjee, n. 2.

12

The Punjabi Suba Movement

A.S. NARANG

The statement, "India is a nation in the making" is not new. It was made long before 1947 when India attained independence. The statement correctly recognises that nations are not born on a specific day. It is a complex set of processes working over a long period that converge to the point of nation making. It is particularly so in the newly emerged post-colonial states where in the process of modernisation there has been a resurgence of ethnic identities which are seeking equivalence with, if not priority over nationalist claims. The ethnic identities have generally been manifested through the claims of language and religion.

Many observers have tried to provide reasons for the rejuvenation of such religious and linguistic identities. These reasons are wide ranging. On the one pole are the primordialists with their primary focus on culture and their belief that ethnic categories and identities are the given entities in society. According to them human nature and human psychology provide the necessary conditions for ethnocentric behaviour. Therefore comes the proposition that while forging of unity through political organisation subsumes the autonomy of the individual and the sanctity of his choice in owing allegiance to whatever structure he prefers, there pre-exist certain socio-cultural structures which the individual is born into and shape his beliefs, orientations and behaviour patterns. On the other pole are those who believe that ethnic conflicts as such do not exist and that these are merely expressions of underlying social and political conflicts between classes, population segments, or interest groups within the wider society for the fulfilment of economic or political interests. In between is the view, that elite competition is the basic dynamic which precipitates ethnic conflict under the specific conditions which arise from the broader political and economic environment rather than only from the cultural values of ethnic groups in question.

It is in this context that in the post-independence Indian politics too ethnicity has emerged as a major instrument of social consciousness, political activity, reallocation and redistribution of resources and share in and access to political power. The national elite, in general, scarcely appreciated the potential energy of ethnic identities. The official recognition to different ethnic linguistic groups in the constitution was resented and criticised on the ground that such an encouragement on the part of the government would help the development of communal problem and could affect the unity of the country adversely. Even the resolve to constitute states on linguistic basis, which was made more than once before independence, was not fulfilled.

In rejecting the ethno-linguistic principle of nationhood, the Indian state sought to base its legitimacy on political ideas all new to the Indian society. Having emerged fresh from the experience of the independence movement, it sought to develop a new ethos for national life of its people. This system based on the attempt for an all inclusive agglomeration and myriad identities and groups through inter-segmental and inter-factional adjustments and changes, as Rajni Kothari points out, proved inadequate when it encountered the large currents of the era of mass politics and large-scale politicisation of the masses following a steady working of the system and its diffusion of democratic norms.[1] Thus, after the first flush of freedom either out of fear on the part of the ethnic groups of being submerged in a larger nation or out of pride in their own group, or because of the aspirations of some leaders to get political power on the strength of ethnic loyalties, demands were now put forth for recognition of ethno-linguistic identities.

The issue of linguistic states in particular became the focus of popular agitations. The new Congress policy of relegating the issue of linguistic states to the background could not last long.

The language became the main instrument for ethnic discourse in the political process because it is perhaps the most distinctive feature of a culture. Linguistic cleavages are certainly more divisive than religious cleavages since they directly hinder personal communication and nobody can turn a blind eye to them. They also involve the state in a more necessary way, for the government has to designate an official language where it can avoid designating an official religion. It has been observed in many cases the world over that the imposition of the language of the dominant majority and a language policy aimed at the assimilation of minorities is the major source of ethnic discord. As for India is concerned separate ethnic collectivities based on distinctively different languages have existed here for centuries. With the progress of social change and the attendant increase of political opportunities in the context of expanding public space, the issues and consequent demands relating to language have become salient facts of national political life. Both minority and majority ethnic groups have used language for fulfillment of their political and economic interests as also an important means for assimilation of or protecting identities. The case of Punjab presents an interesting example of convergence of political-economic interests with those of linguistic-ethnic identities. The demand for and opposition to the creation of a Punjabi speaking state and the role of state in that context brings to light the availability of language as an important tool for ethnic assertions in the political process of a developing polity.

Partition and Punjab

Except for the European powers, virtually every invader had entered India through Punjab. Consequently, there had been going on a process of plurality, interaction among religious and cultural groups as also changes in population patterns. At the time of the arrival of the British Punjab was populated mainly by three communities—Hindus, Muslims and Sikhs—all politically important and ambitious, having been the rulers of the region at one time or the other. Whatever the spoken languages, the existence of the scriptures of three religions written in different languages and scripts, predisposed the elites from the three communities during the process of increased opportunities to use the language as a vehicle for their political and economic aspirations. Therefore, during the religious revivalist movements which were primarily associated with the political aspirations of the elites from different groups, the language came to be associated with group dominance, religious reform and political aspirations. Thus, the issue here during colonial period was not what the people speak, rather what would be the official language. Before independence this conflict was between Hindi, Urdu and Punjabi and after independence, because of partition of Punjab, it became a conflict around Hindi and Punjabi.

Punjab, like Bengal, was greatly affected by the partition. It brought about the most radical change in the life of this region since the fall of Sikh empire. The division of Punjab on communal lines was first of all a severe setback to the growth of Punjabi sub-nationalism. Besides it affected every sphere of Punjabi life, demographic, political, economic, social, linguistic, administrative, cultural and moral. The Hindus who constituted a minority of 30 percent in the united Punjab, now became a majority with 70 percent of the population. The Sikhs who had accounted for about 14 percent before the partition now became the only substantial minority with about 30 percent. The erstwhile majority community the Muslims were now reduced to a political non-entity. The integration of the princely states into PEPSU and rehabilitation of the people from the north-western districts of Rawalpindi, Gujranwala, Sheikhupura, Lyallpur, etc., in Jalandhar, Ludhiana, Karnal and PEPSU, etc., and those from the south-west districts of Multan, Jhang and Dera Ghazi Khan in Hissar, Rohtak and Gurgaon districts further consolidated the Sikhs in the central Punjab and the Hindus in the eastern districts.[2]

One effect of this was that the local refugee tensions which were an overall problem of the state assumed communal colour in Jalandhar and Patiala divisions. In the Haryana region, the displaced population (both Hindus and Sikhs) introduced a new factor in its social, economic and political life and sharpened the already existing feeling among the people of Haryana region that they were exploited by the more advanced people from the erstwhile central Punjab. In the south-eastern districts of the state, local refugee tension created rural-urban cleavages within the Sikhs also. They had different degrees of access to positions of political and administrative power and this altered their respective positions and tactics with respect to political protest and affiliation to political parties.

The partition also had different effects on the Hindus and the Sikhs. A majority of the migrant and local Sikhs were peasant proprietors whose love for land is proverbial. Having lost their land, sacred shrines and cultural centres in west Punjab, they were deeply scared and set out to consolidate their position in the truncated Punjab to fulfil their political and cultural aspirations. On the other hand, the Hindus did not suffer the trauma of identity crisis and economic uncertainty to the same degree as did the Sikhs. The Hindus, both local and displaced who belonged to the urban industrial and commercial groups, were in a more advantageous position in that they identified themselves with the vast Hindu community all over India and could make rapid economic gains.

The urban Sikhs, especially the refugees from west Punjab, were severely hit by the partition. They had to compete with the already established Hindu businessmen and felt that the Congress had neglected them. The only way left for them was to receive good education and to join services. So, they had to ensure that jobs were allocated to them out of proportion to their population. In the changed political and demographic situation the rural peasantry was more inclined towards the Congress. In fact, all over India Congress was trying to forge an alliance with the rural landed classes. In these circumstances the post-partition Akali politics followed nearly the pre-partition pattern, i.e., it broke into two factions, one pro-government (Congress) consisting primarily of rural Jats, and other anti-government led by urban leadership. But since immediately after the partition the leaders of anti-government group Master Tara Singh and Giani Kartar Singh had lost control of the Sikh stage because most of their following had been dislocated and scattered, the pro-government group had a greater say. Consequently the Akali Dal got itself merged in the Congress in 1948.

Demand for Punjabi-Speaking State

The Akali merger in Congress party in 1948 was primarily at the legislative level. Outside parliamentary framework the Akali leadership remained active for protection of the Sikh interest particularly in view of a new constitution for the country being framed. In this the policy of Akali Dal was first to demand for constitutional safeguards and then to campaign for Punjabi in Gurmukhi script as a symbol of their cultural identity.

The Constituent Assembly outrightly rejected the demands for separate electorates and reservation of seats for Sikhs in the legislature. With regard to the Akali demand that Punjabi in Gurmukhi script be recognised as the official language and as the medium of instruction in Punjab, the then Chief Minister Bhim Sen Sachar evolved a formula. The formula provided for a division of the province into two zones, a Punjabi-speaking zone and a Hindi zone. In the Punjabi zone, the medium of instruction was to be Punjabi written in Gurmukhi script. In order to retain the bilingual character of the province it provided for a compulsory learning of both languages in each zone.

This formula was not acceptable to a section of Hindus living in the Punjabi zone, and was not implemented in the schools of the Arya Samaj. In the meantime in the prevailing factionalism in the Congress, Sachar lost support within the party and Gopi Chand Bhargava regained power. Akali Congressmen led by Giani Kartar Singh also supported Bhargava. However, having failed to obtain safeguards and concessions in the new Constitution of India and dissatisfied with the progress on language issue there emerged, once again, division of opinion in Akali Dal as to the desirability of its continuation in the Congress. Under Master Tara Singh's dictum Akali Dal in July 1950 directed its MLAs to leave Congress and return to the Akali Dal (Interestingly only one out of 23 legislators resigned from the Congress).

This led Master Tara Singh, who had already started talking of a Sikh homeland, to make a demand for demarcation of a linguistic state on the basis of Punjabi in Gurmukhi script as the main campaigning issue of Akali Dal. It was clear that so soon after the partition of the country, with the grave consequences that followed in its wake and with the Congress stand on secularism and nationalism no strictly communal demand would be acceptable to the nationalist leadership. Equally clear was the fact that any plan to create a Sikh majority province would be met with determined opposition from those Hindus who were likely to live in such a province. Hence, the demand was voiced not in a communal but in linguistic terms. Harcharan Singh Bajwa, a member of Akali Dal Working Committee (1931-60), in his book *Fifty Years of Punjab Politics:1920-1970*, pointed out the political aspect of demand:

> Now what matters was the vote, the history making potency, chivalry, ambition and sacrifice remained no more as the criteria of sovereignty. On bewilderment, I took along me Bhupender Singh Mann and Gyani Kartar Singh and the trio of us knocked at the door of Dr. Ambedkar. We solicited guidance from him and quick he was in presenting the recipe of our peril. He told us: "If you had cast lots with Pakistan, you would have been a minority there. In joint Punjab you were a minority except in two tehsils which too were not contiguous. In eastern Punjab, too, you are a minority. If you clamour for Sikh state, it will be a cry in the wilderness. Why don't you ask for a Punjabi-speaking state? Congress is committed to linguistic basis for reorganisation of the states. They can defer satisfaction of this demand but they cannot oppose it for long. I have told you the way. You can have a Sikh state in the cloak of 'Punjabi suba'. On hearing this suggestion of Dr. Ambedkar, Bajwa writes, "our faces brightened. We knew that narrow mindedness of Patel had left little scope for our carving out a *de jure* Sikh state. But there was the way to get *de facto* Sikh state. We launched struggle for Punjabi suba."

The Dal placed the demand for a Punjabi suba formally in a resolution which states:

> The callous and unsympathetic treatment of the government has made respectable life impossible for them, they (Sikhs), therefore

> strongly feel the utter necessity of the creation of a Punjabi-speaking province for the protection and preservation of their culture, language and self-respect, particularly when this solution is universally recognised as democratic and which even the Indian National Congress stands pledged.[3]

As such there was no doubt that the demand for a Punjabi suba was for a state with Sikh majority. Although in course of time the emphasis was shifted from the plank of Sikh majority to that of Punjabi in Gurmukhi script as the sole official language but the achievement of Punjabi suba and fulfilment of Sikh aspirations remained always linked. The Hindu opposition on communal lines gave further impetus to this movement.

The Hindu Opposition

It has already been mentioned that the partition had a different reaction on the two communities–Hindus and Sikhs. The Hindus, both local and displaced who belonged mainly to the urban industrial and commercial groups, thought that they stood to gain economically by identifying themselves with vast Hindu community all over India. In Punjab, they after partition could not help in the consolidation of the urban group within the Congress where power centre was shifting from the urban bourgeoisie to the rural rich. In fact, the relationship of the Punjabi Hindus with the Congress had always been tenuous and uneasy. They had supported the Congress in the pre-partition days because of various factors like the presence of the Muslim League, but the party had never really captured the heart of the Punjabi Hindus. After partition, when they saw Congress flirting with the Akali Dal for political power the Punjabi Hindus started developing a 'minority complex' and gravitating towards the trans-Yamuna culture of North India.

The clash of political and economic interests made the communalists among the Hindus even suspicious, hostile and aggressive towards the Sikhs. A majority of them were bitter with the government for conceding Pakistan to the Muslim League, and now that the partition was a fact and majority of Muslims had gone over to the other side, they wanted the Government of India to be strict to all religious minorities. Dr. Shyama Prasad Mukerjee appeared to reflect their political thinking and fulfil their aspirations when he formed the Bharatiya Jan Sangh. Perhaps, the post-partition Punjab situation had a lot to do with the formation of this party. Gerald Heeger points out that "the negotiations between the RSS and Mukerjee to form a national Hindu party were primarily conducted through RSS elite from Punjab and UP".[4]

Subsequently, the Hindu organisations like the Arya Samaj and the Jan Sangh, organised primarily from among the urban Punjabi-speaking cities like Amritsar, Jalandhar and Ludhiana, not only opposed the demand for Punjabi suba but also suggested that the existence of Khalsa was no more necessary and that the Sikhs should come back to the Hindu society. The Akalis responded to this by alleging that the majority community was seeking to deny the cultural identity of the Sikhs. The stand of Hindu parties on language question became the most fractious in this connection.

The communal Hindu organisations and their newspapers led a movement during 1951 census operations to persuade the Hindus to state Hindi instead of Punjabi as their mother tongue. P.K. Nijhawan points out that with regard to language while the rest of India soon recognised the genius of their languages, the Punjabi Hindus remained passionately wedded to Hindi. Among the totality of Hindudom, the Punjabi Hindu was alone, the one who spoke a deliberate untruth. At that time no one could counsel sanity to them. When the RSS chief, the late Golwalker came to Chandigarh in the early sixties, he was quite explicit in stating that not Hindi but Punjabi was the mother-tongue of Punjabi Hindus. But, as soon as he reached Jalandhar, he was made to eat an humble pie.[5] The same was true with some other Hindu leaders who pleaded the case of Punjabi. Some Hindus had gone to the extent of denying the Punjabi even the status of a language. A Hindu-dominated Municipal Committee in Jalandhar passed a resolution soon after independence, favouring Hindi as the medium of instruction in schools within its jurisdiction. Some Akali leaders have maintained that this action in Jalandhar, more than anything else convinced the Sikhs of the communal motives of Hindus in Punjab and they became determined to achieve Punjabi suba.

The Hindus, by and large, felt that it was not really the question of Punjabi but that it was a demand calculated to carve out a separate state in which the Sikh theocracy dominated. As opposed to Punjabi suba they put forward their own demand for a 'Maha Punjab' which would include the territories of Punjab, PEPSU, Himachal Pradesh, Delhi and some districts of Uttar Pradesh. It was widely recognised that primary concern for the demand for Maha Punjab was to maintain the economic and political domination of Hindus in Punjab. But, the demand was not acceptable to all sections of Hindus themselves because of economic and regional factors. The Hindus of the hill areas instead of supporting the demand of the Punjabi Hindus for Maha Punjab, wanted for themselves the state of Himachal Pradesh. Similarly, the Hindus of Haryana region were divided over the demand because of differences of caste and dichotomy between Hindus of the regions.

The Punjabi Suba Movement

By the time of the First General Elections in 1952 both the Akali Dal and the Hindu organisations such as the Jan Sangh and the Arya Samaj had become distrustful of each other and appealed to the religious and linguistic sentiments of voters. However, in the elections, Congress was successful in mobilising political support in the rural areas and came out successful not in general but in Sikh-majority areas (see Table 1). In other words the Akali Dal could not substantiate its claim to be the sole representative of the Sikhs.

To cope with the disadvantageous situation, the Akali leadership decided to strengthen communal solidarity by stirring the emotions of Sikhs with the use of cultural symbols upon which the claims for group rights could be based. The Akali leaders not only presented the demand for Punjabi suba as a necessity to get rid of discriminatory treatment and protect the Sikh culture but they also impressed upon the Sikhs that, according to the Sikh religion, it was obligatory on their part to participate in politics as a group. This approach of the Akali Dal bore fruit and it helped the Dal to retain its rural support during the agitation at the time of pleading its case before the States Reorganisation Commission (SRC).

Table 1

Percentage of Seats and Votes Polled by Political Parties in 1952 in Punjab and PEPSU (Combined)

Political Party	*Total Seats in Vidhan Sabha*	*Percentage of Votes*	*Seats in Punjabi-speaking Region*	*Percentage of Votes in Punjabi-speaking Region*
Congress	122	34.8	60	31.3
Akali Dal	33	14.7	31	24.0
Communist Party	6	5.3	6	6.1
Jan Sangh	2	5.0	-	4.0
Others & Independents	21	40.2	13	34.6

Source: Compiled form India, Election Commission Report on the First General Elections in India 1951-52 Vol.II, New Delhi, Manager of Publications, 1956.

The SRC rejected the demand for a separate Punjabi-speaking state on the ground that it lacked general support of the people inhabiting the area. Instead, it recommended the integration of Punjab, the PEPSU and Himachal Pradesh into one administrative unit. This was exactly what the anti-Akali Hindus had demanded. The Akalis were infuriated at the SRC's verdict. At the same time Akalis were aware of the general elections which were just a year away. They knew it well that, though small and middle farmers, notably from the southern districts of Punjab and from Amritsar district had participated in the *morchas* in large numbers, there was no guarantee of their voting for the Dal. In fact, like in 1952, the Akali Dal had seen in the 1954 PEPSU mid-term elections that the Sikh support to it in agitations did not mean political support in the election as well. So, even while Akalis denounced the SRC report, they were prepared to have some settlement with the government.

The Government of India and Congress High Command were

also keen to end the chronic instability in Punjab. The Akali agitation of 1955 and the subsequent demonstrations had hinted at dangerous implications of a summary rejection of the Akali demands. In this context, Jawaharlal Nehru himself visited Golden Temple in November 1955 and castigated those Hindus who had during the last census claimed their mother-tongue to be Hindi. With both the parties agreeable for a via-media a compromise was arrived at in the 'regional formula'.

According to the regional formula, the PEPSU and Punjab were merged and the new state was divided into the Hindi-speaking and the Punjabi-speaking regions. There was to be a single legislature for the state, but the legislators and ministers from each of the two areas would constitute regional committees with special powers to advise the state government and the legislative assembly on certain subjects. The provision regarding the regional committees meant that any political party with a majority in a regional committee, even if it did not have majority in the whole legislature, could implement its programme on the fourteen subjects that were listed in the formula as regional subjects. After the agreement on the regional formula the Akali Dal once again merged with the Congress for political activities, though it maintained its identity for religious and social affairs.

The Punjabi urban Hindus particularly saw in the regional formula a gradual crystallisation of the regional division and the progressive decline of their power. One possible outcome was the consolidation of the rural Sikhs of Punjabi region and the rural Hindus of Hindi (Haryana) region. Moreover, after the creation of regional committees the leaders of Haryana region might become more conscious of their domination by the Punjabi region and press for a separate state. As such, the Punjabi urban interests, which had all along dominated the state, apprehended the cooperation of the rural people of Haryana and Punjab regions. Their fears further increased when the Congress Chief Minister Partap Singh Kairon included in his ministry two most powerful Akalis (with the exception perhaps of Master Tara Singh), Gian Singh Rarewala and Giani Kartar Singh, along with rural leaders like Professor Sher Singh from Haryana. In contrast, there was less representation of the Punjabi Hindu community in the ministry. Thus, the influence of Punjabi Hindus waned and they calculated that, if the existing government headed by Kairon was forced to resign or was dismissed, some urban Hindu would be chosen leader as the Hindus had a majority in Congress organisation. To achieve this aim, they decided to launch the "Save Hindi Agitation".

Save Hindi Agitation had visible limits to achieve Hindu unity because of regional and class differences. The movement collapsed by December 1957. But, it made Kairon realise that the language provisions of the regional formula could cost him the important Hindu support in both the Punjabi and Haryana regions. The Kairon government, therefore, did not really implement the regional formula.

Failure of the regional plan once again made the Akali leadership to launch a movement in support of Punjabi suba. The decision of the Congress High Command on 28 December, 1959 to bifurcate Bombay into two states–Maharashtra and Gujarat–gave the Akalis further leverage to muster support as now Punjab was the only state which was left bilingual. Akali Dal contested 1960 SGPC elections on the Punjabi suba issue and won 132 out of 139 seats.

In the meantime, as a result of consequences of planning and development as adopted in the country certain fundamental changes in the support structures of political parties were emerging in the country as a whole. In Punjab, the urban Sikh businessmen, professionals and intelligentsia at all-India level were losing interest in the sectarian demand of the Akali Dal. But, in the rural areas, the Akali support was increasing on the basis of its emotive appeal for being a Sikh party as well as its programme tilted towards farmers. The landed farming community was getting dismayed from Congress because of the pricing policy of agricultural production, restriction on grain trade and apprehension about the land reforms.[6] This also created internal rift in the Akali Dal. The conflict was visible in the 1960-61 Punjabi Suba Morcha and came in the open after third general election, culminating in the division of Akali Dal.

Socio-Economic Development and Suba Movement

In 1960-61 the Punjabi Suba Morcha agitation saw the emergence of a new leader—Sant Fateh Singh. Sant Fateh Singh, the Senior Vice-President of Akali Dal had to take over as dictator of the Morcha on Master Tara Singh's arrest. Advised by his suporters who wanted to change the complexion and leadership of Akali Dal, Sant Fateh Singh categorically announced that they wanted a linguistic reorganisation of Punjab irrespective of the fact which community gets majority. His emphasis on language rather than religion earned him the support of some other parties like communists and socialists and softened the attitude of central leadership.

The results of 1962 elections showed a shift in the fortunes and support base of different political parties in Punjab as in other states. Paul Brass'[7] study shows that in Punjab though the Congress had ostensibly come out stronger, there was a considerable shift in its class support.

Table 2

Party Position in the 1962 Elections in Punjab

Party	*No. of Seats Won*	*Percentage of Votes Polled*	*No. Of Seats Won in the Punjabi Region*	*Percentage of Votes in Punjabi Region*
Congress	90	43.7	49	45.7
CPI	9	7.1	9	10.3
Akali Dal	19	11.9	19	20.7
Jan Sangh	8	9.7	4	7.6
Swatantra	-	2.4	-	2.4
Republican	-	2.2	-	2.2
PSP	-	-	0.9	0.7
Independents & Others	25	20.6	5	10.3

Source: Compiled from India, Election Commission Report on the Third General Elections in India 1962 Part II, Statistical, Delhi: Manager of Publications, 1963.

Significantly, its base among the urban and rural Sikhs shrank and it particularly lost its traditional rural Sikh voters' support who now went with the Akali Dal. The Scheduled Caste voters shifted their allegiance from the communist party and the Scheduled Caste Federation to the Congress and independents. Jan Sangh received its major support from urban Hindus. Some urban Sikhs also voted for it. The communists enjoyed the support only of the rural Sikhs, presumably very small farmers, and a section of landless labourers.

After 1962 elections, in which the domination of agriculturist class in Akali Dal came in the open, the rivalry between Master and Sant groups also came in the open. The Dal finally got divided in July 1962. The majority support for Sant group was visible on all accounts.

Once settled in leadership, Sant Fateh Singh spelled out his new approach more clearly. He started campaigning for a state of Punjab exclusively on the basis of language and culture without any consideration of the percentage of Sikh population. The movement also got support from people of Himachal Pradesh and Haryana region who were now aspiring to have states of their own. The central leadership too could no longer resist it and the Sant's unequivocal demand for linguistic reorganisation and emphasis on communal harmony, unity and integrity of the country, left them with no choice but to accept it or otherwise it could be a clear case of discrimination against Sikhs. The Punjabi Hindus, however, continued to oppose the demand and interpreted the new approach as old wine in new bottles.[8]

Sant Fateh Singh temporarily suspended the Punjabi Suba Movement in the wake of Indo-Chinese war in 1962 and offered unconditional support to Nehru government in war. This was an important factor to soften the official attitude. The passing away of Nehru in 1964 and ouster of Partap Singh Kairon further strengthened the Punjabi Suba Movement. But the central government led by Lal Bahadur Shastri still wavered in recognising the need to reorganise Punjab. Sant Fateh Singh paved the way further by postponing his decision to launch an agitation, which included self-immolation by him in view of the Indo-Pak war in 1965. During the war, the role of Punjabis in general and Sikh population in particular was highly appreciated. In view of all these developments, within two days of the cease-fire, the central government appointed a three-man cabinet committee consisting of Y.B. Chavan, Indira Gandhi and Mahavir Tyagi, to examine afresh the demand for Punjabi suba. To assist the cabinet committee, a 22-member committee of parliament was also set up under the chairmanship of Sardar Hukam Singh, speaker of Lok Sabha.

The formation of a cabinet sub-committee and a parliamentary committee to review the Akali demand marked a definite change in the attitude of the central leadership towards the Akalis. This change received further impetus with Indira Gandhi becoming Prime Minister after Lal Bahadur Shastri's death in January 1966.

When Indira Gandhi became the Prime Minister, the Congress was faction-ridden and the state-level bosses exercised a good deal of influence on the party apparatus. Not sure of support from her own party, Gandhi needed support from outside, both to consolidate her position and to win the forthcoming general elections. For that she started looking towards regional parties. In Punjab she thought of Akalis. Thus, she did not wait for the report of the cabinet and parliamentary committees appointed by the Shastri government and asked the Congress President to summon a meeting of the Congress Working Committee to discuss the Punjab issue. In the meeting, a resolution was passed requesting the government to create a new state of Punjab on a linguistic basis. Thereafter, the government promptly announced its acceptance of reorganisation. In September 1966, the parliament enacted the Punjab State's Reorganisation Bill and a Punjab Boundary Commission was appointed under the chairmanship of Justice J.C. Shah with Subimal Dutt and M.M. Philip as members. Finally, Punjab was divided on November 1, 1966.

The new Punjab comprised the districts of Gurdaspur, Hoshiarpur, Amritsar, Kapurthala, Jalandhar, Ludhiana, Ferozepur and Bhatinda besides a part of Sangrur district and Rupar and Kharar tehsil of Ambala district. In theory, the new state was Punjabi-speaking but in reality it was a Sikh-majority state. Also, the Union Government took over Chandigarh and the control and management of Bhakra and the Beas dam projects besides some common links in the shape of a common Governor, High Court, Electricity Board, financial corporations and housing corporations, were retained. All these opened a number of vital questions, immediately after the reorganisation of the state and remain so.

Notes

1. Rajni Kothari, "Integration and Exclusion in Indian Politics", *Economic and Political Weekly,* October 22, 1968, p. 2225.
2. Satya M. Rai, *Partition of Punjab,* Bombay: Asia, 1965, p. 251.
3. *The Spokesman Weekly*, March 13, 1961.
4. Gerald A. Heeger, "Politics of Integration: Community, Party and Integration in Punjab", Unpublished Ph.D. Thesis, University of Chicago, 1971, pp. 155-56.
5. For reference to P.K. Nijhawan, see A.S. Narang, *Storm Over the Sutlej: The Akali Politics*, Delhi: Gitanjali, 1983.
6. For details on this aspect, see A.S. Narang, *ibid.*
7. Paul R. Brass, *Religion, Language and Politics in North India*, Delhi: Vikas, 1966.
8. Satya, M. Rai, "The Structure of Regional Politics in Punjab", (mimeo.) n.d. p. 14.

13

The Naxalite Movement in Punjab

PARAMJIT S. JUDGE

The Naxalite movement began in reaction to clashes between peasants and the police in the Naxalbari area of Siliguri sub-division of Darjeeling district in West Bengal in 1967. Soon it spread to other states of India. In Punjab it may be seen as an extension of its all-India character. However, shortly after it began there developed certain distinctive features of the Naxalite movement in the state. In other words, it may be stated that there were regional variations in the growth and development of the Naxalite movement in India. It is proposed to describe the process of its development in Punjab by taking into consideration three dimensions which are regarded as essential in the conduct of a movement. These are: ideology, organisational developments and the actual unfolding of the events, conscious or unconscious, as the movement grew over a period of time.

The discussion has been divided into five parts. While the first part deals with the background of the Naxalite movement in India as well as the Punjab state, the second part provides a succinct summary of the ideology of the movement. The third part examines the broad strategy of the movement. In this part we have also described the way the state government suppressed the movement. In the fourth part various organisational developments, both at national and local levels, have been briefly discussed. The fifth part contains the concluding remarks.

I

Socio-economic conditions, history of the communist movement, and the Naxalbari uprising may be regarded as the forces that gave rise to the Naxalite movement. Besides the miserable conditions of the majority of the people, two dimensions may be regarded as significant in this regard: (i) failure of land reforms and discontent among the poor peasants, particularly the tribals,[1] and (ii) a tremendous increase in the number of students in the institutions of higher education. "Between 1951 and 1961, the first decade of independence, there was a 81.48 percent growth in enrolment. In 1961-71, it was up further to 108 percent".[2]

So far as the history of the communist movement in India is concerned, it is marked by intra-party conflicts and dissensions. It has been pointed out by many historians of the movement that differences of opinions and views on strategy and tactics led to the formation of various groups within the party.[3] The Communist Party of India (Marxist) came into existence in 1964. There is a reasonable evidence to suggest that even the manifesto of the CPI(M) could not satisfy the aspirations of a section of the communists who were known as "Maoists" or "pro-China communists".[4]

Occurrences in the tribal villages in Siliguri sub-division of Darjeeling district sparked off the Naxalite movement. In fact, these occurrences would have remained isolated events had the Communist Party of China not stamped its support for those communists whose actions led to those events. The Naxalite movement may be divided into six distinct phases:[5] (i) the Naxalbari uprising and its aftermath, (ii) the period between the Naxalbari uprising and the formation of a party, (iii) participation of the party in various rural uprisings, (iv) entry of the movement into some urban areas without any change in tactics, (v) waning of the movement from 1972 as a result of the suppression, and (vi) post-1972 phase in which the movement lost direction and became fragmented.

In 1964, when the CPI(M) came into existence, the Maoist

groups had joined it. In 1967, at the time of the Fourth General Elections, the CPI(M) decided to participate in electoral battles. In February 1967, a United Front government was formed in West Bengal in which the CPI(M) was one of the coalition partners. Under the leadership of Charu Mazumdar and his associates the party wing of Siliguri sub-division of Darjeeling district gave a call to the poor peasants for occupying the land of the landlords. The struggle first broke out in an area under the Naxalbari police station and then spread to the other adjoining villages. The state government reacted with firmness. In the clash that took place between peasants and the police, a police officer died. The police then unleashed severe suppression killing ten persons.[6]

The Naxalbari uprising drew the attention of all due also to the fact that as the workers' party, CPI(M) was party to the suppression as a partner in the government.[7] Moreover, the Peking Radio hailed the uprising as "spring thunder over India". This was a signal to the Maoist groups to leave CPI(M) and it was estimated that 17,850 members left the party.[8] These communists began to coordinate their activities which culminated into the formation of All-India Coordination Committee of Communist Revolutionaries (AICCCR).[9] Charu Mazumdar emerged as the undisputed leader of the movement which quickly spread to other parts of the country. In the beginning mass organisations were involved in occupation of land and other militant struggles against the local big landlords.[10]

In 1969, the Communist Party of India (Marxist-Leninist) was formed. The policy of annihilation of the class enemies as formulated by Charu Mazumdar was adopted by the party as the main tactical line. This discouraged mass struggles and led to an underground guerrilla warfare. However, this policy led to the continuous decline in the intensity of the movement. In an effort to reconcile the cadre having an urban middle class background with the policy, the party and its leaders agreed to spread the struggle in the cities. This was contrary to the earlier strategical line of action. Meanwhile, differences, factions and fights surfaced in the party. In 1972, when Charu Mazumdar died of heart attack in the police custody, the policy of annihilation was withdrawn by the CPI(ML)[11]. The post-1972 period is one of diversity without unity in the Naxalite movement.

It may be noted that Punjab had experienced the first split in the communist movement in 1948, when the Red Communist Party was formed. However, after three years, the Red Communist Party was disbanded and many of its leaders rejoined the CPI. The Naxalbari uprising and the subsequent developments had their effect on the communists in Punjab. It was the CPI(M) from which the Maoist cadre broke away. In addition, there were two more sources of the Naxalite movement in Punjab: the passive and elderly communists, and the radical sections among the students in colleges and universities. By 1968, the Maoists were able to form the Punjab Coordination Committee (PCC) and could start the movement along the all-India lines.[12]

II

The Naxalite movement was a part of the communist struggle to bring people's revolution. In that respect, its differences from the other communist parties were based on the issues of strategy and tactics. However, this was partly the case. The Naxalites offered a different class analysis of the Indian society. Not only that, their views on the revolutionary potential of a class were different from other communist parties. After it came into existence, the CPI(ML) labelled the CPI and the CPI(M) as revisionist and opportunist parties. India was characterised as a semi-feudal and semi-colonial country. It was of the view that:

> Out of all the major contradictions in our country, that is, the contradiction between imperialism and social imperialism on the one hand and our people on the other, the contradiction between the feudalism and the broad masses of the people, the contradiction between the capital and the labour and the contradiction within the ruling classes, the one between feudalism and the broad masses of the Indian people is the principal contradiction in the present phases.[13]

The CPI(ML) also declared that it would follow the Chinese path for revolution in India. It gave the slogan, "Chinese Chairman is our Chariman".[14] As pointed out earlier, Charu

Mazumdar had emerged as the sole leader of the movement. During his ascendance some of the contenders, such as T. Nagi Reddy were marginalised. It was in the second half of 1969 that Charu Mazumdar gave the tactical line for an armed struggle with which the movement became synonymous, viz., the annihilation of class enemies.

While propounding his thesis, Charu Mazumdar pointed out that guerrilla warfare might not necessarily be fought in the mountains and forests. It was possible to start it in the plains. Rather wherever peasants were living the armed struggle could be developed. For conducting guerrilla warfare, mass organisations are dispensable as these hinder the development and expansion of guerrilla warfare. The sole method of starting guerrilla warfare is through the annihilation of class enemies. As he explained, the "annihilation of class enemy, does not mean liquidating individuals, but also means liquidating the political, economic and social authority of the class enemy".[15]

Charu Mazumdar elaborated his tactical line by writing on the mode of conducting guerilla action.[16] The functioning of the guerrilla units should be kept perfectly secret from those party units which have not mastered the style and discipline needed for such work so far. The entire operation by the guerrilla squad should be kept secret even from the political units of the party. The initiative should be taken to approach the poor peasant who has the "revolutionary potentiality and whisper in his ear; Don't you think it is good thing to finish off such and such a jotedar".[17]

After the death of Charu Mazumdar the above discussed tactical line was withdrawn and more emphasis was put on mass work through mass organisations. It is appropriate to point out that many prominent leaders had not accepted the annihilation line. Among them T. Nagi Reddy, C.P. Reddy and Asit Sen are notable figures. In spite of this, the Naxalite movement is generally identified with the annihilation of class enemies. At present, when various Naxalite groups are involved in elections and democratic processes, it is the People's War Group (PWG) in Andhra Pradesh and Madhya Pradesh which has been identified more with the Naxalite movement initiated under the leadership of Charu Mazumdar.

To conclude the discussion on the ideology of the Naxalite movement, it is pertinent to remark that there was more to it than what has been stated here. It may be understood as a reaction of the youth to the vanished hopes. The hope that land reforms would effectively eradicate glaring inequalities in rural India could not be met. The idealist youth lost faith in the proclaimed conviction of the Indian state to carry out its egalitarian programme. As was clear from the interviews with most of those Naxalites who joined the movement when they were young, the commitment to social transformation was not solely derived from the communist ideology. Past, particularly the Sikh history and literature, proved decisive in instilling idealism and hope for the future. The failure of liberal model of the time, moved them to communist ideology as the other hope.

III

The story of struggles led by the Naxalites may be characterised as a movement from insurrection to agitation. Broadly, three phases may be discerned in the movement in Punjab. These are:

(1) Mass struggles which were organised up to 1969.

(2) Implementation of the line of annihilation of class enemies.

(3) Withdrawal of annihilation line and adoption of militant agitational approach.

(i) Mass Struggles

The phase of mass struggles in Punjab was in tune with what was happening in other parts of the country. In the state the Naxalites organised peasant struggles with three-fold objectives: forcible harvesting of crops, seizure of landholdings of the landlords and demand for an increase in wages of agricultural workers. Before the line of annihilation of class enemies was introduced, the Punjab Naxalites had organised three militant mass struggles the gains of which could not be sustained.

The first among these struggles was organised at Bhikhi-Samaon in Bathinda (now Mansa) district.[18] Prominent Naxalite leader, Hakim Singh belonged to Samaon. He was firmly rooted in the social, economic and political reality of the village. Propaganda work to mobilise the peasants for seizing land was undertaken through drum-beating and public declarations. The Punjab Coordination Committee fixed November 30, 1968 for the seizure of land, but it was to be postponed due to lukewarm response of the people of Samaon. Finally, on December 8, 1968, the people in hundreds reached Samaon and the land of rich landlords was occupied by hoisting red flags in the fields.

Such a seizure of land was mainly symbolic in character. Even the authorities did not take much notice of it. When the Peking Radio broadcast the news, police was ordered to take necessary action. Police interrogated the people. Some of the persons were tortured but the leaders of the action could not be apprehended as they went underground.

The second struggle involved the organisation of workers employed by the Birla Farm. During the Ram Kishan ministry, the Punjab government had leased 1,000 acres of land to the Birlas near Ropar for seed multiplication. The leased out land originally belonged to the peasants of surrounding villages. Earlier, the CPI-sponsored Kisan Sabha and Khet Mazdoor Sabha had opposed it. The issue was also raised in the state Vidhan Sabha. "The Estimates Committee of the Assembly recommended abolition of the deal. The United Front government of 1967 promised to cancel it. But the government fell after nine months before it could fulfil its promise."[19]

The Naxalites directed their efforts towards organising the labourers on the farm. About two hundred workers who belonged to various surrounding villages worked at the Birla Farm. Some of them belonged to those villages whose land was allotted to the Birlas. The workers went on strike on April 10, 1969 on the demand for higher wages. The farm management used hired goondas as well as the police to break the strike. One labour contractor who was active in helping the police was attacked by the workers. This provoked the police to use force.

In the process of its interaction with the police the strike turned violent. It was due to this turn that the Naxalites attacked the police station at Chamkaur Sahib on April 30, 1969. In this attack one constable was injured, whereas one of the Naxalites was arrested. This attack gave moral justification to the police to handle the strike ruthlessly.[20]

The last mass struggle took place at Kila Hakima in Sangrur district in June 1969. It is generally claimed that the Kila Hakima struggle is the best example of mass work.[21] This village had a tradition of peasant movement. The clash between the peasants and the police in Kila Hakima on November 25, 1937 was the beginning of the phase of militant peasant movement in Patiala state.[22] Moreover, in this village most of the land belonged to General Balwant Singh who owned 1,500 acres. After contacting the poor peasants of the village and convincing them of the need for forcible occupation of the land of the General, the action was carried out on June 18, 1969. Unlike the Bhikhi-Samaon struggle, the Naxalites remained in the village or the surrounding areas to sustain the seizure of land. On the following day the General reached there with a big police force and started harassing the villagers. A day after the arrival of the police the Naxalites came in the night and set all buildings in the farm on fire. The game of hide-and-seek between the Naxalites and the police continued for about a month. By that time killing of the landlords was adopted as a tactical line. Thus, following the examples of such killings elsewhere, the Naxalites killed the General.

(ii) Annihilations

The Naxalite leaders in Punjab were of the view that at a certain stage of revolutionary struggle annihilation would be necessary. Annihilations were also essential to counter the state terror, they opined. In their perceptions, Punjab was marked by the predominance of middle peasantry and there were very few pockets where landlordism existed. Thus, the campaign of annihilations could be conducted in the limited areas of the state.

As a corollary to the militant line of the movement, Punjab Naxalites evoked tradition of violent struggles in Punjab. Thus, Ghadar Party, Babbar Akalis and the Red Communists became their source of inspiration. Some of the prominent Naxalites, such as Baba Bujha Singh, Hari Singh Marding, Baba Gurmukh Singh

Lalton had been involved in one or the other earlier political movements.

The organisational aspect of the implementation of the line of annihilation was in accordance with the general communist organisational technique. The primary organisational unit was a *cell* which was to operate at the local level. It consisted of five members and its leader also functioned as the secretary. Generally, the decision to annihilate a particular person was taken at the local level.

In terms of the social background of the persons annihilated, the movement may be divided into three phases:

(a) The major targets were the big landlords who were identified as class enemies by the Naxalites. However, this also included moneylenders.

(b) Naxalites attacked police informers who were instrumental in the arrest of their comrades.

(c) When the police unleashed ruthless suppression on the Naxalites by killing them in fake encounters, the police personnel and their relatives were killed in retaliation by them.

It may be pointed out that there is no clear-cut demarcation of these phases, but a general pattern can be discerned. In all, 73 persons were attacked by the Naxalites for killing them out of which 14 escaped death. Among those who became targets of Naxalites' attacks 28 were big landlords, factory owners or big politicians, 12 were moneylenders, 23 were police agents and 10 were police and government officials or their relatives. Major districts of Naxalites' attacks were Jalandhar and Kapurthala (23) and Sangrur (20).[23]

A majority of the Naxalites who were interviewed related that there were some annihilations which were carried out as a result of personal grudges of informants against the victims. This isolated the Naxalites from the people. However, they gave two reasons for such occurrences. First, like any underground movement, the Naxalites functioned through contacts. Some of these contacts were not politically articulate for an appropriate identification of class enemies. Secondly, the Naxalites inadvertently mobilised the already existing factional rivalries in the villages.

Whether the killing of class enemies should be done by modern arms or traditional weapons may appear an insignificant issue, but in the theoretical formulation of the CPI (ML) a great deal of importance was attached to this. Charu Mazumdar advanced the following reasons for his advocacy of the use of knives, choppers, swords, rods, and spears to annihilate class enemies: (a) they were easily available, (b) they could be easily carried from place to place without any fear of detection; and (c) these weapons, being associated with the exploited rural workers, symbolised the hatred they bore towards their exploiters.

When an article in *Liberation* advocating the use of traditional weapons appeared, the PHC rejected it and continued to use modern weapons.[24] On the other hand, the state unit of the CPI (ML) followed the party directive. Soon it turned out to be a farce in the face of fire power of the police and some big landlords. In certain cases the person identified as a class enemy was first attacked with firearms and afterwards was struck with sword or knife to put a mark on his body. In some cases where it was impossible to conduct annihilation with a conventional weapon, firearms were used as it happened in the case of Basant Singh, an MLA and Sikandar Singh, a Deputy Superintendent of Police.

Since the Naxalites were carrying out their activities in complete secrecy, the issue of shelter was very important for them. In theory, Mao regarded guerrilla as a fish in water. In other words, he is supported and provided shelter by the people. However, in practice this was not the case with most of the Naxalites. People who gave them shelter could be divided into the following three categories:[25]

(a) Since a majority of the Naxalites were drawn from among students, college and university hostels were the obvious hiding places, particularly for those who were young.

(b) The houses of relatives, friends and colleagues were another place of shelter for the Naxalites.

(c) The third category of people who provided shelter to the Naxalites were their political contacts. This included members of the CPI and CPI (M) and old Ghadarites and Red Communists who were sympathetic to the movement.

Rarely did the Naxalites take shelter with the poor peasants and working classes. Though they articulated this matter in the interviews saying that these classes were too poor to look after the 'revolutionaries', yet the fact remains that the revolutionaries remained largely isolated from the poor and working class people.[26]

In the end, it may be appropriate to record some actions of the Naxalites in Punjab which were influenced by the cultural revolution of China. In India, particularly in West Bengal, the Naxalites attacked those cultural symbols that signified feudal-capitalist culture of exploitation. This included demolition of the statues of nationalist leaders and libraries, and attacking theatres screening anti-China movies. Charu Mazumar endorsed these attacks.

In August-September 1969, *Shatranj*, an anti-China movie, was being screened in the country. In West Bengal, the Naxalites had burnt theatres showing the film. In Bathinda too Naxalites tried to blow up the theatre, but the police removed the dynamite before it could do any damage. Besides, statues of Mahatma Gandhi were damaged first at Gurdaspur in 1969 and then in 1970 at Phagwara, Ropar and Amritsar.[27]

Before we move on to the discussion of the post-annihilation phase, it is worthwhile to provide a brief account of the way the Punjab government handled the movement. The methods adopted to "curb the Naxalites" activities were thoughtfully planned and executed with thoroughness. On June 5, 1970, Parkash Singh Badal, the then Chief Minister, stated at a press conference, that "the government was vigilant about the Naxalites' activities and would deal with them with a firm hand."[28] Various methods adopted by the state government are detailed below:

One, the Naxalites were identified and classified into different categories on the basis of their level of participation in the movement.

Two, some Naxalites were declared as proclaimed offenders. The police announced cash rewards for those giving information about them.

Three, to isolate Naxalites from the people, the police used the mass media to portray them as dacoits and murderers who killed wantonly and indiscriminately. The police also got printed various copies of *Lok Yudh* a Naxalite magazine, and started harassing innocent people by planting its copies and weapons on them.[29]

Four, the police arrested Naxalites, their sympathisers and the persons under suspicion. Most of the arrested people were tortured to extract further information from them. The Tarkunde Committee found the methods of torture employed by the police extremely brutal.[30] According to a report published in *Zafarnama*, about 20 persons were tortured to death by the police.[31]

Five, the police resorted to the method of fake encounters to handle the movement. In all, 82 Naxalites died of which three were killed in real encounters, whereas 39 were killed in fake encounters. There is no information available about 28 Naxalites as they were killed by the police and their bodies secretly disposed of.[32]

It is obvious from the description of the annihilation phase that in Punjab the Naxalite movement carried out a campaign of killings for a stipulated revolution. The state government successfully prevented the expansion of the movement. It might have continued for some more time, had the CPI (ML) not withdrawn the line of annihilation of class enemies after the death of Charu Mazumdar. With his death a significant phase in the Naxalite movement came to an end. So important this phase was that even now the Naxalite movement is identified with it.

(iii) Post-annihilation Phase

At the time of withdrawal of the annihilation line during the second half of 1972 various trends in the Naxalite movement could be observed. As mentioned earlier, the movement got further fragmented into various factions which took contradictory positions with regard to the strategy and tactics of the revolutionary struggle. However, a majority of the factions moved towards an agitational approach, as against the earlier hostility to the idea of people's politics including participation in elections.

In Punjab, the story was not different. The shift towards mass organisations and struggles took a definite shape. At this moment, the Nagi Reddy group which had rejected the annihilation line had an advantageous position. It had already revived the Punjab Student Union (PSU) which was disbanded after the implementation of annihilation line. The PC which later on became CPI (ML)—S.N. Sinha group, also adopted the line of mass organisations. Shortly afterwards it participated in elections. These two Naxalite groups remained at the forefront of the mobilisation of the students and poor peasantry.

Between 1972 and 1975 we notice two important mass struggles one of which was spontaneous whereas the other was a result of mass work of the Naxalites. The first was student agitation known as "Moga agitation". It originated from the clash between the students and the employees of the Regal cinema at Moga. It escalated into an all-Punjab agitation due to the police firing on the student demonstration on 5 October, 1972 which killed four persons including one student.[33]

For the Naxalites the Moga agitation proved to be very important as they, particularly the Nagi Reddy group, emerged as major contenders with the other political parties. Till the imposition of the Emergency in 1975, the PSU organised many agitations over the local as well as the larger political issues.

The second major struggle occurred at Kala Sanghian—a village in Kapurthala district. In this village, the SN Sinha group organised the Kirti Kisan Sabha—a peasant organisation. It became a powerful organisation as it spread to adjoining villages. The big landowners perceiving it to be a threat to their power looked for opportunity to stop the functioning of the Sabha. A dispute between a leader of the Sabha and his mother over the issue of landownership provided such an opportunity. The intervention of the police and arrest of that leader in response to his mother's complaint precipitated the situation. As the situation became volatile the police came to the village in order to round up all the Sabha activists.[34] The clash between the Sabha members and the police led to the death of two Naxalites in September 1973. The

Naxalites retaliated by killing one of the police agents on April 13, 1976.

During the Emergency period the organisation of mass struggles were stopped.[35] The coming in power of the Janata Party in 1977 created an euphoria in which the Naxalites remained in the background for some time. The PSU organised two agitaions, one in 1979 and the other in 1980. In 1979, the PSU leader Prithi Pal Singh Randhawa was murdered by a rival student group at the Punjab Agricultural University, Ludhiana. In reaction, a strong agitation demanding the arrest of the killers was organised. It continued till the culprits were apprehended. The second agitation was organised to protest against the hike in bus fares. The agitation was initiated by the non-Congress political parties, but PSUs (affiliated with Naxalite groups other than that of the Nagi Reddy group) gave it a militant turn. On November 18 and 20, 1980, the students clashed with the police at Fatehgarh Sahib, Garhdiwala and Dasuya (Hoshiarpur).[36]

The Naxalite-led mass movements began to wane after 1981. The rise of the Sikh militancy in Punjab overshadowed the Naxalite movement. Some of the colleges, which were once a stronghold of the PSU turned towards the All-India Sikh Students' Federation (AISSF). As the Naxalites lost their hold, the militant appeal attracted more and more students to Sikh extremism. A few of the former Naxalites also joined the armed squads of Sant Jarnail Singh Bhindranwala. Nichhattar Singh who was charged with murdering Lala Jagat Narain, the Chief Editor of *Punjab Kesari* group of newspapers, was an ex-Naxalite. Interestingly, the break away group of UCCCRI (ML)-Ajmer Group, popularly known as *Paigam* group, supported the Sikh militants on grounds of nationality question.

However, other Naxalite groups opposed Sikh militancy. As a result they became targets of the militants. Some of the notable Naxalites killed by the Sikh militants were Baldev Singh Mann, Sarabjit Singh Bhidewad and Jaimal Singh Padda. Baldev Singh Mann was a prominent youth leader whereas the other two were well-known peasant leaders. Some Naxalites also confronted the Sikh militants with arms. One of the notable instances was that of the village Harsha Chhina in Amritsar district where the activists of the C.P. Reddy group fought against the militants for a long time.[37] The C.P. Reddy group retaliated by killing some of the Sikh militants who were involved in the murders of their Naxalite fellows.

In the end, we may add that even after the suppression of the Sikh militant movement, the Naxalite groups have failed to mobilise various sections of the working people in the state. They are noticed in the areas where middle class activism is involved. For example, *Jamhoori Adhikar Sabha* (Association for the Democratic Rights) has been quite vocal and active in raising issues, organising seminars and giving press statements wherever they may find violation of democratic rights. During the period of Sikh militancy, the Sabha was able to conduct an extensive survey in the villages of Punjab published a report which was critical of both the state and the militants.[38] In addition, various Naxalite groups have been waging mass agitations through their front organisations since 1993. Some of the Naxalites have also joined the Bharitiya Kisan Union (BKU) which is primarily an organisation of the landowners. Jan Shakti works through organisations such as Kirti Kisan Union and Pendu Mazdoor Union. In association with each other various groups have been quite active in Technical Services Union which is mainly the organisation of the employees of the Punjab State Electricity Board. However, as a political force the Naxalite movement has been rendered weak and without much impact.

IV

Manoranjan Mohanty is of the opinion that the entire Naxalite movement had a pre-organisational character. It was both the weakness and the strength of the movement.[39] Evidence of a spurt in violent activities was always there; however the benefits of such actions could not be sustained. The state of affairs in Punjab in this regard was not different from the conditions that existed in other parts of India. Upto 1970, the Naxalite movement experienced two splits in Punjab. Later on, the movement further fragmented into numerous groups. It is worthwhile to precisely describe these splits.

The First Split

The first signs of conflict within the movement developed in the Bathinda District Committee. The contradictions among the leaders began surfacing even before the formation of the Punjab Coordination Committee (PCC). It all began on the issue of who should be nominated in the combined Bathinda-Sangrur committee. The issue was related to the inclusion of Hakim Singh, a prominent communist, who had been ignored by another important leader in the region, Harbhajan Singh. In the meeting of the PCC, it was suggested to the district committee to include Hakim Singh. As the tension mounted, Harbhajan Singh broke away and formed the Ferozepur-Bathinda Committee in 1970.

The reasons for split put forward by the Ferozepur-Bathinda Committee included their reservations regarding the line of annihilation of class enemies and disbanding of the mass organisations. As the primary concern of the committee was mass organisations and the combination of open and secret struggles, the first thing it did was to ask its members to voluntarily surrender to the police. It remained more or less ineffective upto 1972. The only thing it did during this period was that it declared that it was in agreement with T. Nagi Reddy's line.[40]

The Second Split

In retrospect it seems that the second split in the Naxalite movement in Punjab was a result of mishandling of minor organisational issues by the leadership.[41] When an attack on the police station at Chamkaur was planned, one of the senior leaders was assigned the responsibility of procuring firearms from Delhi who disappeared and could not be traced. One of the Naxalites found him in a private hospital where he was admitted under his real name. This Naxalite along with others in the Ludhiana District Committee adopted a resolution charging the same senior leader as police agent. When these charges were put before the PCC, the resolution was defeated. Subsequently, the Ludhiana committee was dissolved, but the crisis surfaced when the Jalandhar committee also passed the resolution charging the same leader as police agent. This initiated a process in which all sympathisers of the Ludhiana committee were expelled.

The expelled cadres held a meeting on February 25, 1970 and formed the Punjab Himachal Organising Committee (PHC). Hakim Singh was elected General Secretary, the other members of the State Committee were: Babu Ram Vairagi, Baldev Sangol, Darshan Khatkar and Harbhajan Halvarvi. Except for few all the members of the PHC were young communists.

Isolated from the main leadership of the movement, the PHC remained committed to the line of annihilation of class enemies, but it opposed the use of conventional weapons. Between 1970 and 1972, the PHC effectively carried out the official line of CPI(ML).[42]

Splits within Splits

As the intensity of the movement waned, the differences within the movement began to sharpen. It was particularly so in the PHC and the state unit of the CPI (ML). Both the organisations also faced crisis as some of the prominent leaders were either arrested or killed in 'encounters' by the police. The organisational reshufflings also created tensions. Moreover, at the centre the movement began to face splits as the member of the Central Committee of the CPI (ML) and well known communist leader from Bihar, S.N. Singh drifted away from Charu Mazumdar's line.[43] All these factors fragmented the movement that subsequently could be understood as a strange combination of energies being spent on criticising each other. Some of the Naxalite groups which were in existence in the 1980s were: COC, CPI(ML); Proletarian Revolutionary Group (ML)-Saraf Group; CPI(ML)-SNS Group; CPI (ML)-C.P. Reddy Group; CT, CPI (ML); Reorganizing Committee, CPI (ML); UCCRI (ML) (Unity Centre of Communist Revolutionaries of India)-Harbhajan Group); UCCRI (ML) Ajmer Group; and the Hindustan Ghadar Party (ML). Many of these groups have now ceased to exist or have been rendered insignificant by force of circumstances. At the moment about a dozen Naxalite groups are active in Punjab. One notable change which has taken place among these groups is that they have emerged with new names. For instance, the erstwhile UCCRI (ML)-Harbhajan group is now called the Communist Party Reorganising Committee of India (ML) and CPI (ML) C.P. Reddy group is presently known as Jan Shakti. Other groups have also changed their names. Now we have Lal Tara, International Democratic Party CT CPI (ML), CPI (ML)-Liberation, CPI (ML) Party Unity and CPI (ML) SNS Group.

Organisationally, the Naxalite movement in Punjab is a saga of continuous splits and the stories behind the same involved interpersonal differences coloured by ideological articulations.[44] The movement remained pre-organisational in character. A competition between PHC and the CPI (ML) led to more annihilations though the movement remained weak. It created sensation and appreciation among the people, but it was without any sustainable effect. The Naxalites did not have proper organisational structure which could help them to sustain their base.

V

The Naxalite movement was a revolutionary movement which aimed at transforming the Indian society. It was started by those communists who regarded Chinese path of socialist revolution as appropriate for India. Various social and economic factors gave it a boost. The discontent among tribals, failure of land reforms and tremendous increase in the number of students in the institutions of higher education, many of whom with brilliant careers were imbued with a passion for radical social change, may be noted as central to the rise of this movement.

The line of annihilation of class enemies as formulated by Charu Mazumdar has been considered fatalistic by most of the experts. But it may be added that the same line acquired common identity with the movement. Its failure was its inability to assess the 'real' coercive power of the state and the existing level of preparedness of the Indian people for revolution. In the process its militancy, rather than its ideology, attracted more people to the movement.

Despite all its failures, the Naxalite movement in Punjab made its impact in various dimensions of the life of the people. It exposed the lawless ways of police operations giving a fillip to a struggle for human rights. A new movement in the literary cultural field, such as poetry, short stories and popular street theatre also emerged in Punjab. On top of all this, the Naxalites came to be associated with men of great ideals close to the most revered revolutionaries of Punjab—the Ghadarites of pre-independence period.

Notes

1. Ministry of Home Affairs (India), "The Causes and Nature of Current Agrarian Tensions", in A. R. Desai (ed.), *Agrarian Struggles in India After Independence,* Delhi: Oxford University Press, 1986.
2. Suma Chitnis, *The Crisis in Higher Education*, I.P. Desai Memorial Lecture: 10, Surat: Centre For Social Studies, 1997. See also Eric Hobsbawm, *Age of Extremes: The Short Twentieth Century*, 1914-1991, New Delhi: Viking, 1994. Hobsbawm treats rise in the enrolment of students in the universities, particularly in the West as an important event that could be linked to the rise of student power. In India, too, the rise in the number of students could be linked with the expansion of the Naxalite movement.
3. Mohan Ram, *Indian Communism. Split Within Split*, New Delhi: Vikas, 1969.
4. Mohan Ram, *Maoism in India*, New Delhi: Vikas, 1971; Sumanta Banerjee, *In the Wake of Naxalbari: A History of the Naxalite Movement in India,* Subarnarekha, 1980.
5. Biplab Dasgupta, *The Naxalite Movement*, Calcutta: Allied Publishers, 1974.

6. Sumanta Banerjee, *op.cit.*; Partha N. Mukherji, "Naxalbari Movement and the Peasant Revolt in North Bengal" in M.S.A. Rao, *Social Movements in India*, New Delhi: Manohar, 1979.
7. Mohan Ram, *op. cit.,;* Sumanta Banerjee, *op. cit.* Jyoti Basu was the Home Minister in the coalition ministry.
8. Manoranjan Mohanty, *Revolutionary Violence: A Study of the Maoist Movement in India*, New Delhi: Sterling, 1977.
9. However, the Andhra group of communists did not join the AICCCR.
10. Sumanta Banerjee, *op. cit.*
11. *Ibid.*
12. Most of the information on Punjab is based on interviews with the Naxalites as well as the documents. See also Paramjit S. Judge, *Insurrection to Agitation: The Naxalite Movement in Punjab*, Bombay: Popular Prakashan, 1992.
13. Communist Party of India (Marxist-Leninist), "Programme of the Communist Party of India (Marxist-Leninist)", *Mass Line*, Spcial Issue, Vol, No.36, September 13, 1970, p.2.
14. *Ibid.*
15. Charu Mazumdar, *Collected Works, Vol.2.; Chingari*, Vol.4, No.5, September 1972, p.15.
16. *Ibid.*
17. *Ibid.* p.17.
18. Hakim Singh, *op. cit.*
19. Master Hari Singh, *Agricultural Workers' Struggle in Punjab*, New Delhi: Peoples' Publishing House, 1980, p.94.
20. PHC, (Punjab Himachal Committee) "An Analysis of the Armed Struggle in Punjab", n.d.
21. Judge, *op. cit.*
22. Ramesh Walia, *Praja Mandal Movement in East Punjab States*, Patiala: Punjabi University, 1972.
23. Judge, *op. cit.*
24. PHC, *op. cit.*
25. Judge, *op. cit.*
26. *Ibid.*

27. *Ibid.*
28. *Ibid.*
29. Rana Prit, "Police Tricks" in Samar Sen *et al.* (eds.), *Naxalbari and After: A Frontier Anthology*, Calcutta: Kathashilpa, 1976. Author's own investigation substantiates this point. Jaswant Singh Kanwal, *Lahoo di Lo,* Delhi: Arsi Publishers, 1977, also narrates such an incident.
30. Tarkunde Committee Report, "Police Atrocities on Naxalites", *Mainstream*, Vol.15, No.38, May 21, 1977.
31. Amarjit Chandan, "Punjab Vich Naxalbari Lehar de Shaheed", *Zafarnama*, August, 1977 (revised list).
32. *Ibid.*
33. *The Tribune*, October 8, 1972, p.1.
34. Interviews; *The Tribune.*, September 11, 1973.
35. During the Emergency all mass organisations were banned.
36. Judge, *op. cit.* It may be noted that by that time the influence of the Naxalites on students had waned in major cities.
37. Harish K. Puri, Paramjit S. Judge and Jagroopp Singh Sekhon, *Terrorism in Punjab: Understanding Grassroots Reality*, New Delhi: Har-Anand, 1999.
38. All India Federation of Organisations for Democratic Rights, *Punjab: People Fight Back: A Report to the Nation,* Bombay: AIFOFDR, 1987.
39. Manoranjan Mohanty, *op. cit.*
40. Pramjit S. Judge, *op. cit.*
41. Interview with Hakim Singh in August, 1980.
42. *Ibid.* This was also corroborated by Harbhajan Halvarvi and other Naxalite leaders. Also elaborately discussed in Punjab Himachal Committee (PHC) "An Analysis of the Armed Struggle in Punjab", *op. cit.*
43. Banerjee, *op. cit.*
44. Judge, *op. cit.*

14

Trade Unions and Political Parties in Punjab

SANTOSH SOOD

Trade unions occupy an important place in the economic and social framework of industrialised countries, particularly those in which incidence of unemployment is comparatively low. They function as an organised force in the economic field and constitute an important source of political strength for those who lead them. Leaders of unions can negotiate and bargain with employers from a position of strength, particularly when they are backed and supported by a highly skilled labour force that is not easily replaceable. In Britain and many other industrialised countries, trade unions are an integral part of some political parties which have frequently held reins of power. In the USA, "the labour unions have become organisations that select and form leaders who, upon becoming successful, take their place alongside corporate executives in and out of government, and alongside politicians in both major parties, among the national power elite".[1]

In less developed countries, organised workers constitute a small percentage of the economically active population. However, in some of these, they wield a disproportionately large influence on the existing economic and political institutions since they man critically important sectors of economy. From a collective standpoint, unions frequently constitute a group equipped with means through which they present, and occasionally impose, their views upon the larger society.

It is possible to distinguish at least three interlocked concepts which are relevant in a multitude of ways: first, the labour leader, whose importance arises out of the identity of political and union leadership and/or out of the 'quality' of his leadership; second, the industrial worker, who derives his power from his role as possessor and transmitter of industrial skills; third, the leader-labour-union syndrome, potentially an important economic elite which, as a result of its control over major means of production, produces a definite impact on the society as it has power and ability to lead urban masses.

In the specific context of India, the role of trade unions has been closely related to the history of the national liberation struggle. For its ultimate success, the struggle needed the support of the mass of industrial workers as of other sections of the society. At the same time, a trade union movement isolated from the political mainstream could not have made much headway under the conditions then obtaining under British domination. It was hence natural for the two movements to interact at every stage.[2] Although unions were never formally affiliated to any political party, their leaders were often the leaders, or at least active supporters, of one political grouping or another. Many important political leaders were openly associated with the labour movement. Thus, the movement traditionally reflected a cross-section of the prevailing political ideologies, and to some extent even now faithfully reproduces intra-party faction disputes.

According to one view, the working class was mobilised by its leaders not for class-based economic gains but by the professional middle class as an integral part of the nationalist effort to weaken the British hold. The working class developed no autonomous structures and remained dependent on the political movement. This type of association has been described by Stanley Kochanek,[3] Van Kennedy[4] and Michael Bogaert[5] as political unionism. Political unionism covers a diversity of relationships ranging from ideological sharing of views or policies to explicit cooperation and shared leadership. It may be entirely irrelevant to or may, at best, be remotely connected with the employment interests of workers. It is contended that, in the post-independence period, continued political unionism has been mostly used to mobilise electoral support to political parties.

An explanation of the phenomenon of political unionism in India in the specific historical context of the emergence of the trade union movement has been attempted by Rajni Palme Dutt[6] and Sukomal Sen[7]. There was no political movement inspired by socialist ideology till 1920s and the concept of class struggle did not figure in the political movement. Outsiders from non-proletarian classes who sought to organise the working class did not possess an adequate understanding of the aims and needs of a working class movement. Their political ideology was coloured with middle class concepts incompatible with ideas of class conflict. It was only later that a group of young intellectuals of socialist orientation got inducted into the movement and introduced ideas of class struggle. Thus evolved the political consciousness of working class, making a qualitatively new stage in the creation of a leadership of the labour movement.

In the pre-independence period, almost all socialist and communist leaders worked under the umbrella of the Indian National Congress under a system of dual membership which allowed affiliation to their separate political organisations. In the trade union field there existed, however, a common affiliating organisation, All-India Trade Union Congress (AITUC). As a result of differing perceptions of communist and non-communist leaderships on support to the war effort after Hitler's invasion of the Soviet Union, there occurred a major split in the AITUC. In 1947, the non-communist leadership organised the Indian National Trade Union Congress (INTUC) as a rival to the AITUC.

After 1947, other political parties set up their own union organisations to capture the allegiance of the industrial proletariat. The AITUC that had been in existence since 1920 now became the exclusive preserve of the Communist Party of India. The INTUC was controlled by the Congress party. The erstwhile Praja Socialist Party set up the Hind Mazdoor Sabha (HMS). Some splinter left groups formed the United Trade Union Congress (UTUC). Two new major central trade union organisations were set up. The Bharatiya Mazdoor Sangh (BMS) came up in 1955 and was linked with the Rashtriya Swayamsewak Sangh/Jana Sangh (now the Bharatiya Janata Party). The Centre of Indian Trade Unions (CITU), formed in 1970, was linked with the Communist Party of India (Marxist). Outside the formal sphere of these organisations, but mostly in close liaison with them, arose organisations of employees. Even the Akali Dal organised its own trade union, the Punjab Mazdoor Dal. By now, the criss-cross pattern of the union movement includes many other organisations that came into existence as a result of factional splits or on minor ideological grounds. These include the Hind Mazdoor Panchayat, the All-India Red Trade Union Congress, the National Labour Organisation and the National Federation of Indian Trade Unions. A few of these organisations wield a little local influence in some states, while others exist more or less only in name.

In actual operation, almost every major political party in India has its own trade union wing, assigns activities to its trade union front, and helps to administer the union federations at the state and national levels. Significant numbers of the trade union leaders are members or active sympathisers of political parties. A study by Punekar and Madhuri[8] found that as many as one-half of union leaders were party members. A higher figure of 62 percent has been reported by A.S. Mathur.[9]

It thus becomes obvious that the aims of the trade union movement have not been confined to achievement of immediate economic goals. It is plausibly maintained by Kennedy[10], Crouch[11], C. K. Johri[12], Pattabhi Raman[13] and other scholars that the policies of the trade union leadership have been largely conditioned by the association of unions with political parties committed to diverse ideologies. Over a period of time, there have been many strains of thought, different goals and contending sets of leadership. There have been leaders who broadened their aim to include the goal of national independence; leaders who conceived their purpose as the regulation of the factor market; and leaders for whom the purpose of unionism was conterminous with radical politics aimed at a peaceful or revolutionary transformation of social order. Between these extremes, most union leaders have frequently taken intermediate positions at different times.

There is another perspective along which the emergence of the trade union movement in India may be studied. Since its birth took place in the context of curtailed civil liberties and within a colonial economy characterised by artificial obstacles to industrial growth, it developed certain special characteristics. These were reinforced by plentiful supply of unskilled labour coupled with scarcity of skilled labour. Abysmally low wage standards contributed to a pattern of growth and development divergent from the classical one of the colonising country.

Another area of interest is the operational style of the leadership and its structural and behavioural determinants. Specifically, one may consider a particular scenario in which industrial action is by and large spontaneous. The leadership is responsive to those whom it seeks to lead; it is the membership which leads the leaders. In an alternative scenario, the middle level leadership strongly influences the rank and file members who usually follow its initiative. The third scenario is that of the politically or ideologically motivated style determined by affiliation with a particular party. A much greater probability, of course, is that the leadership frames its operational style on a combination of all these factors.

Studies of trade union movement in India have so far been concerned either with its legal or economic aspects, or with its historical development and growth. Four different approaches emerge from studies at the macro-level: the historic approach, the labour-management-state triangle approach, the operational research approach, and the approach focusing on the role of trade union leadership. One may conclude in general that the labour movement is as yet weak, it is influenced by political parties, it is organisationally underdeveloped, and it relies more heavily on government intervention and labour courts than on its own bargaining strength (see Giri[14] and Subramanian[15], for example).

Adherents of the historic approach have attempted to study trade unions as an inevitable concomitant of industrialisation. Their focus is on the earlier developments. The main conclusion is that trade union movement in India, as in some other underdeveloped countries, was born as an adjunct of the nationalist political movement. After 1947, it was further politicised since no non-political leadership could ensure the achievement of economic demands of the organised working class. The political involvement of trade unions has meant the initiation, control and exploitation of the labour movement by political parties, and the role of 'outsiders' has proved crucial in so far as the provision of leadership, cadre and finance is concerned.

A variant of this view is that trade unions and their leaders in underdeveloped countries have to concern themselves with larger political issues because many problems that affect labour can only be solved by the government (Millen[16], Karnik[17], Crouch[18]). On many a labour issue, a union leader may find himself alongside an aligned politician taking a similar stand. Karnik shows that trade unions have always been intimately involved in politics all over the world and at all times. Trade unions can neither perform their primary economic function nor discharge their broader crucial responsibilities without taking interest in the happenings in the wider fields of politics.

The second major view (Ghosh[19], Johri[20]) has focused on the triangular relationship between the labour, the management and the state. In the industrialised West, particularly in the UK and USA, the evolution of unions occurred in the context of bilateral relationship between workers and employers and was generally aided by government policy. In India, the maturing process of unions has been both aided and obstructed by government policy. According to Ghosh, the relationship between the state and the unions is one of limited mutual reliance. Johri holds that the state adopts the extraordinary course of using statutory regulations in a manner that generally restricts the scope of collective bargaining.

The third major approach is that of the dynamics of trade unions in specific contexts. Studies by Pandey[21, 22], Munson[23], Mast[24] and Bogaert[25], who adopt this approach, deal with the development and special problems of unions in railways, printing and textiles industries and among port workers.

The fourth approach, followed by Mathur and Pattabhi

Raman[26], Vaid[27], Munson and Nanda[28], Mohan Das[29], Punekar and Madhuri[30], Sheth and Jain[31], and Singh[32,33,34] is that of focusing on the role of the trade union leadership in different regions of the country.

The issue of political affiliation may be specifically examined from the standpoint of the historical growth of the union movement. As Lichtblau[35] has shown, a significant feature of the movement in most developing countries and some developed ones is the close association between trade unions and political parties. Millen[36] has plausibly argued that political unionism that typifies labour organisations in Asia and Africa has been a product of the milieu in which they have operated. All new countries inherited iniquitous social systems containing distortions and imbalances and a high residue of social injustice. Their political systems have not yet developed the institutions to cope with rapid changes. Economic development is still at a low level. Under such conditions, unions have been drawn into the political process, and political leaders have tried to buttress their positions through trade union support.

Because of the repression by colonial powers, nationalist leaders were forced into clandestine operations or into activities politically less objectionable in the eyes of the colonial administrations. In the Czarist Russia, revolutionary leaders found the trade union movement a useful cover for carrying on political work and organising labour in a leftist orientation. In pre-independence India, trade union work was considered to be a safer (though more arduous) activity than straight political work, though such consideration did not influence at least some union leaders. In any case, political leadership in Russia as well as colonial countries provided the initial impetus to workers to organise themselves, and thus played the role of a catalyst in launching the trade union movement.

Once independence had been won, the union leadership in India was split between two extremes. The left was keen to transform the successful anticolonial struggle into a new struggle for eventual socialism. The right, which had used the working class primarily as an instrument of trans-class national protest, now expected from it an attitude of responsive cooperation with the new government to industrialise India on classic western lines. Industrial workers, on their part, wanted a new deal from their national government. The trade unions hoped that the leaders now in power would concede the economic demands which they had earlier described as legitimate. The unions ignored the fact that these leaders had merely encouraged the trade union movement as part of a larger anti-colonial design and had close links with big business. It was unnatural to expect that, in their new association with the apparatus of political power, they would countenance agitational activities. The movement found itself into a quandary from which it has not completely extricated itself even now. Ornati[37] maintains that the Indian labour movement, as a whole, has still not developed an attitude and an organisation to help it in its inchoate aspirations, and the unions have not found a *raison d'etre* commensurable with that lost with the achievement of independence. Ornati's case is perhaps overstated, but has a ring of plausibility.

The relationship between parties and unions has been viewed from another angle by Bogaert[38] who distinguishes between a political dependence stage and a maturity stage. In the former, the unions are assumed to be directed to a large extent by considerations that are extraneous and even against the employment-related interests of workers. In the latter, unions do not disengage themselves entirely from politics but influence the political apparatus for the furtherance of their interests as pressure groups, instead of being dictated to by political leaders and used for political purposes. The maturity stage is said to have been reached in developed democratic societies.

Whether this model has universal applicability or not, the postulated maturity stage forms no part of the present Indian scene. Capital and labour are at loggerheads with each other and the movement continues to stake its political aims. Chronologically, the establishment of the trade union movement in India slightly antedates its association with political parties, but the rise of the affiliating central union organisations was in the main due to the politically conscious communist and socialist leadership with encouragement from the political left of the

Congress party. All generations of union leadership in India have been deeply steeped in politics. Even in the case of many independent unions, the leadership had, and still has, open or clandestine links with one political party or another. Thus the historical context is that of a political leadership promoting trade unions, and the current leadership is essentially a product of these political developments.

It has been contended that the relationship between unions and political parties in India is asymmetric, with the latter playing the role of the big brother. According to Pattabhi Raman[39], the political involvement of trade unions has meant the initiation, control and exploitation of the labour movement by political parties. Crouch[40], however, argues that "the stronger the personal following of a leader, the less dependent he is on the support of the political party and, at the same time, the more useful he is to the party. Therefore, one would expect stronger unions to be less under the immediate control of a political party".

Political involvement of trade unions is not uique to India. The exact extent varies. As Sufrin[41] points out, it is closer in Europe than in the USA. In Britain, France, Germany, Holland, Belgium and Scandinavia, particular trade unions support particular political parties as a matter of ideology and policy. It is a mater of record that, even in the USA, 77 percent of the leaders from the AFL, and 63 percent from the CIO, belonged to either of the two dominant parties[42]. A British survey showed that 81 percent of full-time officials and 17 percent of shop stewards were members of political parties.[43]

Among various issues that relate to the trade union movement, there is none that is more controversial than the question of the goals of the movement. There is a clear-cut division between two contending schools of thought. One advocates the Marxist-Leninist model of unionism, the other advances the concept of bread and butter unionism.

Marx had visualised the overthrow of capitalism as a historic task of the working class. Lenin had argued that the very fact of existence of working class led to the spontaneous rise of trade unionism. In the absence of political consciousness, trade unions would develop into anti-revolutionary institutions and would serve to integrate workers into the capitalist system. With political consciousness, they had the potentiality of becoming instruments of revolutionary change. Marxists saw the mature movement as having dual aims: to struggle for economic benefits within the constraints of the capitalist system, and simultaneously to strive for snapping the constraints to achieve the break-up of the system itself. The aims were not seen as mutually exclusive. The economic struggles strengthen the unions and win the trust of the workers; this strength, armed with class consciousness, dialectically transforms the class struggle within the constraints into a revolutionary struggle against them.

The Marxist school finds support in the theses of the Webbs, Cole and Laski, except in degree of emphasis. The Webbs include the reconstruction of society by the elimination of capitalism in their list of aims for the movement. Cole emphasises the need for the control of industry by workers. Laski's long range philosophy visualises trade unions as offensive as well as defensive weapons against capitalism. All of them extol class struggle, want business unionism to give place to political unionism, and see the future replacement of capitalism by socialism through the parliamentary process, with Cole and Laski displaying occasional inclination for the revolutionary method.

Non-Marxists either reject the basic proposition that capitalism deserves to be abolished, or maintain that its abolition is a political concept which has little to do with genuine trade union activity. In either case, they are opposed to the induction of politics into trade unions, except in so far as the role of unions as pressure groups working for their members may be termed as political. At the operational level, Sufrin[44] contends that the sine qua non of the trade union activity is an immediate concern with the problems of wages, hours and conditions of employment and other similar issues of immediate economic welfare. Workers' sympathy can be alienated if their shop-floor needs are subordinated to political objectives. Under such circumstances, workers begin to seek unofficial leaders to champion their most immediate needs.[45]

The trade union movement in underdeveloped countries has yet to achieve maturity both by the Marxist yardstick and by the laissez-faire model. The characteristics of the movement have been conditioned by the association of unions with political parties committed to various ideologies.[46] Since the political objectives of the movement in India are almost as old as the movement itself, it has been suggested that unionism here has been primarily dedicated to the establishment of a new society. Its short-term aims are seen to be satisfaction of immediate shop-floor needs of the workers to retain their loyalty, while the long term aims are to be achieved through ideological education.[47]

The philosophy underlying the settlement of industrial disputes has been viewed differently by students of the trade union movement and by trade unionists themselves. Ornati[48] summarises three strands of thought. The first, favoured by West-oriented intellectuals, favours free collective bargaining and pure and simple trade unionism, and is essentially British in origin. The second strand favours collective bargaining without necessarily rejecting conciliatory and persuasive government intervention. The third strand which accepts a planned mixed economy, asserts that objective complexity of issues renders it necessary that market forces must not operate without restrictions.

V.V. Giri[49], a major exponent of collective bargaining, favoured total exclusion of compulsory adjudication from the law of the land since it cut at the very roots of the movement. He saw straightforward bargaining as an incentive for maintaining unity among workers. Ornati[50] views collective bargaining as only a desirable future goal due to the present relative weakness of the movement, erosion of the union bargaining power by massive unemployment, dismal poverty and opposition by employers. Charles A. Myers[51] concurs on the ground that, at the present stage of economic development, India cannot afford the period of labour strife which is the usual prelude to more mature collective bargaining.

Specifically, in the context of India, we may discern some differing strands of perceptions. At the national level, the INTUC leadership holds that, in an economy which aims at planned production and distribution in the interest of social justice, strikes and lock-outs are out of place. It supports negotiations, collective bargaining and voluntary arbitration but takes the stand that the government is entitled, in the common interest, to make arbitration and adjudication compulsory in some cases. The INTUC national stand is not actively repudiated at the regional and local levels, but the approach there is more pragmatic in practice.

The AITUC leadership holds that, in the absence of working class control on the means of production and on the distribution apparatus, or over the state which is the main agency of development in our semi-planned economy, collective bargaining with the right to strike and some measure of state intervention, but no compulsory arbitration, is the right policy. It asks for legislation for compulsory recognition of unions. "In the event of the failure of negotiations and collective bargaining", AITUC says, "the workers should be free either to exercise their right to strike or to refer the dispute to arbitration, for which a machinery should be at their disposal for use at their will".[52] It is thus assumed by AITUC that, given the popular pressure, the state machinery can reorient its policies in favour of the working class.

The BMS leadership regards collective bargaining as superior to any arrangement involving third party intervention.[53] Genuine collective bargaining, in its opinion, implies the ability to apply sanctions including strikes, at least in the last resort. Government intervention is considered acceptable only under exceptional circumstances (threat to the security of state or public health and safety, or on request), and an independent agency is suggested as a device to help in solution of disputes.

In terms of a public image, another dimension is added by the unceasing condemnation of the exploitation of trade unions for political ends in news media. The allegation is widely believed even by many trade unionists. It causes the latter to disapprove of political links except when they themselves are politically committed. It forces political parties to be on the defensive and keep a somewhat low profile in their public pronouncements. The BMS, which operates extensively through its BMS unions, is officially against political unionism. The Congress party, which operates in the movement through INTUC, accuses communists of using trade unions for their own political ends. The left accuses these two parties of hypocrisy, and stresses the need for the unity of the working class movement irrespective of political differences.

It follows from the discussion that we may expect to find a considerable amount of inter-organisational differences with respect to the long term aims of the trade union movement, but little or no controversy in regard to the short term aims, except in so far as these are complementary to each other.

Finally, a brief comment is in order on some relative preoccupation of the leadership. INTUC leaders are perhaps more concerned with development goals, which means development of national economy and maintenance of industrial peace. Since 1950s, the Congress party and INTUC have progressively defined India's national goal as a socialist pattern of society, socialism, and now liberalisation and globalisation. Though the Congress-type socialism was markedly different from the Soviet socialism, since it visualised an indefinitely continuing mixed economy, the borrowing of terms led to some selective (and possibly convenient) borrowing of concepts. In capitalist countries, trade unions are a vehicle of protest against inequalities in the society. In the Soviet system, trade unions had the function of encouraging production, maintaining discipline and acting as social welfare agencies. Through a transference of this concept, it was suggested by many leaders of the Congress party that the proper role of trade unions in India included persuading workers to forego immediate demands and urging restraint, discipline, restricted consumption and greater productivity in order to increase the rate of capital accumulation and check inflationary pressures.

Trade Unions and Political Parties in Punjab: Some Conclusions from an Empirical Study

A few years ago we conducted a study to understand the linkage between trade unions and political parties in Punjab. The study was designed to ascertain the prevailing social and political alignments of the union leadership in Punjab, its perception of its own role and that of others, the nature and extent of its militancy, its point of view on problems relating to the working class in general and the trade union movement in particular, and its style of functioning. We aimed at a study of the role of the state-level leadership of the union organisations in relation to affiliates and the leaders' views on social, economic and political issues.

Our major assumption was that the movement, having developed under the umbrella of political parties, is linked with the respective political sponsors. The leadership tends to be influenced by political linkages both in formulating union policies and in viewing its own role. However, at the plant level, some degree of local autonomy may be exercised by the leadership, sometimes at variance with the policies of the parent bodies. The general style of functioning of the trade union leadership belonging to a particular political party can be affected by the fact of the party being in or out of power at the state level.

The scope of the enuiry was limited geographically to the state boundaries of Punjab.[54] The area of the state of Punjab is 50,362 square kilometres[55] and its total population in 1991 was 20.28 million.[56] The break-up of the population is as follows:

Cultivators	1.92 million
Agricultural labourers	1.45 million
Workers in household industries	0.89 million
Workers in other industries	1.16 million
Total	5.42 million
Membership of registered trade unions (1993)[57]	0.39 million
Membership of registered trade unions (1994)[58]	0.49 million

Since the advent of the green revolution in the sixties, Punjab has made great strides in agriculture, particularly in the cultivation of wheat and paddy. Though the area of Punjab is only 1.5 percent of the area of entire India, it contributes 8.2 percent[59] of the total production of food grains. Other major crops are cotton and sugar cane. Industrially, the state is not adequately advanced, but a number of industries, mostly at a small or medium scale, have sprung up during the last 40 years. These manufacture textiles, fertilisers, engineering goods, sports goods, hosiery products, agricultural implements, electronic goods, etc.

The first trade union in Punjab, the Punjab Press Association, was formed in 1919. In 1994, there were 467 trade unions in Punjab with a membership of 4,94,596.[60] The numerical strength of the various trade union organisations in Punjab in that year shows that BMS claimed 27 percent of this strength, AITUC 26 percent, INTUC 16 percent, CITU and HMS 7 percent each, PMD less than 1 percent. The remaining 16 percent was shared by unattached unions or unions affiliated to other organisations.[61]

In our study, we have avoided the question of the desirability, or otherwise, of political involvement, and have only depicted the factual situation as it exists.

We had a total of 190 respondents of which 27 were state-level leaders, with nine each belonging to INTUC, AITUC and BMS. The remaining 163 respondents were local-level leaders mostly belonging to these unions, but also including some unaffiliated leaders. We found that 58 percent of local-level leaders owned to political links. Surprisingly, the majority of BMS leaders at local level denied that they had any political links. At the state level, all nine AITUC respondents owned to political links with the CPI, eight as members and one as sympathiser; out of nine INTUC respondents, five were members of the Congress party, one was a sympathiser, and three had no political links. The denial of political links by three INTUC respondents at the state level was possibly concerned with factional struggles within the party.

The overall pattern was consitent with the view that, although various political parties actively encourage party links in trade unions at both levels, and particularly at the state level, no individual is debarred at least at the local level unless he is hostile to the party with which the union has political links. It is presumed that a non-political or a political leader will eventually be won over through contact with the politically oriented majority.

Trade union leaders are expected by the members to organise and lead public agitations. Since many of them have political links, they also participate in movements launched by parties.[62] It is reasonable to assume that the extent of conscious participation in such general political activity is a fair index of one's political involvement. We found that nearly all politically linked respondents in the sample were conscious that they had participated in political agitational movements. It also appeared that the interest of some union leaders in the trade union movement originated in their contact with the pre-independence movements, both at the trade union and the political levels—in many cases indistinguishable from each other.

An event not unusual in the life-cycle of a political or union leader in India is imprisonment for an allegedly 'political' offence, for going on an 'illegal' strike, or for other offences of a similar character. The Indian political culture, which has come down to us from the period prior to independence, reveres those who get arrested in such causes as heroes. In fact, imprisonment is regarded widely as an index of one's commitment. Some union leaders are often taken into custody and kept in confinement, sometimes for a long period, although without formally charging them with any specific offence. Occasionally, union leaders are arrested on the eve of a proposed agitation or strike on a complaint lodged by the management to the effect that there is an impending threat to public order. The police arrest the union activists under sections 107 and 151 of the Indian Penal Code (relating to breach of peace) and detains them pending their trial in a court of law; usually, they are released without their being sentenced after the agitation fizzles out or a settlement is reached. It appears that the government uses the weapon of arrest to defuse particular situations, rather than to suppress the trade union movement by imprisonment of leaders through court orders.

Among the local-level leaders arrested for union activities, 48 percent were from AITUC, 35 percent from INTUC, 9 percent from BMS, and 8 percent from unions. Among those arrested for political activities, 58 percent belonged to AITUC, 10 percent to INTUC, 16 percent to BMS, and 16 percent to unaffiliated unions. Data at the local as well as state level showed that the BMS leaders were imprisoned more for political reasons (e.g., connections with the RSS) than for their trade union activities. Respondents belonging to INTUC were, for obvious reasons, imprisoned less for political reasons than for reasons of unions activity.

Our data support the view that there is an intimate link between affiliating organisations and political parties in Punjab. In particular, AITUC is certainly managed by the CPI, INTUC by the Congress party, and BMS by the Bharatiya Janata Party. Even some 'independent' trade unions have political links with these parties. Trade union leaders are encouraged by political parties to become political activists, but no individual is debarred from leadership of a union unless he is actually hostile to the party with which the union has its political links. Non-political and apolitical individuals are sought to be won over through "unity in action". In effect, unions are partly utilised by parties to nurture new political activists. These conclusions have been substantiated by the participation of trade union leaders in political agitations launched by the respective political parties.

Only the INTUC leadership has remained aloof from political agitations because no agitations have been launched by the Congress party. The data also suggest that the relationships between trade unions and political parties are fairly stable: few unions change their affiliation for functional reasons.

The survey showed that most trade union leaders in Punjab are prepared to make at least minor sacrifices for their movement: more than half of them have been imprisoned at least once, and a large majority of respondents from all unions, including those run by supporters of the ruling party, have reported that they had been, at one time or another, subjected to harassment and victimisation at the hands of the employers and/or the police.

During the survey, the respondents were asked to specify the best method in their opinion for settling industrial disputes. Almost all leaders voted for negotiations. There were a few differences in the shade of opinion, some favouring direct and bilateral negotiations, some favouring trilateral negotiations with the government as a participant, while most were undecided on this point. Strikes, struggles and coercive methods as the best methods of conflict resolution were favoured by only nine respondents. Only one respondent felt that straight government intervention was best, while two respondents flatly stated that disputes could not be resolved till socialism was achieved.

We found that the perception of the respondents about the attitudes of the Congress party, CPI, CPI(M) and BJP towards the union movement broadly followed the respective party lines. Not unexpectedly, INTUC leaders placed the Congress party first and BJP last; BMS leaders reversed this order; and AITUC leaders and leaders of unaffiliated unions placed CPI first and BJP last. In all cases, CPI(M) leaders were militantly vocal. On the other hand, the rift between the CPI and the CPI(M) at the political level found its extreme expression in the rivalry between AITUC and CITU at the union level, the perception of AITUC leaders at the plant level was certainly affected by their estimate of the resistance offered by CITU to their leaders.

In operational terms, most trade union leaders tend to apprehend the role of the organs of the state power as the role mainly of: (i) the Central and the State Governments, each of which is conceived of as an interlocking complex of political leadership and the higher levels of bureaucracy; (ii) the district and local authorities whose attitudes assume particular importance in times of stress, since they can refuse facilities for meetings and demonstrations, deploy police, and send impartial or tendentious reports to higher authorities; (iii) the police; and (iv) the judiciary. In addition, the role of the government as an employer also affects the perception of its attitude by leaders of the trade unions.

Some differences among the respondents could be at least partly traced to the policies of the central organisation to which a particular union was affiliated and thus to its political affiliation. There were also some apparent differences in the understanding of the local-level leaders in contrast with the understanding of the state-level leaders. The latter tended to be more cautious in their assessment by returning such replies as "the government is favourable only towards particular unions or in certain situations" or "the government is not much concerned".

At the time of the survey, the central government and the Punjab government were both run by the Congress party with which INTUC has an ideological rapport. Our data show that the assessment of the attitudes of the two governments was broadly similar, except that a marginally greater number of AITUC respondents considered the attitudes of the latter government as hostile, with a corresponding shift downwards in the number of AITUC respondents who considered its attitude to be favourable. There was also a slight shift in the case of the respondents from unaffiliated unions. They specifically stated that their unions had no significant dealings with the state government and their perception was derived from 'general impressions'.

The police has indeed a very poor image as far as the leaders of the trade union movement are concerned. Apart from the universally acknowledged fact of high handed behaviour of police towards the unions, the poor image of the police in the general public has been attested by a number of Police Commissions as well as by the State High Courts and the Supreme Court of India. A favourable rating to the police was given by only 26 out of our 190 respondents; as many as 110 respondents described the attitude of the police as hostile. There were no inter-organisational differences, except that the respondents from unaffiliated union, and in particular those from white collar unions (in whose case the police always proceeds more warily), were less critical of the police.

The judiciary got a mixed rating, with 67 respondents out of a total of 190 describing its attitude as favourable, 65 describing it as hostile, and the remaining 58 either describing it as conditionally favourable or indifferent, or refusing to express any opinion on the subject. There were some inter-organisational differences. At the local level, 47 percent of the respondents from unaffiliated unions, 46 percent from BMS, 35 percent from INTUC, but only 22 percent from AITUC, perceived the attitude of the judiciary as favourable; those viewing the attitude as hostile were 18, 20, 43 and 53 percent, respectively.

There is one plausible reason that suggests itself for the comparatively poor rating of the judiciary among the CPI oriented cadre of the AITUC unions. As probably the most important part of its national programme, the CPI has, in the post-independence period, emphasised the necessity for the transformation of rural land relations. Under its constant prodding as well as because of the previous ideological commitment to Nehruism in the Congress party, almost all state governments did enact land reform measures, but many of these have been struck down by the judiciary on the ground of their inconsistency with the right to property. It is worth noting that many AITUC respondents had rural links.

The BMS unions and the white collar unions included in unaffiliated unions, in line with their liberal creed, have a good deal of faith in the independence of judiciary and regard it as a bastion against the depredations of bureaucratic arbitrariness.

The above remarks may be supplemented by a brief explanation at the political level of the attitudes which may be normally expected from the party lines. As the party then in power at both central and the state levels, the Congress party was the main architect of the labour legislation as well as of the labour policy in general. If the perception of the respondents of the attitudes of the two governments fell short of complete unanimity, the reasons must be sought in their experiences at the local level and pressures from the rank and file. This becomes clearer if we examine the perception of the INTUC respondents about the attitude of the subordinate organs of the state which are responsible for the implementation of the labour policies in down-to-earth situations in which the employers and managements victimise unions, the police sides with the former, and the district and local authorities have a tendency to sidetrack the plaintive union leaders. It is no wonder that INTUC leaders were faced with a real dilemma; their own government would frequently let them down in the eyes of the rank and file. They resolved this dilemma by representing the political government as benign (and even tried to explain some unpopular steps as being in the 'larger' national interest), and shifted the blame to the district and local authorities, the police and the judiciary for the 'wrong' implementation of the policies of the political government. By their logic, they implicitly accepted that the subordinate organs of the state have a relative autonomy of their own, though such a formulation does not form a part of the declared understanding of either the Congress party or the INTUC. Even the classical concepts of the relative autonomy of the legislature, the executive and the judiciary were, in the case of these organisations, tempered with an injunction to the bureaucracy and the judges to be 'committed' to the national interest. The more ideologically conscious CPI accepted the fact of the relative autonomy as an every-day fact of its theoretical understanding[63], and had thus no difficulty in explicitly facing its own dilemma. As a part of its national policy, it extended support to the Congress party government for many years, even welcomed the promulgation of the Emergency and entered into electoral alliances with the Congress party. Though the support to the government was only conditional, the pressure of rank and file, as in the case of the INTUC respondents, led the AITUC respondents to adopt the same alibi: the political government at the centre and in the state is relatively blameless, but the administration at the local level acts on its own in repressing the working class movement.

The perception of the BMS leadership is also understandable in the light of its political convictions. The BJP with which BMS is associated, does not regard the state as a class institution, nor does it perceive any irreconcilable antagonism between the workers and the capitalists. It sees the problem as basically political or even party-political; all that is required is the replacement of the Congress party with a more acceptable alternative as the ruling party so that the 'anti-people policies' of the former are reversed. Thus, the attack is on the central and state governments as well as on the subordinate organs; the latter are viewed as acting in pursuance of a state-directed policy, though more ruthlessly. Since most local level leaders seldom come in direct contact with the government, but find hindrances in their functioning only at the local administrative levels, their individual experiences do lead them to perceive the attitudes of the government in a somewhat more favourable way, though their rating falls short of that given by the INTUC and AITUC leaders.

Our final conclusion is that, at least in Punjab, non-worker trade union activists are perceived by the majority of the existing union leadership as performing a substantial and useful role, though white collar trade unionists (predominant in unaffiliated unions), who have traditionally handled their own affairs at the lower level, are less enthusiastic about their presence in the trade union movement. One might argue that while there was a largely uneducated labour force in earlier years, the organised labour of today is comparatively more educated and is capable of looking after its own affairs without the help of outside activists. On the other hand, it is also true that in contrast with the modest rise in the educational attainments of factory workers, the complexities of modern life have recorded a more than corresponding increase in the complexities of industrial relations. The introduction of professionally trained managements, skilful in negotiations and legal evasions, has in fact further underlined the necessity for professionalisation of labour leadership—a role which many outsiders in the movement have played with distinction in the past. At least, this happens to be the way in which most trade union leaders in Punjab perceive the issue.

It is clear from the above discussion that linkages between unions and political organisations do exist. As regards their influence, our data showed that the national policies of the political parties found an echo in the policies of their associates in the trade union field.

The discernment of the political goals of the trade union movement also followed the party lines fairly closely, at least at the state level. The role perception of the leaders of various organisations was affected by their political linkages. AITUC leaders perceived their political roles more clearly because of the specific guidelines of the CPI about the need to create political consciousness in the working class. The rift between the CPI and the CPI(M) at the political level found its extreme expression in the rivalry between AITUC and CITU at the union level, and the performance of their role by the AITUC leaders at the plant level was certainly affected by their antipathy towards the CITU.

Since the survey, a few political realities have changed, and no doubt there are some discernible differences in attitudes, particularly between AITUC and CITU. However, the underlying hostility still persists and frequently manifests itself at the shop floor level.

Notes

1. C. Wright Mills, *The Power Elite*, New York: Oxford University Press, 1959.
2. Harold Crouch, *Trade Unions and Politics in India*, Bombay: Manaktalas, 1966, reprinted as *Indian Working Class*, Ajmer: Sachin Publications, 1979.
3. Stanley A. Kochanek, *Business and Politics in India*, Berkeley: University of California, 1974.
4. Van Dussen Kennedy, *Unions Employers, and Government: Essays on Indian Labour Questions*, Bombay: Manaktalas, 1966.
5. Michael V.D. Bogaert, *Trade Unionism in Indian Ports*, New Delhi: Shri Ram Centre for Industrial Relations, 1970.
6. R. Palme Dutt, *India Today*, Bombay: Peoples' Publishing House, 1949.
7. Sukomal Sen, *Working Class of India: History of Emergence and Movement, 1830-1970*, Calcutta: K.P. Bagchi and Co., 1977.
8. S.D. Punekar and S. Madhuri, *Trade Union Leadership in India: A Survey*, Bombay: Lalvani, 1967.
9. A.S. Mathur, *Trade Union Elite in India*, Institute of Social Science, Agra: Agra University, 1967.
10. Van Dussen Kennedy, *op. cit.*
11. Harold Crouch, *op. cit.*
12. C.K. Johri, *Unionism in a Developing Economy*, Delhi: Asia Publishing House, 1967.
13. N. Pattabhi Raman, *Political Involvement of India's trade Unions*, Bombay: Asia Publishing House, 1967.
14. V.V. Giri, *Labour Problems in Indian Industry*, Bombay: Asia Publishing House, 3rd ed., 1972.
15. K.N. Subramanian, *Labour Management Relations in India*, Bombay: Asia Publishing House, 1967.
16. Bruce H. Millen, *The Political Role of Labour in Developing Countries*, Honolulu: East West Centre Press, 1966.
17. V.B. Karnik, *Trade Unions and Politics in India*, Bombay: University of Bombay, 1968.

18. Harold Crouch, *op. cit.*
19. Subrateshi Ghosh, *Trade Unionism in the Underdeveloped Countries*, Calcutta: Bookland, 1960.
20. C.K. Johri, *op.cit.*
21. S.M. Pandey, "Rival Unionism in an Industrial Centre: A Study of Kanpur", *Indian Journal of Industrial Relations*, Vol.3, No.2, October 1967.
22. S.M. Pandey, "Ideological Conflict in the Kanpur Trade Union Movement, 1934-1945", *Indian Journal of Industrial Relations,* Vol.3, No.3, January 1968.
23. F.C. Munson, "Printing Unionism in Delhi", *Indian Journal of Industrial Relations,* Vol.3, No.4, April 1968.
24. Mahesh Kumar Mast, *Trade Union Movement in Indian Railways*, Meerut: Meenakshi Prakashan, 1969.
25. Michael V.D. Bogaert, *op. cit.*
26. A.S. Mathur and N. Pattabhi Raman, "Trade Union Leadership in Agra", *Agra University Journal of Research*, Vol.10, January 1962.
27. K.N. Vaid, "Growth and Practice of Unionism: An Area Study", Delhi: Delhi School of Social Work, Delhi University, 1962.
28. F.C. Munson and A.C. Nanda, "Influence of Legal Framework on Labour Leaders and Their Unions", *Indian Journal of Industrial Relations,* Vol. 2, July 1966.
29. S.R. Mohan Das, "Anatomy of Trade Union Leadership", *Economic Times,* Bombay, Vol. 7, October 9, 1967.
30. S.D. Punekar and S. Madhuri, *op. cit.*
31. N. R. Sheth and Som Prakash Jain, "The Status and Role of Local Union Leaders", *Indian Journal of Industrial Relations.*
32. Jaspal Singh, *India's Trade Union Leaders*, New Delhi: National Publishing House, 1980.
33. Jaspal Singh, "Social Background of Trade Union Leaders", *Economic and Political Weekly,* Vol.5, No.34, August 22, 1970.
34. Jaspal Singh, "Trade Union Leaders: A Study in Class Background and Social Mobility", *Indian Journal of Social Work*, Vol. 32, No.1, April 1971.

35. George E. Lichtblau, "The Politics of Trade Union Leadership in Southern Asia", *World Politics*, Vol. 7, October 1954.
36. Bruce H. Millen, *op. cit.*
37. Oscar A. Ornati, "Problems of Indian Trade Unionism", *Annals of the American Academy of Political and Social Science*, Vol. 310, March 1957.
38. Michael V.D. Bogaert, "Dynamics of Political Unionism: A Study of Calcutta Dock Workers", *Indian Journal of Industrial Relations*, Vol.4, No.2, October 1968, pp.199-214.
39. N. Pattabhi Raman, *op. cit.*
40. Harald Crouch, *op. cit.*
41. Sidney C. Sufrin, *Unions in Emerging Societies: Frustration and Politics*, New York: Syracuse University Press, 1964.
42. Mills, *op. cit.*
43. Royal Commission on Trade Unions and Employers' Associations, "Shop Stewards and Workshop Relations" by W.E.J. McCarthy and S.R. Parker, London: HMSO.
44. Sidney C. Sufrin, *op. cit.*
45. K.I. Sams and N. Robertson (eds.), *British Trade Unionism: Select Documents*, Vol.I, Oxford: Basil Blackwell, 1972.
46. Johri, *op. cit.*
47. Ornati, *op. cit.*
48. *Ibid.*
49. Giri was a former trade unionist and later President of India.
50. Ornati, *op. cit.*
51. Charles A. Myers, *Industrial Relations in India*, Bombay: Asia Publishing House, 1958.
52. Government of India, Ministry of Labour, *Proceedings of the Indian Labour Conference* (12th session held at Nainital from 8 to 11 October, 1952), p.243.
53. Bharatiya Mazdoor Sangh, *Note on Industrial Relations Bill*, Bangalore: Canara Bank Workers' Union (*circa* 1978).
54. Before the partition of India, Punjab comprised the entire territory from the river Indus to the river Yamuna, bounded by Jammu and Kashmir to the north, and Sind and Rajputana to the

south, excepting some princely States (Patiala, Nabha, Faridkot, Kapurthala and the Shivalak Hill States). In 1947 Punjab was divided into Punjab (India) and Punjab (Pakistan). In the fifties, the princely States were merged into Punjab. After the 1966 division on a linguistic basis, the present Punjab now (1997) consists of the 14 districts of Gurdaspur, Amritsar, Jalandhar, Kapurthala, Hoshiarpur, Nawanshahr, Ferozpore, Faridkot, Ludhiana, Fatehgarh Sahib, Ropar, Patiala, Sangrur, and Bhatinda.

55. Governmnt of Punjab, *Statistical Abstract of Punjab, 1994*, Chandigarh.
56. *Ibid.*
57. Labour Commissioner, Punjab, *Annual Report on the Working of the Trade Unions Act, 1926, in the State of Punjab for the Year 1994.*
58. *Ibid.*
59. See references 35-37 *supra.*
60. *Ibid.*
61. Figures of the respective claimed though unverified membership (and number of unions affiliated) in 1994 are BMS 1,32,824 (174), AITUC 1,27,626 (75), INTUC 80,614 (66), CITU 36,007 (34), HMS 36657 (10), PMD 1,421 (1), HMP Nil (Nil), others/Independent 79,447 (107). (Report of the Working of The Trade Unions Act, 1926, for the year 1994, *vide* reference 38 *supra*).
62. Various political movements, apart from the freedom movement, may be classified on the basis of their having been sponsored/supported by different political parties. Some examples:

    CPI supported movements: food agitation; gherao of civil supplies officials; against Preventive Detention Act; land grab movement; Kisan morcha; against betterment levy.

    BJP and erstwhile Jana Singh supported movements: Hindi agitation; against Gold Control Order; against bank nationalisation.

    Congress supported movements: agitation in support of the Union Government's decision to nationalise banks.

63. According to the Marxist ideology, the capitalist state is an instrument of the bourgeoisie, with the police and judiciary amongst its instruments of oppression. However, particularly since Gramsci, the relative autonomy of the various components and sub-components of the repressive and ideological apparatus of the state in the context of an overall hegemony of the capitalist class has been increasingly recognised.

15

Agrarian Change and Farmers' Movement in Punjab: A Study of BKU

SUCHA SINGH GILL

Punjab has seen several rounds of mobilisation of farmers in the recent years. They have been mobilised under the banner of Bhartiya Kisan Union (BKU) and consequently this belt has become a stronghold of this organisation. The other organisations of farmers [Kisan Sabhas of CPI and CPI (M)] and new [Kirti Kisan Union of CPI (ML)] have fallen in line with BKU on the issue of mobilisation. In the process, old organisations of farmers, particularly Kisan Sabhas, have been marginalised and BKU has come to dominate the rural scene in the region. Pre-eminent position of this organisation on the rural scene is recognised by non-left ruling political parties to enlist its support in the electoral battles. In mobilisation campaigns of BKU, therefore, these parties, whether ruling or in opposition, do not stand in opposition to it. Their attempt is to harness the organised strength of farmers for their own use to rise in political power. Being not frontal organisation of any political party BKU is free from strings being pulled from behind. The autonomous character of this organisation has enhanced its status in terms of political links and views. This has given a new phase to the farmers' movement as a departure from its earlier phase of being controlled by party politics. In this paper, our objective is to understand the genesis of this phase of farmers' movement. Attempt has also been made to characterise it, discuss limits to its mobilisation process and its vision of the rural society.

Genesis

Three factors are responsible for the emergence and growth of farmers' movement in the region. These are related to the history of awareness and tradition of organised struggle of peasantry, objective material reality and the role of subjective forces which have actually organised and shaped the present movement.

Punjab has passed through a period of active involvement of peasantry in the political process before the organisation of farmers' movement in the present phase. In pre-partition Punjab which comprised a sizeable part of present Punjab and Haryana, peasants were activated by the Unionist Party led by landlords. In princely states the Praja Mandal movement played that role. Kisan Sabha movement of Communist Party of India and Zamindara League of Ch. Chhotu Ram before independence mobilised peasantry and created awareness of usefulness of its collective strength.[1] In post-independence period introduction of universal adult franchise in electoral process and adoption of Panchayati Raj considerably increased the influence of farmers in the whole range of centres of political power starting from village through block samiti, zila parishad to state administration in Punjab.[2] Consequently, the mainstay of dominant political parties of the state in power politics depends on the support of peasantry. These parties have been actively approaching them and recruiting members and cadres from among them. This has involved peasantry into active participation in the political process of the state. Affluent and dynamic farmers have emerged powerful politicians among various political parties. The prominent leaders such as Parkash Singh Badal, Gurcharan Singh Tohra and Harcharan Singh Brar belong to this category of persons. The activated peasantry when faced with declining gains of the green revolution prosperity began to respond to the situation by intensifying its political activities. It threw up powerful leaders in the politics of dominant parties to bargain better terms within the established political process of the country. The other response was developed due to failure/limitations of ruling party leaders to serve the farming community satisfactorily. This led to formulation of independent farmers' movement led by BKU.[3]

The emerging material reality in the agriculture of the state, particularly after the mid-1960s, created an objective basis for development of the farmers' movement.

Punjab was first to adopt new agricultural technology which heralded green revolution in the country. Consequently, the entire area of Punjab achieved highest level of agricultural development in the country. This region crossed the highest productivity level of Rs.1,250 per hectare during 1980-83. Most of the districts of the state have also been experiencing the highest growth rate of output exceeding 3.5 percent per annum during 1970-73 to 1980-83.[4]

Success of the green revolution in the state has been made possible due to availability of assured irrigation by network of canals developed by harnessing water from perennial rivers passing through it and later on installation of electrical tubewells and pumpsets. The state had a favourable man-land ratio and have on the average relatively large size of landholdings (Table 1). The existence of favourable institutional framework has been another factor. Implementation of land legislation created self-cultivation as the dominant mode by removal of whole range of intermediary interests. Along with availability of irrigation and power, creation of infrastructure like credit, regulated markets, network of rural roads, extension and agricultural research facilities by the state proved helpful factors for spread of the green revolution.

When technology of the green revolution was made available in the mid-sixties, it was adopted in this state rather quickly. This included HYV of seeds, chemical fertilisers, later on pesticides, weedicides and mechanised agricultural operations symbolised by use of tractors and other implements. Adoption of new technology involved productive investment and expenditure by the farmers. The farmers with better command over land and other resources were quick to adopt it.

Table 1

Irrigation, Size and Distribution of Operational Holdings in Punjab, Haryana and U.P.

State/region	*Average size of holdings (in hectares) (1980-81)*	*Percentage of holdings between (2-10 hectares) (1980-81)*	*Percentage of irrigated area to net sown area (1983-84)*
Punjab	3.82	54.18	86.4
Haryana	3.52	42.21	60.5
U.P.	1.01	12.77	57.2
Western U.P.	-	18.49*	71.0**
All India	1.84	11.84	29.7

* Data are related to the year 1971 and cover 22 wheat districts largely from U.P. *Source*: Government of U.P., Board of Revenue, Lucknow quoted in Paul R. Brass, "Politicization of Peasantry in a North India State", *Journal of Peasant Studies*, Vol. 7, No.4, 1980.

** Data relate to period of 1976-77 and cover upper and lower Doab regions. *Source*: Government of U.P., Board of Revenue quoted in Zoya Hasan, "Self-serving Guardians: Formation and Strategy of the Bhartiya Kisan Union", *Economic and Political Weekly*, December 2, 1989.

Source: Economic Advisor to Government of Punjab, *Statistical Abstract of Punjab, 1988*, Chandigarh, 1989.

New technology brought increasingly adopter farmers within the market nexus. It involved considerable purchase of various inputs such as chemical fertilisers, insecticides, pesticides, weedicides, HYV of seeds, tractors, thrashers, electric motors, pumpsets, electricity, diesel, etc., from the market. New technology increased area, cropping intensity and productivity of crops, particularly wheat, rice, cotton, sugarcane, etc. This increased the quantity of marketed surpluses by the farmers. Production of the surplus produce increased considerable amount of activities connected with marketing such as loading and unloading of the produce, cleaning, weighing, stocking, storage and transportation. Integration of farmers with the market nexus has increased the influence of changes in market conditions and activities on the life of farmers. Therefore, the issues like availability of inputs, their prices, marketing of surplus produce and its price, matter a lot to the farmers.

New technology is not only a technical factor, it has brought new relations in the sphere of production also. Agriculture has been converted from a way of life to an enterprise. Considerable part of work is being done through hired labour. The component of family labour in field operations has declined and is increasingly replaced by hired labour. Evidence suggests that even small and middle landholders who produce surplus also hire some labourers for work on their own fields. The large, rich and capitalist farmers generally depend on the hired labour for most of the operations while they themselves assume supervisory role.[5] Apart from reflecting the nature of agrarian change, employment of hired labour has increased the role of market nexus for agriculture of the region. This has created distinct market of hired labour involving employers and the employed and also created an area of conflict between them on wage and related issues.

In the initial period of the green revolution, there was a considerable gain to all classes of the farmers.[6] This also increased the viability of the small farmers and contributed to increased solidarity of all classes of farmers on farm input and output prices and against the hired labour in the eventuality of conflict. Most of the farmers in the state are Jat by caste. *Bhaichara* (fraternity) of Jats is an added factor in this solidarity. The level of initial gains and profitability of agriculture raised the level of mark up of returns for the farmers at fairly high level. This also contributed to the rising level of expectations for all sections of people in the rural areas of the region.

Gains of the green revolution could not be sustained in the region. As revealed by data, at constant prices, after 1973-74 wheat crop started giving net income per hectare at diminishing rate in the state. On the average, the negative per annum growth rate of price margin over cost has been 17.09 percent for Punjab in wheat production between 1970-71 and 1980-81 (Table 2). The main cause of this has been decline in net barter terms of trade of agriculture.[7] The movement of prices paid and prices received by agriculture disturbed the parity between agricultural and non-agricultural sectors of the economy. The prices paid by agricultural sector have increased at faster rate compared to prices received by this sector (Table 3). Whereas terms of trade have moved against agriculture in the decade of 1970s, there has been increase in cropping intensity at the rate of 1.42 percent in Punjab. The per hectare yield of wheat has also registered a rise at the rate of 0.58 percent per annum in the state between 1970-71 and 1980-81.[8] Reduced return from cultivation reduced the profitability of the large and rich farmers and increased deficits of the poor. This annoyed all of the cultivators involved in market network creating the objective basis for their mobilisation.

Table 2

Net Income at 1970-71 Prices in Wheat (Rs./hectare)

Year	*Punjab*
1970-71	328
1971-72	426
1972-73	167
1973-74	589
1974-75	430
1975-76	59
1976-77	124
1977-78	72
1978-79	193
1979-80	175
1980-81	54
Per annum rate of decline of price over cost	17.09
Percentage of wheat to net sown area	41.3

Source: Dalip S.Swamy and Ashok Gulati, "From Prosperity to Retrogression:Indian Cultivators during the 1970s", *Economic and Political Weekly*, Review of Agriculture, June 1986 (based on APC data).

Prosperity of initial phase of the green revolution and the process of substitution of hired labour for family labour has created sufficient number of persons available for mobilisation of the farmers. The spread of general education has created opportunities backed by capacity for children of farmers to get schooling completed and large number of them are able to join colleges and even universities. This has produced a large stock of

Table 3

Indices of Prices Received, Paid and Terms of Trade of Agriculture in India (Triennium Ending 1971-72=100)

Year	*Prices received*	*Prices paid*	*Prices received/prices paid by the agriculture sector*
1971-72	102.5	105.1	97.5
1972-73	116.9	112.9	103.5
1973-74	145.0	132.3	109.6
1974-75	166.8	166.9	99.9
1975-76	142.4	168.3	84.6
1976-77	157.0	173.2	90.7
1977-78	164.8	181.6	90.8
1978-79	157.1	183.9	85.4
1979-80	185.4	209.3	88.6
1980-81	213.6	244.8	87.3

Source: D.S Tyagi, "Domestic Terms of Trade and Their Effect on Supply and Demand for the Agriculture Sector", *Economic and Political Weekly*, 28 March 1987, Vol. XXII, No. 13.

educated youth waiting for white-collared jobs which are not available in sufficient quantity.[9] Since physical labour involving work is got done on the farms of rich farmers by hired labour, the educated unemployed youth have little work on the farms. In fact, youth with degrees in their hands have little taste for physical work available on the farms. The spread of education and increased use of hired labour has produced sufficient number of activists among the farmers for mobilisation. They have been joined by retired army and civil officials of rural origin. Their activities have been able to spread the necessary awareness among the farmers to organise themselves independently of established political parties which subordinate farmers movement to their objective of political power. Evidence suggests that a large number of organisers of BKU are educated and articulate persons. A study of Punjab unit of BKU reveals that by 1982-83 roughly 74 percent of the members were literate out of which 40 percent were matriculate and above,[10] against the rural literacy rate of 35.21

percent in 1981 in the state.[11] A total of 29.20 percent of the members were holding or had held in the past the membership of the Village Panchayats/Panchayat Samitis. Among the members of the BKU, 20.38 percent were ex-servicemen.[12]

The Punjab Khetibari Zamindara Union (PKZU), predecessor of BKU, was established by the efforts mainly of eight prominent leaders in 1972. Two of them had held important political offices in the past. One of them was secretary of the erstwhile Unionist Party of pre-partition Punjab and another one was an ex-Akali MLA. Both of them were knocked out of the political process.[13] In fact, Partap Singh Kadian, ex-MLA, played most active role in organising the Union to establish his credibility to join active Akali politics. Thus, initiative to organise the Union came from the politicians in their hour of crisis. Once state unit came into existence it acquired its own dynamism and grew into powerful movement due to ripe objective material reality and necessary manpower availability. Punjab BKU unit, though it came into existence with this name in 1980, was active from 1972 under the banner of PKZU and fought several struggles (1973, 1974, 1974-75, 1977-78) but became very prominent during 1983-84 struggle culminating into gherao of Punjab Raj Bhavan from March 12 to 18 in 1984.[14]

At subjective level initiative to organise the BKU came from politicians. They wanted to demonstrate the support of the farmers to establish themselves in the party politics. But the Union acquired prominence when it became independent of such politicians and its leadership passed on to non-party leaders.

In fact, farmers movement as independent of political parties has been developed in opposition to the practice of politicians using support of farming communities to rise in party politics without properly serving the interests of the community. This is the reason that during campaigns of the Union in Punjab, it has determinedly not allowed politicians both from the opposition and the ruling parties to use farmers' organised strength to their advantage. Along with the failure of leadership of dominant political parties having a base in the farming community to protect and promote adequately the interest of the community another development at subjective level took place. This is related to the shift of emphasis of communist parties' mobilisation strategies. In the wake of development of capitalist agriculture, agricultural labourers emerged as a distinct class bringing on the scene a conflict between all sections of farmers hiring in labour and the labourers on the wage issue.[15] The communists decided to organise the agricultural labourers independently of their Kisan Sabhas. CPI (M) launched All-India Agricultural Workers Union (AIAWU) in 1982.[16] Even before creation of AIAWU, both the communist parties and some Naxalite groups were busy in organising these workers in Punjab on the wage issue.[17] The whole thrust of the left parties and groups moved towards building an alliance between agricultural labourers and poor peasants in their fight against the rural rich on the rural scene.[18] The earlier strategy of the peasant movement led by the left was to unite all sections of working peasants against the feudal oppression and imperialism.[19] As the basis of this unity ceased to exist the organisation of the rich and capitalist farmers disappeared from the agenda of the communists. As objective material conditions became ripe and there existed an activated peasantry in the state and sufficient number of conscious activists from among the rich and capitalist farmers, the farmers movement led by BKU began to fill the vacuum created by failure of leadership of the dominant parties to protect the farmers and strategy of the communists to withdraw from the mobilisation of the upper layers of the farmers.

Characterisation

Farmers' movement has consciously kept itself away from the established political parties to maintain its image of non-party political farmers' movement. In spite of the efforts of the leadership, the movement has remained closer to regional political parties. In Punjab BKU has remained closer to Akali Dal. In fact, many Akali Dal activists and supporters are active in the movement. Prakash Singh Badal has been from the very beginning cultivating good relations with the Punjab unit of BKU and its predecessor PKZU. During his tenure as Chief Minister of Punjab (1977-80) two *morchas* were launched by BKU. One related to supply of defective tractors launched during 1977-78 was successful due to positive role of Badal. The other related to scarcity of diesel in 1979. The Akali government could not satisfy the farmers. Hence, the Union did not support Akali Dal during 1980 elections which indirectly benefited the Congress,[20] and the latter came to power in the state after the elections. Subsequently, the relations between Akali Dal and BKU have improved. The Union was responsible for massive victory of Akali Dal (Mann) in 1989 parliamentary elections. In Akali-sponsored boycott of 1992 assembly and parliamentary polls the BKU faction led by Ajmer Singh Lakhowal played a leading role. But, after formation of Congress (I) government in the state (1992), the Lakhowal faction somewhat distanced itself from the Akali Dals. BKU is generally opposed to communists in the state due to latter's mobilisation of agricultural labourers on wage issue against the farmers in villages. Given the performance and relationship (of both opposition and closeness) BKU in the state has banned its office bearers from contesting elections to assemblies and parliament but has allowed its members and supporters to participate in panchayat and cooperative societies elections and maintained its non-party political image. The constitution of the BKU allows participation of leaders of political parties to be the members but they cannot hold the elected offices of the Union.[21] This allows interaction of the Union with political parties and provides a scope of manoeuvrability by the Union for promoting its cause.

Farmers' movement led by BKU and other such organisations once it became more than a decade old was able to display its forceful hold over the various size-class of farmers. The issue of characterisation of this movement received attention of the scholars. Some scholars have characterised it as a populist movement[22] while others have characterised it as a class movement.[23] Going by the declared objectives and charters of demands and memoranda submitted at various levels by BKU it is clear that the Union is interested in building a just society and wants to remove corruption, exploitation and discrimination of all sorts against the people living in the villages. It is also interested in mobilisation of all rural people irrespective of differences in religion, caste, class and gender. Therefore, the ideology of the movement is to transcend stratification in the rural society and increase mass appeal of the Union to all the people of rural India.[24] Theoretically, the movement is determined to change the present society and appeals to the rural masses not to specific classes and mistrusts the traditional politicians though it is not essentially against intellectuals.[25] This will qualify the farmers movement as populist in character but if we leave rhetoric and go by the practice of the movement then the situation changes. The appeal of the movement is restricted to various classes of the peasantry. Here also, the appeal evokes greater response from the capitalist, rich and middle farmers.

Formally, the demand for minimum wages is included in the list from the beginning of Punjab unit of BKU. However, the participation of agricultural labour has not become possible due to open conflict between agricultural labour and the farmers and openly biased attitude of the Union in favour of farmers in the situation of conflict between the two. Unlike Ryatu Sangh in Karnataka and Shetkari Sanghatana in Maharashtra where they are able to get support and participation of dalit organisations, farmers' movements have made no such progress in this regard in Punjab. Rather there is hostility between the Jat farmers and the dalits who are mostly agricultural labourers. Similarly, the Punjab unit has also listed a demand to secure honourable place for women in society and to eradicate the evils of dowry and liquor consumption. Though women's demand is included, yet the Union is unable to ensure noticeable female participation in the movement. Another demand of BKU related to ceiling on urban property at the level of value of 17.5 acres of land but actually, two factions (Lakhowal as well as Mann-Rajewal) of BKU unit have recently shifted the position by demanding the removal of land ceiling following the similar recommendations by state Financial Commissioner in this regard. Other demands are exclusively related to peasants. These include linking farm prices to index of prices with base year of 1967-68, lowering the prices of inputs such as fertilisers, diesel, electricity, tractors, insecticides, bricks, cement, steel, clothes, etc., establishment of a fund for compensation to farmers in the eventuality of natural calamities, elimination of corruption, smuggling and exploitation by commission agents, removal of octroi on farm products, raising status of agriculture to industry, old age pension at the age of 55 for all villagers, reservation of seats in medical and engineering colleges and other educational institutions and in government service to rural people in proportion to the rural population and free education to the children of those farmers whose holdings are less than 10 acres.

The class character of farmers' movement becomes very clear when specific issues on which farmers have built agitations are discussed. They are mainly related to availability and prices of electricity, diesel, sugarcane, milk, compensation to farmers for damage due to hailstorm, recovery of expenses of account of defective tractors sold to farmers, checking of illegal extortions from the farmers by officials of revenue and cooperative departments and the State Electricity Board and more recently the police repression against the farmers. Most of these issues concern the farming community only. The Union has never started any agitation for special provisions related to poor farmers and agricultural workers and women. The issues which concern exclusively the rich farmers have received priority in agitations of BKU. This explains that theoretically farmers' movement led by BKU resembles populist movement but practically it is a movement of capitalist, rich and middle farmers who are able to get the support of poor farmers partly due to their involvement in market nexus and unity with other farmers on wage issue against the agricultural labourers and partly due to use of ethnicity in mobilisation process. In Punjab use of Sikh religious idiom for the purposes of mobilisation is very common.[26] Though the issue of general development of the rural areas are also raised to remove the urban bias in development strategy yet the movement has not questioned the direction of development. In the state of Punjab the Union (Rajewal-Mann faction) is trying to integrate agricultural capital with industrial capital to strengthen the base of capitalist development in the economy.

Limits to Mobilisation

Ideologically, BKU is committed to peaceful struggle. Its

demonstrations and campaigns take place in disciplined and organised ways. Wherever farmers hold demonstration the Union workers carry their tractor trolleys full of eatables and fuel for cooking. At sites of demonstration and rallies community kitchens are opened and farmers of the nearby villages maintain regular supply of eatables and other requirements. The Union avoids disruption of life and other inconvenience to the common residents of the places where such demonstrations and gheraos are organised. The Union is committed to organise the farmers on secular lines also.

Due to systematic campaigns and building up of organisation for struggle in the villages right up to state level have resulted in successful conduct of the farmers' movement in several rounds. The outstanding example of culmination of this process has been a successful siege of Punjab Governor's residence at Chandigarh between 12-18 March 1984 in which 50 to 60 thousand farmers almost took over the state capital. It was very successful agitation from the point of view of demands conceded and organisational gains for the Union within the state and in the neighbouring state of Haryana. Following this, the Union almost took over the entire rural Punjab and entry of officials of the State Electricity Board and cooperative department, revenue staff and police was banned without the permission of BKU. Ultimately, the Union decided to block the movement of wheat outside the state from June 10, 1984. The momentum of farmers' mobilisation suddenly ended by the decision of the Central Government to bring the entire Punjab and Chandigarh under the control of army and imposition of curfew from 3 June, 1984 and subsequent army action at Golden Temple, Amritsar, popularly known as Operation Blue Star. The Union has displayed considerable resilience and survived in the difficult and disturbed situation. When the entire democratic movement was paralysed due to hurdles put up by state repression on one hand and attack of militancy on the other, Punjab unit of BKU continued the process of mass mobilisation of farmers.[27]

Limits of mobilisation process are imposed by the objective reality and subjective factors like choice of idiom in use of caste, class and religion in mobilisation and differences in the perspective of the organisers. At objective level farmers' movement has a greater appeal to the rich and middle farmers as compared to the poor farmers. Due to antagonism on wage issue, the movement is looked at with awe and suspicion by the agricultural labourers. At subjective level the movement has its own limitations. The Punjab unit of BKU uses Sikh idioms and symbols in mobilisation, therefore, it has not so far been able to mobilise Hindu farmers in the state. Since the UP unit has been organised on the basis of Jat Khap Panchayats it limits the scope for farmers from other castes to occupy high offices in the Union. In Haryana also, the Union tries to use this institution. Though this helps the Union to transcend the class barriers in spread of mobilisation, yet it restricts the scope of the movement at geographical level. The whole of this belt has Jat dominated peasantry which nourishes caste hatred against dalits which is inhibiting factor for winning their support.

The limited perspective of a large number of farmers and the interests and ambitions of the leaders result in factional fights. The efforts of the government to co-opt some leaders to the membership of State Electricity Boards, committees or even to Rajya Sabha nomination creates feeling of jealousy and ignites the desire for such positions among other leaders. This leads to split in the movement. At all-India level also, there are two Inter-State Coordination Committees (ISCC) of farmers: one led by Mohinder Singh Tikait and another led by Sharad Joshi. There was a public scene at Boat Club rally of farmers in 1990 between the supporters of these two leaders. The split in the movement has harmed the process of mobilisation. Farmers' movement in the region is split in three factions. They have been indulging in competitive mobilisation of the same peasantry on the same issues in their respective areas of influence. This has created a lot of confusion and decline in the mobilisation capacity and increased manoeuvrability of the government. On the issue of GATT the two committees have taken opposing positions. The committee led by Sharad Joshi welcomed these agreements while Tikait-led committee opposed them. The spilt in the movement has imposed another limit to the mobilisation process.

Present Status: A Trend Towards Decline

Operation Blue Star (June 1984) and events thereafter disrupted the process of organisation of farmers as the democratic process was completely paralysed. The state was handed over to army and paramilitary forces as civil administration failed completely. A large number of draconian laws were enforced banning even any political meeting and demonstrations. There was some space available for political process after Rajiv-Longowal accord (July 24, 1985) which ultimately cleared the ways for elections in the state in September 1985 leading to installation of Akali Dal ministry in the state. In the changed circumstances, there was some revival of activities of BKU in the state. But, soon, the terrorist activities picked up particularly after 26 January, 1986—the agreed date for transfer of Chandigarh to Punjab. This led to imposition of more curbs on the political process. The political situation was again in the reverse gear culminating into imposition of President's Rule in the state after the dismissal of Akali Dal ministry in June 1987. Democratic movement came to be attacked from both the sides, i.e., state repression/restrictions and terrorist attacks and threat. BKU leadership skilfully manoeuvred by raising the issue of state oppression and was one of the few organisations which did not attract hostility of the terrorists in a big way. BKU activities continued in spite of the state restrictions but on a reduced scale. BKU also successfully projected its existence particularly through newspapers reports. Consequently, the Union became very popular with the peasantry in the situation where the major political parties had withdrawn fearing attacks of the terrorist organisations. Growing popularity of the Union was accompanied by a tussle for the top position among the leaders. This led to split of the Union into two factions in April 1989. One led by Ajmer Singh Lakhowal and another by Balbir Singh Rajewal and Bhupinder Singh Mann. The split was articulated by Lakhowal faction in the form of ideological differences. Opponent faction was labelled as collaborator with the government for agro-processing units and allotment of agencies for agricultural inputs. This allegation got some validation among the farmers with the nomination of Bhupinder Singh Mann to Rajya Sabha by V.P. Singh government. The Rajewal-Mann faction defended grant of licences and agencies on the ground of being in tune with the programme of the Union for diversification of farming for lessening of burden of population on the land. They were of the opinion that Lakhowal was too ambitious who caused split in the movement to become President, though of a faction. Retrospectively looking, the charge of the Rajewal-Mann faction was correct because some of the supporters/district leaders of Lakhowal faction were commission agents and were holders of government agencies for agricultural inputs.

In the post-1989 phase, the Lakhowal faction became more prominent as it was able to attract a majority of cadres and activists of the Union. The other faction was aligned with Sharad Joshi who became chairman of Advisory Committee on National Agriculture Policy appointed by V.P. Singh. The nomination of Bhupinder Singh Mann to Rajya Sabha had cemented this link and confirmed the perception of the opponent faction as being collaborators with the Janata Dal government at the Centre. This helped Lakhowal faction to consolidate its position among the Punjab farmers. At the same time, this offered an opportunity for this faction to share stages with Akali factions which were taking positions closer to the various militant/terrorist groups. Between 1989 and 1992 Lakhowal shifted his interests more towards Akali politics and was one of the key speaker and instrument in the decision of the Akali factions to boycott February 1992 elections to the State Legislative Assembly. Lakhowal's involvement in Akali factional politics and his support to the cause of militant and separatist politics started a hot controversy within the Union.[28] A large number of activists began to question his participation in Akali politics as violation of the constitution of the Union which committed its leaders to non-party politics. Lakhowal retaliated with expulsion of several leaders from Sangrur and Patiala districts in 1992. Consequently, the Union became very weak in these districts. Already the first split (of 1989) had made Amritsar and Bathinda district units as defunct.[29] Thus, out of the then 12 district units four became defunct through splits and the Union was very weak in other four districts, namely, Gurdaspur, Hoshiarpur, Jalandhar and Kapurthala (in some of these districts

Kirti Kisan Union has its strongholds). The second split in Punjab unit of BKU was crystallised in September 1994 when dissidents of the Lakhowal faction established BKU (Ekta) under the presidentship of Pishoura Singh Sidhupur. The third faction of BKU has strong base in Patiala, Sangrur, Bathinda (including Mansa district) and Faridkot districts. At present, the three factions of the Union have their patches of stronghold in the state but none of them is capable of building a statewide movement.

There are two further developments on the BKU front which deserve to be noted. First, BKU (Ekta) has moved towards the leftist peasant organisations such as Kisan Sabha of CPI, CPI(M) and Kirti Kisan Union led by CPI (ML). These organisations have taken up joint rallies and state level demonstration at Chandigarh on common agreed programme. All these organisations are against GATT and Structural Adjustment Programme (SAP) adopted by the government. Secondly, the BKU faction led by Lakhowal organised a Jat (one caste) panchayat at Ludhiana on March 6, 1995 when it was decided that BKU will transform itself into a political party and participate in the election to capture power at the state level. Later on this faction established a political wing and named it Lok Hit Party under the presidentship of Lakhowal. These developments have fragmented BKU's movement in the state. There are three distinct trends in it. One faction has drifted towards the party politics, another towards the leftist peasant organisations while the third faction has moved towards the globalisation and liberalisation programme of the government. The splits and divisions have weakened the movement with a large number of farmers becoming disinterested in BKU due to opposing positions taken up by different factions leading to confusion among the many supporters of the movement. Compared to 1983-84 and even the pre-split situation before 1989, there are clear signs of the decline in the movement with shrinking base, considerably reduced mobilisation capacity and drift/confusion in ideology of the movement. At present, there is no effort to unite the various factions and the leadership is not exhibiting any such potentials.

Vision of Future Rural Society

Farmers' movement by raising the issue of Bharat vs India has pointed out the major distortion in the country's development strategy which has urban bias. In this context it is useful to know the vision of the movement to correct this distortion or way to have better strategy of development. The Union realises the need of reduction of population burden on agriculture and visualises that this can be done by setting up of industries in the rural areas and reserving 75 percent jobs for the local residents of the villages. Apart from protecting sectional demands of the farmers the Union is committed to removal of discrimination against rural areas in the matter of hospitals, colleges, post offices, telephone facilities, etc. Ruralites are to be provided these facilities in proportion to their share in the population. For social justice the Union demands reservation in government jobs, seats in medical and engineering colleges and other educational institutions in proportion to the share of population related to agriculture which Union calculates as 82 percent of the total. It also wants old age pension for every villager at the age of 55 and persons handicapped during mechanised farm operations. Besides, the Union wishes the society free from corruption, adulteration, quota and licensing in imports and exports, removal of sluggishness, ignorance and smuggling which starts from political leadership at the Centre. It further wants end to exploitation of farmers at hands of traders, commission agents and fair prices for agricultural production. Ultimately, the Union demands that agriculture be given the status of industry.

Notwithstanding their demand for imposition of ceiling on urban property, the Union itself has demanded removal of land ceiling provisions. In fact, the Union has been encouraging and helping its members and sympathisers to diversify their activities from agriculture inputs and become commission agents in agricultural marketing. The Union leadership in 1987 started a company, named Punjab Kisan Kheti Udyog Limited, Batala, for standing guarantee to farmers in getting fertilisers agencies and opening shops for this purpose.

The Union leadership (Rajewal-Mann faction) is convinced

that taking up of agro-processing on a massive scale is the only guarantee for remunerative prices to the farmers. It is in this context that the Union supported and campaigned for Pepsi project as the multinational did not comply with the original agreement. The Union created another company, Kisan Ply Ltd., in 1988 later on changed to Kisan Udyog Ltd. in 1989 for manufacture of ply from eucalyptus. The Union has also been trying to get a licence for setting up of sugar mills on its own but the state government has not allowed it. But, in milk processing, the Union was able to sign memorandum of understanding (MOU) with Punjab State Industrial Development Corporation (PSIDC) for three plants. The Union is also of the view that wheat processing should be started in the state and produce DDG (dried and distilled grain), very good for cancer patients and vitamin A can also be produced through computerised processing mechanism. As a consequence, the farmers can be paid very high prices (Rs. 750 per quintal). The Union wants this project to be in public sector to transfer a major part of benefit of value added to the farmers which in Union's view cannot be done if plant is in private sector.

Thus, the vision of the Union is to remove obstacles to agricultural and rural development and provide fair deal to the farmers and integrate agricultural capital with commercial and industrial capital. The Union is not against the capitalist path of development rather it wants the farmers to be integral part rather than subject of exploitation. It is in the latter sense that the Union is intervening for reforms in this path. The concern of the Union for weaker sections is peripheral.

Notes

1. Master Hari Singh, *Punjab Peasant in Freedom Struggle,* New Delhi: PPH, 1984, pp. 180-327.
2. Sucha Singh Gill, "Agrarian Capitalism and Political Processes in Punjab", T.V.S. Sathyamurthy (ed.), *Social Change and Political*

Discourse in India: Structure of Power, Movements of Resistance, New Delhi: Oxford University Press, New Delhi, 1995.

3. Paul R. Brass, "The Politicization of the Peasantry in a North India State", *Journal of Peasant Studies* I, II, Vol. 7, No. 4 and Vol. 8, No. 1, 1980.
4. G.S. Bhalla and D.S. Tyagi, *Patterns in Indian Agricultural Development: A District Level Study*, New Delhi: Institute for Studies in Industrial Development, 1989, pp. 149-50.
5. Sucha Singh Gill, *Migrant Labour in Punjab* (mimeo), Patiala: Punjabi University, 1990, p. 58.
6. G.R. Saini, "Green Revolution and the Distribution of Farm Incomes", *Economic and Political Weekly*, Review of Agriculture, Vol. XI, No. 13, March 27, 1976, p. A-17.
7. D.S. Tyagi, "Domestic Terms of Trade and their Effect on Supply and Demand for the Agriculture Sector", *Economic and Political Weekly*, Vol. XXII, No. 13, March 28, 1987.
8. Dalip S. Swamy and Ashok Gulati, "From Prosperity to Retrogression: Indian Cultivators during the 1970s", *Economic and Political Weekly*, Review of Agriculture, Vol. XXI, No. 26, June 21-28, 1987.
9. K. S. Gill, "Employment and Unemployment in Punjab" in R. S. Johar and J. S. Khanna (eds.), *Studies in Punjab Economy*, Amritsar: Guru Nanak Dev University, 1983, pp. 301-4
10. Kehar Singh, *Farmers' Movement and Pressure Group Politics*, New Delhi: Deep & Deep Publication, 1990, p.52.
11. Economic and Statistical Organisation, *Statistical Abstract of Punjab 1985*, Chandigarh: Government of Punjab, 1989, p. 56; Kehar Singh, *op. cit.*, p. 56.
12. Kehar Singh, *op. cit*, p. 56.
13. *Ibid.*, p. 39.
14. Sucha Singh Gill and K.C. Singhal, "Punjab Farmers' Agitation: Response to Development Crisis of Agriculture", *Economic and Political Weekly*, Vol. XIX, No. 40,
15. Master Hari Singh, *Agricultural Workers' Struggle in Punjab*, New Delhi: People's Publishing House, 1980, p. 12.
16. All India Kisan Sabha (CPI-M), 24th Conference, 8-11

November, 1982: *Proceedings and Resolutions*, New Delhi, 1982.

17. Sucha Singh Gill, *Organisation of Rural Labour in Northern India with Special Reference to Punjab* (mimeo), Patiala: Punjabi University, 1990, pp. 14-17.
18. Inderdeep Sinha, *The Changing Agrarian Scene: Problems and Tasks*, New Delhi: People's Publishing House, 1980, p. 160; H. S. Surjeet, "Upsurge", *Seminar*, No. 267, November 1986; All India Kisan Sabha, 24th Conference 8-11 November, 1982, *Proceedings and Resolutions*, New Delhi, 1982, pp. 22-23; Mehar Singh Manick, *Role of Kirti Kisan Union in Peasant Struggle in Punjab (1978-87)*, unpublished M. Phil. dissertation, Department of Sociology and Social Anthropology, Punjabi University, Patiala, 1990, pp. 103-4.
19. G. S. Bhalla, "Peasant Movement and agrarian Change in India", *Social Scientist*, Vol. 11, No. 8, August 1983, pp. 39-57.
20. Kehar Singh, *op. cit.*, p. 83.
21. Bhartiya Kisan Union: *Historical Facts* (Punjabi), Ludhiana: BKU Publication, 1985, pp. 6-7.
22. D. N. Dhanagare, "An Apolitical Populism", *Seminar*, No. 352, December, 1988.
23. Zoya Hasan, "Self-serving Guardians: Formation and Strategy of Bhartiya Kisan Union", *Economic and Political Weekly*, Vol. XXIV, No. 48, December 2, 1989.

    She calls it rich and middle peasant movement.

    Dipankar Gupta considers BKU movement as such farmers movement, "Country-Town Nexus and Agrarian Mobilisation", *EPW*, Vol. XXIII, No. 51, December 1988.
24. Bhartiya Kisan Union: *Historical Facts*, *op. cit.*
25. Four conditions of populism specified by Ernesto Laclau are (i) ingrained hostility to *status quo*, (ii) appeal to, (iii) mistrust of traditional politicians, and (iv) anti-intellectualism. Ernesto Laclau, *Politics and Ideology in Marxist Theory*, London: Verso Publications, 1979, quoted in D.N. Dhahagare, "Subaltern consciousness and Populism: Two Approaches in the Study of Social Movements", *Social Scientist*, Vol. 16, No. 11, November 1988.

26. Kehar Singh, *op. cit.*
27. *Historical Facts* (Punjabi), *op. cit.*
28. For detailed report on factional fights, see "Report for Punjab: The Struggle Within the BKU", *The Commrade* (organ of the Centre of Communist Revolutionaries of India), Nos. 12 & 13, April-September 1992, pp. 41-66.
29. This was reported by Balbir Singh Rajewal in an interview with the author on December 1, 1992.

16

The Khalistan Movement

HARISH K. PURI AND PARAMJIT S. JUDGE

The Khalistan movement was aimed at establishing an independent sovereign Sikh state through an armed struggle. Its beginnings may be traced to the rise of Sant Jarnail Singh Bhindranwale in Sikh politics; his distinct emphasis on "Sikhism in danger", and his advocacy of violence against the 'other'. The formal declaration of Khalistan was made by his ardent followers from the Damdami Taksal in April 1986, 22 months after Bhindranwale's death. Its collapse was evident by the end of 1992. By then over 25,000 people had been killed in Punjab in the terrorist and counter-terrorist violence, and over 70 percent of the killed were Sikhs. "The violent movement is over and thank God for that", observed Jagjit Singh Chauhan, President of the National Council of Khalistan at the end of 1993. He accused Pakistan of "cynically exploiting the Sikhs".[1] Leaders of the Akali Dal and the SGPC now devoted serious attention to correcting the image of the Sikhs which had been tarnished during the preceding decade or more. They underlined the commitment of the Sikh community to communal harmony, integrity of India, and democracy. The massive electoral mandate given to the Akali Dal (Badal) heralded a definitive reversal to pre-Bhindranwale concerns in Sikh politics.

What were the objectives of the movement and the reasons of its rise and failure? The present study explores and analyses the context and the logic of separatist violence in Punjab.

I

The emergence of nationalism in India since the last quarter of the nineteenth century has been closely associated with religious identification. Michael Ignatief has pointed to the 'relational' aspect in the construction of national identity; that it is defined in terms of the 'other'. He found the connection of nationalism with what Freud described as "narcissism of minor differences".[2] Peter Van der Veer made a study of Hindu and Muslim 'religious nationalism' in India. He found that actually its growth dependend on a conscious sharpening of 'religious antagonism'.[3] One of the direct consequences of the process was the demand for Pakistan which led to the partition of India in 1947. When a demand for Khalistan or a separate Sikh state was raised by some people during the 1940s, it was clearly designed to counter the move for the creation of Pakistan.

The partition of India along religious lines established "a sinister precedent". Its logic created space for narcissistic imagination. The national leadership, on the other hand, was evidently scared. The threat to the integrity and unity of the country were palpable. The centralisation of power and stress on national unity were bound to create reaction. Master Tara Singh's oft quoted questioning: "the Hindus got Hindustan and the Muslims got Pakistan, what did the Sikhs get ?" expressed an undercurrent of an imagined Sikh nationalist grouse. However, the political struggle of the Sikh political leadership in post-independent India centred round the formation of Punjabi suba (a Sikh majority state, in essence) and greater autonomy for the state in the Indian federation. The Shiromani Akali Dal which claimed to be the sole spokesman of the Sikh community did not at any time support the idea of the separate Sikh state. Nor did it favour recourse to a violent struggle for the achievements of its political objectives. Its political rhetoric however was grounded in social separatism and grouses of the Sikh community. State autonomy was conceptualised in terms of political domination of the community in Punjab state. Therefore, for the dissident factional leadership, the alleged opportunism of the ruling leadership and "danger to the *panth*" from the Hindu domination remained a potent instrument for gaining ascendance in Sikh politics. Its impact depended on the overall political context, the actual motives of the factional leaders, and the balance of forces.

Two developments in the mid-1960s augmented far-reaching changes in the world of Sikh politics. One was the formation of Sikh majority state. It unleashed in the Akali leadership exclusive claims to rule in the secular domain of the state politics. Earlier it was confined mainly to the religious domain of Shiromani Gurdwara Parbandhak Committee (SGPC). Competing interests developed variant imaginations of becoming masters in Punjab state. One of these was, for example, reflected in the concept of *Khalsaji ka bole bala* (domination of the Khalsa). The second development related to the prosperity of the green revolution. The new entrepreneurial rich agricultural class which it created, aspired for a share of political power commensurate with their economic clout. These two developments also altered the terms of trade in politics.

The legislative leadership of Akali Dal gained greater importance than religious/SGPC leadership. Its bid for wider support base and alliances favoured secularisation of its political agenda. The Sikh community was not homogeneous. It was divided by caste and class, as also religious sects. The Akali Dal required to win support from sections outside the traditional support base. Its election mainfestoes dropped the exclusively Sikh religious or sectarian issues. So much so that even in the SGPC election in 1979—the domain of religion—the Akali Dal's agenda centred on financial autonomy for the state and it won 95 percent of the seats. The religious leadership was losing its influence.

On the other hand, the emergence of Indira Gandhi at the national scene posed a formidable challenge to the Sikh ruling class in its aspiration for political domination in Punjab. The early experience of the fall of three coalition governments during 1967-70, the centralising nation-building agenda of the Congress and programmes like that of land reforms, increased the threat perception of the landlords and facilitated the construction of the 'other'. Both Indira Gandhi and the Indian government became the symbols of the anti-Sikh Brahminical forces.

Meanwhile, the contradictions of the green revolution made the social costs prominent. The consumer culture, corruption, drug addiction and the fast lane success-at-any cost mindset was seen to be playing havoc with religion and morality. The Sikh youths were found to be ignoring Sikh norms and falling into the ways of the 'others'. By the mid-1970s the gains of the green revolution reached a plateau and thereafter followed gradual decline in the cost-output ratio. On the other hand, widening class differences in the agricultural population increased social tensions and a threat perception among the socially and economically marginalised sections.

The slogan of threat to religion, and assertion of identity appeared in such a context, to be a useful instrument to the competing political interests. More significant in its reach, however, was the emphasis on a particular construction of tradition. Robin Jeffrey expressed his 'continual astonishment' at the new versions of 'rhetorical history' which included the fanciful and the undocumentable.[4] Writings such as *Stupid Sikhs* by Sardar Kapur Singh, SGPC's National Professor of Sikhism, introduced imaginary constructions of recent history for scapegoating the 'other'.[5]

The emergence of the Khalistan movement may be placed in the above socio-historical and cultural context.

II

The demand for 'Khalistan' or a sovereign Sikh state was first made through a paid half-page advertisment in the *New York Times* in USA on 12 October, 1971 in the name of Jagjit Singh Chauhan. Chauhan had been a minister in Lachhman Singh Gill's short-lived government in Punjab during 1967-68. The event passed off without notice. In 1978, a pamphlet on Khalistan circulated by a newly established outfit Dal Khalsa was also regarded as a gimmick. Observers had noticed former Punjab Chief Minister Gyani Zail Singh's hand in the establishment of Dal Khalsa after the Congress party's total rout in north India in the 1977 elections. Another dramatic announcement of Khalistan was made in 1980 by Balbir Singh Sandhu, secretary of the National Council of Khalistan, founded by Jagjit Singh Chauhan in London. The release of Khalistani passport and Khalistani currency notes by him to some journalists in the Golden Temple, Amritsar made a sensational story in the media. All such instances were viewed by the people as the handiwork of some opportunistic individuals. Apprehensions were, however, raised regarding the hidden forces and their hidden agenda.

Passionate commitment and the rationale for a struggle for Khalistan, however, were provided by Sant Jarnail Singh Bhindranwale. He did not overtly advocate Khalistan as the goal of the struggle: "I am neither in favour of it nor against it. If they give it to us, we won't reject it". Yet his message and the method of struggle constituted both the spirit and the dynamics of the movement.

Bhindranwale took over in 1977 as the head of the Sikh seminary Damdami Taksal of Chowk Mehta about 25 Km from Amritsar following the death of his mentor and predecessor Sant Kartar Singh. He was brought up and groomed in the enclosed world of the seminary. It was a life of ritual piety, austere living, regular reading and listening to the scripture and legendary tales of the glory of heroism and martyrdom of the Khalsa in bloody battles. He viewed the Sikh as a divinely created figure of exceptional commitment and courage. The existing state of moral degeneration in the Sikh community concerned him as deeply as the corruption and self-centredness of the religious and political leadership. Bhindranwale seems to have fancied for himself the role of a religious crusader. A battle launched by his predecessor related to stopping the heretical Sant Nirankari sect from following the 'un-Sikh practices'.

Bhindranwale came to public notice after the armed clash between the angry Sikhs sent by him and the Nirankaris gathered at their *samagam* (religious conference) at Amritsar on 13 April, 1978 in which 13 of his men were killed. "This was the first indication of Bhindranwale's role in inciting violence".[6] Then followed the murders of the Nirankari chief Baba Gurbachan Singh in April 1980 and Lala Jagat Narain, Chief Editor of *Hind Samachar* in August 1981. Bhindranwale who was believed to be chiefly responsible for abetting these murders liked to give a loud message to the adversary.

The emeregence of Bhindranwale to quick eminence needs to be explained in terms of the predisposing circumstances in the socio-historical situation. Yet his coming to the centre stage of Sikh politics may not have been possible without the allegedly 'sinister design' of the Congress party. Some elements in the Congress saw in him a potential force for dividing the Akalis. One part of the 'design' consisted of a series of rebuffs to the Akali leaders. The *Nahar Roko Morcha* launched by them related to regional issues of the share of river waters and others. Every time they were near to a settlement with the Government of India, it was allegedly scuttled by the ruling party. The other related to allowing Bhindranwale to call the shots and appear as an invincible Khalsa hero. The failure to arrest him in Haryana was attributed to Chief Minister Bhajan Lal's manipulation on the alleged direction from Gyani Zail Singh, the Home Minister of India. Later, when the Punjab government was able to arrest him, Zail Singh declared in the parliament that there was no evidence of Bhindranwale's involvement in the murder of Lala Jagat Narain. Bhindranwale himself acknowledged after his release: "The government has done more for me in one week than I could have achieved in years".[7] Perhaps, the greater service to his cause was done by the manner in which the Sikhs were humiliated and targeted by the communalised Haryana policemen in order to kill the Akali protest march at the time of Asiad in Delhi in 1982.

Soon after he entrenched himself in the Golden Temple complex to pursue his agenda of a violent struggle, the Akali and the SGPC leaders extended a grudging support to his programme and actions. Bhindranwale and his followers were allowed not only to preach violence, organise collection and supply of weapons inside the sacred temple but also to turn the Akal Takht into a fort. Some of the leaders were believed to have thought that they could fulfil their power aspirations by riding on the back of Bhindranwale. Important to us here, however, is the logic and method of Bhindranwale's programme which became the basis for the Khalistan movement.

1. Bhindranwale's first concern related apparently to moral degeneration among the Sikhs. For a 'good life' of 'purity' as he viewed it, it was necessary to make them conform to the Khalsa Sikh identity. A 'true Sikh' to him was one who was *amritdhari* (baptised according to Khalsa ritual) and observed the Khalsa code of conduct. He made a sharp distinction between *amritdhari, keshadhari* and *sahajdhari* Sikhs. "My responsibility", he insisted, "is to see that your beards remain intact, your hair remain uncut and that you do not go after the evil things of life, like alcohol and drugs".[8] He viewed Khalsa identity as the source of masculine vigour. The construction of masculinity as the defining feature of the Sikh community was therefore the key to self-respect and the fighting sprit of the Sikh *qaum* (nation). Preaching and organising mass baptism ceremonies was a religious campaign with a political intent. "*Santji*", as one of his devout followers observed, "was both a strategist and a saint", a saintly person and a politician.[9]
2. The chief concern in his mind was related to an anxiety that the Sikhs were under seige in the Hindu dominant India. "The Hindu", as he told his close aides "wants the Sikhs to surrender their identity and dignity to his overlordship".[10] The Hindu was a threat to the Sikh religion in the sense of a wily character 'robbing' the Sikhs of their overwhelmingly masculine character. "*Ohnan di nazar tuhadi talwar te hai, ohnan di nazar tuhadi darhi te hai* (they are targeting your sword; they are targeting your beard)".[11]

   Alerting the Sikhs about the designs of the conspiring and the hateful 'other' appeared to be a part of the religious mission. For that purpose "the use of rigorous dualism to define self and other" became a prominent part of the discourse. Further, as Veena Das analysed, the artful linking of contemporary incidents of alleged injustice and betrayal with believed incidents of Hindu betrayal of Sikhs during the distant past—"the creation of contemporaneity between non-contemporaneous events"—formed another element in the discourse".[12] The well-being of the community lay in liberating the Sikhs from the stranglehold of Hindu domination. This was believed to be in consonance with "Raj Karega Khalsa" (the Khalsa shall rule), the destiny of the Sikhs as sung in the daily religious prayer.

3. That the leadership of the Akali Dal and the SPGC were too power obsessed and corrupt to protect the interests of the *panth* constituted a third element. It was an anathema to him that the Akali Dal's government should have, instead of punishing the Nirankaris, taken measures to protect them. As against the power and wealth hungry politicians, the "austere religious saint" had come to save the Sikh religion from moral corruption. It was deeply disturbing to him that the Sikh electorate in the SGPC election in 1979 voted against his protege Amrik Singh in his own area of influence, the Beas constituency. Winning the Sikhs to establish the dominance of the selfless champions of Sikh glory was, therefore, a part of his mission.
4. Another significant element consisted of recourse to violence, killing of the 'enemy', as a religious duty. The Tenth Guru had laid down that recourse to arms was legitimate when all other means failed. To Bhindranwale, that time had come because all the means used by the constituted religious and political leadership of the SGPC and Akali Dal had failed to ensure a place of dignity and autonomy to the Sikhs. Democracy, secularism and constitutional methods appeared to be a subterfuge to keep the Sikhs 'enslaved'. Therefore, his call to them was *shastradhari bano* (take up weapons). Every village must have youngmen with motorcycles and revolvers.[13] Not to use the weapons against the enemies of the faith was a sin. "You are not the son of your father if you do not take revenge for the wrong doing to your nation", he would tell the youngmen who came to him for *sewa* (service).[14] The enemies were the government and its officials and the Hindus—the two being one and the same.[15] Reportedly incensed by Indira Gandhi's remark at Calcutta that the Sikhs outside Punjab were an insignificant minority Bhindranwale reacted sharply: "*Bibi,* we want to tell you that every Sikh has a share of

thirty-five Hindus in the country." In other words, if things do come to such a pass one Sikh can kill thirty-five Hindus and that would balance things.[16]

The preaching went along with action and preparation for a bigger battle. Killing of Hindus, Nirankaris and government officials by armed groups operating from the sanctuary of the Golden Temple accelerated with organised recruitment and training in arms, collection of arms and military fortification of the Akal Takht in the Golden Temple. Observers noted the existence of a parallel centre of power made possible by political connivance of the ruling party at the Centre and the opportunistic factional support by the SGPC and Akali leaders. Commenting upon the silence of the Indian government on the large-scale killings, majority of whom were Hindus, Justice Tarkunde stated that "it looked as if the Centre had given a *carte blanche* to extremists". Just five days before the launching of Operation Blue Star Rajiv Gandhi brushed aside the allegations of Bhindranwale's design by saying that he was a religious saint. The Akalis had a running feud with Bhindranwale. The armed militants of Babbar Khalsa, fiercely hostile to Bhindranwale, acted as security guards of Sant Harchand Singh Longowal, and frequently clashed with Bhindranwale's militants inside the temple. Yet it seemed Bhindranwale suited them because as Longowal put it, he served as their *lathi* (stick) in dealing with the Congress government. The Indian government's perception of the threat led to military action to flush out Bhindranwale and his armed followers.

III

That assault described as 'Operation Blue Star' highlighted the tremendous mismanagement of the affairs of the state by the government. Bhindranwale, Amrik Singh and Shahbeg Singh, the architects of the bloody war inside the holy temple, were killed. But, the destruction of the Akal Takht also delivered a grievous hurt to the Sikhs all over the world. Not the ghost of Bhindranwale, but the collective humiliation of a whole community had ominus implications. As a revenge, Prime Minister Indira Gandhi was assassinated by her Sikh security guards three months later. The orgy of violence in which thousands of Sikhs were massacred in Delhi and other places soon after smacked not only of the breakdown of order but also complicity of men from the ruling party. Rajiv Gandhi and his party, however, cashed on the 'hatred' and the slogan of threat to the nation in the parliamentary elections in December 1984.

The Rajiv-Longowal accord in July 1985, however, came like a sudden burst of light after a long period of darkness. Longowal called it an end to the "era of confrontation". In the state assembly elections held soon after, the massive voter turn-out and the mandate given to the Akali Dal symbolised the people's resolve to move into the future with hope.

The path, however, was not going to be smooth. Surjit Singh Barnala's Akali government was threatened by factional strife in the party. But there was a more formidable challenge from the widely scattered militants who had managed to sneak out during the assault on the Golden Temple. There was also a crop of bitter and angry youngmen produced by the 'Operation Woodrose'. The assassination of Sant Longowal a month after the accord was an early warning. The leaders of the Damdami Taksal, its rival Babbar Khalsa, the All India Sikh Students Federation (AISSF) and those who had forged a militant outfit, Khalistan Commando Force (KCF), were restive for vengeful action. The head priest of the Akal Takht expressed deep anguish over the insulting behaviour of the boys, described as 'hoodlums' and 'ruffians', when they occupied temple in January 1986 by 'brute force', and hurled "direct village variety of abuses" at the priests.[17]

More significant, however, were the series of pronouncements cast in the mould of an 'armed coup' in the religious life and politics of the community. Prominent among these related to the dismissal of all the priests of the Golden Temple and the Akal Takht, dissolution of the SGPC and the Akali Dal and the appointment of a five member Panthic Committee as the supreme commanding body for the Sikhs. New priests were nominated and the apex committee was given the power to remove them from office. The immediate pretext of the Damdami Taksal's takeover was to gain exclusive control over the stipulated demolition of the government built structure of the Akal Takht and the construction of a new one, abrogating the 'agreement' made earlier by the SGPC and the Sant Samaj with the Taksal.[18] The demolition work was started soon after. On 26 January, 1986, the happenings in front of the Akal Takht started a new phase of conflict and violence. At the *Sarbat Khalsa* congregation called by Damdami Taksal, the young extremists gave vent to their feelings against the existing leaders of the SGPC amidst shouts for Khalistan. It created a chaotic situation. The leaders of the SGPC and the priests who failed to act in time now complained about the 'frightening conditions' created in the sacred temple by the "enemies of the panth".[19] A *Sarbat Khalsa* meeting was organised by the Akal Takht head priest. The assembly condemned the armed occupation of the temple by the 'ruffians' and the collection of arms there. By a *gurmata* adopted there the whole Sikh world was 'directed' not to recognise these "brother-killing enemies of the panth".[20]

On the other hand, the extermists themselves appeared to have 'conflicting enthusiasms'. They shared a passion for armed resistance or struggle for Khalistan but were divided on leadership of the movement and strategy for action.[21] Some of their prominent leaders were surprised when Mohkam Singh of Damdami Taksal read out the names of the members of the Panthic Committee. A bitter dispute reportedly erupted between the Taksal and Bhindranwale's father Baba Joginder Singh. Wassan Singh Zaffarwal, a member of the Panthic Committee, stated that when the Baba saw "our weapons", he left the temple.[22] The five members of the committee—Gurbachan Singh Manochahal, Wassan Singh Zaffarwal, Dhanna Singh, Aroor Singh and Gurdev Singh—were little known men gifted neither with religious piety nor political sense. They were not the kind of men who would command moral authority.[23]

On April 29, this Panthic Committee announced the formation of Khalistan. This, it was claimed, was done as per the blessings of "Raj Karega Khalsa" given by Guru Gobind Singh on the Baisakhi of 1699. It, therefore, "fulfilled the dream of the Sikhs to create their own homeland". All the governments of the world and the UN were asked to grant recognition to the new state. The

Government of India was directed to complete all religious and military formalities consequent upon the creation of Khalistan. The Document of the Declaration of Khalistan was a loosely worded broadsheet, unlike several other documents and memoranda prepared by the supporting Sikh intellectuals.[24]

The description of the objectives of the new state of Khalistan included *sarbat da bhala* (good of mankind) and service of society. "This would establish the control of political power by those who produced wealth by honest hard labour". Such conditions were to be created in Khalistan "whereby basic needs of all are met; where feudal and capitalist practices are not allowed and where division on the basis of colour, caste, untouchability, rural-urban and high-low difference will be removed".

The form of government was to remain the same for the time being, "only the seals and stamps of Government of India would be replaced by those of Khalistan". The work of government formation was handed over to "the Prime Minister or the head of the state". The document also announced the formation of Khalistan Commando Force (KCF) "whose commander-in-chief is General Hari Singh". This Force will form the nucleus of the future defence organisation of Khalistan. Sikh religion was to be the official religion of Khalistan.

The Sikhs living in parts of India outside Pubjab were invited to settle in Punjab so that "they don't have to meet the same fate as they did in November 1984". A directive was given to all the political organisations to announce their agreement with and 'loyalty' to Khalistan. The declaration issued a warning to the opportunist Sikhs, described as "Keshdhari Hindus", against any obstruction of the Khalistan programme of Khalsa *panth*. What may appear to be a little odd in such a document was that the Sikhs were particularly instructed "not to snatch or steal arms and other things from the houses of the Sikh."

All the leaders of Khalistan left the Golden Temple soon after the declaration. Some of them such as Wassan Singh Zaffarwal, member of the Panthic Committee, and Gurjit Singh, chief of a faction of AISSF, crossed over to Pakistan. The day after the 'declaration' when the police force was sent into the temple with a view to flush out the militants, there was nobody for a catch.

The sentiment for Khalistan or for sheer vengeful action against perceived enemies apparently prevailed among a large number of militant youngmen. Many among the around 700 released from long detention by the Barnala government were believed to be restive for violent action. About 350 of those who had crossed over to Pakistan during the frightening combing operation (Operation Woodrose) had reportedly returned from Pakistan.

The political fall-out of Barnala's police action in the temple on the other hand created conditions which were favourable to the militants. The detractors of Barnala such as the SGPC chief and the senior Akali leaders who had failed to protect the sacred temple and had been sulking over their humiliation during the four month long occupation of Darbar Sahib by the Khalistani militants now found a new panthic cause to fight for. A vigorous campaign was launched that Chief Minister Barnala must be punished for the 'sacrilege' of the holy temple. As 27 of the Akali MLAs broke away from Barnala, it reduced the government support to a minority in the legislative assembly. Barnala was now forced into the ignominy of seeking support from the same Congress party which had embarrassed and weakened his government through non-implementation of the Rajiv-Longowal accord. A further humiliation followed when the Chief Minister had to undergo religious punishment for the 'sacrilege'.

When J.F. Ribeiro took over as Director-General of Police in Punjab in March 1986, he had found the police to be a highly ill-equipped and demoralised lot. Now, the government was weaker and unstable. The increasing infighting among the Akalis, a pervasive anti-Congress sentiment in the Sikh community and a large-scale inflow of arms from Pakistan created a more encouraging environment for the Khalistani militants.

Little attention was, however, paid to a plan of action or coordination among diverse gangs of militants. That seemed far more difficult in the context of conflictual power interests of the key players. The Panthic Committee had recognised Khalistan Commando Force (KCF) led by self-born 'General' Hari Singh as the exclusive guerrilla organisation. But there were many others such as the formidable Babbar Khalsa which had been virulently hostile to Bhindranwale and did not recognise the Panthic Committee which declared the formation of Khalistan. Its leaders in Canada called 'Babbar Khalsa International' had earned it a notoriety for blowing up of Air India Flight 182 from Toronto to London in which 329 people were killed.

The KCF was one of the prominent militant outfits which emerged after Operation Blue Star. Most of its "400 well-armed guerrillas" belonged to the Majha region consisting of two districts of Amritsar and Gurdaspur. After 'General' Hari Singh's arrest and death in August 1986, 'General' Labh Singh (alias Sukhdev Singh) of Panjwar village in Amritsar district took over its command. Labh Singh had been a constable in Punjab Police earlier. Under them the KCF was structured on the pattern of a guerrilla organisation—the 'General' on top, followed by 'Lieutenant Generals' at the regional level, then 'Area Commanders' commanding their 'cadres'.[25] In practice, however, there was 'extreme decentralisation' and local gangs functioned autonomously. Joyce Pettigrew and Cynthia Keppley Mahmood who conducted extensive interviews with militant leaders and activists provided minute details about their working and mutual antagonisms. Mahmood pointed to "a tendency for general strategy on behalf of Khalistan to turn into personal raids of vengeance on the local level". The titles of 'General', 'Lt. General', etc. were highly 'illusory'.[26] Pettigrew admired the 'symbolic universe' of the movement but discovered that the movement was 'determined' by thriving individualism, family feuds, vendettas and "interest in guns and popularity".[27]

Armed attacks on Hindus which had begun under Bhindranwale's command became later a prominent part of the militants' agenda. Observers took notice of the call given in the Declaration of Khalistan to Sikhs in other parts of India to come and settle in Punjab. The *Sant Sipahi,* edited by Dr. Rajinder Kaur, daughter of the revered Akali leader Master Tara Singh, linked the violent attacks on and commands issued to Hindus living in the villages to leave Punjab with the above mentioned call. "If they started leaving, there would follow riots against Sikhs outside Punjab, making it difficult to live there", it warned. It was noted, however, that "perhaps, this is precisely what the suppporters of Khalistan wanted".[28] A shoot out in Ludhiana in which 13 were killed and 17 injured, killing of 22 Hindu passengers of a bus at Khudda, 24 bus passengers near Hoshiarpur became a part of a chain of successive operations by militants.

One of the prominent actions by the KCF was the daring rescue of Sukhdev Singh Sukha (later General Labh Singh) from police custody at Jalandhar. The robbery of eight lakh rupees at Punjab National Bank in Ludhiana in October 1986 and another of about five crores in February 1987 became highly sensational sources of funds for the struggle. The assassination in Pune (Maharashtra) of General Vaidya who had led Indian armed forces into Golden Temple under Operation Blue Star was another powerful action. Its heroes Sukhjinder Singh (Sukha) and Harjinder Singh (Jinda) infiltrated into the Golf Club of which Vaidya was a member. The letter written to President of India in their name and their execution became a prominent part of militant discourse in Punjab and in Gurdwaras in foreign countries.

A more significant related feature of the struggle for Khalistan was the fierce factional fighting leading to factionalisation and proliferation of organisations and gangs. Gurbachan Singh Manochahal, chairman of the Panthic Committee, gave the first powerful signal of a split by forming his own Bhindranwale Tiger Force of Khalistan (BTKF) in 1987. More serious splintering followed the release of Jasbir Singh Rode, acting Jathedar of Akal Takht, from jail. His statements in favour of *puran azadi* (complete independence) or a Khalsa Raj within India and uniting all the militants for negotiations with the government created among the others apprehensions about his motives. Kanwarjit Singh, who was inducted as a member of the Panthic Committee formed his own breakaway faction of KCF. Avtar Singh Brahma, a prominent Robin Hood-type fighter, founded along with Aroor Singh, another militant organisation—Khalistan Liberation Force.[29]

IV

Operation Black Thunder II, launched in May 1988 to flush out a fresh concentration of militants in the Golden Temple, brought forth the most revolting aspects of the "hot house growth" of militancy. The totally televised operation brought home to the devout Sikhs watching television in their drawing rooms the evidence of defilement of the sacred precincts of the temple and the moral depravity of the men fighting in the name of the Khalsa. A total of 198 'warriors' surrendered to the police; most of them shown walking out with raised hands. Yet another evidence of perversion came to light when 57 dead bodies were recovered from under the debris of the demolished Akal Takht building.[30] The *Sant Sipahi* raised the question dormant in the hearts of many in its cover story *Panthak Gaddar Te Sarkari Agent Kaun* (which are the traitors in the community and agents of the government).[31] "I must say that from early 1987 the movement was taking a direction away from *all the basic* tenets of Sikhism", stated Darshan Singh Ragi, the Jathedar of Akal Takht appointed by the Taksal and the SGPC, lamenting, "We did not know from where this thinking was coming".[32]

The mood in the state police appeared to have turned optimistic, for the first time. "Had there been a better administrative system", a widely respected Inspector General of Police, Chaman Lal lamented after interrogation of around 170 detenues, "crime could have been effectively controlled and checked" earlier.[33] In fact, however, the permissiveness for violence, allowed by a confused political leadership brought in hordes of thugs for spoils. Their agendas were clearly more personal than ideological.

The splits in militant organisations, defections, alliances, new organisations and shifting appointments of 'commanders' and leaders for the next three years or more created a situation of chaos. At the peak of the Khalistan movement one noticed at least four Panthic Committees, three sets of religious priests, four factions of KCF, five groups of All India Sikh Students' Federation and a score of outfits under other names. Media's investigations and police intelligence listed in 1992 over 160 gangs of Khalistani 'terrorists'.[34] KCF (Zaffarwal) leaders alleged large-scale infiltration. They accused Dr. Sohan Singh's Panthic Committee and the allied *char jujharu jathebandian* (four militant organisations) for undermining the movement. But as Cynthia Mahmood and Pettigrew found from interviews with the key players, there were "way too many factions and groups and way too much infighting".[35] The overseas organisations fighting for Khalistan were "as tied up in Panthic Committee politics (rivalry) as those on the ground in Punjab".[36] This infighting involved not only cross-cutting agendas but also large-scale liquidation of rivals.[37]

Conciliatory moves by the government in such a situation were likely to be interpreted differently by rival interests. When Prime Minister V.P. Singh launched his "winning of the hearts" agenda, many people came to believe that the militant leaders might well form the new government in the state. However, the graph of violent killings shot up. The issue for the feuding militants was who should be invited for talks. The claims of the rivals had to be scuttled first of all. Posters for recruitment to militant organisation promised Rs. 5,000 as salary and hefty compensation to the family in case of 'martyrdom'.[38] The year 1990 witnessed the highest number of civilians killed so far, 2,474 and 64 cases of mass killings. As the importance of media coverage of a group's dominance dawned on them, targeting mediamen facilitated terror by press reports. Warnings to professionals and traders through the press led to instant *spashtikarans* (clarifications). Nobody could ignore orders for *bandhs* and for attendance at *bhogs.* Extortions amounted to reportedly over Rs. 100 crores. "The years 1990 and 1991", as K.P.S. Gill conceded, "unambiguously belonged to the terrorists".[39]

A "turning of the tide" was witnessed in 1992 following a no-holds-barred counter-terrorism by the police with 'rewards' and quick promotions for killing listed militants. 'Liquidation', not arrest or trial, as a policy, blurred the distinction between a terrorist, a suspect and an innocent person. When the legendary icons such as Sukhdev Singh of Babbar Khalsa fell, the evidence of their luxury and degeneration shattered the remaining illusions about the mission of the militants.

V

The village view of violence turned out to be very different from that of the ideologues of the movement. The operations and objectives of the 'fighters', as a field study conduced in the villages of Amritsar and Gurdaspur districts[40] revealed, had no relation with ideology, or religious interest. Among a total of 323 *kharkus* (militants) identified and listed by the people in 28 villages, the motives of a vast majority were found to be related to a lust for adventure, weapons, making quick money and kith-and-kin interests. Most of the recruits belonged to families of poor small or marginal farmers; were illiterate or school dropouts and weighed down by a low self-esteem and uncertain future. They ended up joining a militant group more by accident than political design. Access to weapons such as AK-47 assault rifle according to the people of their villages, provided to the militants a sense of 'empowerment'. However, their activities and violence centred on vendetta, family disputes, mercenary interests and assertion of power in their village situations. In the end the individual and collective resistance put up by the people, some of these of extraordinary courage, according to the village view, enabled the desperate and ruthless police force to quickly suppress the violent movement. Joyce Pettigrew who knew more in depth about the working of the militants, reached a conclusion different from that of the villagers. According to her, the Khalistan movement was defeated, "not by the massive array of state force", but "by the features of traditional rural society such as family feuds and vendettas and allegiances based on friendship or on shared hatreds...".[41]

The present study underlines the need to connect the reasons of its collapse with the reasons of its rise. It may also suggest somewhat on the lines of an observation made by Paul Brass in a different context of the politics of religion in the Sikh community, that when hatred and violence tend to become a fundamental basis of a religio-political movement, the movement "takes a life of its own to such an extent" that organisations and actions may be as much shaped by interests, as interests by them.[42]

Notes

1. "Pakistan Exploited the Sikhs". Interview with Jagjit Singh Chauhan in London by Shekhar Gupta and Nirupama Subramanian, *India Today*, December 15, 1993, pp. 65-66.
2. Michael Ignatief, "Nationalism and Narcissism of Minor Differences", *Queen's Quarterly*, Vol. 102, No. 1 (Spring 1995).
3. Peter Van der Veer, *Religious Nationalism: Hindus and Muslims in India*, Berkeley: University of California Press, 1992, pp. 10-12.
4. Robin Jeffrey, "Grappling with Sikh History: Sikh Politicians and the Past", *Pacific Affairs*, LX:1 (Spring 1987) pp. 59-73.
5. Kapur Singh, *Stupid Sikhs* (originally "Sikhs and Sikhism", a lecture delivered at Vancouver 7 October, 1974), Vancouver: All Canada Sikh Federation, May 31, 1975, reprint for private circulation, 1994.
6. Justice V.M. Tarkunde in Citizens for Democracy, *Report to the Nation: Oppression in Punjab*, Hind Mazdoor Kisan Panchayat Publication, Delhi 1985, p. 16.
7. Cited from J.S. Grewal, "Sikh Identity, the Akalis and Khalistan", in J.S. Grewal and Indu Banga (eds.), *Punjab in Prosperity and Violence*, Chandigarh: Institute of Punjab Studies, 1998, p.84.
8. Cited from *ibid.*, p. 72.
9. Tape recorded interview in Cynthia Keppley Mahmood, *Fighting for Faith and Nation: Dialogues with Sikh Militants*, Philadelphia: University of Pennsylvania Press, 1996, p. 70.
10. Ram Narayan Kumar, *The Sikh Unrest and the Indian State: Politics, Personality and Historical Perspective,* New Delhi: Ajanta, 1997, p. 37, 40.
11. Cited from Veena Das, *Critical Events: An Anthropological Perspective on Contemporary India*, Delhi: Oxford University Press, 1998, p. 128.
12. *Ibid.*, 134.
13. Cited in Grewal, *op. cit.*, p. 73.
14. Interview, Joyce J.M. Pettigrew, *The Sikhs of the Punjab: Unheard Voices of State and Guerrilla Violence,* London: Zed Books, p.174.

15. "I only finish those who are enemies of the Sikh faith like policemen, government officials and Hindus", cited from Grewal, *op. cit.*, p. 73.
16. Dalbir Singh, in a tape recorded interview with Joyce Pettigrew. Pettigrew, *op. cit.*, p.34; see also R.N. Kumar, pp.120-27.
17. Singh Sahib Gyani Kirpal Singh, *Akhein Dittha Saka Neela Tara* (Eye Witness Account of Operation Blue Star), Amritsar: Jeevan Printers, 3rd edition, 1999, p. 228 and 234.
18. *Ibid.*, p. 225.
19. *Ibid.*, pp. 229-30, 233.
20. *Ibid.*, p. 254.
21. Pettigrew, *op.cit.*, pp.109-10; see also Keppley Mahmood, *op. cit.*
22. Text of Zaffarwal's interview in Pettigrew, *op.cit.*, pp. 151-52.
23. *Sant Sipahi*, July 1988, p.17.
24. Panthic Committee, *Document of Declaration of Khalistan*, 1986 (all references from this 4-page document).
25. See notes 9 and 14.
26. Mahmood, *op.cit.*, p. 154.
27. Pettigrew, *op.cit.*, pp. 153-54.
28. *Sant Sipahi*, June 1986, p. 28.
29. Pettigrew, *op. cit.*, pp. 82-83.
30. *Sant Sipahi*, July 1988.
31. *Ibid.*
32. Cited from Pettigrew, *op. cit.*, p.46.
33. *The Tribune*, Chandigarh, 24 July, 1988.
34. *The Times of India*, 9 February, 1992; K.P.S. Gill, *Knights of Falsehood*, Delhi: Har Anand Publishers, p. 99. See also Hemish Telford, "Factionalism in Nationalist Movements and the Proliferation of Sikh Militant Groups in Punjab", unpublished paper, Vancouver, 1995, pp. 23-26.
35. Mahmood, *op.cit.*, p. 160.
36. *Ibid.*
37. According to Pettigrew's investigations 'General' Labh Singh was liquidated through a consipracy hatched between Gurjit

Singh, chief of AISSF, Paramjit Singh Panjwar, later head of KCF (P) and Nirmal Singh Nimma. Harminder Singh Sandhu, secretary of AISSF, and former close aide of Bhindranwale was allegedly killed in his home by supporters of Labh Singh. The deaths of Avtar Singh Brahma chief of KLF and Kanwarjit Singh, head of KCF and formerly member of Panthic Committee resulted allegedly from conspiracies by rivals. See Pettigrew, *op.cit.* for more details.

38. Kanwar Sandhu, cited in Pettigrew, *op.cit.*, p. 123.
39. KPS Gill, "Endgame in Punjab: 1988-1993", *Faultline*, Vol. 1, No. 1 (May 1999), p. 51.
40. Harish K. Puri, Paramjit Singh Judge and Jagrup Singh Sekhon, *Terrorism in Punjab: Understanding Grassroots Reality*, Delhi: Har Anand Publishers, 1999.
41. Pettigrew, *op. cit.*, p.140.
42. Paul Brass, *Language, Religion and Politics in North India*, Delhi: Vikas, 1974, p.12.

Contributors

W.H. McLeod, Professor of History, Dunedin University, Otago, New Zealand.

Satish K. Sharma, Professor of Sociology, Himachal Pradesh University, Shimla.

N. Gerald Barrier, Professor of History, University of Missouri, Missouri, Columbia, U.S.A.

John C.B. Webster, former Professor of History, United Theological College, Bangalore.

Spencer Lavan was Professor of Comparative Religion, Tufts University, Medford, Mass., U.S.A.

K.L. Tuteja, Professor of History, Kurukshetra University, Kurukshetra (Haryana).

Mohinder Singh, Director, National Institute of Punjab Studies, Bhai Vir Singh Sadan, New Delhi.

Harish K. Puri, Professor B.R. Ambedkar Chair, Department of Political Science, Guru Nanak Dev University, Amritsar (Punjab)

Mark Juergensmeyer, Professor of Sociology, University of California, Santa Barbara, California, U.S.A.

M.S. Dhami, Former Reader, Department of Political Science, Guru Nanak Dev University, Amritsar (Punjab).

Bhagwan Josh, Professor, Centre for Historical Studies, Jawaharlal Nehru University, New Delhi.

A.S. Narang, Professor of Political Science, Indira Gandhi National Open University, New Delhi.

Santosh Sood, Former Reader in Political Science, Department of Evening Studies, Panjab University, Chandigarh.

Paramjit Singh Judge, Professor of Sociology, Guru Nanak Dev University, Amritsar (Punjab).

S.S. Gill, Professor of Economics, Punjabi University, Patiala.

Index